Black Picket Fences

BLACK PICKET FENCES

Privilege and Peril among the Black Middle Class

SECOND EDITION

MARY PATTILLO

With a new Foreword by Annette Lareau

The University of Chicago Press
Chicago and London

Mary Patillo is the Harold Washington Professor of Sociology and African American Studies at Northwestern University. She is the author of *Black on the Block: The Politics of Race and Class in the City*, also published by the University of Chicago Press, and coeditor of *Imprisoning America: The Social Effects of Mass Incarceration*.

The University of Chicago Press, Chicago 60637
The University of Chicago Press, Ltd., London
© 1999, 2013 by The University of Chicago
All rights reserved. Published 2013.
Printed in the United States of America

22 21 20 19 18 17 16 15 14 13   1 2 3 4 5

ISBN-13: 978-0-226-02119-5 (paper)
ISBN-13: 978-0-226-02122-5 (e-book)
DOI: 10.7208/chicago/9780226021225.001.001

Library of Congress Cataloging-in-Publication Data

Pattillo, Mary E.
  Black picket fences : privilege and peril among the black
middle class / Mary Pattillo. — Second edition.
      pages. cm.
  Includes bibliographical references and index.
   ISBN 978-0-226-02119-5 (pbk. : alk. paper) — ISBN 978-0-226-02122-5
(e-book) 1. African Americans—Illinois—Chicago—Social conditions. 2. African
American youth—Illinois—Chicago—Social conditions. 3. African Americans—
Illinois—Chicago—Economic conditions. 4. Middle class—Illinois—Chicago.
5. Chicago (Ill.)—Social conditions. 6. Chicago (Ill.)—Race relations. I. Title.
   F548.9.N4P38 2013
   305.896′073077311—dc23
                                    2013005615

To Quentin, Michael, and T. A.

CONTENTS

FOREWORD

Given the preoccupation of America with the failings of the poor, social science researchers rarely focus on the middle class. This problem is particularly true of the African American middle class. Originally published in 1999, *Black Picket Fences* offered a fine analysis of a (lower) middle-class neighborhood in Chicago, which Mary Pattillo calls "Groveland." Not only did *Black Picket Fences* receive positive reviews and scholarly awards, but the book has also been influential in social science and policy debates.

Now, a decade later, Pattillo has returned to Groveland. She offers a lucid analysis of the changes that have unfolded over time in this Chicago neighborhood. Her research for this second edition included carrying out in-depth interviews with some of the people she studied in the early 1990s, reviewing countless local documents, and conducting extensive research on changes in the experience of the black middle class in this city and in America. Pattillo enters a conversation, begun by William Julius Wilson, Elijah Anderson, and others, about the role of the black middle class in the city, and the dynamic intermixing of "decent" and "street" folks in the same set of square city blocks.

The first edition of *Black Picket Fences*, and the follow-up, reveal a paradox. On the one hand, the black middle-class families in her study, and across the country, have advantages over white and black low-income families. They own houses; they do not rent. They have often gone to college; they are not high school dropouts. They are much more likely to have stable jobs; they are less likely to be unemployed. Their incomes are above that of many whites; they are not part of the one-quarter of African Americans living below the official poverty line (230, 260). Hence, her study reveals a group of Americans with *privilege*.

On the other hand, the original book and the follow-up also reveal significant challenges. On almost every significant measure, members of the African American middle class fare worse than do comparable whites, and often worse than low-income whites. African Americans live in neighborhoods with many more poor people than do whites. African Americans are also less likely to be able to keep their children in the middle class. For example, over one-half of African Americans who come from middle-income families experience downward mobility: they fall below their parents' income as adults. This pattern, however, is true for only about one-third of middle-income whites. And African American extended families are much more likely to have a relative who is poor than are white families. The unemployment rate of African Americans is about twice that of whites. Private school enrollment rates are lower for blacks than whites. Black middle-class families are more likely to be victims of crime—blacks with incomes "over $75,000 are more likely to get their cars stolen than whites in families earning less than $7,500" (242). Neighborhoods remain heavily racially segregated; and black neighborhoods are more likely to have a lot of poor people in them than white neighborhoods, and high-poverty neighborhoods are found to have many woes, including high crime rates, particularly homicide rates, boarded-up buildings, inferior schools, and limited availability of fresh vegetables and other groceries. Thus, her study of the black middle class also shows significant *peril*.

Not only are these themes true for the individuals in her study, but she found a similar juxtaposition between privilege and peril in the neighborhood of Groveland both at the time of the original study and more recently. On the one hand, unlike blocks of desolation that characterize many cities, she finds "neat bungalow houses" in this 96-percent black neighborhood with lush, trim green lawns, fashionable cars, and clean streets. The value of homes increased over time. New businesses have moved into the area. A bustling youth summer camp offers an array of activities. There is a new library branch. The number of people in the neighborhood who have a college degree grew. Hence, in the ensuing years since Pattillo's original research the neighborhood did not stand still. Instead, the neighborhood remained stable in key ways and, in other ways, thrived.

On the other hand, the proportion of families living below the poverty line in Groveland increased. The unemployment rate also went up in the last decade. The amount of rental housing grew significantly, particularly the number of government-subsidized housing units for poor people. People she spoke with were worried the neighborhood was going downhill. As Pattillo writes, "This position of being 'more advantaged than other predominantly black neighborhoods but less advantaged than white neighborhoods' is the recurring theme of this book" (240–241).

As Pattillo develops her analysis of the experience of the black middle class, I found three themes in the original book and the follow-up to be particularly revealing. First, *Black Picket Fences* helps us develop a language of how social class shapes daily life—a language that has been underdeveloped in America. Since the publication of Pattillo's book, others have built on her work to develop our knowledge further. For example, Karyn Lacy's book, *Blue-Chip Black: Race, Class, and Status in the New Black Middle Class* (Berkeley: University of California Press, 2007) contrasts the experiences of black middle-class families in the Washington, DC, area. Some families choose to live in the predominantly black middle-class communities of Prince George's County, but then send their children to private school. Others, however, moved to the predominantly white suburbs of Virginia, where the schools have a strong reputation. These black middle-class parents worked hard to supplement their children's lives by making sure that they take part in social groups with other African American children. Karyn Lacy has also undertaken a study of the exclusive African American organization for children called Jack and Jill. This class variation among black families was also highlighted in my book *Unequal Childhoods: Class, Race, and Family Life* (Berkeley: University of California Press, 2011). *Unequal Childhoods* used ethnographic methods to show how African American and white middle-class families raised their children via "concerted cultivation," where they enrolled their children in organized activities (rather than have them watch television or play with their cousins). The middle-class parents also reasoned with the children (answering questions with questions), rather than issuing directives. Also, while the working-class and poor parents depended on educators, doctors, and other professionals to provide services to their children, middle-class African American and white parents closely supervised the actions of professionals. I found, of course, that African Americans lived in predominantly black neighborhoods, attended predominately black churches, and experienced racial insults in integrated public spaces, but in terms of child rearing, the middle-class white and black families had a great deal in common, while there was a wide divergence between middle-class African American families on the one hand and working-class and poor African American and white families on the other. This divergence also was reaffirmed when I did a follow-up study of these families a decade later. These studies highlight the heterogeneity by social class of African Americans. Recently, Jody Agius Vallejo has highlighted the diversity of Mexican-American families with her book, *Barrios to Burbs: The Making of the Mexican-American Middle Class* (Palo Alto, CA: Stanford University Press, 2012).

But the class diversity of black families should not blind us to the enduring power of race in residential neighborhoods, which is a second very important contribution of *Black Picket Fences*. Indeed, Pattillo's book also helps us think more about the *black* middle class. Other work has highlighted that white Americans are particularly averse to living in neighborhoods with significant numbers of black residents. Thus, many researchers, including Douglas Massey, Lincoln Quillian, and Robert Sampson, have documented that many African Americans and black Hispanics live in neighborhoods that are almost entirely black. As Pattillo notes, even high-income blacks live with and near poor African American residents, much more so than high-income whites. Also, once neighborhoods become black, it is rare for them to change over. Michael Bader shows that in the few instances when neighborhood change happens, it is because Hispanics move into black neighborhoods. Then, and only then, after Hispanics establish a presence in the neighborhood, do whites occasionally enter such neighborhoods. Whites are even more likely to live around other whites than blacks are to live with blacks, and it is rare for whites to move into racially diverse areas. Many factors play a role, but the significance of race in residential patterns is clear. As a result, blacks tend to live in more economically diverse neighborhoods than do whites.

One of the most powerful parts of *Black Picket Fences* is how it reveals the coexistence of middle-class black families with poor families in Groveland. Middle-class adults are aware of the drug dealing and gang activities in the neighborhood, but they also have personal relationships with individuals involved in these activities. They appreciate the contributions the gangs make to the neighborhood, including providing food for neighborhood block parties or security for neighborhood events. Pattillo shows that the middle-class black families in her study are not naive; they know about the activities that are happening around them. But the families also adapt to the neighborhood reality in order to live peacefully in Groveland.

Third, in addition to contributing to the discussions of class and race in America, *Black Picket Fences* reminds us of the importance of place. The book is part of a rich history of studies of neighborhoods in Chicago. Over one hundred years ago social scientists turned their eyes to the city of Chicago and created a set of influential studies, from a focus on Chicago's Polish immigrants to rich studies of the Gold Coast. This tradition of studies of daily life in Chicago continues to this day, from studies of blues clubs in David Grazian's *Blue Chicago* (Chicago: University of Chicago Press, 2003) to studies of how low-income women learn to distrust welfare case workers, employers, and boyfriends in Judith Levine's *Ain't No Trust* (Berkeley: University of California Press, forthcoming). Robert Sampson's work, especially his recent book *Great American City: Chicago and the Enduring Neighborhood Effect* (Chicago: University of Chicago, 2012), provides the definitive assessment of the variation in neighborhoods in Chicago and the impact of neighborhoods on social outcomes. As he shows, neighborhoods matter.

And, as Pattillo shows us, individuals are rooted in place. She reports that over 60 percent of people living in Groveland in 2010 had moved there before 1999; thus, finding the respondents for the follow-up generally went smoothly. But a number of the young people had moved out of the neighborhood. As these young people grew up and changed, what they wanted from the neighborhood changed. Although involving schools rather than city neighborhoods, Amy Stuart Wells found a similar pattern in her interviews with parents who had attended city desegregated schools (graduating in 1980). Her book, *Both Sides Now* (Berkeley: University of California Press, 2009), reveals that these graduates reported, two decades later, many positive benefits from their high school experiences, including in their friendships, work skills, and life attitudes. But these adults also are not keen to have their children enter desegregated schools in their neighborhoods; they fear the challenges the children would face. So, too, Pattillo shows in her follow-up that the young people who grew up in Groveland are worried about bringing their children to the parks in the neighborhood. Spider Waters grew up going to Groveland Park, but he refused to take his eleven-year-old son Payton there; he preferred to take him to a location where he thought there would be zero risk of violence. The people in *Black Picket Fences* insist that they were fine growing up there, but they worry about having their children take part in neighborhood life in Groveland.

Americans believe in the promise of opportunity. Across the country, people focus on individuals and families. But one of the most important contributions of sociology is to show us how individuals' life chances are *socially structured*. Institutions guide and shape our life options. Groups of people have different life chances. In her fine book, Pattillo highlights a series of paradoxes: of the power and limits of class, of privilege and peril, and of continuity and change. With her work, she reminds us to situate individuals in a geographic context. She shows us that the context is different for black and white middle-class Americans. But she also shows that black Americans are a diverse group. The popular and scholarly conversation in America assumes that when we think and talk about blacks, we are talking about the poor. With her focus on the black middle class, Pattillo helps us broaden our vision of America.

Annette Lareau
Philadelphia, Pennsylvania

ACKNOWLEDGMENTS

Perhaps the most common advice given to students applying to graduate school is: do not choose a graduate program on the basis of one (and only one) professor with whom you would like to work. There is no guarantee that that person will stay for the duration of your graduate career. Even though I now give that advice to undergraduates inquiring about graduate programs, I do not at all regret the decision I made to attend the University of Chicago, with the specific intent to work with William Julius Wilson. Ultimately, Wilson did leave Chicago for Harvard late in my graduate years, but not before I had benefited from his intellectual and professional guidance. When Wilson left, he admonished his students not to simply continue research within the paradigm he has worked to establish, but to add to that body of knowledge, and, indeed, to challenge it. This has been my goal in *Black Picket Fences*.

Wilson provided the resources and the stimulating intellectual environment for me to grow as a social scientist, but—as I believe many scholars feel—I have been a sociologist most of my life. Early in graduate school, I visited Wilson's office and asked for work. He asked about my interests, and I told him of my experience growing up black and middle class in Milwaukee, and the variety of paths that my peers had taken. Of my group of neighborhood and school friends, some had children young, were sporadically employed, or were lured into the drug trade, while others had gone to college, or worked steady jobs and earned enough to start a family. We started pretty much at the same place, but we ended up running the full gamut of outcomes. Some now make six figures—and others are six feet under. I wanted to understand these divergences. My sociological interests were quite personal in that I myself had lost friends and acquaintances both literally in death, and figuratively in that our paths drifted so far apart that there just wasn't much to talk about anymore. Of course, no one remains lifetime friends with all of their childhood or teenage cronies, but I felt there was a story to be told about black middle-class kids like my friends, a story that was not simply about growing apart.

So, in a strange way, I am grateful and owe much to the people I grew up with in Milwaukee—around Roosevelt, Capital, Atkinson, Hampton, and Sherman Park; at St. Agnes, Whitefish Bay, Washington, Dominican, King, Nicolet, Messmer, and Vincent; and in 2-7, 2-4, drill teams and skating crews, Warning League, Unity in the Community, CYO, and Jack and Jill. These insider references translate to mean that we came from stable, but not "ritzy," black middle-class neighborhoods; we went to public, private, and Catholic schools; and we belonged to gangs and gospel choirs. In doing the research for this book I learned that our very local experiences were rooted in broad processes that put us where we lived, affected our choice of schools, and influenced the groups we joined.

I began this project working for Bill Wilson and Richard Taub on the Comparative Neighborhood Study (CNS), which was funded by grants from the Ford, MacArthur, and Rockefeller foundations and perfectly matched my interests because it focused on working- and middle-class neighborhoods. My fellow researchers on the CNS team—Reuben May, Jolyon Wurr, Chenoa Flippen, Maria Kefalas, Patrick Carr, Jennifer Johnson, Jennifer Pashup-Graham, and Erin Augis—were great people with whom to learn how to be an ethnographer, to argue over the particulars of social organization, or to compare findings from our respective sites. While I make only a few explicit comparisons to other neighborhoods in this book, I thank Wilson and Taub for allowing us full use of the CNS data.

I could not have finished graduate school in such fine mental health if it were not for the Center for the Study of Urban Inequality. Aside from the stimulating research and educational functions of the Center, it provided a space for graduate students and friends to work and play in. Lunchtime will never be the same without the regulars at the Center, and my friends from graduate school and beyond—the CNS team, Ray Reagans, Sandra Smith, Mignon Moore, Lori Hill, Jeff Morenoff, Pam Cook, Sarita Gregory, Sudhir Venkatesh, Kim Alkins, Alford Young, and Carla O'Connor. The Center's associate director, Jim Quane, blessed us with his on-target professional advice, Irish humor, knowledge of Chicago eateries, great wardrobe, and cool presence all around.

In writing, I benefited from the always practical and insightful suggestions of Christopher Jencks, who challenged me to write an engaging ethnographic narrative. Richard Taub's "but, what about . . ." questions made me consider other angles and interpretations, or strengthen my original assertions, both of which improved my arguments. Sheri Johnson was most honest in telling me what was right and what was wrong in my analysis, and giving comparative examples from her own black middle-class neighborhood. Robert Sampson's stamp is on this book by way of the classes I took with him and his own research on neighborhoods and crime. And again, Wilson's positive encouragement and reassurance that what I was doing was worthwhile gave me much-needed inspiration.

Throughout the writing of the dissertation and the book, the Internet made it possible to stay in touch with some old and many new friends. Our black (upper-) middle-class cybergroup—Mom, Sheri, Nikki, Adrienne, Peggy, Tommie, Ray, Reuben, Shelby, Jennifer, Cathy, and Michael—and many other on-line debates with Bakari Kitwana, have been the best place to shop fledgling interpretations of the data, get feedback on black culture, or have candid "conversations" about black poverty.

After I left Chicago, I was quite fortunate to land at the University of Michigan, where a Ford Foundation postdoctoral fellowship allowed me the freedom and time to turn a young dissertation into a mature book. I could not have had a better boss and mentor than Sheldon Danziger, director of the Poverty Research and Training Center. He was more than generous with his time, his knowledge, his contacts, his books, and (as all of his students know) his editorial red pen. At the Poverty Center, he assembled an interdisciplinary group of academics and researchers that made for the perfect balance of scholarship and socializing. Special thanks to Mary Corcoran and Colleen Heflin, who helped me test the waters of quantitative research. Outside of the Poverty Center, Geoffrey Ward, Tyrone Forman, and the members of Academics for Affirmative Action and Social Justice added stimulating and grounded discussion and debate to my intellectual stint at Michigan.

At Northwestern, I am grateful to the Sociology and African American Studies departments and to the Institute for Policy Research for allowing me the time and support to complete this book. In particular, I thank Aldon Morris for his advocacy.

At the University of Chicago Press, I am especially grateful to Matthew Howard, whose enthusiasm and optimism energized me through the eighth, ninth, and nth readings of book drafts. Salena

Krug and Leslie Keros improved the book's flow and design, and did so with considerable sensitivity to the people and world I describe.

My parents blessed me with good genes, and my mother especially insisted that I use them. My older sisters and brothers—Cathy, Michael, Patrick, and Sheri—have showered me with love from the day I was born, preparing me for anything, including writing a book. Danny, Van II and III, B.J., and Dave are perfect additions to the family. And thank you, Joseph, for bringing even more happiness to my life.

Finally, the families in Groveland were not just the subjects of my research. I ate, played, worshiped, cried, and protested with them. I hope I have been faithful to those experiences in this book. They made me a part of their lives, and for that I will always be grateful.

INTRODUCTION

The goal of *Black Picket Fences* is to richly describe the neighborhood-based social life of a population that has received little scholarly or popular attention—the black middle class. The black middle class and their residential enclaves are nearly invisible to the nonblack public because of the intense (and mostly negative) attention given to poor urban ghettos. Post–civil rights optimism erased upwardly mobile African Americans from the slate of interesting groups to study. However, the sparse research that does exist unequivocally indicates the continuing economic, residential, occupational, wealth, and socio-psychological disparities between blacks and whites, even within the middle class. In this book I focus on one realm of the black middle-class experience—the neighborhood context—by investigating how racial segregation, changing economic structures, and disproportionate black poverty affect the residential experience of black middle-class families, and especially youth. To accomplish this goal, I report on over three years of research in Groveland, a black middle-class neighborhood on Chicago's South Side.[1]

Even though America is obsessed with race, some policy makers and even more average citizens act as if race no longer matters. The sweeping assaults on affirmative action programs are prime examples. Not even forty years since separate water fountains—which, in the scheme of Jim Crow prohibitions, were much less onerous than the exclusion of African Americans from libraries, museums, schools, and jobs—many Americans would now like to proceed as if the slate is clean and the scale is balanced. African Americans must compete solely on what each individual has been able to accomplish, and how each has performed. Without being too sarcastic, it is as if racism and racial inequalities died just before Elvis, and those who still claim that racism exists are as misguided as someone who regularly spots the King. Even though the facts say differently, such perceptions partially

1

rest on the visible progress that African Americans have made over the last half-century. The upward strides of many African Americans into the middle class have given the illusion that race cannot be the barrier that some make it out to be. The reality, however, is that even the black and white *middle classes* remain separate and unequal.

Much of the research and media attention on African Americans is on the black poor. Welfare debates, discussions of crime and safety, urban policy initiatives, and even the cultural uproar over things like rap music are focused on the situation of poor African Americans. With more than one in four African Americans living below the official poverty line (versus approximately one in nine whites), this is a reasonable and warranted bias. But rarely do we hear the stories of the other three-fourths, or the majority of African Americans, who may be the office secretary, the company's computer technician, a project manager down the hall, or the person who teaches our children. The growth of the black middle class has been hailed as one of the major triumphs of the civil rights movement, but if we have so little information on who makes up this group and what their lives are like, how can we be so sure that triumphant progress is the full story? The optimistic assumption of the 1970s and 1980s was that upwardly mobile African Americans were quietly integrating formerly all-white occupations, businesses, neighborhoods, and social clubs. Black middle- and working-class families were moving out of all-black urban neighborhoods and into the suburbs. With these suppositions, the black middle class dropped from under the scientific lens and off the policy agenda, even though basic evidence suggests that the public celebration of black middle-class ascendance has perhaps been too hasty.

We know, for example, that a more appropriate socioeconomic label for members of the black middle class is "lower middle class." The one black doctor who lives in an exclusive white suburb and the few African American lawyers who work at a large firm are not representative of the black middle class overall (but neither are their experiences identical to those of their white colleagues). And although most white Americans are also not doctors or lawyers, the lopsided distribution of occupations for whites does favor such professional and managerial jobs, whereas the black middle class is clustered in the sales and clerical fields. Because one's occupation affects one's income, African Americans have lower earnings. Yet the inequalities run even deeper than just income. Compound and exponentiate the current differences over a history of slavery and Jim Crow, and the nearly fourteenfold wealth advantage that whites enjoy over African

Americans—regardless of income, education, or occupation—needs little explanation.[2]

We also know that the black middle class faces housing segregation to the same extent as the black poor. African Americans are more segregated from whites than any other racial or ethnic group. In fact, the black middle class likely faces the most blatant racial discrimination, in that many in its ranks can actually afford to pay for housing in predominantly white areas. Real estate agents and apartment managers can easily turn away poor African Americans by simply quoting prohibitive home costs or high rents. It takes more purposive creativity, however, to consistently steer middle-class blacks into already established African American neighborhoods by such tactics as disingenuously asserting that an apartment has just been rented when the prospective renters who show up at the property manager's door are, to his or her surprise, black. Racial segregation means that racial inequalities in employment, education, income, and wealth are inscribed in space. Predominantly white neighborhoods benefit from the historically determined and contemporarily sustained edge that whites enjoy.

Finally, we know that middle-class African Americans do not perform as well as whites on standardized tests (in school or in employment); are more likely to be incarcerated for drug offenses; are less likely to marry, and more likely to have a child without being married; and are less likely to be working.[3] Liberals bumble when addressing these realities because, unlike housing segregation or job discrimination, of which middle-class African Americans are the clear victims, earning low grades in school or getting pregnant without a husband can easily be attributed to the bad behaviors of blacks themselves. For middle-class blacks, who ostensibly do not face the daily disadvantages of poverty, it is even more difficult to explain why they do not measure up to whites. To resolve this quandary it is essential to continuously refer back to the ways in which the black middle class *is not equal* to the white middle class.

This book takes a micro-approach to these macro-realities of racial segregation, disproportionate poverty, and economic fragility. It focuses on the ecological context of black middle-class neighborhoods, which are characterized by more poverty, higher crime, worse schools, and fewer services than white middle-class neighborhoods. The questions that guide this research are: How does this context influence parents who are raising children, and adolescents and young adults who are growing up in such a neighborhood? What are the distinctive choices and transitions that black middle-class youth experience?

The lives of the families in Groveland provide some answers to these questions. Groveland's approximately ninety square blocks contain a population of just under twelve thousand residents, over 95 percent of whom are African American. The 1990 median annual family income in the neighborhood is nearly $40,000, while the comparable figure for Chicago as a whole is just over $30,000. More than 70 percent of Groveland families own their own homes. By income and occupational criteria, as well as the American dream of homeownership, Groveland qualifies as a "middle-class neighborhood."

Yet this sterile description does not at all capture the neighborhood's diversity, which is critical to correctly portraying the neighborhood context of the black middle class. Groveland's unemployment rate is 12 percent, which is higher than the citywide rate, but *lower* than the percentage of unemployed residents in the neighborhoods that border Groveland. Twelve percent of Groveland's families are poor, which again makes it a bit *more* advantaged than the surrounding areas, but worse off than most of Chicago's predominantly white neighborhoods. The geography of Groveland is typical of black middle-class areas, which often sit as a kind of buffer between core black poverty areas and whites.[4] Contrary to popular discussion, the black middle class has not out-migrated to unnamed neighborhoods outside of the black community. Instead, they are an overlooked population still rooted in the contemporary "Black Belts" of cities across the country. Some of the questions about why middle-class blacks are not at parity with middle-class whites can be answered once this fact is recognized.

The mix of residents in Groveland and in Chicago's predominantly black South Side defines the experiences and exposures of black middle-class youth. Groveland residents like twenty-one-year-old Ray Gibbs most insightfully describe this heterogeneous environment.

If a family wanted to feel the different spectrum of life, I think this would probably be a' ideal place to raise children. I mean, you know, you go outside in the suburbs, it's la-di-da-di. Trouble, stuff like that, don't happen. If you want somebody to see probably everything that could happen, you'd move here. Some days you'll have your good days where everything'll be perfect. Then you might have your bad days when yo' kid might have a fight. You know, you'll get to see all the makings of all different type of people. That's to me, that's what this neighborhood is.

Ray Gibbs put a positive spin on the range of activities and incidents that characterize black middle-class neighborhoods. But parents who desire to shield their children from negative influences are less enamored by what Ray seems to think is exciting. Many parents actively attempt to curtail their children's attraction to the less savory aspects of neighborhood life—most significantly, the gangs and the drug dealing.

PRIVILEGES AND PERILS

By the end of my research tenure in Groveland, I had seen three groups of eighth-graders graduate to high school, high school kids go on to college, and college graduates start their careers. I also heard too many stories and read too many obituaries of the teenagers who were jailed or killed along the way. The son of a police detective in jail for murder. The grandson of a teacher shot while visiting his girlfriend's house. The daughter of a park supervisor living with a drug dealer who would later be killed at a fast-food restaurant. These events were jarring, and all-too-frequent, discontinuities in the daily routine of Groveland residents. Why were some Groveland youth following a path to success, while others had concocted a recipe for certain failure? After all, these are not the stories of poor youth caught in a trap of absent opportunities, low aspirations, and harsh environments. Instead, Groveland is a neighborhood of single-family homes, old stately churches, tree-lined streets, active political and civic organizations, and concerned parents trying to maintain a middle-class way of life. These black middle-class families are a hidden population in this country's urban fabric.

The evening news hour in every major American city is filled with reports of urban crime and violence. Newspapers fill in the gaps of the more sensational tragedies about which the television could provide only a few sound bites. Rounding out the flow of urban Armageddon stories are the gossip and hearsay passed informally between neighbors, church friends, and drinking buddies. For many middleclass white Americans, the incidents they hear about in distant and troubled inner cities provide a constant symbolic threat, but an infrequent reality. For the families who live on the corner of the crime

scene—overwhelmingly black or Latino, and poor—daily life is organized to avoid victimization. In the middle of these two geographically
and socially distant groups lives the black middle class.

African American social workers and teachers, secretaries and
nurses, entrepreneurs and government bureaucrats are in many ways
the buffer between the black poor and the white middle class. When
neighborhoods are changing, white middle-class families may find
themselves living near low-income black families, but one group is
inevitably displaced. The neighborhood becomes, once again, racially
homogeneous. More than thirty years after the civil rights movement,
racial segregation remains a reality in most American cities. Middle-
income black families fill the residential gap between the neighborhoods that house middle-class whites and the neighborhoods where
poor African Americans live.[5] Unlike most whites, middle-class black
families must contend with the crime, dilapidated housing, and social
disorder in the deteriorating poor neighborhoods that continue to
grow in their direction. Residents attempt to fortify their neighborhoods against this encroachment, and limit their travel and associations to other middle-class neighborhoods in the city and suburbs. Yet
even with these efforts, residents of black middle-class neighborhoods
share schools, grocery stores, hospitals, nightclubs, and parks with
their poorer neighbors, ensuring frequent interaction within and outside the neighborhood.

The in-between position of the black middle class sets up certain
crossroads for its youth. This peculiar limbo begins to explain the
disparate outcomes of otherwise similar young people in Groveland.
The right and wrong paths are in easy reach of neighborhood youth.
Working adults are models of success. Some parents even work two
jobs, while still others combine work and school to increase their
chances of on-the-job promotions. All of the positive knowledge, networking, and role-model benefits that accrue to working parents are
operative for many families in Groveland. But at the same time the
rebellious nature of adolescence inevitably makes the wrong path a
strong temptation, and there is no shortage of showy drug dealers
and cocky gang members who make dabbling in deviance look fun.
Youth walk a fine line between preparing for success and youthful
delinquent experimentation, the consequences of which can be especially serious for black youth. In the chapters that follow, I attempt
to paint a picture of these choices and crossroads that Groveland
youth face.

I focus on youth for two reasons. The first is pragmatic. A thorough analysis of the many facets of neighborhood life (e.g., schools, politics, leisure, economic health, religion) would be unmanageable. These other important spheres are discussed as they relate to the experiences of young people. The more substantive reason for focusing on youth is that they are a good indicator of the well-being of black middle-class families more generally. Parents want their children's lives to be better than their own, or at least comparable. Substantial downward mobility signals that there are systematic obstacles to ensuring this transfer of class status. While the three years of research in Groveland does not constitute a true longitudinal study of mobility, it was a sufficient time in which to document some of the positive and negative transitions through which youth and young adults passed. These transitions were circumscribed by economic contingencies, the neighborhood context, and cultural pressures. Focusing on the experiences of young people seems to be the best way to draw attention to the particularities of being black and middle class in a neighborhood like Groveland.

CLOSE-TO-HOME ETHNOGRAPHY

There were rarely times during the research in Groveland when I was either an objective or a dispassionate observer. I hope this enriched my Groveland narrative, rather than stifled it. Either way, in the spirit of full disclosure, certain methodological issues merit discussion. (Appendix A contains an extended discussion of methods.)

I spent a total of three and a half years in Groveland. For the first two years, I was a part of the Comparative Neighborhood Study (CNS), which studied four ethnically distinct Chicago neighborhoods, focusing on racial discourse, culture, and social organization. The CNS aimed to match field workers and neighborhoods by race, and have a mixed-gender research team in each neighborhood. As a black female, I was paired with a black male to study Groveland, the black neighborhood. The goal was to conduct some degree of "insider" research, which can be especially fruitful because many of the initial obstacles to entry are minimized.[6] From my first few encounters in the neighborhood, it was clear that Groveland was very similar to the black middle-class neighborhood in Milwaukee where I was raised. Not only did the people remind me of friends and family from home, but we also shared many people in common. There were often fewer than six degrees of separation between me and the residents of

Groveland. With the black Catholics I shared knowledge of black Catholic leaders in the Midwest. I had mutual acquaintances with the young adults who had gone to college on the East Coast. And the neighborhood's political boss was my uncle's best friend. My research partner grew up in Chicago and thus had even more familiar connections. Comforted by this familiarity, I was actively involved in Groveland life. I directed the church choir; I joined the church's community action group; I stuffed envelopes for the alderman's reelection campaign; and I coached cheerleading at the local park, among a host of other activities and memberships. I started to see my Groveland friends at the grocery store, driving on the freeway, and at movie theaters throughout Chicago. I became a part of their lives and they of mine. For the third year of research I moved into Groveland and became even more embedded in neighborhood life.

At the same time, though, these connections and the relative ease of association had important repercussions, especially at the interpretive end. Such closeness to the community made it difficult to problematize certain behaviors, or question the logic behind people's statements. As a fellow African American I was *supposed to know* the answers to many questions that ethnographers must ask in order to go deeper than mere description. There was the constant danger of taking my own insider knowledge for granted, shirking away from probing the residents of Groveland for their own interpretations. Overall, being black facilitated entry and the formation of informal ties, but it was also necessary to consciously assume an outsider position.

I make no claim that the stories and opinions that people shared with me in interviews and in the course of daily conversations encompass the full range of feeling in Groveland. However, over thirty interviews, supplemented by more than three years of writing factual and impressionistic field notes on my every interaction in the neighborhood, further supplemented by my own experience growing up in a not-too-distant black middle-class neighborhood, all bolster my confidence in the claims I make throughout this book. In an effort to be most faithful to the data, the last chapters present two sustained, first-person narratives that hand the microphone over to Groveland residents to characterize their own lives. Their stories are lively illuminations of the processes that I describe in a somewhat more stoic tone. Of course, with the certain but unintended acts of editorial bias and misrepresentation on my part, I still have the final say throughout, even in these extended case studies.

One of the most salient issues in re-presenting the words of others is the issue of language itself. In the informal settings in which much of this research took place—such as the neighborhood park, people's homes, the church basement, or the grocery store checkout—many residents, if not most, used Black English, as did I. My practice in rendering field notes or interview quotes is to delete some of the verbal fillers (e.g., "um," "you know"), as well as false sentence starts that are common in speech. I do try to re-create the pronunciation of words through the use of contractions and notations that signal when the speaker dropped a syllable or sound (e.g., "sayin'" for "saying," "gon'" for "going to"). But I do not translate Black English into Standard English, a decision that requires some elaboration.

It seems obvious that an ethnographer who sets out to capture indigenous experiences would not significantly tamper with the way people talk. But concern for verity is only a partial motivation. The Black English so readily used in Groveland illuminates an empirical point that this book seeks to emphasize. Even though the African American bank receptionist may answer the phone in perfect Standard English, he or she may have a much different linguistic style when in the company of other African Americans. This concept of "code-switching"—i.e., speaking differently to different populations, one in Standard English and the other in the vernacular—can be broadened to characterize the black middle class more generally because it emphasizes the different worlds that whites and blacks inhabit, even African Americans with well-paying jobs or a college degree.[7]

Black English was commonplace in the neighborhood setting, and innovative modifications of its basic rules were even valued among some groups. Speaking Black English while sitting around the kitchen table makes a Groveland teacher no less middle class, but it does illustrate the near completeness of racial segregation. It highlights the importance of race for cultural practices, connecting black middle-class people to the black poor, and differentiating them from whites. As many field excerpts will illustrate, Groveland residents use Black English when talking about the most middle-class of topics—going to college, planning for marriage and the future, working downtown, or owning a home. This might seem discordant to those who view Black English as an inferior language. It might even support a prejudice that middle-class African Americans are not equal to middle-class whites precisely because they do not possess the proper intellectual and behavioral dispositions.

The prevalence of Black English in Groveland has both pluses and drawbacks. As an innovative cultural construction shared among

African Americans across class lines, Black English has unifying potential and performative value. It solidifies the cultural bonds between members of a heterogeneous African American population. However, Black English can also be an impediment to advancement in the predominantly white mainstream. Segregation produces an incubator within which Black English flourishes, but it does not always foster the sophisticated development of Standard English.[8] Black middle-class youth have fewer opportunities to practice and master Standard English in such an environment. The use of Black English by Groveland residents is emblematic of the particular handicaps with which black middle-class youth grow up because of their neighborhood context. In essence, the practice of code-switching represents the linguistic negotiation of two worlds, just as black middle-class individuals similarly maneuver both their racially marginal and their socioeconomically mainstream statuses in other realms.

Chapter 1 provides an overview of the economic and sociospatial position of the black middle class, and highlights what distinguishes members' situation from that of the white middle class. Chapter 1 and the neighborhood history in chapter 2 both describe the impact of broader social and economic processes on the character of Groveland. Groveland's history offers a microcosmic view of the forces that have affected neighborhood formation in Chicago and other similar industrial cities since World War II. Chapter 2 also describes some of the local sights and sounds that set the scenes of interaction.

To illuminate the various obstacles and pressures that black middle-class families and youth face, this book emphasizes the economic, spatial, and cultural contexts that influence decision-making, life transitions, and outcomes for Groveland residents, especially the youth. First, the post-1970s economy stunted the previously impressive growth of the black middle class. Disproportionate public-sector employment, clustering in lower-middle-class jobs, and economic fragility threaten the maintenance of Groveland's families. Chapter 3 discusses the role of a changing economy in the experiences of successive generations who have lived in Groveland, ending with contemporary youth. Groveland's first generation came of age during a period of sustained and rapid economic growth, fostering optimism for themselves, for their children, and for African Americans generally. The adolescents and young adults in today's Groveland—the second and third generations—are facing the uncertainties of changing technologies, stronger demands for an educated workforce, and the rising costs of higher education. There are myriad local effects of these broad economic shifts. Because of downward intergenerational mobility, housing maintenance suffers as inheritors lack the means to keep up their parents' investment. Older adolescents and young adults remain in their parents' homes well into their thirties in order to make ends meet, finish school, or sustain their youthful irresponsibility. And for some, the fast money promised by the ever-present underground economy is difficult to refuse when legitimate economic success is uncertain.

Second, the segregated geography of urban America has ramifications for the spatial context of the black middle class. Social ties across class lines, across lifestyles, and across the law exist partly because of the assignment of most African Americans to "the black side of town." These social ties are the subject of chapters 4 and 5. Groveland is a remarkably stable neighborhood with respect to housing tenure. Some families have four generations living within the neighborhood's boundaries, and others have developed kinlike relationships with their longtime neighbors. Chapter 4 illustrates how these networks promote easy access to both criminal and positive opportunities. The relationships between teachers and gang leaders, or preachers and drug dealers, highlight the appropriateness of the "crossroads" imagery in describing the neighborhood experiences of black middle-class youth. Chapter 5 focuses on three young people in Groveland to further elaborate on how youth steer through various peer networks, family situations, middle-class privileges, and criminal temptations.

Third, I explore the cultural realm through a focus on mass media and popular culture. Groveland youth are targets and consumers of, and active participants in, mass cultural styles that, while imaginative and entertaining, also provide a fashion and behavioral manual for deviance. In chapter 6, Groveland youth are placed within the very American cultural context of mass-media "gangstas." While there are autonomous cultural productions in Groveland, much of youth style—what is said, done, worn, and sung—is the local translation of mass cultural products received through magazines, television, movies, and radio. The popular cultural productions favored by Groveland's youth glamorize the hard life of poverty and scoff at the ordinariness of middle-classdom. Narrowing the scope from a consideration of popular culture and style generally to a focus on one particular fashion item, chapter 7 profiles the rise of the Nike brand to both global preeminence and local vogue. The expensive impulse to consume such fashion items is aroused with every billboard, magazine, commercial, and music video. Gangstas and drug dealers, both on-screen and across the street—with their tales of economic hardships, and their name-brand trinkets to show that they have now mastered the game—embody the messages proffered by the mass media.

To integrate these three realms, chapters 8 and 9 follow in the tradition of the sociological classic *The Jack-Roller,* with its native informant, Stanley. To give character (literally and figuratively) to theory, Clifford Shaw presented Stanley's own rendition of his (delinquent) life story. The final two chapters of this book similarly contain life histories of young adults raised in Groveland. They have completed their adolescence in the neighborhood, and thus provide useful gauges of the impact of such an upbringing. Each weaves together employment concerns, the organization of families and neighborhood networks, and the performance of or resistance to mass cultural messages. Rendered in the first person, these narratives are funny, startling, thought-provoking, and frank, and they address the substantive points raised throughout this book. These two case studies are exemplary of the range of experiences and outcomes of Groveland youth and young adults.

Finally, my conclusion relates the issues confronting black middle-class families and youth to national discussions of race and class. The black middle class is connected to the black poor through friendship and kinship ties, as well as geographically. Policies that hurt the black poor will ultimately negatively affect the black middle class. At the same time, the black middle class sits at the doorstep of middle-class privilege. Continued affirmative action, access to higher education, a plan to create real family-wage jobs, and the alleviation of residential segregation should be at the forefront of policy initiatives to support the gains already made by the black middle class.

❶

The Black Middle Class
Who, When, and Where?

There is a paucity of contemporary studies on the black middle class, making it necessary to define *who* belongs in the black middle class, *when* such a group emerged, and *where* many middle-class African Americans live. The answers to these questions collectively indicate that progress in the immediate post–World War II period led social scientists to prematurely assume that the black middle class was secure, when in fact, deep racial disparities have persisted. Germane to my focus on the neighborhood context, the answer to the *where* question emphasizes the fact that black middle-class out-migration from inner-city areas has been greatly misunderstood. Middle-class African Americans have become more segregated from poor African Americans, but I argue that the increased *size* of the black middle class—not, as some suggest, its increased propensity to move away from poor blacks—has caused these observed changes in the configuration of black communities. In the end, the black middle class continues to live near and with the black poor. These facts influence and circumscribe social processes in Groveland.

WHAT IS MIDDLE CLASS?

"Middle class" is a notoriously elusive category based on a combination of socioeconomic factors (mostly income, occupation, and education) and normative judgments (ranging from where people live, to what churches or clubs they belong to, to whether they plant flowers in their gardens). Among African Americans, where there has historically been less income and occupational diversity, the question

13

of middle-class position becomes even more murky. Just as social scientists wrestle with these issues, so do the residents of Groveland. Charisse Baker, a teenager in the neighborhood, gave her explanation of how class divisions exist within a racial hierarchy.

> Me personally, I don't see rich black people on a regular basis, except on [the television show] *Fresh Prince of Bel Air*. I mean, I know it's black people that are doctors, that are lawyers. But because I don't see them every day, I don't think that we're as divided.

Mr. Simms, a Groveland resident fifty years Charisse's senior, also commented on the compressed nature of the black class structure:

> I guess that there are classes divided on how much money you possess. For black people those are more artificial than real because we don't have where there's a very large upper class. But there are classes. And some are divided on the basis of what they *think* they have, and what they *think* you don't have.

Conversations with Groveland residents like Charisse and Mr. Simms underscore the fluid and complex nature of class categories among African Americans. Although most Groveland residents settle on a label somewhere between "lower middle class" and "middle class" to describe their own class position, the intermediate descriptors are plentiful. Some classification schemes focus on inequality. One resident resolved that there are the "rich," and everyone else falls into the categories of "poor, poorer, and poorest." Other words, like *ghetto*, *bourgie* (the shortened version of *bourgeois*), and *uppity* are normative terms that Grovelandites use to describe the intersection of standard socioeconomic measures and normative judgments of lifestyles and attitudes. Still other people talk about class in geographic terms, delineating a hierarchy of places rather than of incomes or occupations.

Without wading into either the social-scientific or layman's debates over class categories (which are quite extensive), I apply the "middle class" label to Groveland because it meets many of the standard criteria for such a designation. A majority of Groveland residents qualify as middle class by any of the commonly used income-based definitions. For example, economists use a measure called the *income-to-needs ratio* to identify class categories. The income-to-needs ratio divides total family income by the federal poverty level based on the family's size. The lower bound of the income-to-needs ratio for middle-class status is frequently set at two; that is, if a family earns two times a poverty-level income, they are middle class. Almost three-fourths of Groveland's families have an income-to-needs ratio of greater than two, qualifying them as middle class.[1]

Sociological conceptions of class include occupation and education along with measures of income (Blau and Duncan 1967; Poulantzas 1974; Vanneman and Cannon 1987). Studies of the black middle class in particular have used white-collar employment as the marker of middle-class position (Blackwell 1985; Kronus 1971; Landry 1987; Oliver and Shapiro 1995; Wilson 1978; Wilson 1995). In Groveland, 65 percent of the working residents are employed in white-collar jobs, again making it majority middle class. The most strict definition of middle class (for both blacks and whites) includes only those with a college degree. Twenty percent of Groveland's adults have graduated from college. Although not a majority, this is a much larger proportion than the 12 percent (in 1990) of African American adults overall with a college degree.

Finally, aside from these more objective class measures, "typical" middle-class behaviors are readily apparent in Groveland. People mow their lawns, go to church, marry, vote (they *really* vote), work, own property, and so on and so on. While the blanket term *middle class* obscures the particularities of being *black* and middle class (which is the focus of this book), Groveland's residents labor diligently to maintain their families, their investments, and their neighborhood, and to further their achievements.

Having established Groveland as a middle-class neighborhood using contemporary standards, reviewing the history of stratification in the black community illustrates the changing axes upon which class standing has been defined. A historical perspective also highlights the recency of a sizable black middle-class cohort, and the processes by which neighborhoods like Groveland were established. Because most African Americans were economically poor until relatively recently, blacks have used changing criteria to make status distinctions. The identity of the black middle class (the *who*) changes *as* and *when* the general position of African Americans changes. Also, the ways in which social scientists have evaluated such changes in the black class structure have in some ways dictated the amount of attention given to various segments of the African American community.

THE EVOLUTION OF THE BLACK
MIDDLE CLASS

American slavery inhibited the creation of a complete stratification system based on occupation, income, and/or education in the black community. Yet even within the enslaved population, distinctions did emerge that were primarily motivated by the racial hierarchy on which slavery was based. Blacks with lighter skin had particular advantages over their darker kin because of their position in the slave economy. One of the most important divisions was between household or skilled servants and field hands, which confounded "occupation" and skin-tone variation (Frazier 1939). House servants' sustained and close contact with the white upper class allowed for direct experiential knowledge of white lifestyles. These "mulatto" house and skilled slaves, along with a disproportionately mixed-race group of free Negroes, constituted the "old black elite" after emancipation and through Reconstruction (Keith and Herring 1991; Landry 1987). This first black middle class was defined by its phenotypical, spatial, and cultural proximity to the white upper class (Frazier 1939).

The situation changed with the northward migration and urbanization of African Americans in the early twentieth century. The First World War halted European immigration and carried away white workers to fight, spurring the Great Migration of southern blacks to northern cities. Northern industrial jobs beckoned blacks from the failing and oppressive rural economy of the South. Taking an expanded chronological view of the migration, six and a half million southern African Americans migrated northward between 1910 and 1970, altering the spatial configuration of race relations in the North (Farley and Allen 1987; Lemann 1991). Whereas there had been a relatively high degree of residential integration of blacks and whites prior to the flood of black migrants to the North, with the migration, whites began to leave integrated neighborhoods. The physical color line hardened. By 1920, former patterns of residential racial integration had all but disappeared in northern urban centers, creating all-black ghettos, which subsequently required a different kind of black middle class (Drake and Cayton [1945] 1993; Du Bois [1899] 1996; Kusmer 1976; Osofsky 1965; Spear 1967; Trotter 1985).

Aside from a small black intelligentsia, the old black elite earned its living through service to whites. Its status was imperiled, however, as whites moved farther away from black settlements, and increasing European immigration after World War I created a pool of white ethnic competition to black services. The old black elite also exhibited an air of superiority over "common" blacks. As a result, the old black elite did not take advantage of new opportunities that the black ghetto produced—namely, service to the black masses. The new racial ghetto formed the foundation upon which a new black middle class could flourish, one composed of "ghetto entrepreneurs" (Landry 1987). While the African American class structure still did not represent the full diversity of occupations, the "institutional ghetto" (Spear 1967) provided a captive clientele for African American entrepreneurs and professionals. Socioeconomic characteristics became more important indicators of class status. The importance of subjective indices such as skin color and occupational and social association with whites did not disappear, but did subside.

During this time between the two world wars, the black middle class comprised three major segments—small capitalists, professionals, and clerical and sales workers (Landry 1987). Black enterprises were clustered in local personal services—barbershops and beauty shops, cleaners, restaurants, grocery stores, and tailors. Black doctors, dentists, and especially lawyers were restricted to working in the black community. Even though their incomes placed them atop the black class hierarchy, the impact of racial segregation on their incomes was still severe. In the 1920s, a black doctor's income averaged $2,500 per year, while white doctors averaged over $8,500 (Landry 1987). Black clerical and sales workers made the least progress of all during this period. In the South, the prospect of blacks selling to and interacting with a white clientele went against the racial moral order. In the North, there were more opportunities for such service, but among Cleveland's working women in the 1930s, for example, only 3 percent of black females were in clerical or sales positions, compared to almost half of native white females, and 20 percent of foreign-born white women (Landry 1987; also see Cunningham and Zalokar 1992). Clearly, the black middle class continued to differ substantially from the white middle class in that it was anchored by professionals and business people, whereas the white middle class had a sizable contingent of (especially female) clerical and sales workers. In addition to compositional differences in the middle-class populations, the proportion of blacks who were middle class did not top 10 percent until 1960, whereas the white middle class constituted more than 20 percent of the total white population as early as 1910 (Landry 1987).

The unprecedented economic growth and prosperity after World War II, along with the social and political pressures of the civil rights movement, greatly expanded the black middle class in the 1950s and 1960s. The black class structure began to resemble the white class structure, with greater occupational diversity. Between 1960 and 1970, the percentage of black women in clerical jobs more than doubled (Landry 1987). Black women left domestic service jobs in which they had been trapped since slavery. In 1940, nearly 60 percent of employed black women were domestics. That figure declined to 6 percent by 1980 (Cunningham and Zalokar 1992). Between 1940 and 1970, black male professionals and technical workers went from 2 percent to 7 percent of employed black males; black proprietors, managers, and officials increased from 1 percent to 3 percent; and clerical and sales workers from 2 percent to 10 percent of all employed black men (Wilson 1978).[2] The period from 1945 to the early 1970s was extraordinary in terms of opening opportunities for African Americans. Predominantly white educational institutions were admitting black students in large numbers, businesses were recruiting at black colleges, and unions yielded to the pressure of their formerly excluded black coworkers.[3]

The growth of the black middle class piqued the interest of social scientists. In the mid-1950s, sociologist E. Franklin Frazier (1957) incited debate with his unfavorable account of the social life and individual psychology of the black middle class. One of Frazier's students, Nathan Hare (1965), repeated Frazier's opinions in the mid-1960s. Both Frazier and Hare argued that the black middle class imitated the white upper class. Because of this foolish imitation, along with the rejection of and disdain for black folk culture, Frazier (1957, 98) claimed that members of the black middle class "live in a cultural vacuum and their lives are devoted largely to fatuities."

This thesis of a soulless, apathetic, and frivolous black middle class was put forth just at the time when African Americans were launching the fight for civil rights, and as more African Americans from working-class and poor backgrounds were moving up the class ladder. While some of these descriptions may have characterized a segment of the old black elite, they were less applicable to the black middle class of the postwar period. Subsequent studies that looked specifically at the social and cultural life of middle-class African Americans found that while they did stress the importance of owning a home, and involvement in insular, family-centered activities, civic and church involvements were also central to black middle-class identity (Barnes 1985; Bell 1983; Kronus 1971; Sampson and Milam 1975). Upwardly mobile African Americans displayed a commitment to improving the situation of the black poor, and to civil rights more generally. In direct challenge to Frazier's contentions, William Sampson and Vera Milam (1975, 164) wrote that "middle-class blacks are conscious of their blackness, seem to feel an obligation to the race due to their more 'privileged' position, and express a strong sense of group solidarity."

A study of a black middle-class Chicago neighborhood not too far from Groveland was also an explicit test of Frazier's propositions (Kronus 1971). There were not the patterns of frivolous partying, card playing, and conspicuous consumption that Frazier recorded. Politically (a sphere Frazier thought nonexistent for middle-class blacks), the study's author considered 60 percent of the neighborhood residents that he interviewed to be "militant." That is, they responded affirmatively to the following assertion: "In seeking to end racial discrimination, Negro Americans need to stop talking so much and start more economic boycotts and other direct action." During this period of sweeping changes, there were continued ties between the black poor and the black middle class, despite the latter's new homes in nearby neighborhoods. Being middle class did not annul the fact of being black.

Recent studies continue to find allegiances across classes within the black community. Michael Dawson (1994) notes that despite heterogeneity, African Americans are surprisingly united in their political views. Jennifer Hochschild (1995) does find class differences among blacks, but argues that blacks who have made it are actually "enjoying it less" because they continue to feel the constraints of racism, while poor African Americans maintain some faith in the American Dream. In institutions, other scholars show that the black middle class participates in churches and civic organizations that make giving assistance to less fortunate African Americans a priority (Billingsley 1992; Pattillo 1998; Thompson 1986).

Yet despite continuing social and political ties, the reality of class schisms cannot be ignored. In *The Declining Significance of Race* (1978), William Julius Wilson argued that the African American community was splitting in two, with middle-class blacks improving their position relative to whites, and poor blacks becoming ever more marginalized. Civil rights legislation, especially affirmative action, worked well for African Americans poised to take advantage of educational and employment opportunities. The unsolved problem was what to do about African Americans in poverty. They were doing poorly not primarily because they were black, Wilson argued, but because they were unskilled and because the structure of the labor market had

changed around them. Grounded in the conviction that social structure influences the nature of race relations, Wilson saw the growth
in high-wage employment and the rise of political liberalism as fueling
the diminution of race as a factor in the stratification process. The
life chances of blacks were becoming more dependent on their class
position. African Americans with a college education were positioned
to take advantage of jobs in a service-producing economy—jobs in
trade and finance, public management, and social services. And because of affirmative action legislation, firms were motivated to hire
these qualified blacks.[4]

At the same time, the situation for the black poor was stagnating,
if not deteriorating. Black unemployment began to rise in the 1950s.
There was not much difference in the unemployment rate for blacks
and whites in 1930, but by the mid-1950s the ratio of black to white
unemployment reached 2 to 1 (Farley 1985). These changes, Wilson
and others argued, were the result of shifts in the mode of production.
The number of well-paying manufacturing jobs in the central city had
declined as a result of both technological changes and relocation.
These changes permanently relegated unskilled blacks to low-wage,
menial, and dead-end jobs, or pushed them out of the workforce altogether. Wilson's contribution was to direct attention to changes in the
nature of production that disadvantaged unskilled blacks. His prognosis for the black middle class was relatively optimistic, a position for
which he was criticized by other African American scholars. Wilson's
critics rushed to prove him wrong and show that members of the new
black middle class continued to face obstacles because of their race
(Pinkney 1984; Willie 1979; Washington 1979, 1980; see Morris
1996 for a review).

Wilson responded to these criticisms with *The Truly Disadvantaged.*
The title itself was insurance that readers would make no mistake
about his true population of interest, which was not the black middle
class. Wilson reiterated and refined his arguments about the declining
fortunes of the black poor. He also added a spatial component. In
addition to being left out of the labor market, poor blacks were also
being further marginalized and isolated in deteriorating inner cities.
The compelling story told in *The Truly Disadvantaged,* especially Wilson's thesis that the black middle class had "out-migrated" from the
inner city, thoroughly moved interest away from the black middle
and working classes. Attention landed squarely on the black poor. A
research industry was born to test Wilson's ideas concerning this segment of the black community.[5] To be sure, the obstacles faced by

poor blacks in a changing economy and the persistence of black poverty more generally are intolerable facts that merit considerable research and government resources. However, the research pendulum swung to the extreme, virtually ignoring the majority of African Americans who are not poor.

The irony in the timing of Wilson's work and the subsequent lack of interest in the condition of nonpoor African Americans is that, just as attentions were turning away from the black middle class, the initial grounds for optimism were undercut by the economic crises of the mid-1970s. The economy came to a screeching halt, and the black middle class experienced its share of skid marks. Studies in the 1970s found that class background for African Americans was becoming more important in determining occupational status, just as Wilson had posited (Featherman and Hauser 1976; Hout 1984). These trends did not extend into the 1980s, however, when racial differences in the ability to pass on one's privileged class status, or improve the position of one's children, became more pronounced. Data from the late 1980s showed that 60 percent of whites but only 36 percent of African Americans from upper-white-collar backgrounds were able to maintain their parents' occupational status. Whites were also more likely to improve on their parents' occupational status; more than half of whites from lower-white-collar backgrounds moved into upper-white-collar jobs, compared to only 30 percent of blacks. Downward mobility—across generations and within one's lifetime—was also more prevalent among African Americans (Duncan, Smeeding, and Rogers 1993; Oliver and Shapiro 1995; Davis 1995).

The steady and large increases in the percentage of blacks who were middle class waned in the 1970s and 1980s. The black male middle class grew by only 1 percent between 1970 and 1980. Black women continued to make headway in clerical and sales positions, but their gains were slowed in the professional sphere, and they lost ground in business ownership (Landry 1987). In income, the gap between what whites earn and what African Americans earn has not shown signs of narrowing since the early 1970s. For younger workers, the gap may in fact be increasing. The reversal of the trend toward earnings equality is especially pronounced among college-educated African Americans, partly because of their concentration in declining sectors of the economy and the weakened enforcement of equal employment policies in the 1980s.[6]

In the 1980s, the percentage of blacks in middle-class occupations grew from 40 to 45 percent (Wilson 1995). By 1995, the percentage had grown to half of all black workers, while 60 percent of whites had middle-class jobs (Smith and Horton 1997). However, the white middle class has historically contained more upper- (professionals, entrepreneurs, managers, and executives) than lower-middle-class workers (mostly sales and clerical jobs), while the opposite is true among African Americans. The different occupational distributions partly account for continuing earnings disparities. Despite fanfare over the gains of black professionals and executives, most black middle-class families contain combinations of teachers, foremen, government bureaucrats, office assistants, entrepreneurs, firefighters, reception-ists, and so on. When discussed in historical terms, then, the growth of the black middle class since World War II has been impressive. Yet viewed from a comparative perspective, African Americans con-tinue to lag behind whites.

What this social and demographic history indicates is that the de-clining interest in the status of nonpoor blacks was premature. The African American community was in a short time transformed from a population almost uniform in its poverty to one with a nascent middle class—this as recently as the 1950s. But racial disparities in occupa-tion, income, and intergenerational mobility were not eradicated by the few years of progress. The brief period of growth spawned a kind of dismissive optimism, but the economic and social purse strings were once again pulled tight, stalling the advances made by some African Americans. The continuing inequalities between middle-class whites and African Americans attest to the persistence of racism and discrimination, albeit in quite different forms than in the Jim Crow era (Bobo, Kluegel, and Smith 1997). In the next section we see that the same stages that characterize the socioeconomic past and present of African Americans—overwhelming disadvantage, followed by progress and optimism, followed by stagnation and retrenchment— are mirrored in the spatial history (the *where*) of the black middle class.

A MIDDLE-CLASS PROMISED LAND?

George Hicks, one of the Mississippi migrants to Chicago whose story is told in Nicholas Lemann's book *The Promised Land* (1991), epito-mizes the moving patterns of many of Chicago's middle-class black families, including those in Groveland. George Hicks graduated from Alcorn State University, a historically black school in Mississippi. In

1960, utterly frustrated with the racism in the South, he moved to Chicago. Hicks first moved to the Woodlawn neighborhood, which was at that time at the southern tip of Chicago's established black community. When the black community expanded, Hicks moved further south into the Englewood neighborhood, which was the destination of many upwardly mobile African Americans looking for more space and newer housing. When he was promoted to the administrative ranks of the Chicago Housing Authority, he changed residences once more, again moving farther south. Along with him moved other African American families, many of whom were middle class, and all of whom were following the exodus of middle-class whites. This was George Hicks's last move, and the site of Lemann's interview with him. The neighborhood was still all black, and still predominantly middle class. However, Lemann (1991, 278) took care to note that "the parlous state of the black slums in Chicago is a constant looming presence in the consciousness of the black middle class." George Hicks's story illustrates how African Americans, like other groups, have always tried to translate upward class mobility into geographic mobility, but remain physically and psychically close to the poorer neighborhoods they leave behind.

During the period from the Great Depression until the end of World War II, just before George Hicks arrived in Chicago, the boundaries of black ghettos in northern cities solidified. Despite the fact that black enclaves were swelling with southern migrants, black residential options were limited by the lack of new housing construction, and especially the organized and legally inscribed white resistance to integration (Farley and Allen 1987; Sugrue 1996). Single-family homes in the "Black Belts" of major cities were partitioned into ever smaller apartments, kitchenettes, and boarding rooms. Diseases became plagues in such crowded conditions, as did fires, rats, and generally unhealthy conditions (Hirsch 1983). Figuratively, the Black Belt fastened around an obese black community. In fact, the reason that many Groveland residents gave for moving their families into the neighborhood in the 1960s was that they simply wanted more space.

Home-building resumed after World War II, increasing the residential options of blacks who could afford to move (Farley 1996). The congested conditions in the Black Belt, the postwar availability of new housing for whites in the suburbs, and the improving economic means of blacks all contributed to the growth of the Black Belt into previously all-white neighborhoods. This "out-migration" of the black middle class has been a popular explanation for the decline of inner cities. In the 1940s and 1950s, so this argument goes, black neighborhoods were vertically integrated; that is, black middle-, working-, and lower-class families all lived together. Then in the 1960s and 1970s, increasing educational and occupational opportunities translated into residential mobility, and black middle-class families moved up and out of communities that once housed a diversity of classes. They took with them their income, their work ethic, their financial commitment to community institutions, and their example of legitimate success (Wilson 1987). The outcome is the isolation of poor African Americans in the neighborhoods abandoned by middle-class blacks.

However, this out-migration *suggestion* without sufficient consideration of out-migration *outcomes* gives the erroneous impression that the black middle class had escaped the strictures of racial segregation. Little attention is given to where this stabilizing population is moving.[7] The inference is that nonpoor blacks are integrating white neighborhoods, but mostly their exact destinations are left unclear. Wherever they might be moving, goes this popular wisdom, they no longer reside in "ghetto neighborhoods" or "inner-city communities." With these assumptions, and the confidence that the black middle class was on its way to parity with similarly positioned whites, all attentions turned toward the black poor stranded in deteriorating inner cities.

Again, the optimistic projections for the black middle class have not been realized. At the end of the 1960s, the early period of black suburbanization, observers found that "patterns of residential segregation by race within suburbs are emerging which are similar to those found within central cities" (Farley 1970, 512). When African Americans moved to white suburbs, many whites moved out. In general, black suburbs are located near city limits (Galster 1991) and are often the result of the "spillover" of black urban enclaves into suburban municipalities. In other cases, black "suburbs" are actually older and declining manufacturing cities that surround larger cities. East St. Louis, which is one of the poorest cities in the country, is situated in the St. Louis metropolitan area and is therefore a suburb of the city of St. Louis, although it manifests few of the positive attributes of suburbs. In the South, blacks living in rural areas have been redefined as suburbanites as the administrative boundaries of the nearest metropolitan area have enveloped them (Massey and Denton 1993). These classifications can be misleading when simply enumerating increases in the black suburban population.[8]

While some black families *have* integrated white neighborhoods as many commentators had predicted, the black middle class overall remains as segregated from whites as the black poor (Farley 1991). This means that the search for better neighborhoods has taken place *within* a segregated housing market. As a result, black middle-class neighborhoods are often located next to predominantly black areas with much higher poverty rates. Blacks of all socioeconomic statuses tend to be confined to a limited geographic space, which is formally designated by the discriminatory practices of banks, insurance companies, and urban planners, and symbolically identified by the formation of cultural and social institutions. Thus, while the size of the Black Belt has increased, extending beyond the administrative boundaries of cities and into adjacent suburbs, it remains effective in strapping-in the black community.

Researchers at the Rockefeller Institute of Government at the State University of New York at Albany illustrate this point using census data for nine major metropolitan areas, Chicago being one of them. They report that 78 percent of Chicago's African Americans live in majority-black tracts. (Black tracts are defined as more than 50 percent black.) In all nine primary metropolitan statistical areas (PMSAs), including Atlanta, Baltimore, Chicago, Detroit, Houston, Los Angeles, New York, Philadelphia, and Washington, D.C., 68 percent of African Americans live in majority-black tracts. The experience of living in a predominantly black neighborhood holds for middle-class African Americans as well. Sixty percent of black households with annual earnings over $45,000, and 58 percent of black households making over $75,000, live in majority-black census tracts. Although the incidence of living in such tracts declines with household income, these are already high earnings thresholds, encompassing only about 20 percent of all black households.

Viewed from another perspective, 61 percent of black Chicagoans who live in these majority-black census tracts (and 67 percent of African Americans over the nine PMSAs) live in "moderate"- or "middle"-income tracts where the median household income is .5 to 1.5 times that of the PMSA. Groveland falls into this grouping of census tracts. Thus, Grovelandites are not unique in their residential situation. A majority of African Americans in large cities live in predominantly black neighborhoods, and a majority of these neighborhoods are moderate to middle income, not poor. Hence, the experiences of Groveland residents are important for understanding the neighborhood processes that affect many African Americans.

Within these segregated black communities there is an internal, class-based organization that has existed since their formation. The attempts of the most educated and best paid African Americans to move out of very poor neighborhoods are not new phenomena. In the 1920s, E. Franklin Frazier (1939) identified seven zones (each about one square mile) within Chicago's South Side Black Belt. Using a unique set of variables to delineate the class status of each zone, Frazier found sizable compositional differences. The black middle class of that era was clustered in the seventh, southernmost zone. From the first zone (closest to the central business district, and the oldest part of the Black Belt) to the seventh zone, the percentage of southern-born heads of households decreased, illiteracy rates dropped, and the proportion of mulattos rose. Most objectively, the percentage of white-collar male workers rose from 5.8 percent in zone 1 to 34.2 percent in zone 7. The black middle class was very small, but nonetheless attempted to carve out a black middle-class residential space, even at the beginning of the century.

St. Clair Drake and Horace Cayton ([1945] 1993, 658–59) followed in the tradition of Frazier, writing about the effects of segregation on the residential choices of middle-class blacks in Chicago's Black Belt in the 1930s and early 1940s. Their description is still relevant:

> Out of the search for better neighborhoods has arisen the ecological pattern of the Black Belt . . . with its "best," "worst," and "mixed areas." . . . Negroes are unable to keep their communities "middle-class" because the Black Ghetto is too small to accommodate its population and the less well-to-do must *filter into* these "best" areas. [Emphasis added.]

Drake and Cayton described an ongoing "sifting and sorting" of economic classes within the segregated Black Belt. The black middle class pushed southward (and westward) against the borders of the Black Belt, with low-income blacks following their initial forays. In a later edition of *Black Metropolis*, Drake and Cayton ([1945] 1993, 827) noted the particular expansion of black middle-class enclaves in the 1960s: "The South Side ghetto has become more 'gilded' as a large amount of property in good condition has been turned over to middle-class Negroes." Segregation, however, remained pervasive.

Even William Julius Wilson, a leading proponent of the out-migration argument, recognized early efforts of middle-class blacks to segregate themselves. Describing the pre-1960s black community, Wilson (1987, 7) wrote, "lower-class, working-class, and middle-class black families all lived more or less in the same *communities* (albeit in different *neighborhoods*)" (emphasis added). This pattern of a large black community with a diversity of black neighborhoods within it—some very poor, some diverse, and others solidly middle class—survives today. The Black Belt has *core* and *periphery* areas (Jargowsky and Bane 1991; Morenoff and Sampson 1997) created by the constraints of racial segregation, but also by a desire to live among other blacks. Middle-class African Americans have attempted to leave behind their poor neighbors in core ghetto areas—only to relocate to peripheral areas abutting their previous residences. In the contemporary African American ghetto there are still the best, mixed, and worst areas. This situation is the result of both the continuous out-migration of middle-class blacks and the racially segregated housing market they encounter in their attempts to move.[9]

Hence, a rereading of historic and contemporary black residential patterns suggests the following. African Americans have long attempted to translate socioeconomic success into residential mobility, making them similar to other ethnic groups (Massey and Denton 1985). They desire to purchase better homes, safer neighborhoods, higher quality schools, and more amenities with their increased earnings. Out-migration has been a constant process. The black middle class has *always* attempted to leave poor neighborhoods, but has never been able to get very far. However, when the relative *size* of the black middle class grew, the size of its residential enclaves grew as well. *The increase in the number of black middle-class persons has led to growth in the size of black middle-class enclaves, which in turn increases the spatial distance between poor and middle-class African Americans. This greater physical separation within a segregated black community accounts for the popular belief that black middle-class out-migration is a recent and alarming trend.*

The raw number of blacks in the middle class has increased dramatically. In 1960, only 385,586 black men and women in the entire country were professionals or semi-professionals, business owners, managers, or officials. By 1980, that number had grown to well over one million (1,317,080). Similar increases took place in the category of sales and clerical workers, which increased from 391,927 blacks in 1960 to well over two million such workers in 1980. By 1995, nearly seven million African Americans were employed in middle-class occupations (Smith and Horton 1997). All of these new social workers and receptionists, insurance salespeople and government bureaucrats would have to be housed somewhere.

The key dimension of black middle-class out-migration, then, is not that it has increased. There has been steady movement of black families who could afford to move. The difference is that the black middle class is now a much larger proportion of the black community than it has ever been. In the 1930s, there were only two small census tracts at the southern tip of Chicago's Black Belt that were majority middle class. The black middle class was not substantial enough to numerically predominate in any one neighborhood. By contrast, in the 1990s version of Chicago's South Side Black Belt, there is a band of contiguous community areas with a total population of more than a quarter million that could be described as a black middle-class enclave within Chicago's larger black South Side.[10] Over 95 percent of the residents of this stretch of neighborhoods are black, over 60 percent work in white-collar jobs, and the median family income is above the Chicago median. This middle-class area—nearly seven miles long and seven miles wide at the extreme tips—is full of African Americans who "are determined to maintain what America generally regards as 'the middle-class way of life'" (Drake and Cayton [1945] 1993, 518).

While the black middle-class area in contemporary Chicago is sizable, it by no means totally separates blacks of different classes. Residential interclass interaction is most likely in the transitional, or "mixed," areas. These neighborhoods might well be considered vertically integrated.[11] But even the predominantly middle-class areas remain tied to the core ghetto. Administrative boundaries have no regard for the neighborhoods established by the black middle class. High schools service neighborhoods with a diversity of residents. Police districts are responsible for the residents of housing projects as well as those who live in owner-occupied single-family homes. Supermarkets, parks, nightclubs, scout troops, churches, and beaches all service a heterogeneous black population. Also, the poverty rates of the neighborhoods that make up Chicago's black middle-class expanse range from a low of 7 percent to a high of 17 percent. The middle-class way of life is in constant jeopardy in black middle-class neighborhoods because of the unique nature of their composition and location.[12]

The geography and demographic makeup of Groveland are illustrative of its status as a part of Chicago's black middle-class South Side (see appendix B, fig. 1). All but one of the neighborhoods bordering Groveland have lower median family incomes and higher poverty rates than Groveland. The Treelawn community, which is one community removed from Groveland, has a median family income of under $19,000—not even half the median family income in Groveland. Its poverty rate of over 30 percent is almost triple that of Groveland. All of these contiguous neighborhoods are over 90 percent black, illustrating the hypersegregation of Chicago (Massey and Denton 1993). Finally, using a measure of the most violent kind of crime, homicide, there are clear perils associated with living in a black middle-class neighborhood. All but two of the neighborhoods adjacent to Groveland have higher homicide rates. Homicide rates in predominantly white communities in Chicago barely overlap with the levels of violence in the Groveland area. Thus, while there is a concentration of black middle-class community areas, their internal diversity, higher crime rates, and island-like character affect the experiences of the residents who live in them.

The situation in Chicago and Groveland is duplicated across the country. After comparing census tracts in all cities with a population of over 100,000, Robert Sampson and William Julius Wilson (1995, 42) concluded that the " 'worst' urban contexts in which whites reside are considerably better than the average context of black communities." The residential returns to being middle class for blacks are far smaller than for middle-class whites. In Philadelphia, Douglas Massey, Gretchen Condran, and Nancy Denton found that African Americans with college educations had a more than 20 percent chance of coming in contact in their neighborhood with someone receiving welfare, whereas college-educated whites had only an 8 percent chance of such contact. This pattern was repeated for interaction with blue-collar workers, high school dropouts, and the unemployed. Massey and Denton (1993, 153) later concluded that for blacks, "high incomes do not buy entrée to residential circumstances that can serve as springboards for future socioeconomic mobility."[13] In terms of exposure to crime, middle-class blacks are again at a disadvantage, even when they move to the suburbs. Echoing the comments of other researchers, one study found that "even the most affluent blacks are not able to escape from crime, for they reside in communities as crime-prone as those housing the poorest whites" (Alba, Logan, and Bellair 1994, 427).

These comparisons are not meant to suggest that middle-class white neighborhoods are without problems similar to those faced by middle-class blacks. Studies of the fragility of middle-class whites (Danziger and Gottschalk 1995; Newman 1989, 1993); the wayward leanings of some middle-class white suburban youth (Gaines 1991; Monti 1994); and the struggle by middle-class whites to hold on to neighborhood investments (Camacho and Joravsky 1989) all indicate that middle-class status is a precarious standing for many Americans, regardless of race. However, the spatial immediacy of the threats of crime and drugs for many middle-class black neighborhoods differentiates them from similar white neighborhoods.

The problems confronting middle-class African Americans are not solved by simply moving away from a low-income black family and next door to a middle-class white family. The fact that a neighborhood's racial makeup is frequently a proxy for the things that really count—quality of schools, security, appreciation of property values, political clout, and availability of desirable amenities—attests to the ways in which larger processes of discrimination penalize blacks at the neighborhood level. Racial inequalities perpetuate the higher poverty rate among blacks and ensure that segregated black communities will bear nearly the full burden of such inequality. The argument for residential integration is not to allow the black middle class to easily abandon black neighborhoods. Instead, more strict desegregation laws would also open the door for low-income blacks to move to predominantly white neighborhoods, where jobs and resources are unfairly clustered. Yet we need not wait for whites to accept blacks into their neighborhoods, and think of integration as the panacea for current problems. Aggressive measures must be taken to improve the socioeconomic conditions of African Americans *where they are*. By highlighting *where* the black middle class lives, it becomes apparent that concentrated urban poverty has repercussions not only for poor African Americans, but for middle-class blacks as well, while a majority of middle-class whites move farther into the hinterlands. A comprehensive antipoverty agenda would have positive benefits for African Americans as a group, and therefore for the residential environs of the black middle class—although it leaves unchallenged the desire of many blacks and even more whites to live with others of the same race.[14]

2

The Making of Groveland

I pick up my life
And take it with me
And I put it down in
Chicago, Detroit, Buffalo, Scranton,
Any place that is North and East
And not Dixie.

—Langston Hughes,
"One Way Ticket," 1948

The history of present-day Groveland begins in the American South, primarily in Mississippi, Arkansas, and Louisiana, but also in Texas, Tennessee, Alabama, and the other states where Jim Crow laws prohibited African Americans from living freely. At church on Sunday in Groveland, visitors who name a southern state as their home receive a generous round of applause. After service they are greeted with eager questions: "Do you know so-and-so? . . . Where'd you go to school? . . . Is such-and-such church still there? . . ." Southern accents set the rhythm not only in church, but also at political rallies and school meetings, and in friendly public greetings. During summer vacation, children disappear from the neighborhood for visits with relatives "Down South." And soul food is a staple at events from baby showers to retirement parties.

The Great Migration—the movement of blacks from the South to urban centers in the North from the start of World War I through the 1960s—has had a profound impact on the racial makeup of northern (and western) receiving cities. The historical paintings of the African American artist Jacob Lawrence depict the southern train stations crowded with families looking for a better life. Black newspapers published in the North fueled the migration fever with announcements that there were jobs to be had. Chicago was a major port of

31

entry. A woman from New Orleans wrote the following request to the *Defender,* Chicago's black newspaper:

> Gentlemen: I read Defender every week and see so much good youre doing for the southern people & would like to know if you do the same for me as I am thinking of coming to Chicago about the first of June. and wants a position.[1]

With thousands of inquiries like this one, Chicago's black population increased eightfold from 1910 to the 1940s, changing the city into what St. Clair Drake and Horace Cayton ([1945] 1993) called "Black Metropolis."

In many northern cities like Chicago, this growing population was relegated to a geographic space that did not increase with the same rapidity. With no new housing being built from the depression era through World War II, the Black Belt became dangerously over-crowded. But with the ending of the war, blacks and whites alike started looking for new homes, changing the racial geography of the city. The Black Belt grew, and Black Metropolis began to claim more territory as its own. Between 1950 and 1970, block after block, neighborhood after neighborhood dramatically changed from white to African American occupancy. Groveland lay in the path of expansion of Chicago's South Side black community. One Groveland resident put it simply: "There'd be about seven or eight of us [blacks] and about thirty of them [whites]. But, you know, you'd see a white family would move out and a black one moved in, and soon it was more and more of us." Census statistics bear out this story. In 1960, there were only 6 blacks in all of Groveland out of a total population of 12,710. By 1970, just ten years later, blacks made up over 80 percent of the neighborhood's population. By 1990, the neighborhood was 98 percent black (see table 1, appendix B). The neighborhoods that surround Groveland went through similar transformations, some a bit sooner and some later.

Many Chicago neighborhoods experienced some kind of racial or ethnic change during this unstable period, and each employed specific ways of addressing such changes, including violence. Yet in stark contrast to the firebombings, mob attacks, and nightly protests mounted in other Chicago areas, racial change in Groveland proceeded with little turbulence. Some of Groveland's current residents were youngsters when their families moved them into the neighborhood. They remember being chased by groups of white youth, or being the targets of glass milk bottles hurled by their white neighbors, but these were isolated incidents. There were no organized efforts in Groveland to impede the geographic advances of African Americans. In fact, the only organized efforts on the part of Groveland residents were for positive ends. The white priest of the local Catholic church, along with a concerned black parent who lived across the street from the church, created an interracial baseball league to foster friendships between the new and the old residents. One white resident, who later left the neighborhood to enter the priesthood, recalled the role of the Catholic church in easing tensions: "I remember when the neighborhood, as they say, changed. Monsignor Welch said, 'The people who are coming are God's people, and if anything negative happens you will have to answer to me.' Mom and I stayed."

Despite these efforts to stall a complete racial turnover and achieve integration, the neighborhood still changed, and at a rapid pace. Real estate speculators played a major role in inciting neighborhood change. A nine-part series entitled "The Panic-Peddlers" appeared in the *Chicago Daily News* in 1959 (Newman et al. 1959). The articles investigated the dealings of "real-estate sharks" (black and white) in a small area just west of Groveland where black families had just begun to move. The authors published the names, photographs, and addresses of the "blockbusters," who used scare tactics to encourage whites to sell their homes quickly and for a low price. One such scheme involved paying blacks to stage fights in the target area. The actors would recite a full script that often included the threat of gunfire. The speculators hoped that this would escalate whites' fears that not only were African Americans moving in, but so too were crime and violence. In many cases, and despite the work of groups like the church, the Bristol-Groveland Community Council, and the West Groveland Community Association, these scare tactics worked. Once the speculators acquired property hastily sold at a loss by white residents, they quickly marked up the cost to home-hungry African Americans who were willing and able to pay the inflated prices for newer, decent housing. At the same time, whites were being beckoned to new developments in the suburbs.[2]

Groveland did not violently erupt during this transition because the African American newcomers shared many qualities with the former residents of the neighborhood. The predominantly single-family housing and "suburban-style" living in Groveland and the surrounding neighborhoods attracted black families who were able to purchase homes rather than rent. The percentage of families who own their homes in Groveland has not dropped below 70 percent since

1950. In fact, the *only* neighborhood characteristic that dramatically changed during this transition period was the race of its residents. Between 1960 and 1970, the median years of schooling *increased* from 12.1 years to 12.4 years. During the same time, unemployment jumped slightly, from just over 2 percent to 4 percent, but the latter figure included unemployment for both males and females, whereas the former counted only male unemployment. Finally, the percentage of people living below the poverty level *fell* from 6 percent in 1960 to 5 percent in 1970. In many ways, the new black residents were slightly better off economically and educationally than the whites who were leaving.

Socioeconomic similarities translated into like-minded desires and an equal dedication to maintaining the neighborhood. Muriel Wilson, a resident of the nearby Bristol neighborhood, had a keen desire to demonstrate to her white neighbors that her presence did not symbolize the demise of the neighborhood. To the contrary, she was committed to its upkeep. She remembered:

> We were cautious in those days. I'd watch the man next door. I wanted to assure him that I was just as interested in maintaining property as he was. Every time he went to work on his grass, I went out to work on mine. I had nightmares about weeds. [Quoted in Camacho and Joravsky 1989, 46.]

Today, block clubs throughout Groveland instruct residents and guests to drive slowly and look out for children. They prohibit loud music, loitering, and washing cars on the street. Many of the block-club signs begin and conclude with the pleasantries, "Welcome" and "Have a Nice Day!" These are the components of the middle-class way of life that Groveland residents strive to maintain.

Cultural and class similarities mediated the process of racial change in Groveland. The middle-class white residents of Groveland eschewed the violent tactics being used in other Chicago neighborhoods. Although they had strong feelings for the neighborhood and launched efforts to hold on to their property, they ultimately had the economic means and the correct skin color to move to the suburbs that were feverishly built after World War II. Because the suburban move was a general phenomenon for whites at the time, there was no white interest in—only black demand for—housing in Groveland once white families vacated the neighborhood. As Muriel Wilson concluded in her comments about this period, "For the most part, white people just quietly moved. They didn't say anything; they just left" (Camacho and Joravsky 1989, 45).

Many of the first black residents to move to Groveland in the 1960s are still there in the 1990s. According to the 1990 census, over 40 percent of Grovelandites moved into their current residences before 1970. The neighborhood's median age of thirty-six reflects this sizable contingent of older adults, many of whom have retired. This stability has translated into enduring institutions such as strong churches and schools, an active and productive business association and business district, and a responsive neighborhood park. Also, residents have close family and friendship ties. For example, Anna Morris moved to Groveland with her parents and sisters when she was a young girl in the early 1960s. Now approaching forty, Mrs. Morris is raising her own family in Groveland. With such a lengthy family investment in the neighborhood, she easily described her circle of family and friends in both network and geographic terms. "You'd never know it, but it's like one big family around here," she began after a game of volleyball at the Groveland Park gym. "You'd never know all the people that's related." Filling in the details, Anna Morris reported that Diedra, Lucky, and Lance—all regulars at the gym—were brothers and sister. And Spider, who worked at the field house, had shared a locker in high school with Mrs. Morris's own sister, Julie. " 'Cause see I live on this block," she explained as she positioned her left hand as a marker of the street where she lived. "And my mother lives on this block." She held her right hand parallel to her left, showing that she and her mother lived only one block apart. Even her husband's family lives near: "And then Moe's mama lives on this block," she continued, crossing her left hand over her right to indicate her mother-in-law's street, one block away. As Mrs. Morris's family demonstrates, the social fabric in Groveland is thick, nurtured by high rates of residential stability and the growth of extended families.[3]

Groveland is not, however, an island of longtime primary relationships, quiet streets, and committed institutions. A congestion of large auto-body shops and retail stores at the north end and a commercial park at the south end surround the interior of brick homes and green grasses. These physical boundaries are formidable, but not impermeable. Because the neighborhood is relatively small, it is integrally tied to the surrounding neighborhoods both administratively and symbolically. Groveland is united with parts of seven other community areas to make up the aldermanic ward, and the areas that comprise the police district and the state congressional and senatorial districts get progressively larger. Discursively, the frequently used referent "Bristol-Groveland area" illustrates its connection to the neighborhood to the west. The more general and common term, "the South Side," indicates Groveland's symbolic connection to Chicago's black community as a whole.

Also, Groveland is not the same neighborhood it was when the process of racial change was nearly complete in 1970. The changes in the economy that have had a profound impact on urban black communities have also affected Groveland, albeit somewhat indirectly. Deindustrialization, the movement of manufacturing jobs to the suburban ring, and the general stagnation of the economy during the 1970s have left urban black neighborhoods with few job options for those with limited skills. The neighborhoods hardest hit by economic changes have lost businesses; housing has deteriorated and institutions cannot survive, leading to the rise in various social problems. Groveland has been somewhat buffered from the immediate impact of these structural changes. In 1980, almost two-thirds of Groveland's population were employed in white-collar occupations. This group was more likely to benefit, rather than suffer, from economic restructuring that favored technical and professional experience. Still, the neighborhood's professionals and managers live beside residents in lower service positions and manufacturing jobs; the two groups have had to deal with economic changes together.

The deteriorating economic and social conditions in the poorest areas prompt the residents of those areas to continue their attempts to escape, usually into neighborhoods like Groveland. While the racial transformation of Groveland occurred rapidly, class changes in the neighborhood are developing more gradually. They do not, however, go unnoticed by residents. The continuous movement of families out of nearby poor neighborhoods and into Groveland has brought economic heterogeneity to Groveland and neighborhoods like it around the periphery of Chicago's core ghetto.[4] The unemployment rate in Groveland jumped from 4 percent in 1970 to over 9 percent in 1980, and rose again to nearly 12 percent in 1990. The percentage of families with incomes below the poverty line also rose, from 5 to 10 to 12 percent in 1970, 1980, and 1990, respectively. Thirty-five percent of the children at the Groveland Elementary School were classified as low income during the 1991–92 school year (Chicago Public Schools Data Book 1991–1992). The school data suggest that poverty is even more pronounced among younger families. These indicators remain more favorable than the demographics for black Chicagoans generally, but they signal important changes in the character of Groveland.

Twenty-eight-year-old Tommy Smith grew up in the northernmost section of Groveland, closest to the expanding poverty core. His description of the recent changes on his block suggests an unsure future for the neighborhood.

> There may be five houses on the block—no six—six houses on the block that once upon a time was full with residents that grew up and started at the same time as me. They either died or moved away. Out of that, one of those houses is knocked down, one is vacant, one is burned down, and one is empty on a Section 8 listing, and one is, two are empty. . . . And, the people who did move in two of the vacant houses were low-income-housed people. And in that, again, they just did not take care of their property. And did not care much about the individuals surrounding them. And, no, I did not know them very well.

Although most of the streets in Groveland are not experiencing such visible decline, the interrelated issues of population succession, property maintenance, and low-income newcomers are often raised among residents.[5] Most academic examinations of neighborhood change privilege processes of *racial* change, but black neighborhoods can experience class-based changes that similarly threaten their stability.[6] The containment of black urban (and even suburban) communities as a result of larger discriminatory forces ensures that black middle-class neighborhoods are the most vulnerable to processes of class-based destabilization. Groveland parents, like Tommy Smith, devise strategies to manage growing heterogeneity. Other families have picked up and moved out of Groveland, often headed for Chicago's southern suburbs. These movers are replicating the patterns of out-migration and creating new black communities on the suburban periphery of the established Black Belt.

The heterogeneity that some residents are fleeing is apparent when comparing the income distribution in Groveland to the distribution in Beltway, a white middle-class neighborhood in Chicago (see appendix B, fig. 2). Even though the median family income in Groveland is slightly higher than the median family income in Beltway, the poverty rate in Groveland is *four times* the poverty rate in Beltway. The concurrence of these facts is possible because in Groveland, relatively high-earning black families live alongside poor families, whereas Beltway's income distribution contains a clustering of families in the center of the distribution. Groveland's hollowed-out distribution, compared to Beltway's bell-shaped curve, illustrates a polarization of the black class structure (Wilson 1978; Grant, Oliver, and James 1996). At the neighborhood level, the higher poverty rate and more disparate income distribution translate into a shaky balance of residents. Most Grovelandites (poor and middle class) share the desire to keep the neighborhood safe, clean, and thriving, but a smaller proportion than in Beltway have the financial resources to contribute to these goals. The higher poverty rate also places a certain strain on public and social services, most especially the schools, a strain with which the white neighborhood is less familiar. These differences underlie many of the pressures that black middle-class families face that similar white families do not.

Overall, then, the Great Migration, the growth of the Black Belt, constraints on the exodus of middle-class blacks, and economic restructuring have all contributed to the present makeup of Groveland—a racially homogeneous, economically diverse neighborhood. Groveland's business strips exemplify the character of the neighborhood. Its main commercial area is considered the busiest minority shopping district in Illinois, according to one newspaper. Where Common Street meets Ridge Lake Avenue—the two major business streets in Groveland—are four telling institutions. On one corner is an ultramodern branch of a large national bank. According to the Groveland Chamber of Commerce newsletter, it is the busiest branch in Chicago. The facility has ten customer tellers, nine ATMs, and ten personal bankers, as well as drive-through services. The bank handles the business of over fifteen thousand households. The manager of the branch summarized the bank's relationship with the neighborhood: "Groveland is very important to us in that it is a source of our well-monied customers, many of them living in Cedarcove [a subdivision in Groveland], and the older homes between Second and Sixth avenues." The bank represents an institution that supports middle-class Grovelandites, and provides a stable and reliable service to the community. In addition to its formal activities, the branch also donates money to block clubs, and hosts an annual Black Arts fair in its parking lot.

Across the street from the bank is a check-cashing outlet, the Currency Exchange. The fluorescent yellow signage that is uniform across the Currency Exchange chain is ubiquitous in poor Chicago neighborhoods (Wacquant and Wilson 1989). While there are fewer check-cashing outlets outside of poverty areas, the fact that one exists in

Groveland suggests that there is a market for the services offered there. At the Currency Exchange, patrons can cash payroll checks, pay utility bills, buy postage stamps, wire money, buy money orders, or change money—all for a not-so-nominal fee. The advantages are that there is no minimum deposit needed to use these services, services are rendered with the presentation of only one piece of photo identification (at most), and there are no extensive credit checks for authorization. Equally important, the Currency Exchange is open well before and after the bank's usual operating hours. For those with limited savings, who need money regularly and quickly, and who have no credit or bad credit, check-cashing outlets function as expensive but less restrictive local banks—institutions that serve the needs of lower-income Groveland residents.[7]

The businesses on the other two corners of the intersection illustrate different aspects of the neighborhood. Soul Seas is a black-owned and -operated soul food restaurant, identifying with the racial composition of the area and catering to southern black culinary tastes. On the last corner is Keen Bros. Service Station, a black-owned gas station and auto-repair shop. Groveland's businesses and institutions changed with the neighborhood and reflect both its class and its racial makeup. Both the restaurant and the gas station have been in Groveland "about thirty years," that parsimonious time period that many residents use to identify when the neighborhood became predominantly African American. So on the four corners of the busiest intersection in Groveland, the neighborhood's predominantly middle-class composition is represented by the imposing bank structure; the presence of a non-negligible low-income population is suggested by the Currency Exchange; the African American cultural ownership is signified by a soul food restaurant; and black-owned Keen Bros.' thirty years in business is evidence of neighborhood stability.

Away from the commercial streets are many detached single-family homes. There is no public housing, although some of the renters in the neighborhood receive federal subsidies in the form of Section 8 vouchers. Over half of all of the housing units were built before 1950; they are primarily brick bungalows, Georgians, and Cape Cod homes. In the 1950s, Cedarcove, a subdivision in the southwestern portion of Groveland, was financed by Federal Housing Administration and Veterans' Administration guaranteed loans. The area was planned as a "model community," and the housing very much resembles the split-level ranch homes that were built in America's suburbs at the time. But early attempts at integration in Cedarcove could not survive amid the racial transformation overtaking most of Chicago's South Side, and the subdivision, like the rest of Groveland, is now predominantly black.

There are three elementary schools in Groveland—two public and one Catholic—and one public high school. Within the neighborhood, there is a recreational park, Groveland Park, which is a part of the Chicago Park District. Finally, there are eleven churches in Groveland representing ten Christian denominations; six of the churches belong to the Groveland Clergy Association.

Residents actively define the local atmosphere at a much deeper level than the neighborhood demographics can address. Groveland is filled with positive images of African Americans and symbols of black identity. The physical space itself is literally postered and decorated with cultural symbols that establish ownership of the neighborhood, and define the forms of interaction that are sanctioned in that space. The decoration of Groveland Park is a good example. The walls of the waiting room are lined with posters and short biographies of "Black Heroes." Frederick Douglass, Michael Jordan, Michael Jackson, Rosa Parks, Martin Luther King, Jr., Harriet Tubman, Booker T. Washington, Duke Ellington, former New York mayor David Dinkins, and former Planned Parenthood director Faye Wattleton make up an eclectic group of prominent African Americans, past and present. The largest poster is of Malcolm X. The walls behind these posters are painted red, black, and green, the colors of the African American flag. In the hallway is a portrait of Chicago's first (and so far only) black mayor, the late Harold Washington. Original drawings by the young people from the park round out this tribute to historic black figures.

Although such an exhibit may seem unexceptional, its presence is part of the establishment of cultural ownership of the park facilities. The decorations and activities in Groveland Park are reflections of the preferences of the clientele, and are part of the cultural fabric that the residents have woven. Groveland Public Library also has portraits of famous African Americans, and displays artwork that features black figures. Children's books with black characters on the covers, black sorority and fraternity paraphernalia, and posters of black musicians fill the windows along the main business street. Church signs announce Black History Month celebrations during February, and the vestibule of the neighborhood Catholic school features the poem "Black Is," in which the student author lists in a poetic fashion all of the things she defines as black: beautiful, cool, wonderful, great, peace not hate, right, and smart (just like white). Behind the altar in the

Catholic church hangs an African American flag. Kente cloth—a patterned material worn in Ghana—is draped over the altar. The crucifix is carved out of coffee-brown wood. The residents of Groveland exert control over their surroundings and the symbols that will be displayed in order to foster a level of comfort and familiarity.

The sounds in Groveland similarly establish the neighborhood as culturally black. There is often music in the Groveland Park field house. The radio is always set to one of the Chicago stations that play rhythm and blues or rap music. Frequently, the park attendants play their own tapes. When the younger crowd uses the park on Sundays for afternoon basketball, the music of rappers like Snoop Doggy Dogg, Wu Tang Clan, and Scarface predominates. For other groups, gospel music sets the mood. At the end of the Summer Day Camp, the park hosted a program in which the various age groups performed a routine that they had practiced throughout the summer. For the final number, all of the day campers sang the Kirk Franklin gospel hit of the summer, "Why We Sing." By the end of the song, relatives and friends in the audience were singing along. Both visually and aurally, the park reflects the neighborhood of which it is a part.

Through the use of symbols, Groveland's residents, business owners, and church leaders color the neighborhood black. These racial signifiers suggest ownership, contribute to a sense of belonging and pride, and encourage participation in these institutions. Groveland has completed the process of neighborhood racial change, and as a result there is little conflict over the symbols to be displayed in community institutions. Black residents see, hear, and recognize themselves through the display of black leaders, black flags, African cloth, and black music. Their presence as worshipers, shoppers, and day campers is validated by these self-reflecting images.

Certain components of Groveland's landscape, however, transcend racial boundaries. Groveland is a black *middle-class* neighborhood, and as such, many residents have the ability to maintain the neighborhood as any other racial group would with similar social and economic resources. For example, the Groveland subdivision of Cedarcove has yearly contests to judge the best yards and the best holiday decorations. Cedarcove homeowners invest time and money in creatively trimming bushes for the summer, buying decorative bags for autumn leaves, and hanging Christmas lights and knickknacks for the winter holidays. Seasonal winners proudly display a lawn sign that hails their home or yard as the most attractive and best decorated in the neighborhood.

In the same way that the racial signifiers serve to make black residents comfortable, the class signifiers denote Groveland as a middle-class neighborhood. Most houses are maintained in good condition, and block clubs post rules prohibiting loitering, littering, and soliciting. In the summer, a few professional landscapers tend to lawns and gardens. It is the combination of these class symbols and racial signifiers that makes explicit the neighborhood's *black middle-class* identity. These symbols present a reflection for residents and a picture to visitors of the kind of people who have created the space. They are both models of and models for behavior (Geertz 1973). They represent the concerns of residents while also serving as guides for others' behavior. If one neighbor has well-trimmed bushes and flowers, this influences other neighbors to do the same. During one Christmas season, a young woman commented on her decision to put up decorations: "Everyone else on the block had stuff up," she said. "So we figured we better get some stuff." Through these racial and class signifiers, residents provide constant reminders about black cultural ownership and middle-class standards.

Yet such a sweeping portrayal can blur the diversity within the neighborhood in an attempt to highlight the common interests of the majority of Groveland residents. Even within this brief introduction there are hints of the near impossibility of definitively characterizing the social flavor of a black middle-class neighborhood. For example, the stable extended-family ties that Anna Morris described stand in contradiction to the unsettling anonymity that was developing on Tommy Smith's block. Without invalidating any of the preceding descriptions of holiday lights, attractive homes, and friendly neighbors, there are also residents who neither cut their lawns regularly nor plant summer flowers. There are families who have no desire to display pictures of black leaders, have a black crucifix, or fly the African American flag. The people who continue to wash and repair their cars on the public streets boldly disobey the rules that block clubs display on their welcoming signs. The southern charm of the older generation is only occasionally practiced by the streetwise children born and raised in Chicago. Through such behaviors, many Groveland residents challenge the cultural and social order of the neighborhood. They ignore the models for behavior provided by the racial and class signifiers that fill the neighborhood, and they feel no need to learn the styles of interaction. No community is completely homogeneous, and the unique geography and composition of black middle-class neighborhoods like Groveland make them more susceptible to clashes.

Groveland residents experience their share of battles over the rules for social life in the constant renegotiation of what is appropriate neighborhood behavior. These sites of contest, especially as they relate to raising children, are the focus of this book, and ultimately determine the future of the neighborhood.

❸

Generations through
a Changing Economy

U nlike Groveland's first generation, who started their families in the prosperous 1950s and progressive 1960s, teenagers and young adults in Groveland today face a less hopeful prognosis for their economic futures. The gloomy indicators are all but common knowledge. Young workers cannot expect to make as much as their parents, and it will take longer for them to achieve a middle-class standard of living. Young African Americans entering the labor market have a particularly difficult time achieving middle-class status (Duncan, Boisjoly, and Smeeding 1996). Additionally, the economic growth that has occurred in the 1980s and 1990s has been concentrated among the top portion of the "haves" rather than being distributed among all "haves" and to the "have-nots." The gap between the rich and the poor is widening as the middle class is pulled in either direction (Danziger and Gottschalk 1995; Levy and Murname 1992). This could offer some promise that Groveland's black middle-class families are bound for even richer pastures, but in reality, middle-class African Americans run a greater risk of downward mobility than whites, who generally start off as more solidly middle class in the first place (Duncan, Smeeding, and Rogers 1993; Yeung and Hofferth 1998). Add to these economic insecurities the weakened commitment to antidiscrimination efforts and the persistent assaults on affirmative action and it becomes clear why middle-class African Americans are "succeeding more and enjoying it less" (Hochschild 1995).

Perhaps even more important to the black middle class than the uncertainties that plague its own future are the prospects for the less fortunate of the race. "Well-off African Americans are entwined with other blacks, both because they choose to be and because they cannot escape," writes Jennifer Hochschild (1995, 124). The economic and social forces that disadvantage the poor are also widely recognized.

44

Urban communities have been negatively affected by the shift away from well-paying manufacturing jobs to low-paying service work, as well as the exodus out of cities of the remaining good jobs (Kain 1968; Kasarda 1995). At the same time that businesses have divested from cities, so too have governments, further crippling the infrastructure, housing, and social supports needed by city residents (Logan and Molotch 1987). Once again, African Americans have been hit especially hard by these trends. The descriptions and studies of the crime, decay, and hardship that exist in black urban neighborhoods plagued by high rates of joblessness are plentiful. Despite this attention given to the institutional causes of persistent poverty, the persuasive sway of individual-level arguments complicates attempts to address the problems at their structural roots. The black middle class displays a torn ambivalence toward the situation of the black poor. They sympathetically recognize the harms of racism and targeted inequality while simultaneously pointing an accusatory finger at the individual faults of their poor friends, relatives, and neighbors.

There have been many manifestations of the post-1970s economic paralysis for Groveland residents, who personally experience the middle-class crunch, and from only a very short distance witness the worsening predicament of poor blacks. Each generation has been affected differently.[1] The senior generation in Groveland, born before World War II, benefited from the postwar boom and political liberalism that nearly doubled their earnings and opened the doors to jobs from which they had previously been excluded. They also took advantage of residential restructuring that allowed them to buy homes in the neighborhood as the first generation of black Grovelandites. Some of this cohort were members of the new black middle class—teachers, corporate managers, social workers, and government officials, educated at historically black colleges in the South and recruited to staff the professional and managerial jobs opened by affirmative action and growing public projects (Collins 1989, 1993). Next door to these professionals lived black steel-mill and railroad workers. In the 1950s and 1960s, these were coveted jobs that paid enough to buy a nice house and raise a family. Across the street lived postal workers and lower-middle-class office workers. "Believe it, working for the post office he wasn't rich," Kelly Harmon noted about his late father, who had worked for the Postal Service for more than thirty years. "And he put four kids through not only Catholic grammar school, but high school too."

Among the quite diverse senior generation of Groveland residents, many are now retired or have significant seniority and financial security in their jobs. Their frustration with the economic troubles of the late twentieth century is largely vicarious, emanating from the inability of their children to reproduce their middle-class status, and the extra difficulties faced by their grandchildren. The stifled mobility of their children contributes to the decline of the black middle-class enclave they worked so hard to establish.

Groveland's second generation (baby boomers) either moved to the neighborhood in their youth or were born into it in the early 1960s. They entered the work world with the optimism of their parents, but soon realized that times had changed. Most of the second generation have had children, who comprise the third generation of Grovelandites. Some of the early baby boomers (born before about 1957) have children who are entering young adulthood and founding a fourth generation of Groveland residents. James Graham heads one of these four-generation families. "I'm a West Virginian, and I came here [to Chicago] in 1936, was twelve years old," he began of his life story. After a stint in the army during World War II, James Graham returned to Chicago, took advantage of his veteran's benefits, and went to college. As a young man in Chicago, Mr. Graham followed the familiar southward migration, moving from the center of Chicago's South Side Black Belt successively through neighborhoods being vacated by whites. He ended up in Groveland in 1963, with his wife and three children. Over his career James Graham worked an array of jobs— as a radio disc jockey (his college major was communications), an office administrator, and a health-club manager. He also worked for Ford Motor Company in the aircraft engine division plant, and finally he spent some time working for the post office. Most of that time, Mrs. Graham did not work, and the family did well, sending all three children to Catholic schools.

James Graham's second daughter, Renee Jenkins, received her associate's degree in mortuary science, but found that the black funeral business is generally closed to anyone outside of one of the founding families. She now works as a telemarketer. Renee married and had a daughter, Tenasha, but eventually divorced and moved back in with her father. Renee planned to buy the house from her father, but saving for the down payment proved to be too difficult for a single mother.[2] Several times, Renee moved her family into an apartment for privacy and their own space, but she ultimately moved back in with her father in Groveland, two daughters in tow. Living with her father gave her crucial supports. When his grandchildren were young, James Graham remembered, "I changed more diapers on my grandkids than I did on their mothers." His help allowed both of his daughters to continue their educations. "I was helping Renee out as much as I could," he recounted. "They never imposed on me to go dating or something like that. It was just if they were going to school or work, 'Hey, take off. I'll be here.'" This is the strength of extended black families.

James Graham is extending this help to another generation. Almost two years after Renee's daughter Tenasha graduated from high school, she had a baby girl, Andrea, beginning a fourth generation in the Graham family's Groveland history. Both Tenasha and her mother Renee draw from the sturdy financial and household nest that James Graham built when his family was first starting out. But neither Renee nor Tenasha has been able to cultivate much beyond that. The frustrations of James Graham's progeny have various ramifications for neighborhood life in Groveland.

INHERITING HOMES

In Groveland, two simultaneous processes contribute to a decline in neighborhood upkeep. Home inheritance coupled with the downward mobility of Groveland's second and third generations translate into unkempt lawns, broken windows, and crumbling roofs scattered among the houses of those who immediately repair the slightest paint chip. As in the Graham family, many of the second generation of Grovelandites have been unable to follow in their parents' home-buying footsteps. When homes get "passed down" to the next generation, many residents believe that the legacy homeowners have neither the motivation to take care of property into which they have not sunk a significant personal investment, nor sufficient resources even if they were so inclined.

The financial (in)stability of the second generation of Grovelandites (and, by extension, the second black middle-class generation across Chicago and the country) affects the possibilities for regeneration of neighborhoods like Groveland. Mr. and Mrs. Harris, both college graduates and employed in administrative jobs with the federal government, put their daughter, Tracy, through Catholic elementary and high school to direct her on the path to socioeconomic success. Instead, Tracy got pregnant her first year in college, had two more children after that, moved back home, and is now alternately employed with the state unemployment office, or collecting her unemployment benefits from the same office when she is laid off. Tracy strongly shares her parents' concern for the neighborhood and does her part to keep up the house and the block. She keeps her own children under close watch and disciplines other neighborhood kids when necessary, making sure they do not litter or damage the front lawns with rough play. In her Cedarcove subdivision, there were a few cases of owners who were renting out their homes in violation of their homeowners' agreement. Tracy had certain opinions about the renters who lived in these houses.

> In some cases they don't care as much. They don't abide by the by-laws and guidelines that Cedarcove itself has, which is paying the dues annually, keeping your house up, carrying the garbage cans in and out. You know, those various things.

Tracy is clearly concerned about property values and the upkeep of Cedarcove. However, her own tight financial status means that without her parents, she too might struggle to keep the family home in good repair.

Just up the street, Mr. and Mrs. Simms—a principal and a postal employee—have raised four girls, and seen them all graduate from college and one from law school. The two younger daughters—Erin and Elise—both live at home while saving money to buy a house. It is unlikely that Tracy Harris, with three children, no husband, and no stable job, will be able to reinvest in the neighborhood by buying a home there. If she inherits her parents' home, she will not have the economic resources to keep it up as her parents have done with their two professional incomes. Erin and Elise Simms, on the other hand—a teacher and a lawyer, neither with children—are well prepared to take on the financial responsibilities of homeownership. In their case the question is whether they will remain in Groveland, with its older homes and overwhelming residential atmosphere, or move into a more trendy, perhaps integrated, part of Chicago. If the most upwardly mobile young African Americans are siphoned off into other areas of the city—replicating the sifting and sorting that has always characterized the black community—a prosperous future for Groveland and other neighborhoods like it is even less assured.

Many second-generation Groveland residents, because of their own slippery middle-class footing, rely on their parents' stability and stay put in the neighborhood. They will eventually inherit their parents' prized (and sometimes only) possession, the home. But not all are ready for the responsibilities of homeownership. For many Groveland residents who are watching the transfer of homes across generations, the problem of inheritance mirrors the problem of the in-migration of people who have not owned property before, or renters who have not made a significant investment in the home or the neighborhood in which they live. Kim Miles was born in 1960, moved to Groveland with her family in 1963, and now rents a home with her husband just next door to her parents' house. She is a part of the second generation, who will be beneficiaries of their parents' property, but she is a bit leery of the whole practice of passing down homes, especially when the inheritors are struggling financially. In Kim's opinion, her age-mates who inherit property are not compelled to take care of it because, unlike their parents, they did nothing to obtain it.

> Those houses, I think, ended up being where you had somebody that gets really really old and, you know, you don't see a lot of for-sale signs on these houses. They get kinda transferred, you know. [Her husband interjects: "They pass down. They pass down through the family. That's what happens."] And you might get a grandchild that moves in the house that doesn't have the same type of respect for the fact that they grandmother or grandfather or mother or father had to work for that property, to maintain that property. They may have worked, you know, two jobs to pay the mortgage on that property. And so when they get the property, they didn't have to pay for it. So, you know, why take the trouble to maintain?

Despite her apparent pessimism, Kim Miles's overall assessment still shows faith that the neighborhood can survive the irresponsible behaviors of her generation, as long as families like her own also remain in the neighborhood as a counterbalance.

Lauren Grant is an older baby boomer in her forties. She grew up in Groveland, and is now raising her children and a fourth generation of grandchildren in the neighborhood. Lauren Grant inherited her parents' home when they died. Initially, Lauren was just the kind of heiress homeowner that Kim Miles worried about. As a rebellious teenager and young adult in the indulgent 1960s and 1970s, Lauren Grant started selling and using drugs. She became a better drug dealer as she aged, and when her business was good, she moved out of Groveland and into a posh condominium on the lakefront, leaving her two children with her parents in Groveland. But when she started using the cocaine she was selling, her business crumbled. She was addicted to cocaine, but denying that she had a problem.

My mind told me one thing. What I got is the know-how to do this, and can do this again. And I kept getting worse and worse and worse. Alla that money that I had accumulated in all those years left in a matter of a year. That put me back in my mother's house.

Lauren's mother was a conservative, churchgoing housewife who came from a family of teachers. Lauren's father worked for the railroad. They raised their grandchildren while their daughter was living the fast life. When Lauren moved back home, she tried to get back on her feet by opening an informal beauty salon in the basement of her family's house in Groveland. But all the people she knew in the neighborhood were associated with the drug trade, and eventually her parents' basement became a social stop for the neighborhood rogues. "I had a pool table down there, so my clientele switched," she remembered. " 'Cause I started off with the 'normal clientele.' And then I did pimps, players [those who "play the field"], and hoes [whores], you know, and those clientele switched. It was the spot." During this time, and probably related to their disappointment in their daughter's life, Lauren Grant's father died and her mother became ill. In no shape to tend to the house's upkeep, Lauren let her parents' property decay. "When I got in control of it, I just tore it up. Used to be my mother kept it, but she got sick and I was taking care of it. And it just went."

Fortunately, Lauren was able to beat her addiction and is now, in her words, "a part of the neighborhood solution," rather than a part of the problem. With both of her parents deceased, she has inherited the house. She and her husband are now active members of the church to which her mother once belonged. She works as a secretary at the church, and her husband owns a construction business. They are diligent in their efforts to fight against drug houses and other symbols of neighborhood decline. Lauren is optimistic about the future of Groveland and the surrounding middle-class neighborhoods, as long as residents join her and her church in their organizing efforts. Her reflections on the changes in her life, and the changes she has seen in black communities like Groveland, underline the injurious effects of property transfer across downwardly mobile generations.

I can see these neighborhoods, Bristol, Cedarcove, as being model neighborhoods in the South Side area, as long as we stay on top of it. I can remember where black people in the beginning bought property, and where, like me, the property has been inherited. And that inherited property is the ones that seems to me that change the neighborhood. Only because I'm God-centered and I know that what I have isn't mine. God gives it to me and I have to take care of it because it's His and He entrusts me in it, you know. Only because of those reasons do I try to keep the property up, increase the property and all this stuff. 'Cause I didn't work for it, and things that you don't work for are different. You know, it was no struggle. But I'm real grateful.

But when I look at other areas, that's how they changed. And it is a couple places around here, it's a drug house on Fifth Avenue and Richmond Street. Used to be a building. It was on the corner. They closed it up. Right on the corner. I knew that person. She inherited that building and she inherited a huge sum of money. And it's gone. And sometimes that happens. Especially if you have a person who's caught in the grips of a disease. And that's what's happened on Meridian Street. Those people are caught in the grips of a disease and the original owner is no longer capable of taking care of that property. You know, so those kind of things do happen.

From Lauren's own personal experience, she understands how drug addiction can undermine the investments that people have made in their homes and their neighborhood. The house on Meridian Street that Lauren referred to in her comments presents a similar scenario, in which an aging homeowner left the care of the house to the next generation. Ultimately, a teenage boy was killed in the house on Meridian Street, which had become a disorganized drug house when the owner was aged and sick. A nearby resident on Meridian Street explained, "The grandmother is senile, that's who owns the house. But she's senile. So almost everybody up in there is strung out [on drugs]."

Reverend Darnell Johns of St. Timothy's Episcopal Church talked about how the transfer of property has resulted in a drug house across the street from his church:

Directly across the street from me, across the street on the west side of the street, that's becoming a drug house directly. What happened was the woman who owned that house, once she died it just went to pot. She died maybe about a year ago. It was starting, I could see signs of it beginning when she was ill. And apparently she was like the matriarch and wouldn't take too much of that going on in the house. But now there is so much traffic coming in and out of that house all the time so I don't even know who lives there anymore, with the exception of the children. But there is a whole lot going on there.

The examples of houses that were once owned and kept by respectable neighbors being transformed into drug houses represent extreme cases of the threat created by the concurrence of downward mobility and inheritance. Still, the fact that these stories are common in the discussions of the neighborhood's future suggests that if this extreme form of decline is so evident, lesser cases of property transfer and decline must also be an issue. Reverend Johns discussed such general cases:

> I think the other thing that's happened in this community is that it's changed in the sense that you had people who were very stable, lived in this community twenty or thirty years, who are now retiring. But, they cannot retire fully because something down the way and down the line where their offspring, their daughters and their sons, have not been able to maintain that stable lifestyle either through employment or through some other situations.

In another conversation, Mrs. French explained why her daughter, in her mid-thirties and with a young son, had moved back home.

> You know, [her] relationships didn't work and [she] just wanted to start from scratch again. And I guess always comin' back home you can start from square one. You know, it didn't work, lemme go back home and then I'll strike out again.

Similarly, a Groveland teenager described the moving patterns on her block within houses that are owned by one family, but occupied by different branches of that family at different times. "The people have changed," she recognized. "I mean it's like they're movin' in and out. But basically it's the same 'cause it's the same families. Not all the same people, but the same families."

And finally, Kim Miles talked about a house across the alley from her home, repeating her claim that for many young adults in Groveland, the route to homeownership is through inheritance:

> I don't ever remember seeing their house go for sale. So somebody from their family is in that house which is how the houses around here kind of go. Parts of the family kind of moved in, trying to take over and keep things going.

Groveland's first generation labored admirably to buy the homes in the neighborhood and raise their families. They tried to give their children the tools to be able to reproduce their own comfortable status. While some members of Groveland's second generation were debilitated by the raucous 1960s and 1970s, many have worked equally hard to get to where their parents are, if not do better. Erin and Elise Simms, the teacher and lawyer, and Kim Miles, a health professional, stand a better chance of buying their own homes and living comfortable middle-class lives than does Tracy Harris. And even Tracy Harris remains ideologically committed to keeping up the property, even if she will struggle financially to do so. Most worrisome are the new homeowners who are addicted to drugs, and thus nowhere near capable of preserving their parents' investments.

Even the more stable members of the second generation are not facing the optimistic climate in which their parents basked in the 1950s and 1960s. Postwar prosperity ensured that the senior generation of Groveland residents could make their mortgage payments, buy flowers for their yards, and make regular home improvements. National economic uncertainties and personal employment and family setbacks have afflicted the second and third generations, making it difficult for them to leave their parents' nest and limiting their ability to maintain their parents' investments. When homes show signs of disrepair and residents question the character of their neighbors, further disinvestment and disorder are sure to follow.[3]

ADULT CHILDREN AND GROWN KIDS

Groveland's senior generation have rational fears about the tragedies that could befall their children if they let them fly from under their wings. These fears motivate them to prolong their parental support. As members of Groveland's first generation, Lucille Arthur and her husband set high standards for their two daughters, standards that definitely included college. When her oldest daughter did not want to follow the route that she and Mr. Arthur had set for her, Mrs. Arthur worried that she had failed as a mother. In talking with her friends, however, she realized the problems that other parents were facing with their children. With this comparative perspective, Mrs. Arthur knew she was fortunate with her daughter.

She went to work for Friday's [restaurant chain], and Friday's sent her to Houston because, you know, she was very intelligent, very smart, like almost like a straight-A student. But she just didn't have that thing for college. And we tried and tried and tried to get her into college. I mean, we got her there, but she wouldn't do anything. She just wasn't interested. So she went to Houston eventually. You know, I'd be complaining sometime to people, and people say, "Oh, you so lucky. You don't know. Your child ain't on drugs. Your child ain't callin' you every week for money. She supportin' herself." At the time, I just didn't see it that way. I just thought I was just such a failure. But she made it on her own. I didn't have to send her money. She took care of herself. And then she got married. She got a daughter. She bought her a home. So, it turned out okay.

While college was important in the Arthur family, Mrs. Arthur's friends made her see how much worse her daughter's life could be. Lucille Arthur had already talked at length about the prevalence of grandparents raising grandchildren in cases where their children had either died violently or were "strung out" on drugs. When there are numerous examples of children succumbing to these kinds of crises, it becomes less of a priority that your child finish college.

Weighing the possible outcomes, Mrs. Vera Waters had the same positive judgment of her four children. She concluded, "I'm satisfied with their lives. You know, I didn't have to go get nobody outta jail. [Maybe] curfew or something like that. But other than that, I'm grateful none of 'em on drugs." Mrs. Waters believes that there are even more dangers now than when her children were young. She now worries about the third generation. Mrs. Waters's adult daughter, her daughter's husband, and their son all live with Mrs. Waters. Referring again to her satisfaction with her own children's situation, she continued:

I would really wish the same for my grandkids, you know. Even though I know things are different than they were when my kids were growing up. These kids here gon' have it hard because they got lots more stuff to deal with than my kids did. But they gotta stick to these books.

Both Mrs. Arthur and Mrs. Waters fear what could happen to their children and grandchildren. They could easily draw on numerous examples of neighboring families who have suffered through drug addiction, unemployment, or plain irresponsibility. When these are the things that parents fear, one way to protect the children is to keep them under one's own roof. When adult children continue to live with their parents, the parents get the peace of mind of being able to monitor their children's activities. They do not have to worry as much about drugs, or jail, or homelessness as they would if they insisted that their children get out. For the second generation, their parents' support allows them to use their money to save for a car or a house, to get back on their feet after a divorce or job setback, or sometimes simply for their own leisure activities.

Of course, some parents have waited anxiously to get their children out of the house, and are not as amenable to supporting them as other parents may be. Mrs. French, whose daughter and grandson live in her basement, repeatedly and insistently stated that the situation was *only temporary*. She did not plan on sharing her house much longer. But *temporary* dragged on for more than a year as Mrs. French got used to having her grandson around. Her daughter, having all the comforts of home, had little incentive to leave.

The impressive permanence of Groveland families acts as an anchor during shaky times, but it can also confuse the lines of authority within families. When children in the second generation (and in some instances the third generation) find it financially difficult to leave their parents' homes, conflicts emerge, and compromises are made to negotiate the fact that members of the second generation are both children and parents at the same time. They are the children of the senior generation and the parents of the third generation. Lauren Grant, who had her first child in her late teens, remembered how this role confusion was difficult for her and her mother to deal with. "It's conflict when you raise your children in your mother's house," she declared. "Because it can only be one grown person in that house."

On the other hand, there are a number of young Groveland adults who continue to live at home with their parents, but pay their own bills, and are nearly independent. Living with their parents allows them either to save money or to spend it as they please, without the serious repercussions of homelessness or hunger. Terri Jones lives with her parents and has her own catering business, into which she reinvests some of the profits. She also keeps some for frequent travel and shopping sprees. Likewise, Mrs. Waters's son, William, has worked at the same job off and on since he was eighteen years old. In his early thirties now, he has spent only a few years outside of his mother's house in his own apartment, and is now back at home. He gives some of his earnings to his mother and invests some, and what is left over goes toward his car, clothes, and social life. Sharon Maurice is another example. In her mid-twenties, Sharon lives with her grand-parents in Groveland, where she grew up. She has school loans that she is trying to repay, and eventually hopes to have enough money to go back and finish college. She spends most of her free time at church. Terri and Spider are second-generation Grovelandites, while Sharon is the third generation of the Maurice family in Groveland. Being unmarried and childless and having the support of their parents allows them to continue to enjoy the freedoms of youth and maintain a middle-class lifestyle, even if their own incomes alone could not make that possible.

At twenty-two, Tyson Reed is younger than the baby boomers who still live with their parents, but he is also taking advantage of his moth-er's financial security. Tyson recognized, though, that his mother had a certain ambivalence about him living with her. "She wanna be on her own. I guess she just tired of having some grown-ass kids staying in her house. I'on blame her." Tyson's term *grown kids* is an appro-priate label for the entire group. Lauren Grant, who is in her forties, used another appropriate term, *adult children.*

> It's quite a few adult children on my block. When I think about it, it's a lot of adult children on my block. Almost every house has still the adult children, my age, on the block. And I'm still the adult child on the block, I've just inherited the house. That's the only difference. You know, now that I look at it, very few of the people my age or a little under me or over me aren't still there with their families.

Since Lauren's mother and father died, she and her husband are now heads of the household that formerly belonged to her parents. Yet she was raised in that same house on that same block. To her longtime neighbors, especially those of her parents' generation, she is still one of the "children" on the block.

There is variation in who falls in the "grown kids" or "adult chil-dren" category. Some second-generation adults stay with their aging parents to be caregivers, which differentiates them from those who are still on the receiving end of at least some financial care from their parents. In the former case, where an elderly person is sick or incapac-itated, the adult child has clearly taken over the role of "that one grown person in the house." For example, Alberta Gordon moved with her son from the suburbs into the house next door to where she had grown up in order to take care of her aging mother.

I wanted to move back into the neighborhood for several reasons. One, my mother needed assistance in a lot of areas. I wanted to be closer to her. So it's very convenient because when my mother and I get tired of each other I come home. I'm not actually living right there in her home. And so that works out a lot better.

Having a bit of foresight about the conflicts that arise when three generations live under one roof, Alberta Gordon moved close to, but not back into, her childhood home.

But in many Groveland households, grandparents in their fifties, sixties, and seventies still act as caregivers to both their children and grandchildren. When the second generation is debilitated by a drug addiction, the grandparents are the sole caregivers. "We see it all the time," reported an attendant at Groveland Park. "It be the grandparents that bring they kids up here." A woman who worked for a neighborhood doctor concurred: "All of the children come in with their grandmothers. Most of the parents just strung out on drugs and stuff, you know. They just leave them kids with they parents and they out strung out on drugs." Before Lauren Grant took control of her life, this description perfectly fit her three-generation Groveland family. But short of such tragedy, many of the "grown kids" continue their role and identity as children in their parents' homes, while assuming adult responsibilities. They work and contribute to the household finances. They save their money and plan to go out on their own. They marry, and they have children. These distinct family arrangements are adaptations to hard economic times that face the second and third generations of Groveland residents.[4]

SECOND- AND THIRD-GENERATION YOUTH

Economic hardship among Groveland's baby boomers affects the neighborhood youth, the group about which this book is most concerned. In lay understandings, age eighteen or twenty-one commonly marks the transition from being a "youth" to being an adult, while developmental theorists argue that the period of adolescence can extend into the mid-twenties (Feldman and Elliott 1990). Educational, employment, and social institutions ensure that adolescents are not quite adults, but neither are they children. These ambiguities exist because age is not a dichotomous variable and it does not easily lend itself to a precise categorization of people as young and old, youth and adult. Taking definitional liberties, my analysis of "youth" in Groveland encompasses a relatively wide age range. This expanded definition allows for not only a discussion of the situations faced and transitions made by actual teenagers, but also an exploration of some of the results of their teenage years in early adulthood. In essence, defining "youth" as "teens through thirties" enables a set of cross-sectional interviews and interactions to provide some longitudinal insight into the experiences, transitions, and outcomes of young people raised in the neighborhood. Groveland's second and third generations, born after about 1964, do in many respects make up a coherent cohort who reached adulthood through the 1980s and 1990s. Together they face the high and rising costs of education and the instability of the labor market for young workers. And they are all attracted to the liberties of just staying young.

The overwhelming majority of Groveland residents graduate from high school, but the period after high school is filled with ambiguity. A recurring theme in discussions with Groveland's youth is the uncertainty about college attendance and job acquisition. The cost of higher education forces a number of Groveland's teenagers who do enroll in college to "take a semester off," which frequently grows into years. Others must lower their sights from a four-year college to a local two-year school. They often cycle between college and working at temporary, low-paying jobs. Meanwhile they make plans to go back to school, or decide not to go back at all. Youth stay in touch with friends from their childhood who are also "between" jobs (or at a job not viewed as a career), "between" relationships, "between" high school and college, or "between" semesters. Depending on the orientation of the peer group, these continued associations can alternately feed the fire of youthful deviance, or buttress someone's determination to go back to school or make other career plans.

In some ways, black youth are no different from young people of other races in their experiences of uncertainty and drift after high school. This "moratorium period" is characterized by an emphasis on peer interaction and a de-emphasis on work (Osterman 1980). Also, much of the difficulty in getting young high school graduates into career tracks is structural in nature. Gone are the good factory jobs of the industrial era; firms no longer have the organization or the incentive to hire high school graduates and shape them into career employees. The youth labor market is marginalized into low-paying service work in order to protect adult jobs in the higher-paid manufacturing and business sectors. This is the labor market that youth face if they end their schooling with high school or less. The half that choose college or other training after high school are often dependent on their parents, and also not quite adults.

There are important racial differences, however, in this moratorium experience. Of those who do not choose college, young black males are more likely to be out of work and/or out of the labor force than their white peers (D'Amico and Maxwell 1994; Freeman and Holzer 1986; Powers 1996; Skinner 1995). This was not the case in the mid-1950s, when black and white youth worked at about the same rates (Freeman and Holzer 1986; Jaynes and Williams 1989; Osterman 1980). Since then, the situation for black males has deteriorated considerably. Not only does this group have higher rates of idleness—that is, they are neither working nor looking for work, nor in school, nor in the armed forces—they are also idle at much older ages than comparable white and Hispanic youth. When other youth are settling down, young black men are still making transitions from work into idle states (Powers 1996). The periods of unemployment are also longer for black men than for men of other racial and ethnic groups (D'Amico and Maxwell 1994; Freeman and Holzer 1986). Finally, one-third of all black men are under the charge of the criminal justice system, further depressing employment and employability (Bound and Freeman 1992; Freeman 1987; Grogger 1992). African American young women seem to be negatively affected by both their race and their gender with respect to employment and wages (Farkas, Barton, and Kushner 1988).

Because many of the studies of youth employment parcel out the college-going population, they miss important differences between white and black youth who decide on college. African American college entry soared in the 1960s and 1970s, but has slowed dramatically since then, and black male college enrollment declined in the 1980s (Baker and Velez 1996; Mare 1995; Washington and Newman 1991). Comparing blacks and whites who attend college, blacks still lag behind whites. African American students take longer to finish similar degrees. In 1993, the mean time to receive a bachelor's degree was 6.24 years for whites and 7.19 years for blacks, because blacks are more likely to interrupt school and re-enroll later (Smith and Horton 1997), just as the youth in Groveland illustrate. Blacks are also less likely to complete the degree. Of those who were high school sophomores in 1980 (the oldest "youth" in this discussion), by 1992, 5 percent and 11 percent of blacks had attained, respectively, an associate's or bachelor's degree, whereas 10 percent and 26 percent of whites had attained those degrees (Smith and Horton 1997). These differences indicate the more porous nature of going to college for blacks. Because employment is often not a stabilizing force, and college is an uncertain endeavor, adolescents and young adults are often groping for stable ground through older adolescence and young adulthood.[5]

Shifting and more liberal societal norms combine with downward employment trends and sporadic schooling to affect choices such as marriage and childbearing. Marriage has declined for both African Americans and whites (Mare and Winship 1991; Smith and Horton 1997). In 1987 (and the trends continued into the 1990s), over half of black men and women age twenty-four to twenty-nine had never been married. (This was double the 1950 rate.) The figures for whites were also high, but not equivalent: 40 percent of white men and 26 percent of white women in that age group were never married. If marriage marks one of the initiation rites into adulthood, fewer people in their late twenties are heading in that direction. From a different perspective, perhaps marriage is no longer a prerequisite for adult status. As the economic standing of women has improved relative to men's, and as women's unpaid domestic labor is less assured, the returns to marriage for men and women have decreased. Also, the stigma of having children without being married has slightly abated, and thus out-of-wedlock births have risen for both blacks and whites since the 1950s (Jencks 1992).

In Groveland, these macro-level trends translate into a group of late adolescents and young adults—youth in their late teens through their early thirties. Many live with their parents, working here and going to school there. Some have stable careers that still do not allow them to live a middle-class life on their own. Others "hustle," which includes participating in various illegal scams—selling drugs, stealing credit cards, buying stolen goods. This is in stark contrast to their parents, and especially their grandparents, who by their age had already done tours in the armed services, completed school, embarked on a major migration to a new city, gotten married, or gotten a good job. Groveland's first-generation parents have worked to allow their children the comforts of indecisiveness—taking care of their grandchildren when their own children go off on a new whim, keeping a sturdy roof over their heads, and supplying food and utilities. A post–high school education is the clearest route to reproducing their family's status, but for many youth it is also a most difficult hurdle to cross.

EDUCATIONAL LOOPHOLES

Groveland families believe in the promises of education. In 1990, 73 percent of those twenty-five and older had at least a high school diploma (compared to 66 percent of Chicagoans overall), and 20 percent had a bachelor's degree or higher. Even more telling than the census data are the many examples of adults who have gone back to school to obtain either post–high school training or advanced degrees. Thirty-six-year-old Alberta Gordon has a fourteen-year-old son. After joining the army right out of high school, and then working for the Chicago Police Department, she went back to school to become a nurse. As she lounges in her house in a flowered cotton nurse's shirt and green hospital pants, her choice is a lesson to her teenage son of her commitment to learning a new career. Joanne Howell, also in her mid-thirties and with a young son, had the same idea as Alberta Gordon. She is enrolled in nursing school after having worked in a clerical job at a law firm for a number of years. And Bernadette Johnson, mother of two, already has a college degree and works as an elementary-school teacher, but during the summers she takes classes to get her master's degree. These parents are setting examples for their children of the need for education in today's labor market. Reverend Sarah Cherry, co-pastor of Groveland United Church of Christ, affirmed the official data with her assessment of the educational credentials of her congregation: "I would say the education of most of the membership—college. They have some college at least. You know, some college, complete college, and then graduate, all levels. But the average person I would say has some college."

Following the lead of their elder mentors, all of the members of the youth group at St. Mary's Catholic Church have professional career goals and plan to go to college. Charisse Baker, one of the teenage girls in the youth group, wanted to go to the only high school in the city that offered Japanese as a second language because she figured it would ready her for the career she planned in business. (Instead, her father insisted that she go to an all-girl Catholic high school.) Charisse's younger sister, Deanne, wanted to take four years of Spanish, indicating that she had some understanding of changing national and Chicago demographics. As an aspiring doctor, she reasoned that Spanish could come in handy in many cities in which she might practice. Like other young people in the youth group, Charisse and Deanne displayed thorough knowledge of the educational steps needed to achieve a career goal—even if, as is typical of teenagers, their career goals changed by the week.

The information that youth have is evidence of what adults—parents, teachers, neighborhood mentors, and church youth-group leaders—teach them. The St. Mary's Youth Group Career Fair was one place that such information was passed across the generations. A number of the adult church members and their friends attended the Career Fair to act as examples of success. All of the career participants represented white-collar employment. There was a woman who organized tester groups for new products for Kraft Foods. There was a self-employed graphic artist who made promotional designs for small businesses. There was a lawyer, a health professional, and me, an aspiring college professor. A door prize was given to the young person who successfully gathered the answers to a list of questions: What school did this featured guest attend? What was his or her major? What is the name of this featured guest's firm? How many years of school must you complete to become a lawyer (or a manager, a nurse, etc.)? Through these networks and activities, young people garner invaluable information about the educational process and what is needed to succeed in the professional workplace.

In another setting in Groveland, there is similar emphasis placed on education. Among the young men who play pickup basketball at Groveland Park, college provides a place to continue playing basketball, and basketball can sometimes provide the financial means to attend college. Unfortunately, for many young men, these combined college/basketball aspirations are based on unrealistic dreams that eventually go unfulfilled. This was the situation for Kevin, whose high school grades were not good enough to make him eligible to play at a four-year college. Hoping to be spotted by a scout for a junior-college team, Kevin played in various summer leagues in Chicago. His efforts paid off, and he was invited to Southwestern Junior College in downstate Illinois, where he stayed for the two-year program. When he finished at Southwestern, Kevin still wanted to get his bachelor's degree, and he also wanted to continue playing basketball. He again tried to get into a four-year school, but his grades were still not up to par. He commented sourly:

The coach, I let him do this to me. He used to give me a lot of, you know, bogus classes just to stay eligible. But they wouldn't transfer after that last year. He didn't care once he couldn't use me no more. Plus, he had paid for it. That's why I thought I was gettin' over. I ain't have to pay for nothin'. He was givin' us money.

Kevin was learning that he would have to take more responsibility for his own education instead of relying on the promises of others with different interests. After his two years at Southwestern Junior College, Kevin went back to Groveland and spent a semester at a junior college in Chicago. Although visions of playing basketball began to fade, he continued to think about going back to school. He had a good mentor within his own family. His older brother was in school and on the basketball team at a historically black college in the South. Regular visits with his brother kept Kevin on track to re-enroll. Kevin ultimately joined his brother at that school, getting back into college and basketball.[6]

Experiences like Kevin's show that aspirations to go to college are not always easily attained. The plans that young people have are tempered by what resources they and their family have, in terms of both their own aptitude for college work and their financial circumstances. There is often as much "college talk" as there is college attendance in Groveland. Youth often *talk* about college—their plans, the costs, their stints in and out—even when they are not enrolled. Financial hardships are the primary reason for delay. "I wanna go back to school, but I gotta work right now," remarked a Groveland resident in his twenties. "I wouldn't go back to college though. I would go to a trade school. You need money to go to college."

But finances are just one of many impediments to finishing a college degree. Charles Golden's story illustrates the importance of school, the need to work, and the lure of doing neither:

> I'm trying to go back to Grambling [State University] this August. But I gotta get some more credits before I get my Associates. 'Cause when I came back from Grambling I tried to work, go to school, and kick it [hang out with friends], but that was too much for me. Now, all I gotta do is finish up.

Charles needed to work to pay for school, but once he got a paycheck in his hands it was tempting to use the money for his own leisure, rather than putting it toward school. Even though youth express sincere intentions to return to school, once they are working and spending their free time with friends, they begin to accumulate bills that make it necessary to continue to make money instead of going back to school.

Karen Beaumont was a part of the youth group at St. Mary's Catholic Church for all of her teenage years. In her senior year, she was accepted to Roosevelt University in downtown Chicago, and planned to attend the following fall. In August, Karen got sick and missed the first week of school. Instead of trying to catch up, Karen decided to forgo the first semester and continue working at the drugstore where she had worked throughout high school. By the winter semester, Karen had decided not to go to Roosevelt at all, and instead enrolled part-time at one of the city's community colleges. After a year, she got a better job as a customer service representative for a major retail store. Twenty-one and living with her parents, Karen was able to buy a new car, further ensuring that she would have to continue working nearly full-time in order to make her car payments, leaving little time for school. She took classes when she could afford it or when she could find the time, but it became harder and harder to devote full attention to college with the demands of work and the lures of leisure.

While the socioeconomic position of many Groveland residents (moderate incomes, and a sizable minority of parents with a college degree) places a college education within the realm of financial and experiential possibilities, families actually have to come up with the money, and youth have to fight the attraction of material items that working can buy now. The continuation of college talk indicates a commitment to education despite the financial obstacles and the academic challenges. Yet extracurricular distractions, such as Karen's car or Charles's desire to "kick it," may actually pose the biggest threat to attending and finishing college. "Kickin' it" is shorthand for everything leisurely: "He's a year younger than me, except he *kicks it* just as much as I do." "He'll go *kick it* to the show [movies] with us or somethin'." "I got a lotta close friends that live in the neighborhood [from] years of *kickin' it* and doing crazy stuff together." For some Groveland youth, the time between school semesters, working at odd jobs, and living off the kindness of their parents, is the time for kickin' it.

Derek Barnes relayed how the emphasis on leisure not only forestalls finishing college, but can also be risky if a young person associates with the wrong crowd. Derek had just finished his first year of college. His mother is a teacher and his father has been out of his life since he was young. All of Derek's closest friends have similar backgrounds (although many have present, working fathers), and most grew up with him in the Groveland subdivision of Cedarcove. He named each friend and the high school and college each attended.

They all went to the most prestigious high schools in Chicago and were college bound the year after they graduated. The University of Illinois, Columbia College, Bradley University, Fisk University, Alcorn State, and Iowa State make up the mix of state schools, competitive private schools, and historically black universities that his friends attend. But Derek was not so sure that his friends would make it through college, or even go back to school after the summer. He explained:

> They like what's going on in the streets. Basically they just like that quick money. And it's like that with every generation that grew up around here. It's like they'll go to college for a year and after that they're back home living with their parents. And I feel that I can't do that. I'm not coming home after this year. This is my last year coming home.

One of Derek's friends was kicked out of school for having marijuana in his dormitory room. Another was on a basketball scholarship at Iowa State, but left because he was not satisfied with the playing time he was getting on the team. One of his friends is taking time off for financial reasons, but seems to be getting back on track. While out of school, they work odd jobs at Sears or UPS. If their parents have sufficient connections they might be lucky enough to get a job that pays well, but without the college degree their chances for advancement are slim. Some get quick money from illegal schemes like selling stolen credit cards or calling cards. With the earnings from these unstable and risky businesses, Derek's out-of-school friends go to parties, buy clothes, and "kick it" at Chicago's South Side lakefront. Derek understands the allure of hanging out, but he wants to be different from many of his friends. He shared the advice that he has given to his friends about their decision to leave school.

> I suggest like, "Man you doin' good now, but that's not gon' last forever. What are you gonna do after that's over? 'Cause either jail's gon' catch up with you, or death. One of the two. And, I mean, for now it's lookin' good. You got the money and everything, you know, let's kick it or whatever. You doin' good. But it's not gon' last forever. You need to go back to school." And they understand that. But they tell me that school is not about to move. [School's] been around for hundreds of years. I'm always gon' have the chance to go. But I feel that if you lose out on that one year, you're losing out on your life.

For Derek, the possible dangers facing people in his age group include jail and death. These are the same fears that their parents and grandparents have for them, which underlie their decisions to keep their adult children in the house with them in the first place. Even Derek's friends who are working legal jobs continue to hang out with their neighborhood friends who have chosen the illegal route. Associating with such a diverse group can be dangerous even for someone like Derek, who seems committed to taking the legitimate road to success.

One of Derek's best friends, Rashaad Lincoln, gave a similar gloomy assessment of the group they grew up with. Rashaad did not think it likely that young people from his neighborhood would graduate from college. "They might *go* to college," Rashaad began, "[but after] their first maybe one or two years, [they're] back at the crib [home]." Rashaad gave a slightly different reason than Derek for why people were not graduating. The people Rashaad knew got *worse* when they went to college. They were not ready for the freedoms of college life, and were not streetwise enough to stave off negative pressures. One of the young men who grew up in the neighborhood, and then left for Fisk University, a historically black university, was in jail for attempted murder. In Rashaad's explanation, "A couple of 'em, they went away to college, and got, you know, caught up with the wrong people. And things happened. So I guess they payin' the price now."

Rashaad's neighborhood friend in jail for murder is an extreme case of someone who got derailed off the college track, but it could happen to any young person who leaves Groveland, is overly excited by the freedoms of college life, and gravitates toward the wrong crowd. At the other extreme are youth who go straight through the four years, get a degree, and either choose graduate school or begin their careers. Many of these youth who successfully complete college on time have parents who also went to college. Their parents give them insightful advice on how to make it through; their parents can empathize when they have a particularly hard class or when they miss home or when they are struggling with the task of time management. Many of these families can also comfortably afford college costs or are shrewd negotiators with the financial aid office. But between these two poles are the majority of Groveland youth whose families can give lots of encouragement, some helpful advice, and less money. Even if they can give all three, they are in competition with youthful desires to hang out with friends, work just enough to get a car and buy new clothes, and occasionally test the boundaries of deviance to see what they can get away with. The new labor market pays a premium for education, but education comes only *at* a premium. Youth cannot earn enough money to live the life to which they have become accustomed with just a high school diploma, but they also cannot easily afford a college education. With their parents' support (often motivated by fear), they can, however, cling selfishly to the frivolities of being young.

A fourth generation is being born in Groveland. James Graham's great-granddaughter, Andrea, will face a very different world than he. He and his wife began their family believing that their children's lives would only get better and be more prosperous than their own. His daughters and granddaughter are less convinced that they can ensure the success of their children. Since the senior generation moved to Groveland, the economic table has gotten progressively less bountiful. To adjust to these changes, the second and third generations are staying at home longer, sharing the costs of a household in order to live the middle-class life of Catholic schools, newer cars, new school clothes, and, they hope, college. In the worst cases, when the second generation is consumed by drugs or hampered by unemployment, homes passed down through the generations deteriorate and the neighborhood as a whole suffers. More often, there is conflict between the generations over who is the "grown person" in the house, and who has the authority over whom and what.

For the youth—the youngest of the second generation and the oldest of the third—the financial pinch and the changing job market lengthen the time it takes to become self-sufficient. Some parents can afford to send their children through four years at a good private college where expenses top $20,000 a year, while others struggle to pay a semester's tuition at the nearby community college. Other Groveland youth enter a low-wage labor market, or opt for illegal employment. Parents, fearful for their children's safety and committed to their success, extend their care, tolerate their children's drifts, and offer resources beyond the usual period of adolescence. For all of these youth, the allure of kickin' it presents a special roadblock. When all of these groups are bound together as cousins, friends, and neighbors, it is inevitable that they will influence one another, both positively and negatively.

4

Neighborhood Networks and Crime

The spatial context is important for understanding the experiences of the black middle class. Again, racial segregation binds together African Americans of various social positions into a large and diverse residential black community. Such diversity has ramifications for the interactions and exposures of young people growing up in the black community. This chapter focuses on the spatial, or neighborhood, context and describes the networks that form within it.

Groveland is home to one of the top gang leaders and drug dealers in Chicago, as well as to one of the highest-ranking black officials in city government. The young people who grow up in the neighborhood are as easily introduced to the gangs and their drug business as they are to the neighborhood political organization. Yet the two coexist, and maintain what residents refer to as a "quiet neighborhood." In Groveland, residential stability and the strong informal ties that stability fosters do not completely prevent crime in the neighborhood. Instead, they work to circumscribe the criminal activity that does exist by holding the neighborhood delinquents within the bonds of familial and neighborhood associations. The result is a system of interlocking networks of legitimate and deviant residents that sometimes paradoxically, and always precariously, keeps the peace.

SOCIAL (DIS)ORGANIZATION THEORY

Social organization is goal-oriented. Social *disorganization* is defined as "the inability of a community structure to realize the common values of its residents and maintain effective social controls" (Sampson and Wilson 1995, 45); hence, social *organization* refers to the effective efforts of neighborhood actors toward common ends. These ends are similar across populations. Regardless of the social class or racial composition of a neighborhood, most people share a "common goal of living in an area relatively free from the threat of crime" (Bursik and Grasmick 1993, 15). Disorder—public drinking, loitering, street harassment, corner drug-selling, vandalism, abandonment, and litter—is neither desired nor condoned in any kind of neighborhood. Disorder breeds neighborhood dissatisfaction and withdrawal, and increases crime rates (Skogan 1990).

Social (dis)organization theory contends that if a neighborhood is socially organized, it will produce and experience less crime. One of the central neighborhood-level variables that positively affects social organization is residential stability, or the low incidence of movement in and out of the neighborhood. When neighbors live with one another for long periods of time, they form friendships and take responsibility for each other's well-being. They are more likely to participate in block activities, and more inclined to speak out when they have a concern about something or someone on the block. Most important, having watched the neighborhood children grow up, they feel comfortable monitoring local youth, and disciplining them if necessary. Young people bound by the ties of their parents and by the respect built up over years of being neighbors are compelled to mind the instructions of local adults.[1]

The flaw in social organization theory lies in the assumption that dense networks always work *against* crime. An alternative formulation might be that stable neighborhoods can more easily develop organized criminal subcultures because of the very fact that neighborhood familiarity is high. In the 1950s, Richard Cloward and Lloyd Ohlin described contexts where the "neighborhood milieu [was] characterized by close bonds between different age-levels of offenders, and between criminal and conventional elements" (Cloward and Ohlin 1960, 171). In these cases, neighborhood stability actually fostered the formation of an alternative opportunity structure based on organized crime. The profits from organized crime benefited both the criminal and the law-abiding residents. These relationships across the law provided the basis for the criminal enterprises of Irish, Italian, and Jewish immigrants alike (Ianni 1971, 1974; O'Kane 1992; Whyte 1943). Although the color of their faces has changed, delinquents in contemporary poor neighborhoods still provide important social and economic resources to their law-abiding friends, kin, and neighbors (Jankowski 1991; Sullivan 1989; Venkatesh 1996, 1997). Bootleggers, fencers, pimps, and drug dealers do not always hoard their profits for themselves. Rather, they provide for families, support neighborhood institutions, and are generous with friends. One former drug dealer in Groveland remembered being a hero when she contributed to neighborhood events:

> I could remember one [drug] house I had. When the block club would have block club [parties], we'd donate all the hot dogs and the pops. And they looked forward to that. And I mean, what is fifty or sixty dollars? You know, it wasn't no money.

These minor philanthropic acts may not counterbalance the devastation wrought by the dealers' illegal and violent businesses, but their drug money is nonetheless an integral revenue source for some marginal families and neighborhoods.

Because many of Groveland's lawbreakers are not poor, and to the contrary have middle-class backgrounds, crime in Groveland requires a complex incorporation of the various considerations in this book. The changing employment market and racial segregation ensure the continued confinement of blacks of various socioeconomic statuses into a fixed geographic area. Concentrating disadvantage often means concentrating crime (see appendix B, fig. 1). Added to these socioeconomic and neighborhood concerns is a cultural layer. The emphasis on emulating media toughs, and on having the newest outfit and shoes to match, also affects social organization and social control in Groveland.

At the neighborhood level, neighborly and family connections affect the management of youth behaviors, including crime. Residential stability is important for the creation and maintenance of social networks. Because Groveland is very stable, thick kin, neighborly, and friendship ties are the norm. These networks positively affect both the informal and formal supervision of youth. (*Informal* social control refers to the effective daily management of behaviors in casual settings, whereas *formal* social control involves actors who represent local institutions as well as official law enforcement agents.) But at the same time that dense ties are good, they also have negative repercussions. Just as organized crime existed in ethnic and poor neighborhoods, Groveland's dense networks similarly allow for organized criminal enterprises. Neighborhood familiarity does not necessarily stop residents from getting involved in gangs and drug dealing, but it does keep them connected to nongang adults and youth who constantly monitor their illegal operations, demanding that they conform to neighborhood norms of order.

Moreover, the gangs and the cliques of drug dealers are real parts of

Groveland's organizational infrastructure. The leadership of the Black Mobsters, the local gang, levies considerable social control on its members. Groveland's gang leaders were raised in the neighborhood. They often concur with the norms of the church and block-club members, and hold their youthful charges to similar standards. Both factions spurn disorder, actively combat graffiti, and show disdain for activities that may invite negative attention, such as loitering or public fighting. Also, both groups explicitly desire economic prosperity. The "occupational status" of the neighborhood drug dealers mirrors that of neighborhood residents who work in the legal sector. Such interlocking networks, and the similarities in interests and behaviors, make it difficult for law-abiding residents to totally rid their neighborhood of the criminal element.

For the most part, the two groups agree on goals, but disagree on strategies. Living in a black middle-class neighborhood requires that law-abiding residents compromise some of their attitudes—such as the scorn for drug dealing and the violent enforcement that goes with it—for the achievement of a "quiet neighborhood." This unique, adaptive strategy for social organization rests on a tenuous integration of and intermittent truce between the networks of gang members and the business of drug dealing on the one hand, and the activism of church leaders, block-club members, and local political officials on the other.

NETWORKS INTERTWINED

"GANG BUSTED" read the headline of a Chicago newspaper. The article continued:

> In a blitzkrieg of police work reminiscent of the lightning attacks of the 1980s on the El Rukn street gang and the Herrera family of heroin peddlers, about 250 law-enforcement officers swooped down Thursday to make arrests after the indictment of 39 alleged Black Mobsters.

This "victory" for Chicago law enforcement—the article's subtitle read, "We Ripped Off the Head of the Snake"—has had less than predictable results in the neighborhoods on Chicago's South Side, including Groveland, much of which is Black Mobster territory. Social organization in Groveland is partially dependent on the social control levied by neighborhood gang leaders on their local troops. Keith, a twenty-six-year-old resident, described the neighborhood before the bust as follows:

> One of the biggest gang leaders in Chicago, on the South Side, live right around the corner. And he ain't gon' let nothin' happen in his neighborhood. He don't want a lotta stuff goin' on 'cause he don't wanna lose his house. He control alla [all of] these little gangbangers. Like he got together with some of the churches and stuff and got that liquor store closed over there. You know, I won't say he all bad, 'cause he does do a lot of good things for the community. But he do 'em for the wrong reasons.

The former supervisor at Groveland Park also talked about the complex position occupied by the Black Mobsters in organizing the neighborhood:

> The kids really protect this building. No graffiti, well sometimes we'll get some, but they don't let that go on. No fighting, no break-ins. 'Cause there are gangs around here. I forget what they call themselves, Black somethings. But this is like a neutral zone. The gym show this weekend, Friday and Saturday, they [the gang] did security. They bought blue security T-shirts to match the kids' and they were all over the building. They had walkie-talkies and everything. They were in the front halls and all around the back. There were about thirty of 'em and we didn't even have to use the police. 'Cause, you know, I had called the police to provide security 'cause we must have had about two thousand people in here over the weekend. But they were better than the police.

Gangs are a reality of neighborhood life in Groveland. And as both Keith and the park supervisor conveyed, gangs are not uniformly depicted as the scourge of the community. Residents must reconcile the "good things" that gangs do (and the good people that are in gangs) with their "wrong reasons."

The density of neighborhood networks and the prevalence of family and fictive kin ties underlie the tangled relationships among gangs, drugs, and the forces that fight against them. Intimate networks are created and maintained when people live near one another for long periods of time. Seventy-five percent of Groveland residents own their homes, which economically ties them to the present and future of the neighborhood. Once families move into the neighborhood, they stay. A full 70 percent of the residents in Groveland moved into their homes before 1980, which means they had lived there at least ten years at the time of the 1990 census. In the area of Black Mobster rule, almost half of the residents moved into their current residence before 1970. Since African Americans did not begin to move to Groveland until the early 1960s, the group that moved to the neighborhood before 1970 was probably part of the first wave of black Groveland residents. These demographics indicate the stability necessary to form intimate social bonds, and bonds from childhood remain very much alive among adults in the neighborhood.[2]

The Vincent family illustrates these enduring ties. Husband and wife Kim and Joseph Vincent both grew up in Groveland, although Kim lived in the neighborhood first. "Where I grew up we were like a family on the whole block," Kim described. "You know, the next-door neighbors babysat me and now I babysit their kids, you know. I'm their godmother and their mama's my godmother. So it's like a family."

Before Joseph Vincent moved to Groveland himself, he would come to visit his cousins, who lived on Kim's block. When Joseph first saw Kim, he told his cousins he would marry her. Kim and Joseph both agree that it was love at first sight, although it took nearly fifteen years of off-and-on dating before they finally got married. After getting married, they bought a two-flat building in the neighborhood and rented the bottom and basement apartments, and Kim started her own business in their top-floor apartment. When their family grew, they bought a single-family house four blocks away (still in Groveland) and rented out the apartments in the two-flat. Some days after school, their eight-year-old son drops his bags with his mother and walks the three blocks to visit his grandparents, who continue to live in the house where Kim grew up. Many residents in Groveland have these kinds of extended and family ties.

The Vincent family has three generations in Groveland—blood relatives. But when unrelated families live near each other for so long, over time they become just like real family. Fictive kin networks flourish in Groveland (Anderson 1978; Chatters, Taylor, and Jayakody 1994; Stack 1974). Neisha Morris's description of a part of her family tree illustrates how time erases the lines between blood and nonblood "relatives." Neisha explained, "My uncle was her godfather. So that's why I say we cousins. It was like we've been knowing each other since little babies. You know, on pictures together. I been knowin' her forever, so that's why I say she my cousin." Neisha's family is not alone in absorbing others into their family. At Groveland

Summer Day Camp, three-year-old Dove clung to Parker, one of the camp counselors, boasting, "That's my cousin. That's my cousin." Yet despite Dove's insistence, she and Parker are not actual cousins. Parker's mother is Dove's godmother, which in the ways of fictive kinship lines makes them cousins of a sort.

It is also not uncommon for more than one generation of a family to live in the same household. Twelve percent of all Groveland residents live in "subfamilies" (Chicago Fact Book Consortium 1995). Subfamilies are usually childless married couples, or married or single parents who live in the household of another family unit. This commonly refers to a multigenerational or extended-family household. Reverend Darnell Johns, pastor of St. Timothy's Episcopal Church in Groveland, described this phenomenon:

> Let's say a young woman who used to live in this neighborhood, she gets married and goes on her own. She has two or three children. She and her husband are having a difficult time and they break up and she moves back home with her parents. And so what happens is that she ends up being here with the children, and then the grandparents end up having to extend the whole parenting again.

Reverend Johns pondered aloud the effects of this type of family organization. He was concerned that the "cultural difference between a grandmother and a grandchild" would hamper communication and weaken the authority of the grandparent. This lapse in control, argued the Reverend, "creates a whole host of new issues and problems." Particularly, the break in communication is a break in social control. Reverend Johns reported:

> These people who are speaking [about problems in the community], it often is many of their children and many of their grandchildren who are contributing, you know, to the problems of the community. And it's just denial. It really is. You've kinda given me some food for thought. Maybe that's a good forum or workshop, you know, to have at church—the generational dilemma in our community.

The "generational dilemma" that Reverend Johns referred to points to a complication in child rearing and supervision in the neighborhood. The extended-family network has long been a positive feature of African American families (Billingsley 1968; Stack 1974). Yet having numerous adults in a household does not always translate into more or better supervision of youth. Instead, there may be confusion over who is "the one grown person in the house." The lower energy levels and limited financial resources of grandparents also strain the family relationship, grandparents' love and commitment notwithstanding (Chase-Lansdale, Brooks-Gunn, and Zamsky 1994). At the same time, Reverend Johns's comments foreshadow the ways in which dense networks can connect upstanding members of the community to neighborhood delinquents. These relationships make it difficult to uniformly crack down on neighborhood crime because few (grand)-parents are able to see their own (grand)child as being one of the rotten apples in the neighborhood bunch. Even fewer are able to believe that they are deserving of harsh punishment.[3]

Numerous extended-family networks, specifically those spanning generations, do, however, increase levels of familiarity within the neighborhood. At Groveland Park's annual Halloween party, Nicholas, a sly seven-year-old boy, tried to use his family connections to get a free prize. He had not competed in the costume competition for which the children were given prizes, but went up to the prize table anyway to see if he could swindle one from Ms. Mandle, who watched over the treats. After an unsuccessful claim that he was too shy to participate in the contest, his last resort was to say to Ms. Mandle, "Do you know Ms. Terry?" Ms. Mandle said she did. Nicholas replied, "I'm her grandson. Don't you think it would be okay if I could get a prize?" Ms. Mandle was unimpressed. "I know who you are," she answered. "And you're not getting a prize." It did not work on this occasion, but in countless settings like this one, old and young residents do benefit from their shared relationships.

These are the innocent uses of neighborhood networks. But mutual familiarity also means that residents, especially youth, are exposed to antisocial networks as well as legitimate ones. The schools provide one local arena where disparate groups come together. Because the lives of classmates can take different trajectories, many Groveland adults have acquaintances on the other side of the law, if only by default. Thirty-three-year-old Kelly Harmon is in his second year of an M.B.A. program at a Chicago university, while a childhood friend of his was caught in the city's roundup of the Black Mobsters. Kelly reported:

I actually went to school with one of the top [Black Mobster] lieutenants who graduated, who lived on Third and Granger. I knew that family very well. But now he's in jail. The top lieutenant whose name was, whose nickname was Lance, is in jail. He's facing an array of charges, so he's gonna be there for a while. But his little street minions are still there.

In Groveland, everybody knows Lance. He went to the local public schools; he and his siblings participated in activities at Groveland Park, and now their children also attend Groveland School and frequent the park. Lance's position in the neighborhood is more multifaceted than the narrow title "gang leader" might imply. He is a father, uncle, neighbor, and former classmate, and, as was already mentioned, Lance has been a community activist, participating in the successful effort to close down neighborhood liquor stores.

Each of Lance's "minions" also shares this plurality of roles, and this has the effect of making some residents feel safer. Strangers are a certain cause of fear (Anderson 1990; Merry 1983). Yet, as sixteen-year-old Charisse Baker described, gang members in Groveland are rarely strangers.

> I mean, I know most of 'em. Because it's not like anybody came into the neighborhood. Most of the people in this neighborhood are like grandparents now, so they've been here a long time. And it's a lot of their kids and grandkids. So it's still people that I grew up with, and people that I saw all the time. People I went to school with. So, it's not a change. I mean, I see them more and I realize what's going on more. But it's not a case, I don't feel unsafe, you know.

Forty-year-old Alberta Gordon echoed these sentiments:

> I don't carry a knife. I don't carry Mace. I don't feel that this is something [I need to do]. And I feel that if anything happens to me coming home it will not be someone in this neighborhood because they know me. They know my sister. They know my brother.

Ms. Gordon got agreement from her teenage son, Michael, who chimed in:

> They gotta deal with my grandmother. The reason why, you know, I don't get messed with is because basically they know my grandmother and she's known around this whole area. She taught a lot of the gang members when they were in second grade. The gang members now, your big [ones], she taught them.

Unlike Nicholas, who never got a prize out of Ms. Mandle at Groveland Park's Halloween party, Michael went on to give an example of how he has indeed reaped the benefits of his grandmother's favored neighborhood status.

Grandparents, grandchildren, cousins, neighbors, classmates—this density of relationships in the neighborhood, forged through high levels of homeownership and long-term residence, has created an intricate system of socialization that produces top-level city politicians as well as high-ranking gang leaders. Moreover, for many residents, this web of networks and their embedded position within it generally make for a "quiet neighborhood."

The structure, however, does break down. Fifteen-year-old Brandon Johnson was shot and killed one January afternoon on one of Groveland's quiet streets. His obituary chronicled his activities, listed his affiliations with local institutions, and illustrated his intense involvement in neighborhood networks. It read:

> He confessed his belief in Christ at an early age. He was a member of St. Timothy's Church under the direction of Reverend Darnell C. Johns. He was a youth member at St. Timothy's Church. He attended Benton Heights Career Academy as a sophomore. He played Basketball/Football at Benton Heights. He was a member of the YMCA where he played Basketball. He had just started a part time job at Ridge Lake Groceries. He was a counselor for the City Wide Program during the summer.

Brandon's abbreviated biography shows that he was actively involved in positive local and citywide activities. One involvement the obituary did not mention, however, was Brandon's peripheral gang affiliation. As one of his peers described him, "Brandon was like a real good person. He wasn't really *too* into gangs or whatever." Another youth tripped over her words when trying to characterize Brandon, illustrating the duplicities in his identity and the sympathy she felt for his too-early death.

> He was trying to change. You know, he was a little, he was bad. Really bad. I mean, not he, I mean, well he got killed. He was changing his life around and he was actually good, you know. He was turning it around.

The details surrounding Brandon's death were as sketchy as the opinions on his gang affiliation, yet both point to the intricacies of overlapping neighborhood networks. Brandon lived with his mother, stepfather, grandparents, and siblings in the house in which his grandparents had lived for nearly thirty years. His mother and grandparents were churchgoing people, and clearly passed that orientation on to Brandon. His grandparents had been involved in the church-sponsored "March against Drugs." Ironically, Brandon was killed in an identified drug house where he had been visiting his girlfriend. His funeral was attended by a mix of members of his church youth group, classmates from his high school, and a group of young men who, in other locales, had been known to flash gang signs, wear gang paraphernalia, and use the greeting used by gang members. All of these associations, however, did not alter the perception of Brandon as "like a real good person" who was "turning it around." This plurality of associations and roles, which is characteristic of the networks in Groveland, confuses and complicates social control efforts.

INFORMAL AND FORMAL SOCIAL CONTROL IN GROVELAND

Brandon Johnson's death prompted a special community meeting called by the pastor of his church. Nearly thirty neighbors and family members attended to discuss the need for increased police presence in the neighborhood, expanded activities at Groveland Park, and reinvigoration of the block clubs. These concerns are repeatedly raised in casual conversations and neighborhood meetings, and there are ongoing efforts by a number of individuals and community groups to further this agenda. These efforts and the players involved in carrying them out rest on one side of the seesaw of Groveland's social organization. At a Local School Council meeting, Mr. Wilson expressed the consensus in these groups and the approach they take to working on problems. He pointed out, "We have to take responsibility for all of our children. The same children that are beating up on our children are also our children. They go right around the corner when they go home. They are our children."

Most responsibility for "our children" is taken on informally, using the strong extended-family and friendship ties within the neighborhood. Alberta Gordon discussed this informal control:

> Some of the kids call me Ms. Gordon. Some of 'em call me Mama G. And I told them the reason I want them to feel comfortable in calling me Mama G is because I grew up calling people on this block by their last name or "Aunt" whoever the person was.

For instance, Tanya's mother, I still to this day call Aunt Sarah. It was a [matter of] respect and [a kind of] extended family. So there are a lot of young people that I do know that call me Mama G.

And I have no problem in telling them that they're wrong about doing something. And no problem in going to their parents because I know their parents. . . . [And I] have told their parents in return, if [my son] Michael is doing something and you know it's wrong, correct him and then let me know so that I can deal with it.

At Groveland Park, Ms. Spears put Ms. Gordon's sentiments into action, as the following interaction illustrates.

A teenage girl walked up to Ms. Spears to ask a question, but before she could get it out Ms. Spears spotted that the girl was wearing an electronic pager. Ms. Spears asked her sternly, "Whose beeper is that?"

The girl responded, "It's my father's."

Ms. Spears continued with a barrage of questions and directives, "What are you doing with a beeper? You don't need a beeper. Give it back to your father. I don't care if it's yo' brother's, mother's, father's—you don't need a beeper. It's not becoming. Take that beeper back to your father right now!"

The girl responded, "He's right in there. He knows I got it."

Ms. Spears said in a serious voice, "Take it to him right now."

The girl turned around and walked inside to do as she was told.

Associating a pager with drug dealing, Ms. Spears thought it was inappropriate for a respectable young girl to be suggesting such an association. Being a neighborhood disciplinarian requires a certain amount of respect, which Ms. Spears has cultivated in the nearly twenty years she has lived in Groveland, raising her children and now her grandchildren there. She is also an employee of the Chicago Park District and for many years has worked at Groveland Park, which is across the street from her home. She is seen by many of the youth as a grandmotherly figure, and she addresses most people, young and old, with the sugary pleasantries "honey" and "baby." Her longtime residence means that she can intervene in behaviors that she feels are inappropriate, and be confident that her intervention will be acceptable with their parents.

Similarly, William "Spider" Waters has lived in the neighborhood most of his more than thirty years, went to the local schools, and works at Groveland Park. He uses this neighborhood-level legitimacy to coordinate men's pickup basketball on Sunday mornings. Spider is the keeper of "the list"—the roster of names used to determine the next team to play. He frequently deviates from the list, moving up his friends' names or giving some players special choice in their teammates. His final decisions are respected. When tempers flare and the playing rules are ignored, Spider always has the last word. Once, after a controversy over a personal foul, Spider ordered loudly, "All you muthafuckas that lost, get the fuck off the court." When the losing team did not move from the court, Spider responded, "Fuck that. The muthafucka is closed. Gimme my got-damn ball." He took the basketball and turned off the lights in the gym, announcing, "Shop is closed!"

Spider always handles conflict with this same blunt and direct swiftness. Spider's amiable relationship with Lance and the Black Mobsters augments his status as an official park employee, and gives him further authorization to settle disputes and make decisions within the park, especially among the young people. The key to promoting comfort and feelings of safety is to lessen anonymity. Yet the more familiar people are with one another, the more illicit networks are absorbed into and normalized by mainstream connections. This is the conundrum that plagues social control efforts in Groveland.

"Concerned residents" are enraged by gangs and drug activity. When informal mechanisms fail to control these activities, residents turn to the next level at which social control is exerted—local organizations and institutions (Hunter 1995). These two levels are not separate, as the above examples illustrate. Employees of the local park are also longtime neighborhood residents, as are church leaders, business people, and police officers. Local organizations and institutions are only aggregations of the informal private ties that individual residents possess, increasing the ability to address the concerns that residents cannot tackle individually.

Community meetings (of block clubs, police beats, the Local School Council, church groups, the Chamber of Commerce) are the places where residents air their many complaints. Gangs and "gang-bangers" top the list of residents' concerns. At a Local School Council meeting, Principal Wilson told council members that the gang situation at Groveland School was negligible. Ms. Jones interrupted him, flailed her hands in dismay, and argued:

Mr. Wilson, I've been here several times and I know we got a security problem. Don't give me that! The gang members be up in here and they ain't in here to see nobody they know. They be looking for people, somebody they gon' jump on. Don't give me that!

Mr. Wilson tried to respond, but Ms. Jones continued:

The security here is not enough. I know in fact that they be in here. And I know your security staff can't even handle this. I was downstairs and one of your staff—and I'm not going to say his name—[she says his name anyway] Mr. Winters—said to one of the guys in here, "Can I help you?" And the boy said, "We Mobsters and we don't need no help!" So don't tell me we don't need security!

Ms. Jones's charge to the school principal conveys the frustration that residents feel over the rising gang activity in their neighborhood. According to an older man attending a local police beat meeting, gangs are "worse than anything. They can just take over!" The formal neighborhood institutions direct their efforts at preventing this takeover.[4]

The residents who express their concern and anger over changes in their community—young people playing loud music, leaving trash on their lawns, stealing backyard furniture—frequently recognize that putting up gates around the entire neighborhood would not rid Groveland of the problems they are experiencing because the troublemakers are natives. One woman at a beat meeting complained of young men "gangbanging" (i.e., congregating) on her corner, and of one man in particular who she thought was in charge. But, she said, "I didn't wanna give this young man's name [to the police] because his mama is such a sweet lady." Her comment illustrates that while dense neighborhood networks and the resulting familiarity can improve some informal efforts at social control, it can thwart the use of public or formal means of control.

Many local institutions do, however, boast successes. The Chamber of Commerce has been active in efforts to keep the main commercial strip and the entire neighborhood thriving. One of the Chamber's executive board members talked about how the organization "got the pay phones out on the streets set up so that there are no incoming calls and no coin-generated calls after a certain time. This was particularly to stop any drug dealers from using the phone."[5] The Chamber has also been successful in utilizing the city's "Graffiti Blasters" program to promptly remove any graffiti from area businesses.

In addition to their proactive efforts, businesses are also supportive of other local organizations and institutions. When a group of block clubs teamed up with the alderman's office to plan an antidrug march, many businesses donated materials and food to help out. One organizer announced, "Mr. Brown over at Diamond Groceries is donating all the hot dogs, buns, and relish we need." The president of a Groveland block club said he could always count on the local grocery stores to donate food for his annual block party, and the area bank to donate money. Similarly, when the Catholic church's youth group planned an overnight retreat, two fast-food restaurants donated food; and when the same group planned a career fair, a local music store donated door prizes. Residents and organizers depend on the businesses to support their efforts to provide positive activities in the neighborhood.

The churches spearhead social organization efforts in Groveland. Groveland United Church of Christ hosted a string of community meetings at which organizers made specific demands of the alderman, the police, and the public-school principal. They targeted three drug houses in the neighborhood, two of which were eventually closed by the city. The church also complained of gang activity on the public elementary-school playground and demanded that the police monitor the playground to make it unattractive to gang recruiters. At the next meeting, the police sergeant responded to these demands: "Immediately following the last month's meeting, we made arrests of some kids with spray cans on the school grounds. We will continue to work toward these goals," he averred. St. Mary's Catholic Church was successful in getting a security guard placed at Groveland Park, as well as more programs and activities for teenagers.[6]

Concerned residents focus their energies and activities on curbing youth delinquency. This illustrates the centrality of gangs and drugs to the organization of their opposing forces. Nearly all of the projects proposed by these activists are concerned with connecting young people to positive activities and groups, and deterring deviant behavior. There is also considerable discussion of the physical maintenance of the neighborhood, but this is frequently connected to the irresponsibility of idle young people (indiscriminately referred to as "gangbangers") who trash the neighborhood. Yet for all the institutional support and commitment of key leaders, the force against which they are fighting also has a strong organization, powerful leaders, and the buffer of actors who negotiate both worlds.

THE BLACK MOBSTERS:
ORGANIZATION OF A DIFFERENT SORT

The Groveland Park field house was a gang stronghold until the Chicago police cracked down on the Black Mobsters. "Folks" is the gang "nation" under which the Black Mobsters are positioned (see Hagedorn 1988 for a discussion of the "People" and "Folks" nations in Milwaukee). "What up, Folks?" was a conspicuous greeting at the field house. So, too, were six-pointed stars, hats tilted to the right, T-shirts with the picture of their jailed gang leader, and the color blue. Despite these visible gang symbols, members of the "organization," as they called it, consistently declared:

> Ain't no gang problem around here. You come up to the park and you don't see no graffiti or nothin' like that. These people around here think we got a gang problem. This ain't nothin' like Lorry Park [another park on the South Side]. I used to work up at Lorry, and say you used to bring your son up there to play. The boys would come up to him and take his ball and jump on him. And when he started to fight back because you taught him to stand up for hisself, they would be talkin' 'bout, "You don't need nobody else. Come get with [our gang]."

Groveland's Black Mobsters stop short of bullying the non–gang members who use the park. However, in routine park activities there are many times when "Folks" use their organizational strength to control the park. Once during a league basketball game, a member of the "organization" was not getting much playing time. Someone from the stands called out, "All us over here came to see Pope play. Pope, go on in there and get you some time, man. Folks don't sit on the bench. They play. You B-Mobster ain't you? Then use yo' Mobster weight." Pope moved to the scorer's table and checked himself into the game.

Compared to the intimidation that occurs at Lorry Park, these shows of dominance are relatively low-profile. Fights are rare; there was only one during the more than three years of this research. There was no graffiti and only three documented cases of vandalism at Groveland Park. Although residents complain that the Park District no longer plants flowers and has become lax about grounds maintenance, there are few blatant signs of disorder. The occasional gang-related organizational meetings are perhaps the most visible negative harbingers. On one Sunday afternoon ten young men played basketball in the field house gym. Suddenly a group of about ten men in their early twenties emerged from the field house basement and rushed into the gym. They wore their jeans baggy and their baseball caps tilted to the right. They lined up around the court near the gym exit and the locker room. More came after them. Some gave each other the Black Mobster handshake. Then, just as quickly as they had filed in, they left through the gym door. Later the same afternoon, forty more youth, this time young teenagers, repeated the sequence of events, hurrying from the field house basement and taking over the basketball courts, and then leaving just as quickly. These episodes were rare, but could easily alarm any nongang resident in the park at the same time.

The same way that the church people used Groveland Park to hold Bible studies, and the local block club held regular socials in the park, the local gang also used their park for organizational meetings. When Lance, his employees, and his bodyguards congregated at Groveland Park (before the "gang bust"), they sometimes talked in hushed tones and acted in ways that betrayed their innocent veneer—making several trips to their cars, leaving abruptly in the middle of a conversation, or casting frequent and alert glances out the window. As a young man who was a regular at the park recognized:

> I guess they say we got a gang problem up here. But I guess we don't even think about it like that because we know all of 'em, you know. We grew up with all of 'em. But, I guess from the outside looking in it might be kinda intimidating.

Most often the young men played basketball, joined in on volleyball games, coached the younger boys, played dominoes, or just socialized. They were neighborhood residents using their neighborhood park, and this is how the supervisor treated them. She explained:

> I don't know, well I do know, but I can't be sure of what anyone does. So I'm not going to be telling people they have to leave. My supervisors come down here and they tell me not to let 'em sit out in front there. But, again, what am I going to say? I can't tell them to leave because they're just sitting out there. I mean, I do understand the concern. You know since I've been here there hasn't been one fight. I don't hear a lot of profanity. I mean, I know people curse, but there haven't been any problems. I mean, they all grew up together. They live here. Plus, some of 'em have kids here, so that's an extra part of it. I mean, I can't tell people to leave.

As an official of Groveland Park, the supervisor is a part of the formal social control apparatus. Yet she is reluctant to condemn the gang members who frequent the park because, as residents, they have legitimate reasons to use it. They have children in park activities and friends throughout the neighborhood, which justifies their presence.

The "civility" of the Black Mobsters at Groveland Park is part of their more expansive efforts to legitimize their illegal businesses. Newspapers describe the Black Mobsters as Chicago's largest street gang, and its tentacles span the Midwest. One resident described Lance's dominion as spanning the country. "Tell 'em, Reggie," he goaded his friend, but then continued the story himself. "This Lance's spot. Lance is the man over alla them. He the man in the city. He a real Mobster. He run the Mobsters in the city, down south, Texas, and up north in Minnesota." The organization has been involved in an assortment of endeavors. The police investigation of their activities uncovered money-laundering schemes through concert promotions, political organizations, neighborhood restaurants, and even social service establishments.

But while their citywide strength is considerable, their territorial hold in the Groveland area is limited to an area four blocks long by ten blocks wide—just about half of the official community area. To the south and east are four other neighborhood-based gangs, all of which belong to the rival gang nation. To the north and west are Ruthless Mobsters, also Folks, but a different faction from those in Groveland. While this territorial crunch produces some turf battles, the organization is concerned with turf only as it affects drug sales. "The only thing they care about is makin' money," Charisse Baker argued. "Everybody else [says], 'This my territory, you not supposed to be over here,' [but] they don't care about nothin' but makin' money."

Lance manages the Black Mobsters' business on the South Side of the city, but he keeps Groveland relatively clean—partly because he wants his family safe, and partly because residents are active in fighting against such activity. As a result, there are few drug houses in the part of the neighborhood controlled by the Black Mobsters, and almost no corner drug-selling. Linda Brewer, who grew up on the same block as Lance, described what happened when a family tried to sell drugs in Groveland outside of Lance's organization:

Lance told them they couldn't sell the drugs. It really really got bad and people was comin' [from] outside the neighborhood.

A coupla people got robbed and raped and beat up, you know. And a coupla people got in there and started drive-by shootin's and stuff like that. So he told 'em they couldn't sell it. 'Cause now he was worried about his mom, you know. So, now alla the sudden he said they couldn't sell drugs around here.

Faced with the unsupervised sale of drugs in Groveland, and the disorder that it was causing, Lance put a stop to this upstart enterprise. These prohibitions illustrate Lance's centrality as an agent of neighborhood social control.

There is significant irony in the fact that having an organized gang in the neighborhood has, in some respects, translated into fewer visible signs of disorder, less violence, and more social control. Lance operates from a profit motive, albeit an illegal one. Aside from that, he wants his family safe, he wants his neighborhood clean, and he wants his children to have healthy activities. The fact that Lance and his minions are indigenous Grovelandites plays a role in these parallel interests of gangs and the upstanding citizens who fight against them.

MIDDLE-CLASS MOBSTERS

If there is a system of occupational stratification within organized crime similar to that which exists in the legitimate sector, Groveland represents the middle managers in both milieus. Neisha Morris described the activities of her boyfriend, Tim, who sold drugs:

Well, see, Tim don't sell drugs on the corner. He did do that type of stuff, but [now] he got a pager. People can just page him. He don't sell drugs to people. He sell drugs to the niggas that sell drugs. He not at the stage no more where he just sell to hypes [drug addicts] $10 bags, little bags. You know, one of his friends like wanna buy some work [drugs] and they'll like pay $800 for something and they work what they got from him. He say they bag it up and they sell it to hypes, like that. I guess he done moved up in the world. And it's people that he buy his stuff from [that] got mo' money than him.

In her explanation of Tim's duties, Neisha described an occupational hierarchy (Padilla 1992). Tim was promoted from selling drugs on the corner to buying in bulk and selling to independent distributors who work the corners he once occupied. Above Tim are suppliers even more wealthy than he, who are likely to be subordinate to some even more powerful and wealthy drug dealer. In this occupational chain, Tim is not a laborer at the bottom of the totem pole. Having moved off the corner, Tim is now able to work from his home. He is a low-level manager, a small business owner. In the underground economy, he is like his neighbors who work similar jobs in the legitimate employment sector. As in the distinction between blue- and white-collar work, most Groveland residents—legitimate and criminal—have "clean jobs."

Another middle-class characteristic of the drug trade in the neighborhood is that Groveland is a bedroom community. Most drug-selling takes place outside of the neighborhood and the profits are brought home to families like Neisha's. At the park, there was never an exchange of drugs, drugs present, or obvious drug users or addicts. Corner drug-selling is rare in the section of Groveland controlled by the Black Mobsters. The drug houses that are allowed to exist in the neighborhood were described by one resident as "drug salons," highlighting a hierarchy of drug-selling establishments. In "drug salons," customers buy their drugs and leave, rather than congregating and creating the social disorder that accompanies drug use (Williams 1992). "Around here they'll sell on they porch, and they'll see a hype comin', then they get off the porch and go serve 'em. Yeah, it's a calm area around here," reported one Groveland ex–drug dealer. His friend agreed, saying, "I'll say all the people over here go to the other side to sell drugs. That's where all the places to do it. They'll go on the other side."[7] The money is to be made elsewhere, outside of Groveland. Like the residents in Groveland who commute to their legal jobs, Groveland's drug dealers do most of their business outside of the neighborhood. The proximity of Groveland to low-income markets highlights the importance of geography in explaining crime in Groveland. A major caveat is that the violent repercussions of the drug trade can often spill over into their own territory.

Within the drug-selling world, as in the legitimate sector, there is also a visible lifestyle hierarchy. Those at the top, like Lance, drive fancy cars, wear expensive watches and jewelry, and are surrounded by helpful underlings. Over the years, those underlings (or minions) acquire fancier (but used) cars, begin to wear more name-brand clothing, and make more frequent trips to the barber. As the Groveland Park supervisor relayed to her white friends who had a particular image of gang members: "I mean, really, these guys aren't using the pay phones, you know. They have cellular phones and car phones," she informed them. "These guys wear Fila and shop at Burberry's [designer brand and upscale clothing store, respectively]. This is not like, you know, guys hanging on the corner smoking."

In addition to possessing the accoutrements of middle-class status, on some issues Lance demonstrates behavior bordering on prudery, as a conversation about one of his parties illustrates. "We had all kinds of food and shit," Spider boasted. "I stuffed myself. Man, I was full as hell. We had all kinds of waters too." A friend who was eager to hear what one of Lance's parties was like asked Spider, "Y'all didn't have no liquor?" Spider answered, "Naw. You know Lance don't have that kind of shit." Lance's distaste for alcohol is common knowledge around the neighborhood. And as a good businessman he especially prohibits drug use by his "employees" and associates as well (Taylor 1990).

Much of this insistence on order stems from a concern on the part of Lance and other members of the organization for the safety of their own parents and grandparents, siblings, and children. Even more important, however, Lance was raised in this middle-class neighborhood. His behaviors illustrate his own desire to comply with the social norms. As Tracy Harris described, "At Groveland Park, [the Black Mobsters] were the ones outside every morning to make sure that the kids got to the park safely. And they stopped traffic and directed traffic. And got the kids in the park." Tracy believed that the members of the Black Mobsters in Groveland were taught to be successful, and they are now passing those middle-class orientations on to their children.

> They got themselves in a situation and they used that situation to the best of their advantage. And they're working it. And that's what it's about. It's like any other job. They're working the situation to their advantage. And because they have some semblance of class, intelligence, and some decent upbringing, they bring that back into the group in which they're in. And when they raise their children, they raise their children with the same effects as they were raised—to achieve something, to go somewhere.

The comparable class position of many of the Black Mobsters and their law-abiding neighbors makes getting rid of them even more difficult for concerned residents. They share many of the same values for an attractive and safe neighborhood, and both groups want socioeconomic security, but they have divergent strategies for achieving those goals. And because the outcomes are often similar, the neighborhood's betterment groups have a difficult time convincing their less-involved neighbors that there is even a problem to begin with. Apathy, based on what one resident called a "false sense of security," plagues organizational efforts in Groveland. "The problem is, they won't get involved until there is an incident," lamented one member of St. Mary's Outreach Team about the lack of participation by the residents of the Cedarcove subdivision.

Many residents feel secure precisely because much of the illicit activity is kept within the bounds of acceptable neighborhood behavior. Neighborhood fights, for example, are rare, a fact that makes rallying the troops difficult. As one older resident put it, "I never seen one. 'Cause I call a fight several blows exchanged. Now wait a minute, there was a fight maybe about twenty-five years ago." The paucity of incidents is partially a function of the gang's deliberate control of such behavior, yet any incidents that do occur are usually gang-related. Hence, there is a twist to the semi-effectiveness of gang organization: If no gangs existed, there would be no need for the protection that gangs provide. The same ironic logic holds for the coordinated, yet competitive, sale of drugs.

The fact that a high-ranking gang leader lives in Groveland does not significantly distinguish it from other neighborhoods regarding the integration of licit and illicit networks. Residents of all kinds of communities have frequently supported, and often defended, their crime bosses as fervently as they would any other product of their upbringing. Gang members everywhere are connected to parents, cousins, teachers, and even pastors, although to varying degrees across places. These connections mean that residential stability and network density can both facilitate and impede social control. Groveland's particularities as a middle-class neighborhood are the people to whom the illicit networks are linked, the unique strategies of organizing a diverse neighborhood that sits near higher-crime areas, and the particular forms of illicit activities. The neighborhood organizers have myriad attachments to the neighborhood troublemakers. These links help in informally influencing behavior, but can hinder involving public agents of social control. Simultaneously, the social position of gang members and those involved in selling drugs mirrors the legitimate occupational status of other neighborhood residents. With some "reminders" by legitimate community organizations, they also operate under similar rules of conduct, and with similar goals. The criminal minority—already a part of the kin and neighborly networks that exist, and often contributing to the support of local families—is given a degree of latitude to operate in Groveland. This balancing act is an adaptation to the unique geography and resulting composition of Groveland as a black middle-class neighborhood, whereas families in white middle-class neighborhoods are not so immediately and extensively confronted with gangs, the drug trade, and the accompanying violence.

5

Growing Up in Groveland

The kin-based branches of the Gibbs family tree spread far and wide in Groveland. The family's trunk—Mr. and Mrs. Gibbs—moved into Groveland in 1961. They raised their six daughters there. Anna Gibbs Morris is one of the three daughters who have chosen to raise their own families in the neighborhood. Last year, Anna Morris's nineteen-year-old daughter, Neisha, had the family's first great-grandson, Tim Jr. The Morris family represents over thirty-five years in the neighborhood, with four generations, in one square block.

Much has changed since the Gibbs family moved into Groveland. One such change has been an increase in gang activity. Little Tim's father, Tim Ward, Sr., is in a gang, as were many of Neisha Morris's boyfriends before Tim. Drug dealing often goes along with being in gangs. Neisha's mother Anna feels both anger and sadness as she watches Neisha's boyfriends fall prey to the fast life.

I'm so sick of all this shit. 'Cause, you know, Neisha done lost too many friends to all that shit. You know, Neisha just can't take it no more. She lost two boyfriends. And she really took this last one hard. I just hate to see her go through alla that. The first one was like her first boyfriend. You know, he was a nice boy. I liked him. But they just be out there doin' they thang. And they shot him. This last one, Sugar, we just buried. You know she had waited about a year after her first boyfriend and she started seeing this boy Sugar. They shot him in the head. He was in a coma for six months. For the past six months we been goin' to visit that boy in the hospital. We all thought he was gon' pull through. And I really took this second one hard. They done lost ten friends already. Close friends too. But still, they still choosin' these little boys who [are] out there like that.

I mean, they ain't bad people, but they get caught up in all that stuff sellin' drugs.

The Gibbs family vignette illustrates the permanence of many Groveland families through changing surroundings. Having introduced in chapter 4 the importance of the spatial/neighborhood context for binding together a diversity of families and neighbors, here I elaborate on the local context by focusing on the cohort of adolescents and older youth to which Neisha Morris belongs, and examining the range of resources and exposures of this group.

Contextual particularities of black neighborhoods, even black middle-class neighborhoods, fuel consistent racial disparities in social indicators such as educational attainment and performance, marriage and childbearing, and levels of crime and violence. The impact of the unique middle-class black neighborhood works partly through processes of adolescent socialization. Higher poverty rates in black neighborhoods and in black communities beget greater lifestyle diversity within them. Middle-class black youth grow up with friends from a variety of social backgrounds. As a result, middle-class parents have less control over the experiences to which their children will be exposed—less than they would in a more homogeneously middle-class setting. While parents do try to control their children's interactions, other avenues continue to be alluring and enticing for their children. This is Anna Morris's dilemma: that her daughter Neisha, after losing ten friends to violence, is still "choosin' these little boys who [are] out there like that . . . sellin' drugs." While black middle-class youth have a number of resources that smooth the bumps of growing up, they also face unique roadblocks. The possibilities for downward mobility (not to mention violent death) among middle-class black youth as a result of the heterogeneous lifestyles to which they are exposed are reminders of the limited protection that middle-class status provides for African Americans.

BOTH STREET AND DECENT

Theorizing from his ethnographic research in a number of poor black neighborhoods, Elijah Anderson (1991; 1994) discusses the continuum of lifestyles that exists in such contexts. At the two extremes are "decent" and "street" behaviors. "Decent" families are "loving," "committed to middle-class values," and "willing to sacrifice for their children," whereas the code of the streets revolves around the maintenance of respect, often through violent means (Anderson 1994). "Street" families are especially prevalent (although not the majority) in poor neighborhoods, and there the code of the streets is the dominant mode of public interaction. Although Anderson's categories are related to one's material class status, "street" and "decent" are not fixed attributes of either poor people or middle-class people. Many poor families practice "decent" behaviors despite formidable material obstacles, and the middle class can act in "street" fashion. As Anderson (1991, 375) states, the culture of street families "is characterized by support for and encouragement of an alternative life style that appears highly attractive to many adolescents, regardless of family background."

But Anderson only briefly develops the idea of the malleability of street and decent orientations, and the diversity of behaviors at the individual, familial, and community levels. Families and individuals seem to be either street or decent. While decent parents want their children to be able to navigate the streets, they generally shield their children from street influences. In most cases, according to Anderson, street families produce street children and decent families raise decent children. What I aim to do in my discussion of Groveland youth is develop a much more nuanced picture of families, the choices young people make, and their outcomes. A dynamic intermediate position of balancing street and decent lifestyles is a much more common orientation in Groveland than either fully street or fully decent. While the street/decent dichotomy is useful in some ways, I argue that it is inadequate because, in daily practice, most of the "action" is going on in the middle.

The use of Black English and slang by neighborhood residents of all ages is a good example. Most studies of Black English have focused on its use in poor black communities. But as discussed in my introduction, and as illustrated in various of the field notes, Black English is also widely used among the children of African American professionals, and even among some of the professionals themselves, especially in casual settings. Language in Groveland constitutes a cultural arena where the significance of race is clear; Black English unites African Americans of different classes. Knowing the latest slang word or peppering stories with curse words symbolically maintains middle-class connections to the streets, especially for youth. For example, Tyson Reed explained that he not only had a different *manner* of speaking with his friends from college and his friends from the neighborhood gang, but he also had a *separate set of topics* to talk about.

"You just gotta know when to speak upon stuff," he advised about the craft of code-switching. But he went on to share how such linguistic maneuvers can also be confusing. "Sometimes now, I be slippin' and be forgettin' who I'm with. Like sometimes I be slippin' when I be with my ghetto-ass friends." Tyson's deliberate code-switching is part of the practice of balancing street and decent orientations that characterizes Groveland youth (and adults).

In black middle-class neighborhoods there are substantial resources to present nonstreet alternatives for young people. At the same time, the streets have a definite appeal to youth traversing the rebellious period of adolescence. And as Anderson (1994, 82) points out, being street-savvy "is literally necessary for operating in public." Black middle-class youth interact with friends who embrace components of both street and decent lifestyles, and neighborhood adults set both street and decent examples. Three Groveland youth—Neisha Morris, Tyson Reed, and Charisse Baker—typify the active negotiation of these two lifestyles within their family, peer, school, and neighborhood contexts. Each of these arenas is nestled within the next, going from the most immediate context of the family to a larger look at the neighborhood. All three young people share similar neighborhood exposures, but their schooling, peer, and home lives are very different.

Neisha Morris (whose family opened this chapter), Tyson Reed, and Charisse Baker are connected through family and friendship ties. Neisha has a first cousin named Ray Gibbs who also grew up in Groveland; both are grandchildren in the four-generation Gibbs clan. Ray Gibbs and Tyson Reed are best friends, played football together at Groveland Park, and went to college together. Charisse Baker is more peripheral to this group, and would probably not recognize the other two young people on a Groveland street, but she does have a weak tie. Neisha's current boyfriend, Tim Ward, grew up in his grandmother's house two blocks from Charisse's family's home. Tim also played basketball under Charisse's father at the local Catholic school gym. Charisse has a crush on Tim's younger brother—a crush that her father forbids because Tim's younger brother is in and out of jail. Charisse stays informed on the gossip of Tim's relationship with Neisha, although Charisse and Neisha have never met.

NEISHA MORRIS

Neisha's family life can be characterized by the neighborhood-based kin ties described in the first vignette. In addition to her mother's

family, Neisha's father also grew up in Groveland, and his family remains in the neighborhood. Neisha's mother, Anna Morris, is a dental
assistant, and her father is the supervisor of a South Side park. She
has a nine-year-old brother, Nate. Her parents were married for over
fifteen years. They recently separated because Neisha's father had a
drinking problem. Her father's unpredictable and, according to
Neisha, "crazy" behavior played an indirect role in Neisha's getting
pregnant at age eighteen. To avoid her father, she moved in with her
nineteen-year-old boyfriend, Tim Ward, at his grandmother's home.

> [My father] was too strict on me. That's when I met Tim and I
> started spending the night with him every night. I got to the
> point where I felt like Tim took me away from my father, and
> havin' to come home, and havin' to be bothered with that.

When Neisha got pregnant, she returned to her mother's house, bringing her boyfriend along with her. By that time, Neisha's parents had
separated. With Mr. Morris out of the household, Tim's income from
selling drugs was a welcome help to pay the bills.

The fact that many black middle-class households are just a few
steps away from financial hardship is most apparent when there is a
sudden shock like Mr. and Mrs. Morris's separation. Together the
Morrises made over $40,000, but the bulk of that income was from
Mr. Morris's job as a park supervisor. And, as in most black families,
income from their jobs was the only means of support in the Morris
household.[1] With Mr. Morris gone, Neisha's mother looked for creative ways to keep the family comfortable.

Neisha's extended family provides both positive supports and examples of negative outcomes. Many of her first cousins who grew up
in Groveland run the range of possible current situations. One cousin
is in jail in Iowa for assaulting someone who owed him money. Her
cousin Ray, after being shot in the stomach, decided to make some
changes in his life. He joined his friend Tyson Reed at Grambling State
University, a historically black college in Louisiana. Another cousin
graduated from college and is a graphic artist for a downtown design firm. Her closest cousin, Kima, has an informal beauty shop in
her grandmother's home to support herself and her three-year-old
daughter.

Among Neisha's closest girlfriends there is somewhat less diversity.
All three are young single mothers like Neisha, searching for career
direction.

My close friends—Libra, she's in college. She goes to Chicago State for nursing. Well, all my friends just had kids. So, Trenique's baby is one. Deshawn is one. And my friend Roxanne, his birthday is Thursday, so he makin' one. So, it's like Trenique didn't finish at Benton High School 'cause she got pregnant. So she went to school and got her GED. So now she in school to do hair, cosmetology school. And Roxanne, she not working either. She just trying to find out really what she wanna do with herself, you know.

As in most friendships, Neisha and her three girlfriends have much in common in addition to being young mothers.[2] The children's fathers are all in the drug business, as is Neisha's boyfriend, Tim. Drug money fills the gaps between what their parents provide, what public aid and food stamps provide, and what they need to support themselves and their children in the style to which they are accustomed.[3] "I can't take care of me and my son off no aid check, not the way he can take care of us," Neisha commented about the discrepancy between public assistance and her standard of living with her boyfriend's support. "It's like I won't have a lot of the stuff I want because my mother has to take care of her and my brother and this house." Yet Neisha knows she cannot fully rely on the unstable income of a drug dealer. "I got to do stuff for myself 'cause that [drug-dealing] lifestyle, you could have it one day and the next day it could be gone."

For the Morris family, drug money is one of the safety nets that support their once middle-income family. Because of Tim's illegal income, Neisha can avoid welfare, although she does receive food stamps. Mrs. Morris does not approve of Tim's business, but she also does not find it reprehensible. Her opinion of drug dealers was not uniformly negative.

It all depends on that person, what they do. It all depends on the way they carry theyself. Certain of the things they do I don't see them do. See what I'm sayin'? So, what I see of them might be what I like. Maybe what somebody else sees is something different.

Mrs. Morris is content that Neisha's boyfriend does not store drugs in her house, and does his business away from her family. What she sees of Tim—his boyish shyness, the encouragement he gives Neisha to go back to school, and his affection toward his son—is what she likes.

The integration and balancing of street and decent orientations is apparent in the Morris family. Mrs. Morris keeps her garden colorful and her lawn meticulously trimmed. The glass table in her living room never had a smudge on it, an impressive feat with children in the house. The commitment to legal work on the part of Anna Morris, and Tim Sr.'s participation in criminal enterprise (which is also hard work), exist simultaneously. Neisha is an unmarried teen mother, but chooses not to receive welfare. The extra money she might get from public assistance would only add unwanted bureaucratic hassles and stigma to her pot of resources. And, as Mrs. Morris stated in the opening vignette, she abhors the violence that accompanies the drug business. Yet she cannot abandon her daughter, and therefore improvises with various means of keeping the family afloat.

A description of Neisha's schooling similarly depicts the simultaneity of street and decent orientations. Neisha did not attend the local public elementary school. Instead, she was bused to a racially mixed magnet school. "I had some real high scores on my Iowa tests," Neisha remembered. "And they told me to pick another school that I wanted to go to. And that's the school my mother picked, that offered a' enrichment program there." Mrs. Morris was proactive in putting her daughter in a challenging academic environment, a clearly decent strategy to facilitate Neisha's future success. However, young people do not always see the benefits their parents are trying to bestow upon them. Neisha could have continued on to the magnet high school that most of her classmates attended, but she was weary of the long commute and wanted to be with her neighborhood friends. She started at one high school and then transferred to Benton.

Benton High School is in Treelawn, a neighborhood with nearly three times the poverty rate and half the median family income as Groveland (see appendix B, fig. 1). Benton is not the closest high school to Neisha's house, but the two closer schools have worse gang problems, and one of them in particular is dominated by a rival gang. The Black Mobsters are the dominant gang in Groveland, but they have little clout at the closest two high schools, which is why many Groveland teenagers choose Benton over the closer schools. Even though Benton is designated as a "preparatory academy," so that non-neighborhood students like Neisha must achieve certain standardized test scores to get in, the overall graduation rate there is only 59 percent. Neisha described the mix of students at Benton.

It's a lotta kids that's strictly into that school, strictly into going to school, all type of activities, honors, this and that. But a lotta people just be there to cut classes all day. Just to go to gym and lunch. And sometimes just come to school and don't even go in the building. And they bring down the school, the whole school. So basically it's half and half.

Neisha did graduate from Benton High, but she was not part of the honors group—not because she was not smart, but because her attentions turned to her friends and to boys.

The examples set by Neisha's family, schoolmates, and neighborhood friends present various roads for Neisha to travel. Both of her parents worked in stable jobs with good incomes. They remained married for fifteen years, until Mrs. Morris could no longer cope with Mr. Morris's drinking. Their home and yard were manicured. Neisha's mother chose a competitive magnet school, but also allowed Neisha to make her own decisions about high school. Of Neisha's neighborhood friends, including her cousins, some went to college and have careers, while others just made it out of high school and have started a family. Many of the young men in Neisha's life are captivated by the fast-money drug business. All of these situations have been affected by the mix of people who live in Groveland.

TYSON REED

Tyson Reed was a member of the Black Mobsters in Groveland. The leader of the gang took a special interest in him and Neisha's cousin Ray Gibbs because of their leadership skills. Tyson spent a few years selling drugs and trading guns as a member of the Black Mobsters. Many of his gang friends have, according to his friend Ray, "faded or disappeared." Ray elaborated:

It's probably three things. Well I should say four things: either in jail, still out here doin' nothin' with theyself, some died and then the other few like us probably trying to do something with theyselves like go to school, or get a job. Just get away.

Tyson and Ray have tried to get away from the gangs and drugs in Groveland by going to Grambling State University together.

Because of the schools Tyson Reed attended, his networks are much more far-reaching than the boundaries of the neighborhood. "You gotta think about it," he instructed.

I grew up in Groveland, but [I was] always on the West Side.
I went to Presley, and kids got bused in to go there, so I knew
a lotta people. Then I went to Dayton, kids got bused in to go
there. Then I went Down South and went to college, so I had
a lotta friends there. Not to mention in between I played football—got a lotta friends—[and] wrestled.

Tyson went to elementary school at Presley Academy, a public magnet
school outside of Groveland for which there is a long waiting list. A
majority of Presley students perform above national norms on standardized tests. After Presley, Tyson attended Dayton Prep, a public
high school in a racially mixed, middle-class neighborhood. While
Dayton High School has changed over the years, and it is neither as
racially mixed nor as middle class as the neighborhood that surrounds
it, it continues to send over 85 percent of its students to four-year
colleges, and it is one of the few Chicago public schools to which
college admissions officers from elite universities make regular recruiting visits. The list of magnet schools that Tyson attended was the
result of his mother's insistence on a good education. Tyson's mother
is a high-ranking official in the Chicago public school system. She
had just received her Ph.D. a few weeks before I interviewed Tyson,
and he proudly showed off her diploma. His mother's own continued
schooling illustrates the stress placed on education in the Reed family.

Tyson's immediate family includes his mother and his twin sister.
His father has been out of his life since he was a boy. All of what
Tyson had to say about his father was filled with intense anger because
of his father's absence. "I know where he at, but I don't wanna fuck
with him," Tyson snapped. Even though he does not want a relationship with his father, he explicitly recognizes the problems that arise
because of absent parents:

That's a real problem right there with the black community today, with our kids and stuff. People just don't care. I mean,
when the kids [are] young really it's the parents' responsibility,
well duty, to be around 'em. You know, be around they friends,
be around your family or whatever. Matter of fact, outta all my
friends, I'll say 90 percent of them either live with their mother
or live with their father. Only like 10 percent of my friends live
with both of their parents.

From his own experiences, Tyson is convinced that he would not
have gotten involved in gangs or drug dealing if his father had been
around.[4]

Tyson also harbors anger at his mother for having a boyfriend who seemed to try to take his father's place. At twenty-two years old, Tyson has far from a close relationship with his mother, but he is beginning to realize the advantages he has gained from the kind of education his mother provided for him. He talked about this burgeoning appreciation.

> 'Cause you gotta learn how to appreciate stuff you got. I ain't never really appreciated what my mother used to do for me. Like sending me to Presley and Dayton. I ain't never appreciate that until, until I started to get fucked up a lot, and, you know, I really got on my own. I was like, "Damn, if it wasn't for that I'll be just as dumb as this mufucka over here." You know what I'm saying? Really, when you really think about it, you'on appreciate it till it's too late.

Once Tyson began to appreciate it, he started to use it to his advantage. He has just one course to complete to receive his B.A. in criminal justice at Grambling. He has plans to go to law school once he finishes college. In the meantime, he plans to work for the Chicago Board of Education, a job secured through his mother's connections.

CHARISSE BAKER

Because Charisse is the youngest of the three youth, much of her adolescent life is still unfolding. She is sixteen and lives with her mother and younger sister, Deanne, across the street from St. Mary's Catholic Church and School. Charisse's mother is a personnel assistant at a Chicago university, and is taking classes there to get her bachelor's degree. Mr. Baker is a Chicago firefighter. While her father and mother are separated, Charisse sees her father many times a week at the after-school basketball hour that he supervises at St. Mary's gym. He and Charisse's mother are on very good terms, and Charisse has a loving relationship with both parents. Mr. Baker is as active as any parent could be, attending the father/daughter dances at Charisse's high school, never missing a big performance, and visiting his daughters often.

Charisse and her sister are being raised by the neighborhood family in addition to their biological parents. "We [are] real close. Like all our neighbors know us because my dad grew up over here. Since the '60s." Charisse is a third-generation Grovelandite just like Neisha Morris. Her grandparents moved into Groveland with Charisse's then-teenage father when the neighborhood first opened to African Americans. Charisse's parents lived in other neighborhoods when they were first married, only to eventually settle back in Groveland a few houses down from Mr. Baker's parents. Now Charisse is benefiting from the friends her family has made over their years of residence in Groveland, especially the members of St. Mary's church, who play the role of surrogate parents. When Charisse was in elementary school at St. Mary's, her late paternal grandmother was the school secretary, and so the Baker girls were always under the watchful eye of their grandmother as well as the staff, who were their grandmother's friends. And in the evenings Charisse's mother would bring her and her sister to choir practice, where they accumulated an ensemble of mothers and fathers.

After St. Mary's elementary school, Charisse went on to St. Agnes Catholic High School for girls, her father's choice. St. Agnes is located in a suburb of Chicago and is a solid, integrated Catholic school where 100 percent of the girls graduate and over 95 percent go on to college. Many of the students come from lower-middle-class families like the Bakers. Charisse told a story about a recent St. Agnes graduate that illustrated the importance of education at St. Agnes, as well as the economic status of its students.

> I was hearin' about this one girl who went from St. Agnes. She got a full scholarship to Stanford. And she was, you know, she was a minority. She was talkin' about how e'rybody in Stanford drivin' to school with they little Rolls Royce and Corvettes and she was on her little ten-speed. She was like, "That's okay!" She gettin' her education.

The possibility of a Stanford scholarship, as well as the graduation statistics at St. Agnes, make it easy to understand why Charisse's parents chose it over the closer, and free, Benton High School.[5]

Most of Charisse's close friends went to St. Mary's and now go to St. Agnes with her, but her choice of boyfriends shows modest signs of rebellion. From her father's perspective, the mere fact of having boyfriends is rebellious, but Charisse still manages to have a very full social life when it comes to boys. Many of Charisse's male interests are older than she, and irregularly employed—although some are in and out of school. She meets many of them hanging out at the mall. One evening, members of the church's youth choir sat around talking about their relationships. Charisse cooed while talking about her present boyfriend, who had just graduated from high school but did not have a job and was uncertain about his future. But in the middle of that thought, Charisse spontaneously changed her attentions to a new young man that she had just met. "Charisse changes boyfriends like she changes her clothes," her sister joked, indicating the impetuous nature of adolescent relationships.

While these young men are not in gangs or selling drugs, many of them do not seem to share Charisse's strong career goals and diligence in attaining them. Some of them would not gain the approval of her parents. However, this full list of boyfriends has not clouded Charisse's focus. In her always bubbly, fast-talking manner, she declared:

> Okay, I would like to go the University of Illinois in Champaign-Urbana. I would like to major in marketing and I'm considering minoring in communications, because I talk a lot. And once I get a job, I get stable, then I can pursue a relationship. I'd like to get married and I want five kids. 'Cause I love children. I really do. I love children.

Charisse has a clear vision for her life—school, marriage, children. The content and order of these plans subscribe to a very traditional life sequence, perhaps more traditional than anyone ever really follows (Rindfuss, Swicegood, and Rosenfeld 1987). Her parents have made decisions about Charisse's schooling that will prepare her for college, that have instilled in her the Christian values in which they believe, and that have steered her toward a group of like-minded friends.

Yet Charisse's family, friends, and acquaintances are not all angels. "Any of my uncles might be in jail," Charisse responded when asked if she knew anyone in jail. She continued, "I know one uncle I haven't talked to, he could be on parole. And I have a cousin who I know is on parole in Detroit, so he can't see nobody." About her neighbors, Charisse recalled, "I know Harris is in jail. He live around here. You know his brother Big Tim [Neisha's boyfriend]." These relationships show that Charisse is not completely sheltered from a different, perhaps more street-oriented, crowd in either her neighborhood or her family. While Charisse's closest family and friends stress positive behaviors, her larger network provides a more diverse set of experiences and exposures.

RESOURCES AND PARENTAL STRATEGIES

Many Groveland parents possess financial, social, and human capital that greatly facilitate parenting, a crucial distinction between them and poor families. All three of these youth—Neisha, Tyson, and Charisse—have familial financial resources that have provided access to private schools, paid for sports equipment and dance lessons, and generated some spending money for movies, the prom, and an occasional trip or vacation. Some of the financial capital of Groveland families goes toward endowing neighborhood institutions. There are thriving local businesses; Groveland Park hosts a full Summer Day Camp and other recreational activities; and many of the churches are well supported. These are the things that money can buy.

The families of these three youth also have important social connections to the work world. Even though Neisha dislikes her father, his job with the Chicago Park District helped her get a summer job. She admitted, "My daddy got a promotion to another park. He's a park supervisor, so I'll probably work at his park, you know, through the summer." Tyson also took advantage of his mother's connections and planned to work for the Chicago Board of Education. And Charisse's younger sister, who was not yet even sixteen years old, spent her summers filing and answering phones in her mother's office, while Charisse worked at a beauty salon owned by a family friend and member of St. Mary's Church.

Finally, Groveland parents have valuable skills and knowledge— human capital acquired through both academic and on-the-job training. Parents impart these resources of information and know-how to their children. Tyson's mother's knowledge about and experience with Chicago public education surely influenced her decision to place her son in magnet schools. The fact that she attended college and graduate school no doubt facilitated Tyson's and his sister's college application process, and Tyson's aspirations for law school. And because of their white-collar employment, both Neisha's and Charisse's mothers work with computers, fax machines, and other high-tech office equipment. Familiarity with such technology is now a prerequisite for future success. Groveland youth are in many ways privileged because of these resources. They enjoy opportunities that their counterparts in poor black neighborhoods do not.

At the same time, Groveland is not far removed from poor neighborhoods where resources are few, and parental strategies run up against the stubborn obstacles of underfunded and understaffed schools, crumbling housing, poor city services, drugs, and violence. The neighborhood is a part of a larger and poorer black community on Chicago's South Side. Groveland residents share many South Side institutions with other neighborhoods. The character of middle-class black neighborhoods and black communities generally increases the options, many of them deleterious, from which middle-class black youth have to choose during the rebellious adolescent period. Even though parents have strategies for raising their children that include steering them in positive directions, they cannot be with their children at all times. Charisse's covert relationships with boys illustrate that fact. Once parental strategies are chosen and enacted, there is inevitably youthful rebellion against those plans. But the shape of this rebellion cannot go too far outside of the options presented in the young person's social and spatial milieu. Some youth emerge from this course unscathed. On the other hand, many find themselves left with a variety of battle scars—gunshot wounds, criminal records, new babies, subpar educations, or one less friend.[6]

Parental strategies are quite recognizable in the life stories of Neisha, Tyson, and Charisse. All three have clear ideas about what their parents do not want for them. In response to the direct question "What do you think your parents definitely don't want for you?" Charisse and her sister answered in agreement: "No drugs. Drug addicts sittin' in a crack house, standin' on the corner tryin' to get high. With three babies! On welfare." Neisha's answer to the same question also stressed self-sufficiency. "[My mother] don't want me to be on [public] aid all of my life." Just as they have similar understandings of what their parents want them to avoid, they also have parallel notions of what their parents positively hope for them. As Charisse put it: "That we be successful in whatever we do. So we ain't constantly callin' them for no money." Neisha expanded on her parents' hopes for her success:

> I guess they just want me to really basically go to school, have a nice job, be able to take care of me without depending on somebody else to take care of me, you know. [My mother] want me to have a job and food and enjoy the finer things in life instead of just stayin' around. Like she be sayin' she wish she coulda did this and wish she coulda did that, and I still got all them opportunities. They just want the best for me. Want me to experience more than Second Avenue. You know, more than this right here.

These parental desires are not at all surprising. Most parents want the best for their children, and prosperity is a key component of parents' "decent" plans.

Groveland parents use explicit strategies to encourage their children's expedient development into self-sufficient adults. Charisse's parents raised her in the Catholic church and school; Neisha took every dance class ever offered at Groveland Park, and she still wants to be a dance instructor, with the full support and urging of both parents; and Tyson's mother used magnet schools to get her son a solid education and steer him toward college. For the most part, these strategies were accepted by each youth, and they developed an interest in these activities apart from their parents' master plans. Yet there were some strategies that did not work, and such disagreements illustrate the different conceptions that young people have from their parents about what their lives should look like. During the rebellious period of adolescence, young people draw from both the street and decent activities available in the neighborhood environment.

ADOLESCENT REBELLION IN THE NEIGHBORHOOD CONTEXT

Tyson Reed resisted being pushed in the direction his mother had planned for him. He talked about the kind of son his mother wanted him to be.

> Without all the gangbanging. Without knowing the people I know. She really ain't want me to play football. She wanted me to be on the swim team. 'Cause I been swimming since I was like three months old. So I know how to swim real real good. And she would say, "Well why'on't you get on the swim team?" Yeah, awright, that's gay as hell. I mean, when you think about it, it ain't gay, but you thinkin', I'm a male, seventeen, eighteen, nineteen, twenty, whatever. In college, high school. How the hell I look competin', "Oh, I'ma beat you swimmin'." When I can run up and physically hit somebody. You know what I'm sayin'? Or even basketball, you can show your abilities or something. How I look, "Oh, I'm gonna outswim you. I'm faster than you." I mean, even with track, I think it's more manly than swimming.

Tyson dismissed his mother's desire for him to be a studious young man on the swim team with sarcastic obstinacy. His mother's suggestion of swimming as the sport of choice indicated to him that she could not possibly understand the masculine pressures he faced as a young black male. His rebellion was based on common adolescent concerns of gender identity and a tough image.

The absence of Tyson's father compounded his search for a masculine identity, and further fueled the anger toward his mother. In search of male role models and a fellowship of young men, Tyson got "plugged," Chicago slang for joining a gang. According to Tyson's friend, this was not difficult to do. His friend explained the process of becoming a Black Mobster.

> It start off like two or three people'll join a gang, but you hang with them. So you too close to 'em to let somebody beat up on 'em. Somebody mess with them, you in it. So now they look at you as, you know what I'm saying, you with 'em. So now they want you too. But pretty soon you start doing everything they doing. Everything they doing except being plugged. So you just plug. That's when it start.

Tyson's friend's description of getting plugged is a clear illustration that youthful rebellion can go as far as the local options allow. Tyson did not have to search far to get involved in the Black Mobsters and their drug business. There was no elaborate initiation or probationary period. Plugging was as simple as being friends with the boy next door, who was supposedly in a gang, but who himself may have been guilty of the charge only by his association with some other gang-identified friend.[7] The absence of Tyson's father, and then the departure of an uncle to whom he had been close, allowed for Tyson's exploration of delinquent neighborhood networks. His recollection of how he got involved in selling drugs interweaves the search for a male role model and the options offered by the neighborhood.

> When I really needed somebody to teach me something, my uncle was there trying to help me. But after he went to college, and I was still in grammar school by myself, it wasn't nothing else to do but go across the street and do what I had to do. Awright, my mama might have a good job, but if my homey [friend] and me go up across the street and he get on and start sellin' drugs, now you honestly think I'ma sit there? That's a form of peer pressure, I know. But you gon' see him make all that money and y'all together. You there anyway, fuck it. You might as well make you some money. That's how I felt about it, you know.

In Tyson's words, the crossroads that he faced are apparent: a young man, feeling directionless because of his father's and uncle's departures, recognizing that his mother has a good job and that that should count for something in his decision. Yet his friends are a strong force at this point in his life (the peer pressure he referred to), and fast money in the era of hundred-dollar-and-up sneakers has an almost irresistible allure. And most important for this focus on neighborhood context and options, just across the street was the short distance Tyson had to travel to make the decision to sell drugs.

In a neighborhood like Groveland, gangs and drug dealing are attractive to these middle-class youth because of the fast money they are supposed to provide. Although Grovelandites frequently describe the neighborhood as "middle class," being *black* and middle class does not allow for a lot of excess. This was definitely the situation for both Charisse and Neisha, whose families packaged financial resources— sometimes illegal ones in the case of Neisha's family—to pay the bills. To get the extra money to buy the newest sneakers or the latest hairstyle, some Groveland youth turn to the Black Mobsters and their drug business. Still, Tyson's professional mother had a high income and an average-sized family on which to spend it. What could possibly be Tyson's rationale? "Your parents give you what you need and sometime they get you what you want," Tyson explained. "But when you sell drugs, *you* get you what you wanted." Tyson's decision to sell drugs despite his family's financial resources was due in part to consumer greed, and in part to the ease of opportunity, which resulted from the diverse neighborhood composition.

The higher poverty rates in black middle-class neighborhoods mean that a nontrivial minority of the families in them will have fewer resources to connect their children to positive activities like dance or swimming, and buy for them the status symbols of contemporary youth consumer culture. For this more disadvantaged portion of the population, the economic attraction to selling drugs is the strongest, and the commitment to decent behaviors is most attenuated (Sampson and Wilson 1995). Middle-class youth—eager to rebel and thrilled by the risks—are often drawn into these orientations. Their parents could provide some luxuries, as Tyson's mother could, but never enough to satisfy the wants of a consumer-minded American adolescent. Many black middle-class youth like Tyson are simultaneously in search of a male peer group and role models, excited by the sheer deviance, and desirous of the flashy material goods that an illegal income can buy. Other youth who are middle class only by the skin of their parents' teeth have clearer economic motives. For all, the opportunity for delinquent rebellion is readily available in Groveland. Tyson did not have to search far to get involved with the "wrong crowd."

Like Tyson's, Neisha's family situation affects the nature of her rebellion, which is in turn circumscribed by the neighborhood milieu. Neisha's parents stayed together for most of her childhood years, provided for her financially, and enrolled her in positive activities, and her extended family continues to give her much love and encouragement. Yet her father's problem with alcohol means that his presence often has negative consequences. When he was still in the household, he was very strict and did not want Neisha on the phone with boys, let alone dating them. Still, Neisha, like Charisse, found a way to have a thriving social life, including boyfriends. Many of the boys Neisha chose, however, have gone a similar route as Tyson. Although Neisha's mother spoke somewhat negatively about her daughter's choice of boyfriends in the opening vignette, she cannot simply forbid Neisha to date them. The reality is more complex than that. Many of Neisha's boyfriends have grown up in Groveland, and Neisha's mother has known many of them for years. She knows where they live. She knows their families. Aside from their seedy involvements, she also knows their friendly, funny, and respectful sides. These longtime neighborhood connections make it difficult to completely sever relationships with the neighborhood delinquents.

For example, Kareem, who holds a leadership position in the Black Mobsters, was one of Neisha's boyfriends before Tim. Kareem, of course, was not *born* a gang member. Before the Black Mobsters, Neisha's mother, aunts, and grandmother all knew Kareem as just another neighborhood kid. Mrs. Morris could not see Kareem and the other young men in the gang as anything but little boys. She said about them, "You know all these little boys, like Kareem and them? I ain't scared of them." How could Mrs. Morris be afraid of Kareem when he had such a humbling crush on her daughter? Neisha described her early neighborhood memories of Kareem, and how they eventually started dating.

> Kareem been likin' me for the longest [time], even before he had money. I remember seein' him, he used to be sittin' on some crates over by the store with some ol' raggedy T-shirt on, and his fat just hanging. Well, this was before he had money. He would just keep on talking to me and kept on and kept on.

Then, you know, he started makin' money. And I ain't think he even liked me any more. So, you know, I wasn't even thinkin' about it. But then, he just kept tryin' to get my number and shit. Finally, I just gave it to him. And that nigga called me about a hundred times that day. He just kept tryin' to talk to me. The first time we went out he gave me $300. I was like, "What's this for?" But, you know, I really started likin' him. He really real sweet and all.

Kareem is much more than a high-ranking gang member and drug dealer. He is the fat little boy who sat in front of the store, he is "real sweet," and he has been persistent with his attentions toward Neisha. Neisha could undoubtedly find a boy in the neighborhood not affiliated with the Black Mobsters and not selling drugs, but money and power—no matter their source—have always been aphrodisiacs. The neighborhood cycle that fostered Tyson's entrance into the drug business also operates in Neisha's case by shaping her choices of young men to date.

For both Neisha and Tyson, family strategies and circumstances interact with neighborhood options. Parents use strategies to positively direct their children, but onerous family situations can undermine some of these plans and turn young people's thoughts to what else the neighborhood has to offer. The absence of Tyson's father and the frequent cruelty of Neisha's sent them both looking for alternative avenues on which to mature. Because of the diversity of local lifestyles within Groveland, and because street and decent networks are connected at several family and neighborly junctures, it was not difficult for Tyson to get plugged, and for Neisha to be attracted to drug dealers.

Charisse Baker's neighborhood experiences differ in some important ways, although it is more difficult to thoroughly appraise Charisse's choices because she is younger than the other two. A number of factors in Charisse's upbringing converge to provide her parents with considerable control over the choices she can make. Her parents are separated, but her father continues to be a daily and positive presence in her life. And Charisse's intense involvement in the church leaves her little time for much else. Describing how she spends her free time, Charisse joked, "I got a lot of stuff that I have to do at the church. But I don't know if that's considered work or free time?" She listed her involvements in St. Mary's, including the parish pastoral council, youth group, youth council, gospel choir, and the hospitality committee. The extra parenting that she is subject to by church members makes her all the more accountable for her actions.

Charisse's rebellion, like Neisha's, is through boys. And also like Neisha's, her extended family (church and kin) know many of the residents in Groveland—the good and the bad. But unlike Neisha, whose father pushed her away from the family, Charisse and Deanne have a very good relationship with their father. This bond fortifies their conscience when choosing boyfriends and deciding what to do with them. Charisse's sister, Deanne, recalled her father's talk with her about boys.

> I think one good factor is the way my father approached me about boys. He told me when I was like only six or seven. I mean, I was thinkin' 'bout boys but I wasn't goin' to a big long extent or nothing. He sat down, and he was like, "Deanne, boys'll tell you anything to get you in the bed." [She laughs as she remembers her father's words.] I'm thinking that's not true. You know, I'm in second grade. I ain't thinkin' along those lines. He specifically said all boys. He said they'd tell you anything. He was like, "They'll tell you they love you. They'll tell you anything to get you in the bed." He was like, "Don't do it!" He had that look on his face like if you do it, you in trouble. So, I didn't do it. Later on I found out that all boys aren't bad, but a lot of them are. So I kinda got the hint.

What would happen if either Charisse or her sister were to get pregnant? Charisse answered without hesitation.

> I would run away from home 'cause I think my parents would actually try to kill me. I think my daddy would kill me. I'm not being sarcastic at all. I would run away from home. I would call [my friend] Khadija and say, "Khadija, I gotta go." And I'd be up. And that's all seriousness. That's why I ain't doin' nothin', so I'on get nothin'.

Charisse's good relationship with her parents means that their words stick in her mind. While she tests the boundaries when it comes to boyfriends, she is not inclined to disregard altogether her parents' advice and lessons.

The fact that Charisse's parents have been able to more closely supervise and influence her behavior does not mean that the neighborhood context is unimportant. To the contrary, the church is also a part of the neighborhood context, as are the Catholic school and many of the people who participate in these two institutions. Charisse's family's involvement in the church and school integrates positive family and neighborhood contexts for Charisse. Just as Tyson and Neisha were easily introduced to drug dealers and gang members, Charisse's friends come from families who are paying a premium to send their children to Catholic school. The members of St. Mary's parish include Groveland's state representative, an executive at the Coca Cola Company, an executive assistant at the Urban League, entrepreneurs, teachers, and board members of community organizations. They are examples of success for Charisse to follow. At the same time, Tyson and Neisha also have positive role models in family members and friends who also exemplify hard work and success, and Charisse is by no means sheltered from the neighborhood troublemakers. Charisse knows the neighborhood gang members. She grew up with them just as Neisha did. Some of the young men who play basketball at the church gym under her father's supervision are gang members. Since Mr. Baker grew up in Groveland during the time when the gangs were first forming, he knows many of the founding members as well as the younger cohorts. Mr. Baker's familiarity with the gangs gives Charisse and Deanne a certain feeling of security. Deanne commented, "I want people to know that that's my daddy 'cause I'on wanna be messed with or anything." These associations, and her father's lessons, make Charisse streetwise. Yet within her independence exist the rules and limitations that her parents have set for her, guiding her neighborhood relationships.

(YOUNG) WOMEN, (YOUNG) MEN, AND FAMILIES

Neisha and Charisse are teenagers, and Tyson has just passed into his twenties. Their conceptions of sexuality, their personal understandings of gender roles, and their ideas about starting a family are in a crucial stage where what they have observed and learned will soon be translated into their own adult decisions and eventually shape their future. There is a gendered experience of growing up in Groveland. Boys and girls, young men and young women are equal beneficiaries of the resources of their middle-class parents, and so both genders have in front of them similar educational and career options and opportunities. But males and females face very different "street" temptations in the neighborhood context. The different kinds of street behaviors are themselves gendered (see also chapter 7). Boys and young men join gangs and sell drugs (as Tyson did for the somewhat gendered reason of wanting a father figure), and girls and young women get pregnant before they are married. Of course the existence of an unwed mother means that there is necessarily an absent father out there somewhere, but this is given less attention than the woman's culpability, and even her moral worth. Still, as the stories of these three youth show, street behaviors exist within a range of other activities, aspirations, and values. Neisha has "decent" plans of getting certified to work for the Chicago Park District, moving out of her mother's house (possibly to the suburbs), and raising her son with Tim Sr. She has seriously reflected on the decision she made to have a child at a relatively young age. She remembered her mother's caution: " 'Havin' this kid is all right, Neisha, but it ain't what you think it's gon' be.' " Contemplating this point, Neisha concluded, "If I woulda known what I knew now, I would have waited." What could easily be labeled as a street behavior—i.e., Neisha's out-of-wedlock motherhood—is not nearly as unidimensional as the popular rendition might suggest.

The same point can be made when dissecting the street and decent labels as applied to certain family forms. Stressful family situations have had an impact on the routes that Neisha, Tyson, and Charisse have taken, and will probably continue to influence the choices they make as adults. Neisha's mother and father stayed married until Neisha was seventeen years old, although her father's drinking problem meant that the Morrises were a two-parent family in name only. On the other hand, Charisse's parents separated when she was in elementary school, but her father is perhaps more involved than most fathers-in-residence. Neisha and Charisse take in their parents' experiences and examples, and their views on marriage reflect those examples. Even though the Bakers' marriage did not work out, we heard Charisse's optimism about marriage fitting neatly in her long-range plan of school, marriage, and then lots of children. Neisha, on the other hand, is more hesitant. "We was just talkin' about that a coupla minutes ago," Neisha reported, referring to a conversation she and Tim Sr. had about getting married. She continued with a skeptical "but."

But we just both still young. I'm only nineteen, he only twenty. So, I feel like, you know, ain't no rush to get married. You know, you never know what might happen. You know, we cool for how we are now. And if we still together in a few mo' years, then we gon' get married.

Neisha's comments and those of many others in Groveland point to a tolerance and sometimes a preference for flexible family forms. Social scientists are clear on the facts—that two-parent families almost always have more resources to put toward their children's development, and that children from single-parent homes are at higher risk of dropping out of high school, having a teenage birth, and getting in trouble in school or with the law (Garfinkel and McLanahan 1986; McLanahan and Sandefur 1994). But this is a separate question from the family decisions at the local level. Charisse may profess her plans to adhere to the "normative" sequence of family formation, but she also babysits for a best friend who doesn't have a husband, and she is not ashamed of her own fatherless household. The majority of family households in Groveland (57 percent) are headed by a married couple. But this dry demographic does not capture the lived family fluctuations. Both the Bakers and the Morrises are still officially married. Neither couple has undergone a divorce or a legal separation. Mr. Morris moved around the corner to his mother's house, while Mr. Baker moved about a mile away. Neither husband/father is absolutely absent from the household. Who could say for sure what the response was to the "marital status" question when the census taker came to these homes?

Groveland youth watch these elastic families, growing when a cousin or grandfather moves in and contracting with a husband's or sister's departure. There is no one way to characterize what the youth and adults believe about marriage and families. Words often follow "decent" formulations, but deeds are less dogmatic in their unfolding.[8] Tyson, whose own parents separated when he was very young and who further commented that he had very few models of two-parent families, had mainstream plans for his future family life. "That's why I always said whenever I have some kids or whatever, I'ma stay with one person. I'ma get married one time. And I ain't gon' be trippin'." The test of these beliefs will be his practice. And if his beliefs and his practice contradict one another, is Tyson to be classified as street or decent? Moreover, if "street" connotes some type of dysfunction, then even that label is problematic when applied to non-nuclear families. Mrs. Morris was acting in her children's best interest when she made her husband leave. For her children as well as for her own financial and emotional reasons, she stood by him through years of counseling and periods of sobriety, which were overshadowed by episodes of violence. Her new "female-headed household" status seems quite unlike the dysfunctional connotations of "street." Neisha's out-of-wedlock childbearing may fit more squarely in that category, but even Neisha's situation is affected by family and neighborhood pressures outside her own control. The most important conclusion to draw from these stories is in fact the least satisfying one, because it complicates the neat bipolarity of street and decent, and introduces the multiple realities that families and youth experience that influence their own choices and decisions.

Each of these three youth had some roadblocks along the way, but nevertheless, Tyson will soon graduate from college, Charisse is determined to be successful in business, and Neisha still has aspirations to be a dance instructor and will have much help in raising little Tim. Despite their rebellious forays, their street and decent balancing acts, and the fragility of the collective resources on which they depend, Neisha, Tyson, and Charisse may still be poised to duplicate their parents' middle-class status. While this is true for a good portion of young people growing up in Groveland, there are three important qualifications to such a conclusion.

First, the need to reconcile street and decent lifestyles does not end with adolescence. Adults must also maneuver the neighborhood context, as well as their peer and family relationships. While people may choose their friends, they cannot choose their relatives. Imagine the reunion of Neisha's, Tyson's or Charisse's extended family. The possible stories and gossip—from what cousin is on parole, to which nephew graduated from college, to whose teenage daughter is pregnant, to where a sister landed a new job—run the gamut of street and decent activities. And since for many Grovelandites the extended family is the unit that makes middle-class status possible, it would be unwise for anyone to distance him- or herself from the family, even if remaining close means interacting with some unsavory characters. In all likelihood, Neisha will be able to do well only with the support of her family and the generosity of their resources. So as youth age, there are certain family imperatives, and similar friendship demands, for staying versed in both street and decent ways of life.[9]

Tyson is most explicitly determined not to lose his street edge as he grows older. Even though he is planning for law school, he stays in touch with his neighborhood friends who are still dabbling in drug dealing and maintaining their membership in the Black Mobsters. He is committed to making his future children street-smart as well. "Even if I do become a big-time lawyer, judge, or whatever, e'rybody ain't gon' be able to do that," Tyson reasoned. "So I can always know somebody in the ghetto. I'ma send my kids right over [to their] uncle such-and-such and cousin such-and-such house to let [them] know how it feel if [they] didn't have this." Negotiating street and decent lifestyles is a continuous process for black middle-class individuals embedded in especially heterogeneous neighborhoods, families, and friendship groups.

A second qualification is that a too optimistic reading of these stories disregards the fact that these three young people are the ones who are persevering. This is especially relevant for Tyson, for whom, as a young black male, mere survival has been an accomplishment. The stories of his friends who have "faded or disappeared" would be less sanguine. Neisha, Tyson, and Charisse in many ways represent those who have been or are still being successful in maneuvering their family, peer, school, and neighborhood environments. These young people are still working toward their parents' desires for them of self-sufficiency and happiness. Those who did not succeed now exist only as stories of lost friends and relatives: "Ms. Strong's daughter is on drugs," or "My cousin Ronnie got killed last year." Such reports are indicators of the uniquely perilous road that black middle-class families traverse in raising children.

And finally, the role of other factors in these young people's lives, such as personal agency and family situations, should not be underestimated. Neisha scored high enough on standardized tests to attend a magnet high school, but instead wanted to be closer to her friends, and so attended a less rigorous school. Tyson could have been his mother's angel by staying out of gangs and joining the swim team, but he chose otherwise. Charisse could still choose not to go on to college as her parents have planned for her, in favor of having a baby because she loves children. Without minimizing the importance of individual agency, the neighborhood context exists above and beyond individual and family circumstances. Choices are made within the limits of what options are presented to these young people, and many delinquent options can be realized in Groveland with great ease.

In sum, then, categorizing families as either street families or decent families misses many crucial nuances. The Morris, Reed, and Baker families are all "decent." Each employs specific strategies to guard against street influences. But is Charisse's family more decent than Neisha's because Neisha's father drinks too much, or because Charisse's family regularly attends church? Is Tyson's family more decent than either Neisha's or Charisse's because his mother holds an advanced degree and a professional job? Is Neisha's family the most decent because they have the best-kept yard, prettiest flowers, and cleanest house? Instead of demonstrating mutually exclusive categories, their lives illustrate how street and decent orientations are tangled together—in the neighborhood context, in the same family, and even within the same person. Tyson is, after all, a gangbanger with a college degree (almost). The simultaneous privileges and continuing constraints faced by the black middle class make the intermediate position of balancing street and decent a most common strategy for negotiating a variety of family situations and local and community-wide settings. All of these neighborhood-level processes operate within a mass-media and consumer-culture environment that intensifies the excitement of rebellious delinquency for youth, which is the subject of the next two chapters.

6

In a Ghetto Trance

Revisiting the classic texts on black life is always a reminder of how little some things have changed. St. Clair Drake's and Horace Cayton's ([1945] 1993, 589) description of the people they called the "wild children" of the 1930s and 1940s has its counterpart in scholarly and popular discussions of today's incorrigible youth. Drake and Cayton capture the interconnectedness of style and actual delinquency, which is relevant to the focus on mass culture in this chapter. They write about youth of their era:

> Parents were without money to give children for the shows, the dances, and the "zoot suits" which lower-class adolescent status required. There were few odd jobs. Purse-snatching became general in lower-class areas and even in the main thoroughfares. . . . Studies of delinquents show that their behavior is partly "rational" (e.g., desire to get money for a show) and partly the search for a thrill or excitement.
>
> Bronzeville's wild children were not so numerous as the frightened upper and middle class thought, but there were enough of them roaming the streets during the Depression, stealing, fighting, and molesting pedestrians, to cause everyone—including lower-class parents—to talk about the "youth problem." Much more prevalent were the thousands of lower-class young men who were never arrested as delinquents but who skirted the borderline of crime. These were the "cats" who, clad in "zoot suits," stood around and "jived" the women.

In the World War II era in Chicago, young people did not wear their hats cocked to the side to represent their gang affiliation, or blast the latest rap song from their car stereos. But they did wear zoot suits and call each other "cat," which incited the same fear among their elders as contemporary gangbangers and gangsta rappers do in the

1990s. Simply donning the threads of a zootsuiter in the 1930s and 1940s was enough to get a young man labeled delinquent, even if his only objective was to look good to his peers. Because styles continue to be policed, and continue to have significance to fellow style-wearers, a particular type of jacket or certain color shoelaces in the present day can carry the same risk as the zoot suits of a foregone era.[1]

Drake and Cayton also point to another fact that remains true today. While some youth snatch purses or sell drugs for both economic and amusement purposes, more young people "skirt the borderline." Despite the collective hysteria, most kids are law-abiding. The problem is that parents, shopping-mall security, police officers, grocery-store clerks, and even other youth have a hard time distinguishing the delinquents from the wannabes because they share many of the same styles. In their dress, in their language, in their hairstyles, and in their walk, the many lawful youth take on the stylistic affectations of true "wild children" even though they infrequently, if ever, cross the line in their behaviors.

Finally, there is one point that Drake and Cayton overlook. Black working-class and middle-class youth are not exempt from the thrill and excitement of either stylistic deviance or actual criminal behavior. For that matter, neither are young rich and middle-class whites. There is little glamor in being simply middle class. In riches there is showy extravagance, and poverty demands a noble struggle. To be middle class—more precisely, lower middle class—is to be blah. Such youth of all races may be even more captivated by popular-culture styles that release them from the bonds of middle-class civility and mediocrity, and allow them, if only through their new outfits, to conspicuously transgress.[2] Styles, however, have repercussions.

Two things separate voyeuristic middle-class white youth—such as those who took on the cool of jazz, the swinging hips of rock and roll, and now the "fuck the world" attitude of gangsta rap—from their African American peers like those in Groveland. First, white youth are given the benefit of the doubt by white authority structures. Their stylistic displays are less harshly sanctioned relative to the surveillance of black youth who follow the same fashions. Two youth wearing the same baggy pants and hooded sweatshirt (or the same blue suit, for that matter)—one black, the other white—are not read the same by the department-store salesperson who keenly keeps her eye on the black shopper, while the white teenager could be stealing a watch. The race of the wearer affects the degree to which certain styles are criminalized.[3] Second, the neighborhoods and communities in which black youth live and interact consist of some peers who take their styles more seriously. Amid economic pressures, some youth pierce their ears on the right or left, tattoo their bodies with specific anthems, or invent an elaborate handshake in order to organize their criminal enterprises. For them, their outfits, language, and walk signify more than simply staying in style, and they may take offense at someone who wears the styles too lightly. The opportunities to merge styles with actual delinquent behaviors are more plentiful in a place like Chicago's South Side, and the chances that a stylistic faux pas will have negative consequences are higher in the neighborhoods where black middle-class youth live.

THE GHETTO TRANCE

In the vestibule of St. Mary's Catholic School are two pieces of student art. One display is a "Spotlight on Poetry," and on another wall hangs a "drug-free mural" assembled by the school's sixth-grade class. On the mural are pictures of a marijuana leaf, a pack of cigarettes, and a bottle of alcohol. All three pictures have a large X drawn through them, and in the center of the mural is the word NO. Each student in the sixth-grade class signed the display to show support for the message: "Shenika Brown—Class of '96 in the House." "Corbin Humphrey aka Hi C." As in the closing pages of a yearbook, various students had their unique tags appended to their names, some more innovative than others. One student duo did not give their real names at all. They instead signed: "Dr. Dre and Snoop Doggy Dogg." In 1993, just before this mural was drawn, producer/rapper Dr. Dre and rapper Snoop Doggy Dogg had a chart-topping song, "Gin and Juice." The lyrics—"Rollin' down the street smokin' indo, sippin' on gin and juice" ("indo" is a potent strain of marijuana)—undermine, to say the least, the drug-free theme of the mural. It was a case of a practical joke that had escaped the inspection of the sixth-grade teachers. Or perhaps the adults in charge did not know who Dr. Dre and Snoop Doggy Dogg were, and treated this moniker as they did "Hi C" and the many other nicknames. However the signatures made it onto the public mural, the irony illustrates the infusion of popular "ghetto" or "gangsta" images into the routine lives of young people in Groveland.

Ghetto does not carry the same meaning when used by different groups. Social scientists commonly use the word to refer to all-black and predominantly poor neighborhoods. I have used it in this book to refer to the segregated Black Belts in which a diversity of African Americans live. But when funkster Rick James sang "Ghetto Life" in the early 1980s, he was only partly referring to his upbringing in an actual ghetto. More generally he was alluding to a mentality—one that might have its roots in the social conditions of the ghetto, but transcends that space. Similarly, when Ice Cube raps about certain pop stars as having their "ghetto-passes revoked," he is referring not only to their having moved out of the physical ghetto, but also to their having changed their walk, talk, and style in order to cross over into the mainstream. *Ghetto* (as a noun or an adjective) does not always carry with it a negative stigma. Belief to the contrary, Too $hort raps, "There's money in the ghetto." A Houston rap group self-identifies as the "Geto Boys." And in the ghetto, raps the group Westside Connection, "gangstas make the world go 'round." But even before rap music, and before Rick James, soulster Donnie Hathaway repeatedly draped a simple chorus of "The Ghetto" over a silky rhythm and bass line that suggested none of the pathologies often attributed to the ghetto by outside observers. *Ghetto*—like *soul, cool,* and *bad* before it—is a mood (never all-encompassing) that transcends the racism and poverty that motivate it. That mood is partly expressed through language, and dress, and bodily movements, and accessories; that is, through style.[4]

In the 1930s and 1940s it was the zootsuiters. In the 1950s, the jitterbugs and the hipsters held stylistic sway among urban African American youth. The 1960s and 1970s were owned by blaxploitation pimps, hustlers, and badasses. The late 1980s and 1990s have been the domain of gangsta rappers.[5] Groveland youth are participants in ghetto styles. Every generation of black youth has been influenced by some form (and usually many forms) of ghetto-based cultural production that was one part social commentary and resistance, one part deviance, and two parts fun.

EXPERIENCE AND AESTHETICS

Journalistic descriptions of the graphic sex and violence in gangsta rap music are plentiful. Social scientists and cultural critics also clamor to define and deconstruct the causes and effects of this musical genre. It is impossible to deny the sordidness of this strain of rap music when it includes lyrics like the following, by the late gangsta rapper Eazy-

E: "Now back on the streets and my records are clean/ I creeped on my bitch with my Uzi machine/ Went to the house and kicked down the do'/ Unloaded like hell, cold smoked the ho'." How are we to interpret such lyrics? Are they truthful portrayals of "the other America," or are they fantastic concoctions that are entertaining and profitable?

One camp argues that rap music, including gangsta rap, tells the story of the black underclass (Dyson 1994; Lott 1992). Gangsta raps, ghetto movies, underground magazines, and self-produced music videos are rooted in the material conditions of black urban poverty. They chronicle what happens in poor neighborhoods, what residents experience as victims of racism, and the frequently illegitimate paths they must pursue to survive in such a world. The styles that correspond to this version of ghetto life are ever-changing due to the ephemeral nature of popular consumer materials. Yet the overall commitment to a ghetto demeanor outlives a certain brand of sneakers. While this public biography is not necessarily transformative, some argue that it does offer a sobering and unsanitized depiction of what social scientists attempt to represent in their scholarly research on the same conditions. It tells a story of a world that consists of "crime, guns, drug-selling and drug-using, sexual exploitation, irresponsible parenthood, Black-on-Black homicide, women as inferiors and objects, gang-life, 40-ounce drinking as routine, and extreme materialism" (Kitwana 1994, 50–51). These stories are also told by sociologists, anthropologists, and historians, but devoid of the emotion. To be sure, this is but a small sliver of life in any ghetto, and gangsta rappers' depiction of it is far from objective.

Another interpretation of the genre privileges aesthetics over materialism.[6] The tales of gangsta rappers are not in any sense objective renditions of their lives. Gangsta rappers are as much captivated by the characters of Clint Eastwood, Steven Segall, and the macabre creations of Freddy Krueger and other big-screen serial killers as they are interested in telling true stories about their own local experiences. Gangsta rappers do not create their violent and sexist stories in a vacuum, but are perhaps expertly ensconced in a tradition and history of American popular-culture violence (Nightingale 1993). Hip-hop culture and rap music, including gangsta rap (goes this line of reasoning), are primarily for leisure enjoyment. The music is for dancing, or for relaxing, or for attracting someone's attention driving down the street. The words are to establish who can integrate the most disparate cultural references into a fantastic story, while never losing the beat.

Rap music falls in the tradition of African American rhythmic creations, transformed by the unique technology available to the generation that produces it. And rap lyrics are creative hyperbole in the spirit of an oral tradition received from Africa, sustained through slavery, transplanted to the urban north, and finally mass-produced in the postindustrial era for all to hear (Toop 1984; Rose 1994). This syncretic aesthetic is apparent in the fashion sphere, where hip-hop enthusiasts share clothing items with preppy northeasterners, blue-collar construction workers, and 1970s pimps all at once (see Kakutani 1997). Ghetto styles appropriate myriad cultural messages and signs that cross racial, class, gender, and even historical boundaries.

Undoubtedly, gangsta rap music and the other components of hip-hop culture are both materialist commentaries on being black in the United States (and, frequently, on being black and poor) *and* contemporary renditions of black musical and oral traditions that integrate various cultural materials and in which the beat and the lyrical battle are central. Using both frameworks, Eazy-E's lyrics, quoted above, can be interpreted in the following way: He did not in actuality kick down his ex-girlfriend's door and discharge rounds of bullets from his semiautomatic weapon, ultimately killing her. He would probably be in jail if he had. At the same time, he probably had seen an Uzi in action, or heard women referred to as bitches, or might even have victimized women himself. Eazy-E's overall accomplishment, like that of many Hollywood writers and directors, was to imagine such a gruesome story line, amass detailed words and references to narrate it, and place them atop a beat that made his fans bob their heads.

Gangsta and ghetto styles can be separated, therefore, into material themes of "economic fragility . . . ethnic interaction . . . and post 1960s disillusionment" (Rose 1989, 37) on the one hand, and on the other, the creative genius of setting those stories to a funky beat with layers of borrowed and original melodies. Just as the styles themselves have both a material and an aesthetic genesis, Groveland youth follow ghetto styles both because they can identify with the actual content and themes, and because the act of consumption and translation is highly pleasurable. At the material level, the black middle class remains a vulnerable group clustered in lower-middle-class occupations and, because of its recency, lacking any substantial wealth. And because black middle-class youth live near areas of concentrated poverty and among higher proportions of poor people than the white middle class, they do have some experiences with the gritty urban reality described by gangsta rappers, depicted in black urban cinema, and re- ported in newspapers and magazines. They also experience some of the economic pressure, and recognize the stigma, of being African American. The fact that some Groveland youth described Groveland as a ghetto is an illustration of the affinity they feel with the material themes of gangsta styles.

To focus on the structural positioning of Groveland youth, how- ever, is to ignore the pleasure they receive from participating in— and, indeed, contributing to—a certain popular-culture niche. In pur- suit of leisure, Groveland youth play gangsta verbal games, buy the emblems of ghetto fashion, and swagger like the main characters in a black shoot-'em-up movie because it makes passing the time enjoy- able; it works in courtship rituals; and it feels good to look good, sound good, and smell good. Moreover, Groveland's youth are more than simply mindless repositories into which mass-culture producers pour the ingredients to make millions of consuming gangstas. The images they watch in videos and movies are as much a reflection of themselves as they are a stylistic road map for them to follow. In their basements and at parties, and hanging out on the street, at the lakefront, or in the popular parking lot, Groveland youth, like other black urban youth across the country, create the new words, or new ways to wear a simple scarf, that later make their way to Hollywood or New York. Black kids use consumer materials in ways their corporate creators did not intend, and conventional words are redefined (as well as respelled) with ingenuity. As quickly as black youth incorporate a popular ghetto trend, they are reinventing another.

The appropriation and unique rendering of gangsta styles by Groveland youth for sheer entertainment would not be problematic if the stylistic realm existed separately from and had no repercussions in the material realm. Instead, symbols feed back into the material world. The stylistic forays of black middle-class youth exist in an eco- logical milieu where others are not just dressing up. Sometimes, when you dress like a gangsta, talk like a gangsta, and rap like a gangsta, soon enough you *are* a gangsta. The style itself may constitute devi- ance and thus be subject to official sanctions. Rules in malls and high school dress codes exemplify the criminalization of certain styles. Also, there can be tragic consequences when such styles are misread by gangstas for whom the identity is more than a symbolic act.

Groveland youth are caught in a ghetto trance to varying degrees. There is, of course, a distinction between ghetto styles and actual de- linquent behavior. As Drake and Cayton pointed out, many youth had the zoot-suited look of criminals but were really guilty of nothing more than admiring women. Analytically, this distinction between style and crime makes sense, but in practice, where the styles themselves might be read as delinquent, the categories are less starkly distinguishable. At one end are young people who embody the full package of gangsta styles *and* behaviors, while at the opposite extreme are those who scoff at the gangsta styles altogether. I offer three analytic types along this continuum. While this classification suffers from the same narrowness as the street and decent labels, I emphasize the fact that midrange behaviors are the most common, and even the extreme types are not pristine categories.

Some Groveland youth now exist only in the stories of their friends and relatives because they were *consumed* by the gangsta image, most often through violence. Those who were once consumed but were able to get out of the fast life before they too were just a memory are now grateful to be able to reminisce. Style and behavior are inseparable for this group. The second category, which constitutes the majority of Groveland youth, are *thrilled* by ghetto language, styles, and stories. They not only admire the popular styles disseminated through videos, movies, and magazines, but they pay close attention to the performances of the gang members and drug dealers within Groveland itself, and in Chicago's larger black community. They have friends who are gang members from whom they learn the handshakes, nicknames, and signals, but they do not join themselves. They excitedly recount the local tales of urban danger, but manage to avoid being too close when they actually occur. These young Grovelandites occasionally dance over the line that separates image from personification, style from behavior—but most often they recognize that their commitment is primarily symbolic. Finally, there are youth who are *marginal* to the subcultural practices that comprise the ghetto style, but even this group boasts of having "ghetto friends."

CONSUMED

If the connotations of the slang title "OG," which stands for "Original Gangsta," were not so gendered, Lauren Grant would definitely qualify. Mrs. Grant, in her early forties, is an ex–drug dealer and addict. Even though Mrs. Grant is proud to no longer be a part of the problem, her past is never too far behind her. Because she continues to live in the Groveland home where she grew up, her past is also never far away. She vividly recalls the lures of the 1960s, the decade of her adolescence. Her story foreshadows the processes through which the next generation of Groveland youth would also travel, but with different cultural icons and symbols.

Lauren Grant moved to Groveland in 1967 when she was sixteen years old. Although her parents were working class—her father "worked for the railroad" and her mother was "the homemaker type"—many members of her extended family were teachers.

> You know, I have a real bourgeois-type family background. And, you know, I didn't like those people. Maybe I could think back and maybe it was envy or something. Or maybe not envy, just rebellious, you know. Thinking, "Who do they think they are?" And doing everything I could to be the opposite of that.

The mix of her bourgeois family background and the ghetto styles she would take on made Mrs. Grant particularly bicultural.

> I had this personality where I could fit in anywhere I went. You know, anywhere. If I was amongst a room full of teachers, I could fit there. I could fit in church people 'cause I went to church the majority of my life. I played for a choir. I directed a choir. I could fit there. I could fit in the streets with the drug dealers. I could fit with the drug users. I could fit with the car thiefs. It was just so many places I could just walk in and, like a chameleon, turn colors, you know.

The stylistic tools available for Mrs. Grant to use in the 1960s and especially the 1970s came from the blaxploitation films of that era (see Bogle 1989; Van Deburg 1997). While these films were frequently commentaries *against* crime and vice, their flashy and attractive depictions of pimps and hustlers meant that they were remembered as celebrating the fast life. Mrs. Grant recalled her reaction to the gangsta rappers of her day.

> I grew up with *Superfly*. And I was like, "I could do that." I never watched the end of that picture. They didn't end that picture right. You know, and I can get real deep. Yeah they knew what they were doing putting these movies out. And they knew the whole popularity was either gonna go drug dealer or pimp/whore. And you know, that's basically what happened. . . . And then the little pleasure-seeker that I was, I would do anything and I would overdo anything that looked good, tasted good, felt

good to me. And like I said, that picture had a profound effect on my life. So, when I came up, I was gettin' ready to get this money. And I set out in life to get this money.

Mrs. Grant believed that with the right stylistic props, she could *be Superfly*. She was consumed by the image, and it started her on a downhill road.

Mrs. Grant began selling pills in high school to get new shoes. It was not that her parents did not or could not buy her shoes. Mrs. Grant was an only child and, from her own description, was quite spoiled. Still, her parents could not afford all of the things she would later accumulate from selling drugs. Her small-time drug pushing in high school led to ever deeper involvements in the drug business. "In the process of going up the ladder, I had different [drug] houses in different areas. It was like a corporation," she reported. Mrs. Grant acquired more expensive trinkets and accessories as her business grew. Her purchases rarely satiated her "pleasure-seeking" personality and did not do much to improve her general well-being (one more car was not a necessity at that point), but they did give her a feeling of superiority in the expressive realm. Driving down the street in her "triple white Cadillac" or "Rolls Royce" entitled her to the envious stares of those less resourceful. "They were looking," she remembered. "I was a show-off."

Even Mrs. Grant's retelling of her years of vice has components of the verbal posturing that permeated the lyrical dialogue of the blaxploitation films of her era. Such boastful loquacity is equally a part of rap music and hip-hop culture in the 1990s. Mrs. Grant did not have just a nice car, but a *triple white Cadillac*, drawing out the layers of description. "I had everything material that a person could want," she remembered. By her own recounting, she was flashy. "I'm in a condo up North and, you know, the glitter," she said, summing up that time of her life with a telling word, *glitter*. It felt good (though not all the time), looked good, and tasted good.

In addition to having expressive functions, Mrs. Grant's story is also rooted in her material experiences. She at some point decided to stop mimicking the costumes and mannerisms of the movie characters in *Superfly*, and instead started reproducing the behaviors of the actual drug dealers in her own environment. After watching their operations, Mrs. Grant recalled feeling especially qualified for crime.

I used to hang out with a lot of [the gang leaders and drug dealers]. I wasn't afraid of 'em. Actually, I was so arrogant, the main

gang leader, I could remember thinking that I was more notorious than him. You know, "Who does he think he is?" You know,
"He doesn't know me."

Lauren Grant was tantalized by the hustlers on the big screen and
taught by the ones in her own neighborhood. The same is true of
contemporary youth, whose mass-media superstars are incarnated in
the drug dealer down the street.

But not surprisingly, Mrs. Grant's felonious largesse was short-
lived. Soon she started using the drugs she meant to be selling, and
then "the fall came." "I didn't know a monkey can't sell bananas," she
quipped. Having started off participating in the pleasures of the 1960s
and 1970s versions of ghetto styles, Mrs. Grant became consumed
both by that cultural make-believe and by the real hustlers with whom
she competed. As she looked back on it, her rationale for the decisions
she made seemed less clear to her. A bit confused by her own
life, she reflected:

> My background didn't dictate the life I started living. . . . I mean
> I grew up in a church. My family's educated. I was well ex-
> posed. I traveled as a child. I was well exposed. I played classical
> music. I played at the Opera House. Monetary gain, you know,
> during that '60s era and getting involved in this drugs and
> wantin' this money. And you end up, and you don't know how
> you got there.

Mrs. Grant, a religious woman now, thanks God that she is able to
look back at bad times and forward to better ones. Yet she sees much
of her own story being repeated today in her daughter's life. A new
generation of neighborhood criminals has attracted Mrs. Grant's
daughter, just as she was drawn into drug dealing when she was
young. Her daughter eventually became "a part of that element," wor-
shiping fast money. Mrs. Grant knows all too well the hazards of the
crime business. "My daughter has obituaries like this," she lamented,
holding her hands an inch apart to indicate the stack of paper memories of a new consumed generation. In the 1990s, the names are different. *Superfly* has been replaced by *Menace II Society*.[7] Cadillacs have
survived in the South and Midwest, joined by vintage luxury cars
on the West Coast, and sport utility vehicles on the East. And the
neighborhood drug dealers have merged into organizations of various
levels of criminal and civic sophistication. What remains is the sheer
pleasure in participating in ghetto styles, and the often irrevocable
consequences if the style becomes a way of life.

Twenty-two-year-old Tyson Reed had at one time been consumed by the gangsta life. When he was a sophomore in high school, he stabbed his mother's boyfriend with a kitchen knife. Tyson spent one week in jail on charges of attempted murder, but when the boyfriend was released from the hospital he dropped the charges. In Tyson's senior year in high school he faced weapons charges after the police raided his bedroom in his mother's house and found a small cache of guns there. He escaped conviction again, but this time his mother kicked him out. (Tyson's football and wrestling coaches and the vice principal at his school eventually persuaded his mother to take him back in.) Tyson was a member of the Black Mobsters gang in Groveland, and sold drugs within their organization, but again, he was never caught.

Tyson's involvements speak to much more than the influence of popular-culture gangstas on his development (see chapter 5). Deep resentment over his father's departure clearly fueled his anger toward his mother's boyfriend, and rap music did not dictate that Tyson should store guns in his house. However, Tyson's own rendition of this era in his life demonstrates the importance of media gangstas—and their local embodiment in the neighborhood gang leaders—to his own stylistic and behavioral development. For example, in the case of drugs, which are a conspicuous component of the gangsta lifestyle, Tyson recognized the connection between behavior and the popular-culture images most celebrated among his friends.

> Some people just followin' a fad. Like everybody and they mama back in the '70s, e'rybody used to smoke weed. Nowadays, every video you see, "Hay, rollin' hay" [the lyrics to a rap song about marijuana]. Smokin' weed. Tupac, smokin' weed. Snoop Doggy Dogg talk about gettin' high and gettin' drunk all day long. That's all they talk about. So that's why I think some people do it. 'Cause it's the in thing.

Even with this insight, however, Tyson was not able to see his own complicity in the enactment of popular-culture images. He disparaged people who superficially mimic the styles of media gangsters. "Now that you in college or now that you moved to the suburbs, now you wanna be Tupac," he said about the people who can dress in ghetto styles only because they live at a safe distance from where real gangstas live. "But back in the days, you was a straight ho," he continued. "You was a punk. But now you wanna be hard." Tyson believed that his own biography was more authentic. He was not just dressing up, but living the life that Tupac created in his videos and movies.

> At least I know, man, I know what'll happen if I sell drugs. At least I done had the money before. I know how it feel, you know, so even if I wanna do the experience again I know what'll happen, or what'll not happen.

Tyson began to change when he realized the futility of crime, especially since he was in many other respects positioned for legitimate upward mobility. He reasoned:

> I got $6,000, but what I'ma do? I can't go buy no car. I can't go buy no house. All I can do is buy all the Nikes and Guess? [brand name] I need, you know. And after a while, it ain't no purpose to that.

Like Lauren Grant's, Tyson's own personal biography did not dictate his involvement in the Black Mobsters or in the neighborhood drug trade. His mother was an educator, and through magnet schools tried to ensure a solid education for her son. Yet Tyson's formal education existed alongside his education among the neighborhood gang members, and within a cultural era that mass-produced ghetto-style entertainment. As a result, Tyson explicitly considered himself bilingual. Echoing the words of Lauren Grant, Tyson believed he had the ability to interact in a variety of social settings.

> Believe it or not, when I'm around my friends from the ghetto and that's hoodlums and all that, I'on sit down and talk about, "Yeah did you know that Albert Einstein was born on . . . ?" What the fuck they wanna hear that for? So, when you around people you gotta know whatever they into and you into. That's what you talk about. If you into killin' mufuckas, you'on talk about, "Man, I got a' A in class today." You talk about, "Man, you see that new Uzi they got?" You know what I'm sayin'? Or into sellin' drugs, you say, "Man, you see the D.A. trippin'?" Or if you big in school, "Man, I'm trying to get in Law School and stuff." So, you just gotta watch what you say, and where you are, and who you with.

Tyson's consumption by ghetto styles was both grounded in his material and family circumstances, and pursued for aesthetic enjoyment. Concretely, Tyson's mother had a particularly hard time raising a son without a father figure in the household. Tyson actively searched for male role models and companions. He found them in the nearby Black Mobsters. But while the materialist argument works for illuminating the neighborhood and family forces that allowed Tyson to easily translate gangsta styles into actual drug dealing and gun toting, it falls short when taking Tyson's middle-class background into account. Youth (and adults) do not rob or steal simply because their legitimate options for making money are few, and the costs of getting caught do not outweigh their need. Such economic theories of crime have limited explanatory value, and overlook the fact that crime is "seductive" (Katz 1988). Snatching purses, shoplifting, passing bad checks, using unfairly received stock tips, and even murder can all be transcendently exhilarating for the perpetrator. Even if the act itself is rather mundane, or even distasteful, the criminal booty can be used to buy things that carry gratifying symbolic weight in American materialist culture. And inasmuch as ghetto styles may themselves be delinquent, such practices may provide similar hedonistic rewards to adherents. In sum, deviance—whether real or stylistic—titillates.[8]

After all, Tyson did not retell his drug-dealing history with sullen regret. Instead, he all but boasted about his recurring ability to "get over," to be above the law. His description of stabbing his mother's boyfriend was vivid. He re-created the scene as if he were momentarily transported back to that moment, once again feeling the rush of adrenaline.

> And as I moved like this my hand rubbed against [he goes into a drawer and pulls out a large knife], rubbed against a knife. It was about this big. It was just a big one, you know, a big butcher knife. My hand hit it. And I grabbed it. I cupped it. And I walked toward him and I said, "Man, get yo' big goofy-ass self out." And I walked up to him. He walked towards me like, "Tyson, what's goin' on?" I was, "This what's goin' on."

Tyson gestured out the stabbing motion, but remembered that he had not known that he actually stabbed his adversary until he saw the blood. When he realized he had actually drawn blood, Tyson distinctly remembered *not* being afraid, but rather bolder. "I'm finna ["fixing to"] shoot this nigga," he remembers thinking after the initial attack. "For some reason, I wasn't scared. I just jumped hard or whatever." During the actual event, Tyson was probably filled with more emotions than he could relay. But over years of recounting the stabbing, it was transformed into something like a scene from a thriller movie.

Perhaps more stomachable than the excitement of violence illustrated by Tyson's story are the thrilling rewards of selling drugs. Unlike some dealers, Tyson did not use his profits to buy food or necessary clothing items, or to contribute to the family's finances. Tyson spent his money at the mall, buying the latest ghetto-style gym shoes and jeans by the bundle. He made flashy purchases "just to talk to some broads. Just to let my homey [friend] talk to some broads." Like Lauren Grant, Tyson bought things because he knew people were looking. The purchases looked good to him and, he suspected, to the girls who were watching. Adolescent flirting and posturing are important for explaining the influence that ghetto styles have on young people. While there may be true materially based motivations for some young men to be actual gangstas, most of the rewards from selling drugs are expressive—a new car, a shiny watch, or the twentieth pair of sneakers. These adornments help men jockey for the attentions of young women. The same is true of girls' in-style accessories (also see chapter 7).

Even as Tyson moves away from actual deviance, he still enjoys the expressive components of the gangsta aesthetic. He and a group of his friends own a family of "pet" pit bull terriers. The dogs are named after legendary crime bosses—Bugsy, Luciano, and Tyson's dog, Meyer Lansky, named after the "brains" behind mob operations. Tyson's and his friends' interest in ethnic mobsters demonstrates the hybrid nature of gangsta styles and maintains their connection to their gangsta pasts, however figuratively. Tyson uses his college education to learn about the history of organized crime, the debates around the legalization of drugs and drug policy, and the genesis of black gangs. As he crosses back into mere stylistic participation in ghetto life and away from actual crime, Tyson sees his criminal background and knowledge being used for new purposes.

> I was kinda interested in law 'cause I used to be a criminal. And when I first started reading about laws and stuff, it was helping me be a better criminal. But once I stopped doing it, I started getting interested in it.

Tyson's story elucidates the material and aesthetic components that facilitate the translation of popular styles into personal biographies. But both the importance of popular styles and the fun of experimenting with criminal behavior fade over time. And even when they were most consumed, neither Lauren Grant nor Tyson Reed was a unidimensional "gangsta." During the interview, Tyson was not brandishing a weapon, or smoking a joint, or standing as so many stereotypes depict young black men standing—with their hands on their crotches. Instead, he stood in the kitchen, cleaning the oven for his mother and washing down the grease-splattered walls. He wore his school's College Freshman Week T-shirt, sweatpants, and a pair of ancient Nike basketball shoes. And his aspirations were like those of many upwardly mobile young people: "I'ma live in a suburb of a city. I'ma have a phat, phat-ass crib." Translation: Tyson plans to join the exodus to suburbia and buy a large and luxurious house there.

Tyson is not unlike many white middle-class youth who are also in a ghetto trance. There is ample overlap in the styles of black and white youth. The difference is that they live in very different environments. Tyson Reed and Lauren Grant both had ample opportunity to embody the stylistic trends that they followed.

THRILLED

Despite the general concern and even hysteria about the Tysons and Lauren Grants in urban neighborhoods (at least their past incarnations), most Groveland youth are not so invested in ghetto styles that they become real criminals. As Drake and Cayton pointed out in the 1930s, "Much more prevalent were the thousands of lower-class young men who were never arrested as delinquents but who skirted the borderline of crime. These were the 'cats' who, clad in 'zoot suits,' stood around and 'jived' the women." This group of youth are *thrilled* by the rebellious possibilities of gangsta styles.

Some young people who start off thrilled may end up consumed. As Tyson remarked, "People now, they just freelancing, and that'll get you dead or in the penitentiary." Freelancers, as Tyson referred to them, run the real risk of being harassed by police who actually have code books warning against particular color combinations, or certain hats. Freelancers are also in danger that their conspicuous styles will send an unintended signal to someone whose commitment runs deeper than his or her outfit. These gambles notwithstanding, most of the young people in this category consciously, and sometimes quite explicitly, manage their image and actions so as to avoid real trouble. For thrilled youth, their enactment of popular gangsta culture is almost entirely for the aesthetic capital gained by displaying the right clothes, language, and demeanor. They usually know when playtime is over. One Groveland parent spoke about how, in an instant, youth's allegiances can quickly revert to middle-class banality.

> They say they're involved [in gangs]. You know, kids need to feel that they belong just to exist in the world. How much stock I put into it is little to none. But they'll claim they represent [a certain gang]. And if push came to shove and they were told they had to get out there and do something, you know, [they'd say,] "No, I don't represent anything. I represent school."

Many of the members of the youth group at St. Mary's Catholic Church fall into this thrilled category.

The youth group can attract more than twenty-five members on a good day, but for most meetings, attendance settles at about ten regulars. A still more "core" committee of about six or seven makes up the overlap between the youth group and the youth choir. The majority of the St. Mary's youth-group members attended St. Mary's Elementary School and have gone on to Catholic high schools, some of which are the most prestigious high schools in Chicago. Most of them attend Sunday Mass regularly, if not every Sunday, and the core group is especially active in various church committees and activities. Those who are most active have parents who are also faithful workers and leaders in the church. They all come from lower-middle-class or middle-class homes. Their parents are teachers, computer programmers, entrepreneurs, and administrative assistants, and a few parents work in blue-collar jobs. Even though the group's demographics suggest that they are slightly more middle class than the neighborhood as a whole, one teenager described herself as being a member of the "upper poor" class, a characterization that was echoed by her peers.

Tuesday is youth choir rehearsal. But since the youth choir is scheduled to sing at Mass only every fifth Sunday—i.e., every three months—there is no pressing need to rehearse each week. As a result, many Tuesdays turn into informal rap sessions at the church rectory, providing a stage where the members of the St. Mary's youth group practice their ghetto styles, recount authentic urban ghetto tales, and display their ghetto outfits. It is a safe place because everyone is, in essence, freelancing. They are sure that no one will mistake them for real gangstas and turn their play into a perilous reality.[9]

Because they are teenagers, many of the conversations concern dating and relationships. Stories about school, classes, grades, and teachers are also prominent. Because they are members of St. Mary's, church gossip constitutes another prevalent topic of discussion. A theme that runs throughout their conversations is the excitement that occasional rabbling episodes—fights or shootings, rumors of somebody being pregnant, someone being arrested for drugs—thrust into an otherwise mundane and even boring life. Sarita Arthur whined about the boredom of her magnet high school: "Like the worst thing you ever hear at my school is like somebody got stabbed with a ruler or somethin' like that. You don't never hear of no fights or nothin' like that." Rashaad Lincoln was equally dispassionate about his top-ranked Catholic school: "My school is so boring. Don't nothin' never happen there. People get sent to the office for things like yellin', like verbal stuff. I mean, it gets so boring." Popular gangsta styles offer a way to compensate for this middle-class routine.

Highlighting the spectacular nature of their experimentation with gangsta styles (Hebdige 1979), Sarita Arthur and Rashaad Lincoln spent one Tuesday evening reminiscing on the dramatic skits they had created for youth-group functions over the years. The first skit they described involved two main characters fictionally named Ta-Dow and Gina. Ta-Dow, a curious proper name, was also (and by no coincidence) the name of the leading man in an extended video by rapper Snoop Doggy Dogg. The story line of the youth group's play was as follows: Gina, played by youth-group member Karen Beaumont, told Ta-Dow, played by Rashaad himself, that she was pregnant with his child. Ta-Dow vehemently denied being the father. While Gina's mother lamented the defilement of her daughter, Ta-Dow's uncle scolded him for having unprotected sex. The clear moral of the story: Practice safe sex. Or better still: Abstain. Rashaad and Sarita reenacted this rather simple plot, playing their roles as they had in the actual performance, and adding embellishing side commentary:

Rashaad put an imaginary phone to his ear. "Man, I told her that baby wasn't mine. I did her just like Caine in *Menace!*" he reported, flashing a sly grin. Caine, the main character in the black gangsta movie *Menace II Society*, had also denied paternity when an old girlfriend called to tell him that she was pregnant. Sarita took over the storytelling. She played Gina's alcoholic mother, who had warned Gina all along that Ta-Dow was no good and "wasn't nothin' but a hoodrat." She told Gina that she was dumb, and that she was angry at her for getting pregnant. Yet despite her anger, Gina's mother eventually broke down in tears. Sarita delivered her regret-filled lines as Gina's mother: "He did you just like yo' daddy did me. But, I'm not gon' let you have to deal with this alone. I don't want you to have no abortion. I'ma help you out." Meanwhile, Ta-Dow's uncle, played by youth-group member Eric Cochran, overheard Ta-Dow's telephone conversation with Gina, and his categorical denial that he had gotten Gina pregnant. When Ta-Dow hung up the phone, his uncle lectured him. "Boy, you done gone and put yo' thang just up in anybody. I told you you gotta put a condom on it. Boys runnin' around doin' stuff and later things is fallin' off." Not able to control her laughter, Sarita interjected, "Eric said something about things swelling up like pickles." Eric's foul but funny description of the results of a venereal disease was a reminder that the skit was supposed to be entertainment.

The next skit Sarita and Rashaad re-presented involved a drive-by shooting. This time Sarita was out of her chair acting while Rashaad took the narrator's role. In this playlet, Sarita was walking down the street when another character started shooting in her direction. Sarita ran to the other side of the room to act out the role of the shooter. She formed her hands as if holding a gun, and pulled the trigger. She hurried back to where she had been standing to pick up her role on the other side of the bullet. As the bullet approached, Rashaad's character rushed to her, trying to push her out of its path. But Sarita "got caught in the crossfire." Her character fell quickly to the floor, but Sarita bounced back up in laughter. Sarita remembered that she had almost started laughing at the real performance because people were in the audience yelling, "Dang! She dead!" In a monotone voice, the play's moderator confirmed the audience's suspicions: "She died." Sarita and Rashaad laughed together at their acting skills, at their recollection of the crowd's reaction, and at the moderator's detachment.

The skits put on by the St. Mary's youth group are modified cases of art imitating life. More accurately, they are art imitating someone else's life. Sarita has never actually witnessed a drive-by shooting, although she definitely knows people from the neighborhood who have been shot, and she occasionally hears gunshots near her house. Likewise, Rashaad is not a teenage father, yet he has close friends who are expecting babies and others whose girlfriends have had abortions. Thus, the inspiration for these skits is neither personal experience nor their own material circumstance, but rather fragments from the lives of people they know. Integrated into these secondhand story lines are swatches of language and themes borrowed from popular ghetto-style productions like *Menace II Society* or a Snoop Doggy Dogg music video. To the extent that gangsta styles are themselves imitating the lived experiences of some segment of the African American community, the youth group's skits could be characterized as art imitating art, which in turn is imitating life.

Despite youth-group members' personal, albeit somewhat removed, familiarity with the themes of their skits, the productions are by and large for "play" time. They are performed at youth retreats and church slumber parties amid an agenda that includes spiritual activities (usually a religious speaker or focused prayer time), food, sports, dancing (usually to the "clean" versions of popular rap and rhythm-and-blues songs), and movies. The adult chaperones might wish that the skits explicitly addressed some moral question that was appropriately resolved at the conclusion. To some extent, the skits do deal with moral issues that confront contemporary teenagers. However, the youth-group members are more interested in showing off their acting skills—assuming the role of a recalcitrant ex-boyfriend, mimicking gunplay, or re-creating the emotions of a drunken mother—than in performing a parable. They are pleased with their creative ability to take a topic, build a story, and present it in such a way that it elicits laughter and sometimes tears from their audience of peers. Clearly situated in the land of make-believe, the youth-group members enjoy the freedom to act out gangsta styles with no repercussions.

In addition to re-presenting their skits, the teenagers at St. Mary's are eager to report on their experiences with neighborhood violence. One Tuesday, Sarita started off a round of "shooting stories." Sarita shared how one evening she was sitting in the back room of her home, which was enclosed in windows. She was playing on her personal computer when she heard a loud bang. Sarita jumped out of her seat. After the shock, she sat back down to continue typing. Soon, her father came running into the room yelling frantically, "They out there shootin' on the street!" All of the youth immediately laughed at Sarita's father's frightened reaction. They were amused by the frenzy of their parents' generation, who had not yet been numbed to the sound of occasional neighborhood gunfire. Another youth-group member quickly followed Sarita's account with her own shooting story.

Each account of neighborhood violence is rendered with the same giddy delight that saturated Tyson's recollection of stabbing his mother's boyfriend. And in the same excited manner, the young people in Groveland recall scenes from popular movies and videos, or confer on the dramatic details of some popular gangsta icon's life. They describe actual neighborhood events as if they are a movie, and describe scenes from movies as if they occurred in real life. They also integrate mass-culture references into their own daily routine. Sarita described a typical gang member in Groveland as a "brother on the corner with little popcorns comin' out his head [her creative description of a type of hairstyle] with a plaid shirt on lookin' like he on Crenshaw Boulevard." Because Sarita has never visited Los Angeles, it is likely that her only experience with its Crenshaw Boulevard—a street in L.A. where on Sundays black youth would park their cars and create their own social event—is from a scene in the movie *Boyz 'n the Hood.* Such appropriation of terms or references from gangsta rap or films on ghetto life is commonplace in Groveland.

Among the members of the St. Mary's youth group, Rashaad is possibly the most thrilled by ghetto styles. He once told Tenasha Jenkins, a fellow member of the youth group who was looking for a job, "You could come work for me," intimating that he oversaw some mysterious gangsta crime ring on the days when he was not manning the phones in St. Mary's rectory. "See, this is all a front," he claimed. "I can't be just comin' home with a G [a "grand"; a thousand dollars]. So I gotta look like I'm doin' somethin'." Warren, another youth-group member, challenged Rashaad's assertions with a joke. "Man, yo' parents know you didn't get no G from workin' at St. Mary's." Yet Rashaad insisted, "Ya'll don't know what I do when I leave here." Warren came back with, "Man, I call you every night at 9:15 and you at home." Rashaad squirmed out of the trap of ordinariness with a smirk: "But you don't know where I'm at on the weekends."

Yet away from his familiar surroundings at St. Mary's and in Groveland, Rashaad is much more cautious about such brazen stylistic signals. At one impromptu rap session, Rashaad told about going to a neighborhood about one mile from the notorious Robert Taylor Homes public housing project on Chicago's South Side. He spoke with a comical lightness that belied his memories of being "scared as hell." Rashaad was accompanying Virgil, a friend of his from Groveland who wanted to buy some marijuana, to an area called "Shanktown" because the local gang faction referred to themselves as "Shanks." Rashaad and Virgil got out of the car when they arrived, and they were approached by a group of young men asking, "All is well?" and holding out their hands for a handshake. Rashaad knew this was a way to ask if he was also a Shank. Knowing this was not the time to perpetrate, Rashaad gave a standard hand slap and said, "Naw man, I ain't down." While Virgil made his purchase, Rashaad spotted that one of the Shanks had a "big ol' shiny gun" down the front of his pants. Rashaad held up his own shirt to illustrate where he could see the gun. Unashamed, he repeated how scared he was. Inside, he said he felt like holding his head in his hand and yelling, "I wanna get out of here." Finding some retrospective comedy in it all, he wished he could have wailed, "I want my mother!"

Rashaad of course made it out alive and well. For all his talk about being a gangsta, he clearly recognized the limits of his commitment. He was, by his own admission, "scared shitless" in this alien area with true gangstas who carried real guns. His description of the gun was as if it was the biggest, shiniest, scariest thing he had ever seen. Ghetto styles are alluring and enticing as a fashion statement, and even as a state of mind, but as a lived experience they were utterly frightening. And it was not that Rashaad had never seen a gun, or did not know real gangbangers in his own neighborhood. However, the immediate anonymity of the situation contrasted with his familiarity with the gangbangers in Groveland. In Groveland, they are not menacing faces with secret introductions and handshakes, but rather kids who have grown up next door and who have mothers and fathers who belong to the same block club as his parents—just as the Shanks are to somebody else in their own neighborhoods.

MARGINAL

As with most classification systems, the distinctions between those who are consumed, those who are thrilled, and those who are marginal are somewhat arbitrary. Though both Rashaad Lincoln and Sarita Arthur are thrilled, Rashaad flirts with consumption, while Sarita is frequently more marginal to ghetto styles. Whereas Rashaad speaks excitedly about being a gangsta, boasts of his relationships with OGs, flaunts his knowledge of Groveland gangs, and experiments with crime, Sarita is somewhat disdainful of those same styles. She frequently mocks the thought processes of her female peers who don the feminized version of gangsta styles. "Aw, girl, you know I gotta get my hair done. And I just got my nails done." Her voice changed from her own natural southern rhythms to an exaggerated shrill, accented with mouth motions as if she were smacking on a piece of gum. She lifted up her hands, making believe that she wore fake fingernails. Pointing to each fingernail, she continued, "See this one? I got my mama name on this one, my daddy name, my baby name, my booboo [boyfriend] name." Sarita's audience was in stitches over her impersonation of the type of girl that one rapper referred to with affection as a "gangsta bitch." While at various times Sarita has her own set of fake nails, she is adamant about separating herself from girls who are consumed. Yet despite this occasional condescension, Sarita has more knowledge about and is more thrilled by gangsta styles than those who are truly marginal to the culture.

Groveland youth who are marginal to the gangsta styles are often critical of the styles and the people who sport them. Groveland Park, for example, is associated with gangstas because it is a frequent hangout for the members and leadership of the Black Mobsters in the neighborhood. Even though law-abiding families and children are in the majority at the park, it nonetheless has a shady reputation among some Groveland residents. The park's reputation is not primarily a result of its being truly unsafe. Even though there is a considerable gang presence, the park is, in the words of its supervisor, "a neutral zone." The Black Mobsters are more concerned about ensuring the park users' safety than threatening it. Despite their respectable behaviors, their *styles* are read as dangerous by some parents and marginal youth. Groveland Park's supervisor understood this concern, even though she felt them to be harmless.

> Sometimes they'll try to come in here and just stand around and talk, about five of 'em or so. And I tell 'em they can't be standing there. You know, parents come in and see them there, they got on all this gold and beepers. They thinkin' it isn't safe. So I just tell 'em to go to the back or somethin'. Just don't be standin' in the front hallway. And they usually go.

In the absence of actual antisocial behavior, simple gold chains and beepers become objects of fear for those who do not participate in gangsta styles. Add to these trinkets oversized clothes, baseball hats, cellular phones, dominoes, and the rap music that frequently blares from their portable CD player, and the total effect frightens marginal Groveland youth and adults into avoiding their public park altogether.

Twenty-five-year-old Sharon Maurice is well aware of her marginal position. She described herself as "naive" and "sheltered," and said that her friends affectionately called her "sadity," an old black vernacular term for "snobbish." Growing up under her grandparents' charge in Groveland, she was not allowed to go off the block. "When we did come out it was only for like ten minutes," she recalled about her limited neighborhood exposures.

> You know, when we ride the bikes, you could just ride up that
> street, get off, turn back around. I mean you couldn't even ride
> across the street to go up the other street right across. . . . I've
> never been the in-crowd kind of person. . . . I was sheltered.

Sharon's grandparents kept her under close watch.

> One of the girls who stayed like right [across the street], if I was
> allowed to go out, I could go over to her house. And we would
> eat popcorn and I wouldn't tell my grandmother. But I still
> would have to eat dinner when I came home. But then we didn't
> go outside. That's how her mother kinda was too. So she got
> all her toys inside.

Sharon Maurice spent most of her childhood and adolescence with
her paternal grandparents (with whom she still lives) because her
mother was an alcoholic and her father had remarried and started a
new family. Her splintered family situation left the door open for
Sharon to experiment with ghetto styles and behaviors, but her family
used certain strategies to keep her from that path. They kept her so
busy that she had little time to spend with anyone that her parents
or grandparents did not arrange for her to be with. The short time
she lived with her father and stepmother, she and her stepsister were
enrolled in everything.

> My stepmother was very very [into the] society thing. She would
> bring us up in, I don't wanna say like, but how white people
> bring up they kids. Ballet, tap, ice skating, clarinet, piano. I
> mean, you know, we never had free time. Monday it was this,
> Tuesday it was this. If you weren't doing that, you were practic-
> ing for this.

Her father added a style component to this regimen. "My father was
from the military so our shoes were shined. Our outfits, we were like
beige to black. Our uniforms were starched. We were Vaselined
down. That was him."

In junior high school Sharon moved in with her mother. She initially felt as if she had been liberated from her austere father and his
demanding wife. But her mother's drinking problem quickly sent her
back with her grandparents. Despite the changes in environment,
Sharon's family managed to keep her ultra-busy. For high school, her
grandmother enrolled her in an enrichment program at the University

of Chicago, which supplemented her curriculum at Benton High School and accounted for nearly all of Sharon's free time.

> Separate classes, homework every night. When you came in for the summer, you would be doing the freshman work for Benton. And then when you got to Benton, you'd be doing the freshman work that you did for the summer. But then over at the University of Chicago, you'd be doing the sophomore work. . . . It was so hard. Every night was homework, which would have been fine, [but] we even had classes on Saturday. So it was like every day. Sunday, church.

It was not until Sharon went away to college at Jackson State University, a historically black school in Mississippi, that she became more knowledgeable about ghetto styles. Jackson State, she joked, "should be called Chicago State at Jackson." Her classmates were "Chicago people tryin' to be hard, knowing when they got home they were like nothing." From her judgment, Jackson State was full of freelancers. She referred to her friends from college as her "ghetto friends." "They're streetwise. They're very very streetwise," she said in explanation of what she meant by "ghetto." She followed this definition with an example.

> We were standing out in front of the church and it was this car that came skidding by and everybody just ran in church and I'm standing out there like, okay. Like I knew I mighta should have ran, but it didn't mean anything to me at that particular time. And then everybody said, "You didn't even run!" I was just like, "Y'all didn't even take me with you!" But everybody knew to run except for me. So I call them my little ghetto friends. Because I guess in comparison to what I know about the street, if they don't tell me then I wouldn't know.

Sharon's ghetto friends, who live in other parts of Chicago, occasionally tell her stories about situations in her own neighborhood.

> They kinda connectin' me to what's going on outside. Like they'll say, "Did you know that it was a gang war over there by your house?" And I'm like, "No, I didn't." They said, "Yeah, they were meetin' up. . . ." And I'm like, "Oh, for real?" I missed that. You know, I'm just in the midst of going going going.

Along with her lack of awareness of the consumed element around her, Sharon's stylistic tastes equally illustrate her noninvolvement in popular ghetto culture. She listens mostly to gospel music, and some rhythm and blues. Her pastimes include going to plays, reading spiritual books and motivational writings by African American women, and occasionally going to the movies. About her clothes, Sharon said:

> I really don't buy clothes. This is strange, but the guy I date buys my clothes. He's just like, "Oh, this is cute." So when I see things, I'm like, "Oh wow, I really have to buy this 'cause I finally found something that I like." If not I will wear my grandmother's clothes 'cause she dresses really nice.

Sharon contrasts her disinterest in clothes with the shopping habits of one of her ghetto friends.

> I went shopping with my friend and she's like an expensive type of person. I'm not. If I could get like a $30 pair of pants and like a $12 shirt, I'm set. That's the outfit that'll be just fine. But she's like into like Bloomingdale's, and we were in there and we were looking at the sales rack, which was not like the sales rack. It was like $200 marked down from $900. So, I mean, of course $200 looks good. And so I would never go back to Bloomingdale's. I wouldn't even, I can't even remember what stores were in there 'cause that was crazy, name-brand stuff.

She is even more opinionated when she talks about her ghetto stepsister:

> My sister has a pager. [She] doesn't work, doesn't do anything. The girls get their hair done like every week. They have nails. And I'm like, I work every day! Either I have no interest for that or I'm working to pay some bills. You know, I'm always questioning that little part. Now what happens to that money? Is that hairstyle like really really needed?

At almost every turn, Sharon indicated her own marginal status to and partial distaste for the in styles, as well as her lack of street wisdom.

However, marginality is quite different from total disengagement or detachment. Being marginal means existing on the outskirts of a certain cultural or behavioral terrain, while maintaining a connection. Sharon's connection is through her ghetto friends, as well as through her work with the youth group at Groveland United Church of Christ. "I guess since I work so much with the kids, you have to pay attention to what they're doing and what they're saying," she commented about how the young people at her church were keeping her in touch with local ghetto styles.

> 'Cause if you don't, they'll be doing some kind of gang stuff. And I'm kinda naive. I don't know what that is. So, every little thing that they do, I'm like, "Well, what is that?" And I know if the girls start laughing, it's got something to do with some little gang or something that they've created.

Sharon is especially concerned about a few of the teenagers in her youth group whose older siblings are in the neighborhood gangs. As she watches her thrilled youthful charges, she is worried about their future. "They know the colors that they wear, their shake, they know what everything is," she said about some of the kids at Groveland Church. To keep them from being consumed, Sharon replicates the strategy her family used for her. "They're here Monday, Tuesday, Wednesday, Thursday, Saturday, Sunday," she said. "The only day that they have to be in trouble would be Friday."

Being marginal means being "kinda naive," as Sharon described herself, but not totally oblivious to her surroundings. She has friends and family members who are thrilled, and even consumed. Short of total seclusion, it is impossible for a black middle-class young person growing up in a neighborhood like Groveland to be completely isolated from either the stylistic displays of ghetto life or the actual behavioral manifestations. Young Grovelandites receive gangsta messages through popular-culture productions, but they also see the flashy styles of the drug dealers in their own neighborhood. With this dual influence, Sharon's degree of marginality is not very common among Groveland youth. If only for the aesthetic pleasures of staying in style, most of Groveland's teenagers and many young adults buy the correct brand names, utter the newly created slang, and share the most up-to-date, star-filled gossip. For added excitement, some may venture beyond the styles into petty crime. Still others may believe, as Lauren Grant did, that they can *be* the gangstas created by Hollywood, who in many ways resemble the gangstas across the street.

What causes some young people to be consumed and others to remain within the safety of thrilled or marginal status? Consistent with overall gender differences in criminal offending, teenage girls and young adult women in Groveland are much less likely to be consumed than boys. Stylistically, some of the young women earnestly participate in conspicuous consumption. Their hairstyles are impeccable, their fingernails a work of art, and their adoration of the consumed young men apparent. "A good brother don't get no play," Rashaad recognized, while a "ruffneck" is the male persona of choice among consumed and thrilled young women. Girls' behaviors are most rooted in the expressive realm. They wear ghetto styles for the same reason that Elizabeth Taylor wears designer dresses and gaudy diamonds—to be beautiful and to be seen. Gang membership and selling drugs are almost nonchoices for most of the teenage girls, with Lauren Grant as a noted exception. Instead, girls might be consumed through their association with consumed young men.

"If you wanna make a nigga mad, after you had his baby, have another one and it ain't his," Diedre Gasper insisted in a conversation between young women at Groveland Park. She continued, "Shit, that'll make they shit know [that they don't own you]. They can have babies all around the city, but don't let you have one." But her friend cautioned, "They kill you for some shit like that." To this another participant added, "Shit, just for talkin' to another nigga, they be shootin'." This group of women all had children by young men who were selling drugs, men consumed in both affect and action. There was a certain volatility in their relationships with their boyfriends that illustrated the contentious but exciting game of courtship among some Groveland youth and that resulted from their boyfriend's jealousies and their own determination to be in control of their sexuality. These women's consumed character was in that they passively condoned and perhaps aided their boyfriends' vices. It was part of what made their boyfriends attractive in the first place, just as Tyson Reed suspected that his new clothes gave him an edge with women.

Yet despite the existence of young women who are consumed by consumed men (and the few who themselves take styles to their behavioral extreme), the behaviors and activities of young girls are still more circumscribed and controlled than those of boys. Neisha Morris thought that teenage girls in Groveland were more likely to graduate from high school than teenage boys. " 'Cause the boys get to doin' they thang. You know how boys more so branch off easier than girls." And Charisse Baker said that the gang leader around her block would not even allow girls into the gang because he did not want them to get hurt. The gendered differences in supervision and perhaps even temperament and attraction to public deviance account for the disproportionate representation of girls in the thrilled and marginal categories, and their underrepresentation among the consumed.

No other distinction is as evident as the gender differences in how deep youth fall into the ghetto trance. The presence of a male role model does seem important for young men. Tyson is convinced that he would not have gotten so involved in the Black Mobsters had his father been around. His mother clearly possessed the money, the connections, and the desire to put Tyson on the right track. What she lacked was time, another pair of eyes, and perhaps a special insight into the pressures of being a young African American man. Echoing Tyson's desire for a father, sixteen-year-old Jeremiah Height also saw his relationship with his father as crucial: "People join gangs 'cause they feel it's no love at home. 'Cause I felt like that once and I wanted to join 'cause I thought my father didn't love me." On the other hand, both of Rashaad's parents are there for him (and very gainfully employed). He does not express the same kind of inner turmoil that Tyson and Jeremiah discuss, but he is still seduced by the trappings of ghetto life. Even though a disrupted home life can prompt youth to take to the streets, there are examples of young people from single-mother homes who are marginal, and those from two-parent homes who get shot. The ultimate and all-too-real danger is that thrilled youth who do not *expect* to be consumed end up that way anyway. Rashaad divulged his petty criminal involvements. Like an eel, he always seems to slither out of real trouble. But the line is thin.

Groveland youth can be consumed as victims, their innocent stylistic signs misread by some real gangsta (or some overzealous police officer). At Jackson State, Sharon Maurice's friend was shot at a party. "That was a case of he was from Chicago, [and] he thought he was bad," she said pityingly. Or thrilled youth can casually be absorbed into actual delinquent networks. Ray Gibbs, for example, and his childhood friend Skip were in the Boy Scouts together before they both joined the Black Mobsters. It was an uneventful progression for them—from thrilled to consumed. Ray's bullet wound and Skip's death show the consequences of that progression. Following the very same fads that white middle-class youth adopt, Groveland's teenagers and young adults are situated in an environment where their contemporary zoot suits are loaded with expressive meaning, but can also bring on lethal trouble.

7

Nike's Reign

Groveland youth use their own bodies and the accessories that adorn them as status markers and symbols of identity. For the girls and young women, each long, acrylic press-on fingernail is accented with intricate colored brush strokes and sometimes even a hint of glitter. For young men, the placement, color, or brand of a baseball cap may pledge allegiance to a certain gang, or may clearly distinguish someone from that crowd. From the top of a girl's twelve-inch-high french-twist hairstyle to the underside of a pair of Nike Air Jordan basketball shoes—which carry the infamous "Jump Man" trademark—and with all the personalized tattoos, Georgetown jogging suits, Girbaud jeans, fourteen-carat-gold necklaces, Karl Kani leather jackets, and Tommy Hilfiger boxer shorts in between, Groveland's young people are walking mega-malls, forever trying to stay in material dialogue with their friends, as well as with their enemies.

Groveland styles are proof that black youth are particularly vulnerable to the messages they view on television about what to buy, why they should buy, and who they could be (or, at the very least, be like) if they buy. Black youth are conspicuous consumers. They watch more television and view it more favorably and as more realistic, and they respond more positively to marketing stimuli, than their white peers.[1] Using the example of Nike sports apparel, this chapter illustrates the coincidence of the growth in mass marketing with the rising brand-consciousness of Groveland youth. Nikes are just one component of an elaborated discourse about clothes and other personal fashion items, their worth, and their meaning to young Groveland residents. The story of Nike in Groveland elaborates on the previous discussion of ghetto styles. By exploring the targeting of black youth by mass marketers, and the status-enhancing properties of consumer goods, the draw of the streets becomes more comprehensible.

THE BLACK MARKET

In the 1960s, not only were African Americans slowly brought into the economic and political spheres of American life, but they were also incorporated into some social and cultural spheres as well. As television became more generally accessible, it was possible to visually reflect the diversity of Americans. Advertisers then recognized blacks as an important and sizable target market. Black newspapers had been trying to convince white businesses of the loyalty and eagerness of black consumers since the 1930s; they urged companies to spend advertising dollars in their publications. Yet it was not until the late 1960s, and especially the 1970s and 1980s, that white companies took heed (Nightingale 1993; Pitts et al. 1989). Since the 1960s, the use of African American actors in advertising has increased, and black celebrities have proved particularly successful for reaching black audiences (Lee and Browne 1995; Williams and Qualls 1989). The success of advertisers' increased use of black models, celebrities, and cultural themes has meant the inclusion of blacks, particularly black youth, within the reaches of marketing culture.

People use material goods to level the playing field, buying things they often cannot afford in order to give others the impression that they can. African Americans have done this for years, and with decidedly more vigor than whites. The real gap in economic status can be minimized at least symbolically by just looking good. Historian Carl Nightingale (1993, 143) writes that for blacks, material items have always "been the stuff of intense emotional importance." African Americans use material goods as symbolic affronts to the power of whites. From the early 1950s through the 1960s, poor black men were more likely to buy expensive and prestigious cars (such as Cadillacs) and goods (like Scotch) than poor white men. A 1949 issue of *Ebony* magazine gave an answer to the query of "Why Negroes Buy Cadillacs." "Basically, a Cadillac is an instrument of aggression," argued the article's author, "a solid and substantial symbol for many a Negro that he is as good as any white man" (quoted in Nightingale 1993, 144). In dress, too, blacks consume more and are more fashion-conscious than whites with comparable incomes (Alexis 1970; Stith and Goldsmith 1989; Nightingale 1993). A new car, good whiskey, and a designer suit are not simply to level the field with rich whites, but they make a statement to fellow blacks as well. A Cadillac (like Lauren Grant's "triple white" one) serves to sort among the African American community. The driver buys it to signify first to him- or herself, then to friends, and finally to "the white man," that he or she has made it. This affront, however, is always at the symbolic level. It does nothing to alter the actual inequalities that consumers try to overcome. Because of its limited transformative utility, Cornel West (1994) blames consumer culture for the formation of decadent "market moralities."

Young people in Groveland are sometimes uncritical in their acceptance of fads and fashions, but they also use those fashions to resist and reinterpret their racially marginalized position, and they surely wield their clothes and accessories as weapons among each other. All the while they are enacting these seemingly contradictory behaviors, they are having fun. Nikes are an important component of the style of Groveland, and young people like those in Groveland are a big part of Nike's profits. The story of the two together illuminates the cultural milieu in which Groveland youth are embedded.

IT'S GOTTA BE THE SHOES

On a Wednesday evening in early February, I sat with Spider in the small office next to the gym in Groveland Park field house, where volleyball was supposed to begin at 7 o'clock. It was nearing 7:30, but I enjoyed the leeway to sit around and shoot the breeze. Spider always kept me entertained with his stories about the neighborhood, told with the detail of a painter. Spider and I were joined this night by Chris, a nineteen-year-old young man who carried the belly of a forty-year-old couch potato. Chris didn't seem to have any set schedule. He hung around the gym at all hours, making me pretty sure that he didn't have a regular job. That is, he didn't have a regular *legal* job. I had become convinced that Chris worked for Lance, the notorious South Side gang and drug kingpin who grew up six blocks away from Groveland Park. Lance would drop by Groveland Park quite often. It was a home base, and it was familiar. Lance would talk to Spider, use the phone, play dominoes, and get business reports from any number of young workers like Chris.

This evening, the television droned in the background. When there was a lull in the conversation, the TV guaranteed that we all had something to look at, instead of staring into the uncomfortably silent air between us. In one of the quiet moments, I noticed that Chris had on new gym shoes. These particular shoes were the newest of the new. Not only were they a new purchase for Chris, but they were the most recent addition to the line of Air Jordan basketball shoes created by Nike. In the local sneaker shorthand, they were called the "North Carolinas." I inspected the impeccable white shoelaces, the soft white leather upper, and the gleaming light-blue patent-leather trim along the bottom (God's favorite color, according to Tar Heels). But before I could comment on how I liked them, Vince—the six-foot-three-inch, 275-pound park instructor—walked in and stepped on Chris's $150 toe, leaving a smudge that damned those shoes to the far reaches of the attic.

The dream had ended. The way I saw it, there were two lines of action that Chris could take. He could turn on his old friend Vince with a strong right to the nose, and demand retribution, not only for the monetary value of the shoes, but for the lost days when Chris could have used them to impress women, his neighborhood friends, and the admiring preteen boys who kept him feeling like he was Michael Jordan himself. Or he could run to the nearest water fountain, grab a clean towel, and engage in the usually private ritual of making once-worn gym shoes once again presentable.

Instead, no one saw it the way I saw it. It wasn't until a year later that I would see Chris whip out two $100 bills to make a whimsical bet. Another time, he pulled out a wad of $100 bills while he and Spider talked quietly among themselves about something I was clearly not meant to hear. I did not know at first that Chris had money like that. Once I did, I could interpret his unruffled composure when Vince stepped on his new shoes. While he paid big bucks for those shoes and for the awesome looks they could bring, it was well within his means to replace them with some other, even more spectacular, piece of status. Spider was the only one to comment on Vince's ruination of Chris's newest of the new North Carolinas. "He don't care," Spider said, directing his explanation to me. "Shiiit, he wear them outside."

At least Spider understood my astonishment. Some people don't wear their immaculate new gym shoes outside, unless God has painted the sky with Carolina blue, and the weatherman has forecast no rain, snow, or dog shit. Some people (like me and Spider, I guess) see those shoes as investments. And such a sudden depreciation in any sane person's investment would call for, at the very least, an irritated growl at the person who made the market crash. But for Chris, who could wear his gym shoes outside, these were the concerns of peons. Luckily, I figured all this out quickly enough not to give myself away as the ultimate peon, who would have cried had the same tragedy befallen her. When I had regained my composure, we picked up the conversation, reviewing the players in the NBA with whom Chris shared the distinction of sporting the "North Carolinas."

How had it come to be that what Chris wore on his feet could prompt a full conversation with impressive knowledge about which famous people wore the same thing on their feet? How could the most trampled piece of our wardrobe, taking from some wearers three hundred pounds of abuse with every step, and subject to the violence of someone else's three hundred pounds if we're not careful, inspire such high regard? What's more, gym shoes are charged with protecting the part of our body that, when we were children, we considered almost as gross as our private parts. Feet sweat, they breed fungi, they grow calluses, and with the new exercise craze, they are often pummeled into unsalvageable deformation and ugliness. And worst of all, feet stink. Still, we are willing to pamper them in $150 gym shoes, while we may spend only $1.49 on the soap to wash our faces with. Why? The reason is part of an intricate story of marketing decisions, local cultures, timing, and originality on the part of both producers and consumers.

In the late 1960s, before Chris was even born and in faraway Oregon, entrepreneur Phil Knight dreamed up what has become the Nike empire. According to an executive at a Portland investment firm who worked with Nike at its inception, "They managed to create a need where none had existed" (Labich and Carvell 1995).[2] Nike began with shoes for runners. Phil Knight had been a distance runner on the track team at the University of Oregon. After Stanford Business School, he thought that there might be a market for high-quality running shoes. He began by importing a Japanese brand and selling them out of the back of his car. Frustrated with the slow returns, Knight and his old track coach created their own brand. They paid a Portland State design student $35 to think up what is now worth over $6 billion— the Nike "Swoosh" (Lane 1996). By the 1980s, Phil Knight's concerns were no longer the possibility that a heavy rain might wash out his car trunk and spoil the day's sales. Instead, his company had graduated to sponsoring athletes in the 1984 Los Angeles Olympic games, competing with the world's largest shoe companies.

While the Olympics were a far cry from hawking in Oregon, there was still more work to be done. Nike athletes took home only 63 gold medals, compared to the 259 gold medals that Adidas athletes won. Equally upsetting was the fact that an upstart shoe company had acquired the right to market the Reebok brand in the United States. They made rapid inroads in sports apparel through their domination of the women's aerobic market. In 1980, Reebok profits were a mere $300,000, but that figure jumped to $1.5 million by the next year. Despite the exposure of the Olympics, Nike now battled with Adidas and Reebok over the market of feet and bodies. Nike needed new ways to be number one, and stay number one.

Like most companies, Nike did not begin to recognize the black consumer market until the 1970s. Before that it was considered a substantial risk to use blacks as product endorsers, no matter how prominent they were. But after the turbulent 1960s, there wasn't much more that could ruffle America's feathers. So on the sidelines, Nike moved into basketball. To their number-one hoops consultant, Sonny Vaccaro, basketball meant moving into the black market. In his first meeting with Nike executives in 1977, Vaccaro told them, "Nobody's taking on these young kids in the colleges. *Black and East is basketball. It isn't pros. It isn't West Coast white kids.* You guys are missing the playgrounds and you're missing the colleges and that's what it's all about" (Strasser and Becklund 1991, 286). Nike took Vaccaro's advice and gave him the authority to corral the East Coast playground scene and the college game.

One strategy Vaccaro used to get to the young kids on the playgrounds was the Dapper Dan basketball tournament—half All-Star game, half auctioning block. The top high school players in the country received the honor of being invited to Pittsburgh to play against one another and show off their skills at the Dapper Dan. The top college recruiters were also invited to appraise the players and mutter among themselves about who might be bidding on whom. By 1978, 17,000 people attended the Dapper Dan tournament. Most important, it was officially sponsored by Nike. This meant that the most spectacular of players were outfitted in what would become the most spectacular of urban fashion symbols. After the weekend's festivities were over, the teenage participants were sent home as uniformed ambassadors of Nike.

Hooking the high school players was relatively easy compared to making headway in the college game. College basketball was a bit more sticky because of the watchdog National Collegiate Athletic

Association (NCAA). To infiltrate the colleges, Vaccaro had to use the connections he made from his Dapper Dan tournament to court college coaches. Backing Vaccaro's plan to woo college coaches, Nike gave him a hefty expense account to meet with coaches, wine and dine them, and make offers of free shoes for themselves and their teams, and yearly trips for the coaches and their wives to warm, relaxing, Nike-sponsored getaway destinations. This was not a new strategy. Converse had long since figured out that the way to the urban basketball market was through the college player, and the way to the college player was through the college coach. The major difference was that Vaccaro had a special knack for this business. By 1979, fifty college basketball coaches had signed on with Nike. At twelve players a team, that meant there was a new army of six hundred college basketball players wearing Nikes. The players in those college programs later became the personnel of the pro league, so that by 1984, about half of the National Basketball Association's players wore Nike.

The NBA was just an idealistic dream for Tommy Smith, who was growing up in Groveland in the 1970s. He played basketball every day on the playground of Groveland Elementary School, a few blocks from his house. Shooting hoops into the late evenings, Tommy saw himself and the other kids who hung out there as rising athletes. But when he reached the tenth grade, Tommy was routinely buying jeans that were just thirty-one inches in length. This was his signal that he was not "rising" much above about five-nine, a little too short for the pros. His basketball career dreams faded, but he did not stop playing, because basketball was more than a dream. It was the divider between the in and the out crowds. "I was on the basketball team my senior year," Tommy remembered. "I've never been much of a student council person, or student government or anything like that in college or in high school. I was more of a cool type, and those things kept you away from that." Nike was just starting to work its way into the urban market when Tommy was in high school, looking to be cool.

How I came across Tommy's first Nike memory was quite serendipitous. It is amazing how the human brain works to recall information. Major events in our lives seem to act as anchors for a host of less significant activities that surrounded the event. Someone may remember the exact date he changed jobs because it was the same day that John F. Kennedy was killed. Someone else may remember taking an uneventful trip to the museum only because when she got home that evening her infant child took its first step. I thought that, perhaps,

Tommy would remember his first talk with his mother or grandmother about sex or drugs; that it would have been such a monumen-
tal occasion (either for its gravity or for its awkward hilarity) that he
would be able to tell me about it in detail. Instead, he came up relatively blank on the subject. His mother's friend Pam was the one who
talked to Tommy about the birds and the bees, although the details
he gave of that conversation were pretty vague. What he did remember was that Pam was the bearer of great gifts—his first pair of Nikes.

> [Me and my mother] never had any talks. She had a friend
> named Pam Rhodes, and that's where I think my girl talk and
> my, as I think about it, and my drug talk came from. From her
> friend Pam, who bought me my first pair of leather gym shoes,
> when Nikes first came out. I think I was in the seventh grade,
> seventh or sixth. I think it was seventh. She bought me my first
> pair of white Nikes with the black stripe and the suede around
> the toe.

At twenty-nine years old, Tommy described the new Nikes of his
childhood as if he had stored them in a glass case in a sacred room,
peeking in on them periodically ever since. Remembering those shoes
brought back his mother's old friend (her first and last name), chronologically situated the occasion in his seventh-grade year, and called
up the less significant lessons he was taught about girls and drugs.

Tommy was in the seventh grade in the late 1970s, just around
the time when Sonny Vaccaro convinced Nike of the gold mine in
black neighborhoods. From the Dapper Dan tournament and the
ranks of predominantly black and wildly popular college teams like
the Georgetown Hoyas to little Groveland Elementary School playground, Nike made inroads into the black urban basketball market,
just as Vaccaro had imagined it. And Tommy was probably one of
the first of his friends to have a pair. Tommy was cool. Tommy was
a trendsetter. Tommy had Nikes before anyone else in the neighborhood. Even as he got older, Tommy continued to see himself at the
cutting edge of fashion. Reveling in the originality that he was proud
of as a child, Tommy talked about his shopping routine.

> I just wouldn't go where everybody goes. I'm that individual
> that likes to be unique. And I like the compliments. I have a
> necklace, for instance, that's a gold beer or pop top. And every-
> where I go, people, you know, wow! So, that's the kind of re-
> sponse I like to get. I don't want, "Oh, I got a pair of those." I

don't really enjoy that. So, I try to go places that people usually wouldn't go or don't go.

As Tommy sat behind the desk in his home office sharing his strategies for being unique, he was dressed in an attractive but plain blue-and-gray striped shirt and green army pants. On his feet he wore a pair of blue Nikes that matched his shirt. It was true, I had not seen them on anyone before, and I had made it a practice in Groveland to greet people and then immediately size up their footwear. Maybe he really *did* know "unique" places to shop where other people did not go. Tommy was setting trends. And he had the admiration of those who were less innovative, those not patient enough to look for a gold pop-top charm (especially since cans no longer feature pop tops). Others settle for a gold cross, or the first letter of their name, or maybe even their whole name. (In an entirely different setting, an equally innovative fashion connoisseur had a gold charm of Michael Jordan's "Jump Man" logo, where the ball at the end of Jordan's outstretched arm was a single diamond. He of course got lots of wows for that.) With every "wow" Tommy knew he was on the right track to being unique.

But Tommy found himself in a bit of a dilemma. His eleven-year-old son, Corey, was also a part of that admiring crowd, not to mention the twenty boys that he counseled at the group home where he worked. The boys at the group home were not really Tommy's concern. Someone else would have to worry about where to get the $150 for their gym shoes. Most likely, Tommy's charges at work would just not get any new gym shoes. Instead they would be condemned to coveting Tommy's expensively covered feet every day that he arrived at work. Now his son was another matter altogether. "He wants Air Jordans this, he wants this and that," Tommy said, but he was not convinced that buying new Nikes was the best thing for Corey. "First I let him know exactly what those shoes really cost," he began.

> And they're exploiting the people who makin' 'em in the first place, and then overcharging me to get 'em for you. But then I'll let you know that you're gonna have to get these $100, these $150 shoes yourself. And you're not gonna wanna spend *your* $150. And then we go through that.

"But, Dad!" I can imagine Corey protesting to his father's reasonable explanation for why he should not expect an oblong box that smelled anything like leather and rubber under the Christmas tree that year. I can also imagine eleven-year-old Corey accompanying his father on the shopping trip of the week, traveling far from the neighborhood and down confusing side streets to find the obscure store that sold Tommy the few-of-a-kind Nikes of which he was so proud. It is probably safe to assume that most fathers are not giving introductory lectures to their children on the political economy of gym shoes. Most kids just beg and they get. Corey could possibly get if he continued begging, but he had to first endure Tommy's internal conflicts over staying in style while supporting a system that, in his estimation, cheated both the makers and the buyers.

Tommy had some ammunition for his somewhat leftist convictions. When our conversation was winding down, Tommy got up from his chair, left the room for a moment, and returned with a book he had been reading entitled *Wealth and Poverty*. He sat back down and began answering a general question I had posed.

> Why do I think all this is happening, which is the people in our community striving to do what they wanna do and yet and still these things are happening? This answers your question exactly, key, important.

From there, Tommy began to read extensively (but not verbatim) from the book's text.

> Capitalism. Can a, can a man live in a free society if if if they feel no reason to believe that that society is just? Okay, um, a man cannot long tolerate the sense of spiritual meaninglessness in their individual lives, so they cannot long accept the society in which power, privilege, and property are not distributed according to some moral um meaningful criteria. Um, capitalist freedom leads to a vulgar and decadent civilization, afflicted by um libido for the ugly and trivial, the shallow and the ungodly and lacking in discipline and courage, or the values to be worth preserving. Capitalism is not only morally vacant, it also perpetuates gross immorality, racism, sexism, environmental abuse. It is a practical failure as well because it brings on inflation and unemployment. Above all, capitalism creates and perpetuates um the differences between the rich and the poor, rich countries and poor ones, men and women, and destroys the balance between men and women, I mean, between man and nature, consumption and individual appetites and social needs. Capitalism is an edifice without an inherent foundation in morality and religion, and that therefore it engenders a shallow and dubious

order of human life. The system is immoral because it is based on greed.

I had not expected to stumble upon a Marxist in my ethnographic interviews. I was even less prepared for a Marxist in Nikes.[3] Nike's production practices made it difficult for Tommy to reconcile his politics with his participation in the dialogue of commodities. In the end, though, and however tortured he might have been, Tommy seemed to have found a way to wear his Nike gym shoes with confidence.

In the early years, Nike had small factories in Exeter, New Hampshire, and Saco, Maine. But even then, most of the manufacturing was done in Korea and Taiwan. In 1985, the Maine factory closed because of the unremarkable fact that American workers just cost too much money. Korean and Taiwanese workers earned just over $1 an hour in the 1980s, while American workers were making between $8 and $11 for producing the same quality shoe (Strasser and Becklund 1991, 559). After 1985, only a small factory in Oregon remained open in the United States; the rest of production was overseas. By the 1990s, even Korea and Taiwan were becoming too expensive. Nike began expanding to Indonesia, Vietnam, and Thailand, where the labor was cheaper and the governments promised a cooperative and eager workforce. By 1996, an $80 pair of Nike shoes in the United States cost the company about $2.60 in labor costs (Gargan 1996). As a result, Nike came under fire for its labor practices (Jones 1996). But the berm around Nike's seventy-four-acre corporate campus proved too tall and too thick for much of this criticism to get through. Moreover, Nike's popularity was too well fortified by the star personalities of its athletes for much of anything to get through.

The first solid brick in Nike's wall of athletic fame was basketball player Michael Jordan. In 1984, Michael Jordan decided to leave college to enter the NBA. Shoe companies lined up to dress his feet. Nike was trailing in the athletic shoe race with Adidas (worldwide, and in the heart of Michael Jordan), and saw Reebok picking up speed in the inside lane. Dapper Dan coordinator Sonny Vaccaro met with Nike executives to discuss what to do about Nike basketball. They had a lot of players on their team, but there was no go-to guy to get them closer to their ultimate desire: "To get Swooshes on everybody's feet. . . . To Swoosh the world" (Strasser and Becklund 1991). Nike was founded on risk, and it was once again time to gamble. It was all or nothing.

Nike offered Jordan "all"—a reported $2.5 million over five years, which included annuities, signing bonuses, and, most important, royalties from his own shoe, a first in the endorsement business. Adidas offered Michael Jordan close to nothing—$100,000, and no special shoe. In October of 1984, at the Palmer House Hotel in Chicago, just before he was to play his first regular-season home game with the Chicago Bulls, Michael Jordan signed with Nike, and history was made. The Michael Jordan/Nike marriage approximated the divine. Describing the scene at an Air Jordan photo shoot near a Chicago housing project, an ex–Nike executive (Strasser and Becklund 1991, 566) wrote:

> When Jordan left the playground, the kids mobbed him and begged for one of his Air Jordan T-shirts. A little girl standing in the middle was Jordan's favorite. He bent down, handed her the shirt, much to her delight, and walked away. The mini-mob followed him to the car, wanting to touch and be touched by him.

This larger-than-life portrayal is no exaggeration of Michael Jordan's stature among youth. B. J. Brown—a quiet Groveland fourteen-year-old who made the interview process feel more like a visit to the dentist's office than a friendly conversation—was finally able to muster up a few thoughts when I asked about his role models. He wanted to be like Michael Jordan, simply because "e'rybody like him. I wanna be like somebody, somebody bigger." There's no discerning whether Nike made Michael Jordan a superstar or vice versa. But there is no denying that the two together have become a part of many American dreams.

With the right publicist, the St. Mary's boys basketball team in Groveland could make a case for being showcased in one of Nike's and Michael Jordan's clever commercials. On the team of ten fourth-, fifth-, and sixth-grade boys, each player had star quality for a different reason. One of the boys was nearly five and a half feet tall, pretty impressive for a sixth-grader. "Girl, and you see how big his feet are," his mother pointed out to another mother in the bleachers during an evening game. "He gotta get men's clothes already. He gon' cost me a fortune." Another player stood out for his athletic skills. He was the shortest player on the team, nearly swallowed by his jersey and shorts. But he was also the most creative, handling the ball like a seasoned pro, and shooting with a confident touch. What nickname did the St. Mary's boys give to the best player on their team? Baby Jordan, of course.

Baby Jordan and seven of his teammates wore Nikes. (The two unfortunate misfits—or fashion rebels—had on Converse and Champion brands.) Four of the pairs of Nikes were Air Jordans, and two of those were the most up-to-date edition. When Steven, one of the boys who had on the new Jordans, was fouled and went to the free-throw line, his mother commented about his gym shoes, "Girl, them the ugliest things I ever seen. His grandparents bought him those. He told them exactly what he wanted for Christmas and his grandparents bought him those. I think they the ugliest things. Butt-ugly!" Ugly or not, Air Jordans were a hot ticket. If Steven's mother refused to buy them for him, he had surely found some way to get them.

Elsewhere in Groveland, Ray Gibbs was growing up just when Sonny Vaccaro got really good at targeting black youth, and just around the time when Michael Jordan became Nike's ticket to success. But as a youngster, Ray Gibbs was not nearly as cool as the eight Nike-clad boys on St. Mary's basketball team. He wasn't as cool as Tommy Smith either, who got his first pair of Nikes five years before Michael Jordan made them popular. In 1984, when Ray was nine years old, he was still subject to the unfashionable consumer decisions of his mother.

> You know when you a shorty everybody mother used to put 'em on some Pro-Wings. You used to think you had some name-brand shoes on. Come to find out it was a big disappointment when you got to school and the older kids start [asking], "Whatchu got on there?" "Aw man leave me alone." In those days, I mean it was kinda funny. I mean, it didn't hurt you as much. But, you know, nowadays some of us wouldn't be caught dead going into Payless [shoe store].

On the sunny day nearing noon when I talked to the older and more fashion-conscious Ray Gibbs, he had long since said goodbye to Pro-Wings. Running late for our scheduled interview, Ray was just getting out of the shower, and spent much of the time we talked putting lotion on his basketball-calloused hands and dry knees. He had thrown on blue shorts and a T-shirt. His choice of footwear was a pair of Nike Air Max. Top of the line. In this particular shoe, he could go walking in the morning, maybe lift some weights in the afternoon, and play a leisurely pickup basketball game in the evening. Introducing the cross trainer.

Even though Michael Jordan jump-started Nike in 1984, bringing in over $100 million in new revenues, Reebok just would not go away. In the 1987 straightaway, Reebok overtook Nike with $1.4 billion in revenues. Again, Phil Knight and the other top managers needed something new. The answer, they decided, was in the "air." Nike designers wanted to capitalize on the "Air" moniker that had done so well selling Michael Jordan's shoe. The expanded Nike Air line, featuring this strange invention called the "cross trainer," fit the active lifestyle of people who were generally into fitness, but not avid athletes— like Ray Gibbs. Mixing this new idea with old marketing strategies, Nike got versatile football and baseball star Bo Jackson to be the poster child for this versatile shoe.

To regain the lead over Reebok, however, Nike needed a double whammy this time. So, along with the new ad campaign featuring Nike Air, cross trainers, and Bo Jackson, Nike also went back to Michael Jordan, who had been "the most successful athlete endorsement in history" (Strasser and Becklund 1991, 574). This time, Nike (and its ad agency) brought in black film director Spike Lee to simultaneously market black culture and the shoe itself. Nike was no doubt aware of the studies showing that African Americans especially identified with brands that used themes from black culture in their advertisements.[4] Their marketing tactics were a success, and Nike regained supremacy in 1990, with revenues of $2.24 billion.

Over his twenty-two years, Tyson Reed's contribution to that mammoth sum has surely been no more than a tiny fraction of a percent, even though he has always been a Nike loyalist. He played football at Groveland Park and at his high school, and wore Nikes for all his games. The worn and grimy pair that he had on as he cleaned the oven during our conversation was probably left over from his old football days. During his high school years, Tyson was determined to stay in style. He remembered begging his mother for new shoes and clothes, with no success. So Tyson searched around for other ways to get what he wanted. Recall that it was Tyson who asserted in chapter 5: "Your parents give you what you need. And sometime they get you what you want. But when you sell drugs, *you* get you what you wanted." He went on to elaborate on this sentiment: "And then from there, you'on think about my mother. Man, I'on give a fuck if my mother don't never buy me nothin'. I'ma buy myself something."

When he was sixteen, Tyson felt he was a man because he could use his drug profits to buy whatever he wanted. And the first things he wanted were clothes and shoes.

Man, no bullshit, every time I used to mess with [sell] drugs for like one day, I used to make like $1,800. And I'm sixteen making that kinda money. You know what I used to do? I used to go to the mall. I went to the mall one time, I ain't gon' never forget it. Tricked off! Just to talk to some broads. Just to let my homey [friend] talk to some broads. I went, I swear to God, I spent $1,200 on Guess? jeans. Not shorts. On Guess? jeans, that's it. Then I went to Foot Locker and brought [sic] like eight pair of gym shoes. And that ain't shit. I know people now who go in Foot Locker and spend $5,000.

Tyson punctuated his memories of teenage wealth with the intonation of an excited twelve-year-old. He flashed back to the days when he was on top of the style world. He remembered how the drug money and the things he could buy with it were sexy enough not just to get a girlfriend for himself, but to make his friends attractive as well. That's a double-duty dollar.

Tyson eventually got out of the drug business. Since then, he believed, he had gained more respect for money. His impetuous spending sprees were things of the past, but his taste for Nikes was not. Nike need not worry about losing Tyson Reed to financial sobriety, for in him they still had a loyal follower. But with less disposable cash to work with, Tyson had to come up with a new solution to the problem of affording his favorite footwear. Tyson described his new shopping strategy.

If I want some gym shoes, instead of going to Foot Locker and buying one pair of gym shoes, I'll go to one where I know somebody, and get me about four or five pair of gym shoes. So I'll get like a couple pairs free or something.

"Buy one, get three free" was Tyson's new motto. Buy one pair of shoes and get four pairs in the bag. In fact, Tyson's consumer fraud–inspired math was just about right. In 1992, the retail price for a pair of Nike shoes was just about four times what Nike paid for that pair from its Asian manufacturers (Clifford 1992).

Two blocks up a Groveland street, at Neisha Morris's house, a young Tyson was in the making. Neisha's son, Little Tim Ward, was not yet one year old. About the time when some children are repeating simple words like *cat* or *dog,* Tim will be jumping straight to two syllables—*Ni-ke.*

Neisha sat relaxed in her mother's living room, which was fur-
nished with new off-white furniture, a plush brown rug, and a large
painting of a quaint nature scene on the wall. Neisha had taken on
the demeanor of a new mother, affectionately asking, "What's wrong,
Boo?" when Little Tim made any gurgling noise. But she did not miss
a beat as she told me about the neighborhood and her life. In the
privacy of her home, and in the company of women, Neisha lounged
around in just a long faded T-shirt and discolored slippers. This was
a long way from the style she exhibited when she went to Groveland
Park gym. In theory she went to the park to play volleyball, but really
she went there to flirt with the young men who hung around the gym
talking to Spider or Lance. Neisha, her cousin Kima, and their friends
treated volleyball hour like a fashion show—Coach purses, primped
hairstyles, leather coats, Timberland boots, and Nike gym shoes. They
staged grand entrances, they smiled models' smiles, and they walked
with their eyes to the lights.

But when Neisha had Little Tim and got more serious with Big
Tim, her trips to the gym became less frequent. She began to move
into life's next stage—motherhood and girlfriendhood. Neither role
lessened her sense of style, but the energy that she had once put into
keeping *herself* "clean" was now redirected to her son. Little Tim surely
could not understand what he was worth when he was all suited up
in his pricey clothes and gym shoes, but the fashion statements were
worth much more to his mother than what they cost in dollars. Neisha
was proud that the mothers of her generation made sure that their
babies looked good.

You know, I see older people that have kids. They just be lookin'
nasty and dirty, you know. But like our age group, I guess 'cause
maybe we are more materialistic and into things like that or
something, but our age group keep our kids clean, you know.
Everytime I go out the door, unless I'm just really runnin', Tim's
always dressed. Dressed and I'm dressed. And my friends, they
kids be dressed. Even though, like my friend Shauna, her boyfriend [is] not there for her. So she can't really, she buy her baby
gym shoes like once a month. [Whereas] Tim been here for five
months and got seven pair of gym shoes. That don't make no
sense. Every Jordan that done came out from the white ones, to
the black ones, to the black and white ones, the all-black. He
got all four of them plus the Dennis Rodmans and two more

pair of Nikes. And my friends, you know, they might buy they kids shoes once a month. I feel like, you know, some of 'em are under me, you know.

If babies are not even walking at five months, do they really need shoes? They do if shoes are not for walking. Shoes are to gauge who is "under" someone, or who doesn't have it as good. "It's a lotta people that's below average," Neisha judged. "You know, [people] that my mother give my old gym shoes to, or my old clothes to, or they just don't have it. They don't have Nike gym shoes. They don't have this, they don't have that."

The pecking order was clear to Neisha when she looked toward those less fortunate, but she was less able to focus on her own situation. Mrs. Morris had just recently kicked Mr. Morris out of the house. He no longer contributed much to the household bills, and there was Neisha's nine-year-old little brother to take care of (and to outfit in Nikes as well), house payments, car payments, and Little Tim. Mrs. Morris had a stable job, but Neisha was not working (although she received food stamps). And Big Tim's drug business was not something on which Neisha could fully depend. Her situation was not as privileged as she had projected, but she was nonetheless going to get full fashion mileage out of that collection of resources. Her pity for her less-well-off friends became her own words to live by. "It ain't always what you got," she counseled. "It's how you make with what you *do* have."

In using her son to pledge allegiance to the Nike Swoosh, Neisha was only following the lead of the "role models" created by the mass market. Nike is, after all, nearly as venerated as the red, white, and blue itself, and its citizens have proved to be loyal. At the top of the list are the professional athletes, who sometimes make more from their shoe contracts than they make playing their sport. These enormous endorsement contracts ensured that two Nike-ists on the 1992 gold-medal U.S. Olympic basketball team—Michael Jordan and Charles Barkley—would drape the American flag over their shoulders in order to conceal the blasphemous Reebok symbol on their warm-up suits, which they were compelled to wear, since Reebok paid the high price to sponsor the team. But it does not even take millions of dollars to elicit such fanaticism. Nike corporate salespeople—young, fresh, and moderately paid—make sure their clients understand the depths to which they believe in Nike and the eternality of their allegiance. Tattooed on some of their calves, ankles, shoulders, and inner thighs is the Nike Swoosh (Labich and Carvell 1995). It is indeed possible (and perhaps probable) that when Little Tim grows up, he may wear some brand of gym shoe that has not yet even been thought of. But for now, the zealous devotion to Nike exists from the top of its ranks to the very smallest of its disciples.

While Neisha was just following a fad by buying her son Nikes, and Baby Jordan's teammates were less than creative in deciding on a nickname for him, Groveland's Black Mobsters did occasionally push the fashion envelope in their use of brand names.[5] One afternoon, Kareem and Lucky, two Groveland Park regulars and members of the Black Mobsters, walked around the gym looking important in their jobs as Lance's bodyguards. Lucky's outfit was the most obviously coded. Lucky wore a blue Georgetown warm-up suit. When Georgetown basketball players wear their warm-up suits before a game, the message is benign: this is the uniform of Georgetown players, and as a team we all dress alike. At Groveland Park, however, the Georgetown uniform enjoyed added popularity because its colors were the same as the colors of the Black Mobsters. It is unlikely that Georgetown's African American basketball coach, John Thompson—respected for his "uplift the race" views in the area of college sports, but less known as a $200,000-a-year Nike "consultant"—intended for his team's predominantly blue uniforms to correspond to the color scheme of one of Chicago's most notorious gangs. But Thompson should take solace in the fact that Georgetown is not alone; a number of college and professional sports teams are unwitting accessories to the crime of gang-style posturing.[6]

Lucky's simple blue-is-the-color-of-the-Black-Mobsters outfit was a blatant use of popular fashion for locally significant ends. Kareem's fashion statement, on the other hand, took a bit more decoding. On the chest of Kareem's white T-shirt was a blurry picture of Michael Jordan encircled in a cartoonlike border. The caption read, "What's up, Folks?" Recall that the Black Mobsters are a part of the Folks gang nation. In effect, the decal portrayed Michael Jordan issuing the Black Mobster greeting, "What's up, Folks?" Despite this T-shirt's symbolic claim, Michael Jordan is, of course, not a member of the Black Mobsters or the Folks nation. The mere suggestion of gang affiliation is probably an affront to Michael Jordan's wholesome image. But as a popular-culture icon, Michael Jordan's image is prone to manipulation, just as in the more obvious (and less creative) practices of appropriating team colors, cocking a hat to the side, revering Italian gangster movies, or imitating the body language of big-time rappers.

The layers of signification in Kareem's T-shirt, while not immediately apparent, are noteworthy. In 1992, Nike and the National Basketball Association fought over the right to market Michael Jordan's likeness on sports apparel. Initially, Jordan gave sole rights to Nike, which meant that neither Jordan's face nor his likeness could appear on anything that Nike did not make, such as Bulls or Olympic jerseys with the team's picture. By the end of that year, however, Nike and the NBA had reached an agreement to allow the NBA to use Jordan's likeness after all (see Vecsey 1992). It was unlikely, however, that the makers of Kareem's T-shirt cleared their creation with Nike or the NBA. And they were probably not paying royalties to the superstar himself. They had, in essence, stolen Michael Jordan for their own purposes. It was also in 1992, during the Superbowl, that Nike premiered its "Hare Jordan" commercials. The "Hare Jordan" concept teamed Michael Jordan with popular Warner Brothers cartoon characters. There was Bugs Bunny—whose signature saying is, of course, "What's up, Doc?" And there was fellow animated animal Porky Pig, who ends all his shows with, "That's All, Folks." Michael Jordan plus Bugs Bunny plus Porky Pig equals "What's up, Folks?"

Kareem's T-shirt was not one-of-a-kind, but rather represented the Black Mobsters' small-business ventures. It played on the communal adoration of Michael Jordan (especially in Chicago) while simultaneously pledging allegiance to the Black Mobsters. The Black Mobsters' T-shirt business communicated a certain refusal to pay for the use of Jordan's face. Why should Folks pay for Michael Jordan's image when Nike and the NBA (among others) have made it abundantly available for the stealing? After contributing so much to the coffers of both the NBA and Nike, and since they admired him as much as most Americans, the Black Mobsters were determined to make a little money off Michael Jordan themselves. Folks appropriated, repackaged, and redefined all-American Michael Jordan to be an all-American Black Mobster.

POSTSCRIPT

Nike's defeat seems assured by the cycles of capitalism; the only question is when. Revenues for 1994 neared $4 billion, and 1996 revenues surpassed $6 billion, with $550 million in profits. Phil Knight's challenge to his employees to make Nike a $12 billion company by the year 2000 shows that Nike is not going to fall without a fight (Lane

1996). And there will be quite a few challenges. In 1996, Nike lost one of its celebrity endorsers when basketball player Chris Webber decided that the $140 price tag on his signature Nike shoe was just too much to ask young people like the ones in Groveland to pay. Nike seems unaffected by his departure, however. In 1990, the civil rights organization Operation PUSH announced a boycott of Nike (Jackson and Schantz 1993). PUSH charged that Nike did not reciprocate the support that African Americans gave it through their purchases of Nike gear. PUSH claimed that blacks made up 30 percent of Nike's clientele. Nike put the figure somewhere between 10 and 15 percent, and boasted that three-fourths of its yearly $10 million in philanthropy goes to inner-city neighborhoods. The ever-increasing Nike revenue figures suggest that the PUSH boycott has also had little effect (Royko 1990).

In 1995, Reebok and Nike controlled over 40 percent of the global market in athletic footwear, and Phil Knight was the sixth richest person in America. In the year 2005, both giants could be cut down to the mere 10 percent global share (5 percent domestically) to which the once mammoth Adidas has been reduced. Someone will always be on top, and someone will be on the bottom. There will always be money to be made, because there will always be fashion battles to be won on the streets of Groveland. Tyson Reed explained it with profound simplicity.

> With kids, I would say, nowadays, regardless of if your parents own Sony, or regardless if your parents work for Sony, or regardless if your parents buy tapes from Sony, e'rybody and they mama gon' be listening to the same thing, wearing Jordans. If you po' you gon' have on Jordans. If you rich you gon' have on Jordans. If you middle class you gon' have on Jordans. Your parents buy 'em when you rich, you gon' have 'em. If you middle class, you work for 'em and you get 'em. If you po', you sell dope, you gon' have 'em.

The race to stay in style by whatever means continues. At present, those young Grovelandites with the Swoosh on their feet are in the lead.

It is not enough to investigate the economic and spatial contexts in which Groveland youth are embedded. The cultural context is crucial to fully understanding the crossroads that black middle-class youth face, the "street" and "decent" balancing act that they perform, and the diverse trajectories that their lives take. Nike is just one part of the popular-culture and mass-market context. There is nothing so peculiar about the company that it should warrant a full chapter of discussion, except for the fact that it reigned over other sneaker brands during the time of my research. Yet a similar point could be made about any number of fashion or consumer items: there is a local discourse that surrounds the act of purchasing and the act of showcasing the latest styles. Styles are generated by the strong messages delivered in advertising, and transformed through local processes of redefinition. It is clear that Nike has made a strategic pitch to the African American community, especially its youth, and that Nikes have in turn been incorporated into a dialogue of symbols that matter for courtship, for self-esteem, for aesthetic enjoyment, for gang affiliation, and for distinction-making in Groveland. The fashion trends are also a part of the "ghetto trance" discussed in the previous chapter. Groveland youth grow up within a popular-culture milieu that targets them as consumers and inundates them with exciting images of the gangsta lifestyle. White youth receive the same messages, but the *interaction* of popular culture with the economic and spatial realities of the black middle class (and of course the black poor) imbues the gangsta image with more serious repercussions for black youth.

❽

William "Spider" Waters, Jr.
Straddling Two Worlds

The purpose of presenting a first-person case study is to see the world through the eyes of someone in Groveland, using his or her unique perspective to illuminate key social mechanisms. Stanley's narrative in Clifford Shaw's 1966 classic, *The Jack-Roller,* gave some substance to popular sociological theory. The major variables of social disorganization theory—neighborhood heterogeneity, residential instability, economic distress, and family breakup—were all parts of Stanley's delinquent childhood. In the same way, the African American "self-portraits" in John Gwaltney's (1980) *Drylongso* infuse theoretical perspectives on race, class, and gender with character and emotion. Following in this tradition, William Waters, Jr.—or "Spider," as he is known in the neighborhood—provides insight into the issues discussed throughout this book.

Spider was the "Stanley" (Shaw 1966), or the "Doc" (Whyte 1943), or the "Herman" (Anderson 1978), or the "Tally" (Liebow 1967) of this research.[1] His longtime residence in Groveland—he was born in 1961, and moved to Groveland in 1965—his job at Groveland Park, and most of all his gregarious personality make him a friend to many. He also works at the Chicago Mercantile Exchange in downtown Chicago—"The Merc," in his shorthand—making him familiar with a world outside of Groveland. Like the now-infamous informants before him, Spider is notable not because he so perfectly personifies the average Grovelandite. To the contrary, his peculiarities and inconsistencies are what make him such an interesting person to learn from. He tells and revels in incredibly violent stories, while he treats most people with impressive kindness. He has a filthy mouth, yet scolds the younger boys for merely talking too loudly when the church people use Groveland Park for their Bible study. He smokes a lot of marijuana, seems never to miss a day of work, and sometimes works on his day off. He uses heavy Black English, but claims that two of his

167

three best friends are white. As the black middle class seems to stand between the black poor and the white middle class, Spider similarly straddles both worlds.

Spider loves to tell stories. After an evening at Groveland Park in his company, I always returned home with a head full of detailed and colorful narratives, which I labored to recover with some precision, but I rarely succeeded. The taped interview I did with him late in the research allowed me to be truer to his own language and emphasis.[2] But while the stories in this chapter are drawn primarily from the taped interview, I had already heard many of them during more than three years of field work. Spider is one of the few people about whom I truly feel "saturated" with information, having heard some stories more than three or four times. This repetition assures me that either Spider is an expert liar (and has convinced his friends to corroborate), or he really has done and experienced the things he talks about.

How much Spider's descriptions match the actual details of a particular event is another matter. Clifford Shaw (1966, 3) introduces Stanley's narrative by remarking, "It is not expected that the [subject] will necessarily describe his life-situations objectively. On the contrary, it is desired that his story will reflect his own personal attitudes and interpretations." There is surely much exaggeration, posturing, omission, and manipulation in what people tell themselves about themselves, and even more in what they tell others. Spider's rendition of his life is no different. But it adds excitement and drama to my own otherwise "objective" academic tale. Many of my points about geography and migration, adolescent temptation and rebellious thrills, Black English, black middle-class balancing, and generational change are represented in Spider's story, and in Terri Jones's narrative in the following chapter. But with my editorial comments left to a minimum and relegated to the endnotes, I hope to encourage readers to draw their own parallels to theory and experience.

FAMILY DISCIPLINE

My mother from Mississippi. My father from same [place] where Clinton from—Little Rock, Arkansas. But my father, he don't like to say that 'cause Clinton the president, and, "I smoke[d] weed but I didn't inhale." Get the fuck outta here you dork. [My father came up to Chicago] when he got out

the army I guess, yeah. My older sister Benetta and my younger sister Beatrice, we went to Mississippi for two years. When we was kids in Mississippi we slept with our doors open, front and back. Well I mean we locked the back door and we just close the front door. You ain't have to lock it.

My grandmother made us go to church. And you in Mississippi, you got on that little bitty salt-and-pepper suit, with the tie. You sweatin'. And you got this little fan. You fannin', and you ain't fannin' nothing but hot air. 'Cause see in Mississippi the church is different 'cause you get to singin' and, you know, they be feedin' you good. Everything was fresh. Last year I went to Mississippi to see my grandmother before she passed away.

[Up here] my mother used to go to church. I forgot, it's somewhere on, some big church on Highland [Avenue] or somethin'. I'on ["I don't"] remember. I ain't like it. It was boring. See when I was a kid, my mother used to make me go to church and when you start making me do something, I'on like doin' it. When I was a kid she made me, but when I got to a certain age I used to ask her, "Do I have to go to church?" She said, naw. Awright, I stopped going. I mean, I got a Bible. I read my Bible e'ry now and again. I ain't touched it in ten years, I ain't gon' lie to you. But I'm like this: I believe in God, yeah. . . .

. . . I was the oldest boy. Ooooh, I got my ass beat. Child abuse, shit. I woulda been the poster boy for child abuse I got my ass whooped [whipped] so many times. I mean, my mother whooped me with a' extension cord, Hot Wheel, them Hot Wheel racetracks, shit. Just 'cause I was the oldest boy. And [my father] used to beat my ass for fuckin' up in school, gettin' suspended from school, throwin' erasers and eggs at teachers. I'd erase the chalkboard and scrape all the stuff down and I'll go up to this girl. I go, "I bet I'll make your face turn white."

She goes, "Get outta here, Spider. You so damn stupid."

I said, "Naw, naw, serious, serious." And I get mad too. I be like, "Naw, serious, serious. I bet I could make your face turn white. It's magic."

She like, "Okay." She'll sit there.

And I go [snaps his fingers], "Bam, your face is white."

She be like, "You stupid ass. My face ain't white."

And then I blow all the chalk in her face. I go, "It is now." Get in her eye, she start crying, I get suspended.

I'm a kid, and you want me to take this gold slip that says, "William acted real silly in class today." And I'm supposed to take this home to my father? Now I think I was weighin' about sixty pounds in grammar school—well I think I got up to ninety when I was in eighth grade—but in fifth and sixth and seventh grade. I'm supposed to take this gold slip of paper home and show it to my father and then get my ass beat?

When I got in the eighth grade that's when he stopped whoopin' me. I was gon' kill him one night. And I told him this too. I told him this about two years ago. I was standin' over him like this with a' eight-inch butcher knife. Hell, he was 'sleep. I wouldn'ta did it no other way, shit. Then, I said, fuck it. I went back, I put it back in the kitchen and I went back to sleep. And then when I got older I told him. I said, "Man, I was gon' kill you one night, Will. For real." I said, "Man, you had beat my ass so bad, man, and it felt like somethin' was burnin' on the inside." . . .

. . . When my mother and father got divorced, my father made sure her house was paid for. He drives a limo. My mother and father, they was workaholics like me. We wasn't rich, we wasn't poor, but we wasn't, we, you know. My father moved [to a north suburb] because he said it was a lotta crime here in the city. They broke into our house. I came home [from work one day] to put me on some blue jeans, 'cause you know you couldn't wear jeans [at the Merc]. So I put on blue jeans and a nice T-shirt or something. Get home, it's a nice sunny day. It's broad daylight. It's about 12:30. I walk into the house, sit down. [I'm thinking] my brother and his girlfriend musta got into a real fight. Man, they trashed this fuckin' place. But you know how you walk past somethin', or they show you in the little cartoon, "Somethin' is missin'. Figure it out." But you can't figure out what. So I go, fuck it. I go on downstairs to my room. I go downstairs in the basement. They done kicked my door off the hinges. And I'm like, wait a minute, I know I locked my door when I left this mornin'. So we had these little windows that opened up from the bottom like this. It was part my fault too 'cause the windows was dry rottin'. I had money in the bank. I shoulda went and bought the glass windows, block windows like I said I was gon' do. They kicked the window in. They took my brother's TV, his VCR. They took my TV and my VCR. They took two gold chains, a couple gold nuggets, and a gold ring. Now, I had a thousand dollars under my waterbed mattress [that they didn't get]. I got some Altec speakers in my basement right now. They like, they 'bout $800 apiece. They ain't take them 'cause they was too heavy. They ain't touch my stereo. They just took my TV and my VCR.

So, I just went down to the bank. I took out, what, $700 out the bank and went to Hardy's Glass. I took three days off work. 'Cause my boss was, "Man, you gotta come in." "Man, fuck you and yo' ["your"] job. This mufucka broke in my house. If my family ain't secure, I ain't secure. You could fire me. Do what the fuck you wanna do, but I'm finna ["fixing to," i.e., "going to"] put these glass-block windows in this house."

But, I figure [moving because of crime is] just an excuse. 'Cause I'on care where you go, you gon' find crime. You gon' find it's everywhere, you know what I'm sayin'. But this, the last straw that broke the camel's back. When my father moved he bought a LeSabre. I think a '79 LeSabre. Him and my uncle, they rebuilt the engine. It ran good. It ran great. This was like in 'bout '81, '82. And then he got drunk one night. So he was rentin' a room from some lady on [South] Michigan [Avenue]. Now, she got a two-car garage, so I guess he was so fucked up he ain't wanna put that car in the garage. Or he was that lazy he ain't feel like doin' it. Some kids stole the car. He had like a bookbag, all his electric equipment in there—an electric toolbelt and alla ["all of"] that shit—briefcase, leather jacket. They stole the car, they took everything, they totaled the car. And that was the last straw. And he said, fuck it. He went and bought him a house in the suburbs. He probably moved there in '81. Yeah '81, '82, yeah.[3] But before he moved, he paid for my mother's house, and then that's when he moved. I liked it. It's quiet out there. Then, when it got too quiet, I come back out South for some good ol' South Side violence. Hear some guns shootin' off in the alley behind the crib. Damn, I feel at home.

EARLY NEIGHBORHOOD EXPERIENCES

We moved in this neighborhood in 19, I'd say about 1965. 'Cause see we lived on, okay where's that [nightclub] the Blues? It's about on Northern and Ridge. We used to live down there.[4] And that's when the Blackstone Rangers [gang] was real rough over there so my mother and father worked extra hard to buy the house over here in Groveland. My father, some days he was a butcher, he was electrician, he was mechanic, he was everything to get that house for us to live in. Like back in the day, when we was growin' up, say for instance when I was a freshman at Franklin [High School]. The people at Franklin didn't like us 'cause they had this mentality. They go, "Y'all think y'all better than us." So we would separate ourselves from those guys. 'Cause, you know, our parents would go the extra length. "Ma, ma, you know, I want the new Converses that came out." They'll try to work extra hours to see you got the Converse, keep you happy. You keep your grades up, they get you what you want, you know. And it's a few apartments around here, but it's more houses around here. Now when you go over [north of here] it's a lotta apartments over there. A lotta people was on drugs and, I mean, they used to chase us home every day.

But see as far as us growin' up, it was like I can come over to your house, your parents would feed me, you know. I could take my bath. I had somewhere to sleep. If I disrespect your parents, both your mother and father had the authority from my parents to whoop my ass if I got outta line. See when we was growin' up we was all together. You know, we got, we still got whites livin' in this neighborhood. The Japanese people still own that house right there on the corner, the Sasakis. 'Cause it was like a close-knit community. Well this how it was when we were the second black family on our block. We had Irish, Japanese, all kind of everybody. And if ain't nobody at [my house], the Irish, Mr. O'Brien, he was always at home. And he eat cabbage and cornbeef, you know, that's all they ate. And we ate that. And then when it's 8:00, no 8:30, you was in the bed, period. You don't wanna go to sleep, he whoop yo' butt. Then when my father come home the next day, he'll come down there and get us. Well [Mr. O'Brien] already had clothes for us, dress us, we go to school. Or Larry, he would take us to school. He had a '57 Chevy. He used to drive us to school. Then when you get home, my father'd ask, "Hey Mr. O'Brien, how did Spider 'n'em ["and them"] do?"

"Aw, they behaved real good. I ain't have no problems out of 'em."

"Good, good."

But see like as far as me growin' up, race didn't play no effect in our neighborhood. 'Cause race is taught. Racism is taught to kids. Like when we was kids growin' up around on Poplar Street. Man, we runnin' around in the streets. And if you come in like the Sasakis' house, if the wife is makin' dinner, hey, you could come in there and eat. You know, you go in the bathroom, you wash your hands, you sit down, you say your grace, then you eat. And it wasn't no, well we had a few that said, "Whatchu doin' up here. Yo' kind don't come up here." "What the fuck you mean our kind?" Then you look, then you go, "Yeah my skin is darker than his, and his hair straight and mine kinda nappy, but what make him better than me?" Then you see [a white] kid run and fall, "Man, look, his blood same color as mine. So what make him different from me?" That's what I couldn't never understand.

See back when we was growin' up, I was always taught: Yes ma'am, no ma'am. Yes sir, no sir. You speak when spoken to. You come when called. You go to somebody else's house, you don't want nothin', don't touch nothin', don't ask for nothin'. You go on out in the world here with me and embarrass me, you gon' get it twice as worse when you get home. And everybody knew everybody. It wasn't like, "Oh well who is that?" You know, people come over, they welcome us to the neighborhood.

GANGS AND TROUBLE

I go with my gut instinct. 'Cause I used to sneak outta my house with my friends to get out here to learn these streets. 'Cause I feel like this: the world to me is just like a jungle, you know what I'm sayin'. You got yo' prey, and you got yo' predator. . . .

. . . I say, I ain't got no gang problem [at Groveland Park]. I'on know what you talkin' about. Ain't no gangs up here. You know, ain't no graffiti. Niggas ain't gettin' shot up in here. What they talkin' 'bout I got a gang problem? I mean, I ain't gon' tell nobody they gotta go. I got kids that come to our programs. Ain't no gang problem here. I ain't a part of a gang. I'm a part of a' organization. Society, they put that on. They put that label on you. I say a gang ain't organized. They just go out and do stupid shit. And see, I feel like this too, I mean, I show anybody love, any gang. It don't bother me. Like them KBs [King Boas] used to come up to Groveland Park. I'd be like, "KB, what up?" They favorite line is "Peace out." I hate that shit, "Peace out, man." [So instead] I be like, "Awright, my brotha."

But see people don't understand that organization always existed. 'Cause see I figure it's like this—just like in California—it's like it go down from generation to the next generation. And that's it. See first it grew from [when] we was "G City Mobsters," the kids. Some people knew. It's just like now. I'on know nothin'. You'on see nothin'. I ain't hear nothin'. I'on know nothin'. Two and two is eight. Like that's how you would play it.[5] 'Cause we was like in seventh grade. And then you had the older guys that was in eighth grade. We call them Sweathogs. 'Cause if they catch you by yo'self, they just beat the shit out you. I mean they don't hit you all in the face. Just hit you in the body, in yo' thigh and in yo' arms and in yo' chest. And that's as far as it went. Wasn't nobody threatenin' nobody, people shootin' at people with guns and all. It wasn't never like that.

Lance grew up with my sister. He used to come over [to] my house. Him and my sister and my auntie was [friends] like that. They was good friends. They all went to school together. We knew him 'cause his little brother Lucky and all us, we all went to school together. And [Lance] was his older brother. It was just that his age group that was growin' up was way wilder. They was like more advanced than us. It's just something that went down, and he accepted that, and it was just like that. He made a decision in his life and that decision wasn't forced upon him. He chose that decision.[6] Just like I made the decision to do what I wanna do. That's, I'on bother nobody, I'on want you botherin' me. So, if you do somethin' to me, I'ma try to do somethin' to you. 'Cause see

people don't understand it's a business. You seen the movie
King of New York? Just like Frank White.[7]

So we all knew each other. But if you got outta line, everybody know who you could go to talk to. I mean everybody
tried to make it out like [Lance] was this monster and all. It
wasn't even nothin' like that. And my father knew [about all
this]. My father was like, "Dude." He said, "I have taught you.
You know right from wrong." He said, "I mean, you got sense
enough to know, 'Okay, here's a gun. Go shoot dude.' 'I'on
wanna do that.' 'Why?' ' 'Cause that ain't right. I mean dude
ain't did nothin' to me. I'on know dude.' " And see that's really
why Lance really likeded me and Vince growin' up around
here. 'Cause ever since Big Lance knew me, I always worked
with my uncle and had a hustle, and kept money in my
pocket. He knew I smoked weed. He didn't like it, but ain't
nothin' you can do. You can't tell me what to do.

'Cause, see, we felt like this: this is our home and whatever
happen, we gon' defend it to the death. Period. Like most of
the parks you go to you see graffiti all over the walls everywhere. We ain't have that up here. See when we was growin'
up, we catch you writin' on this park, first thing we do is
surround you. And we go, Why you doin' this? Why you de-
facin' the property? And they couldn't answer. They just look.
Well what you cryin' for? We ain't did nothin' to you yet. Why
you cryin'? Why are you writin' on the building? Now stop
crying 'cause we still gon' whoop yo' ass. I'on care how many
tears you shed. We gonna whoop yo' ass and send you home.
Or we'll whoop yo' ass and we'll take you home. Hey, yo' son
was finna deface the park, so we whooped his ass and we
brought him home. Now yo' father get outta line, we gon'
whoop his ass. And if he whoop our ass, we gon' go get somebody bigger that's gon' whoop his ass.

[Once] we was comin' up here [to Groveland Park]. Awright, this what happened. I got shot. My buddy Clifton Tiller,
he got shot. We was comin' up here to go swimming. We was
in our teens, yeah, about sixteen, seventeen. 'Cause see it was
all our group. We comin' up here to go swimming. It was
about twenty guys [not from the neighborhood] come zoomin'
through here on bikes. You know, we was like, Damn! Like
a fuckin' bike-a-thon and shit. So it's two guys that's strag-

gling. I don't know if they bringing up the pack or what. But one of the guys in our group named Hakeem, he said something. So dude stopped his bike right there at the entrance of the park. Dude stops his bike, gets off his bike, and put the kickstand down. So, me, Tiller, and Ivy, we look at each other. It was me, Tiller, Ivy, Warren McNair, my sister, ah, who else was with us? This guy named Paul somethin'. And some more of us. It was about nine, ten of us. Maybe fifteen. Dude stopped his bike and like, "Watchu wanna do?"

[I'm thinkin'] "Aw, dude, you finna get yo' ass whooped, mufucka. You's just a superhero. You and yo' boy." 'Cause as long as I've been growin' up my father always told me like this: Don't hit nobody unless they hit you. Don't go around lookin' for no fight. If you don't bother nobody, they shouldn't bother you. But if trouble come your way, hey, I'm just gonna accept it and whatever happens, it happens. I'm not finna run from nobody.

But his boy kept tellin' him, "Man, get on the bike. Let's ride. Let's ride. Fuck that." So my boy Ivy standin' next to me. Warren McNair was in the middle. I was standin' here. Ivy was standing there. So when Ivy swung a chain [dude] duck[ed]. And when I punched him, then that's when his boy upped the .25 automatic.

Now, he coulda killed us if he wanted to. That's how close he was. But you could tell dude ain't wanna do no damage 'cause he was shootin' at the ground. And the bullet ricocheted and it hit me in the leg. It just ricocheted off the ground and hit me. I ain't even know I was hit. I pulled it out myself. It was alright. But Clifton Tiller, my buddy, he had the bullet. I just got hit with like a fragment. Clifton Tiller had one wedged in his shin. They was gon' have to cut his leg off. Who else? Ah yeah, Floyd Riggs. He got shot. And Warren McNair, when he turnt to run, the bullet ricocheted off the ground, hit him in the butt and went across his testes and came out through the other side. So, he leant on the wall, he stuck his hand down in his pants. Then he came up, he sees a hand full of blood, and he just passed out. Then we all went to the hospital. 'Cause Mr. Leonard—he on the [Groveland Park] Advisory Council—he came out there and, you know, he had some kind of towel. The ambulance and the police was over here like that [quickly]. And, you know, didn't nobody die from it.

EDUCATIONAL POTENTIAL

I got a good education from Groveland [Grammar School]. The only activity my father really encouraged, "Mufucka, you finna bring all yo' books home. Think you a smart-ass." 'Cause I was like the class clown, and the teachers used to tell my parents. I'm I'm I'm real hyper. That's why I smoke a lotta weed. It keeps me calm. And when I was going to school, teachers would give me work and I would finish it. Then I'd act [like] a goddamn fool. And they be like, "You cheated."

"I don't, I didn't cheat."

Like my physics teacher at Franklin [High School]. He was like, "You cheated."

I go, "I didn't have to cheat."

"Well, how did you, how did you finish this?"

I go, "I went home, I read the whole book."

He goes, "Why'd you do that?"

I go, "I ain't have no choice."

"What do you mean you didn't have a choice?"

"Well when yo' father standin' over you, and he lookin' like God, and you just this little bitty creature like this. And you lookin' up at him." And my oldest sister, he gave her permission to whoop my ass if I fuck up. So in grammar school I had to bring my reading book home, my spelling book. What else you get? Reading, spelling, math, science, what else, ah, spelling. And what's that other big red, the dictionary. I had to bring each, all them books home.

When I went to Franklin, Vince was in my class, and this guy named Neck. My teacher thought I was cheatin' offa Neck and Vince. I go, "I'm much smarter than both of them." And this is physics. And I took the whole book home. And back in grammar school, from me fuckin' up, and [my father] makin' me bring all my books home, I got into that cycle. So, I would read a chapter, like try to read a chapter every hour 'till about 9:00 [P.M.]. Then I go to sleep. So the physics teacher—Mr. Krumkowski at Franklin—he sit me over in a corner. He took all my books away from me, and he said, "Here, it's a double period. You should be finished during the second period." I finished in the first period. He took the test. He looked at it. He graded it. He was like, "You cheated." He looked at my hand.

I go, "Dude, I ain't have to cheat."

He go, "Well how did you know all this?"

I go, "I read the book."

"You read this whole book?"

I go, "Yeah."

"Why?"

I go, "I ain't have a choice. My father made me do it."

And then he would say, he straight told me, he goes, "You not even supposed to be in this class. You'on belong in this class."

I was like, "Why?"

"You belong in the Honors Class or something."

So I was goin' to school at the Shedd Aquarium. He set something up and sent the papers down there. They go, "Yeah, you right." So, I would take my woodshop like in the morning. Then my last class was supposed to have been physics, but I would take biology. And once I finish biology, they would send him the tokens and stuff. So, man, I'll just catch the bus to the Shedd Aquarium.

I used to love bio [too]. My teacher, what's his name? Dr. Pallat. He said I shoulda been a doctor. 'Cause me [and] this chick named Stephanie—she had good handwriting, so I made her my [dissection] partner. 'Cause she wasn't touchin', she was screamin'. So, I told my teacher, I said, "I wanna cut my frog open alive."

He was like, "What? Are you sick?"

I said naw. So, he gave me the ah, whatchu call that? The formaldehyde or whatever you put in the jar. Put the frog in there and put another thing on top. And he jumpin' around all crazy. Then all the sudden, he slow down. It knocks him out. Then, I take him and pin him on that little pan with the tar. And then he goes, "You gotta be very careful with the scalpel." 'Cause if you just dig in, you gonna fuck up all the internal organs. So, I just took it and all you gotta do is touch it. And I gently glide it across. Then, I opened it up, and this shit fascinated me. I was like, damn! Then, you know, you could see the spleen and the heart. Then you draw your little diagram. And I draw what I saw. Then, she'll take her little notes and I'll be explaining. It lived for two days, and [then] it died.

I wanted to go to college but I really couldn't afford it. And I really wasn't gon' put all that pressure on my mother and father. And plus I wanted to get out here in the workforce and try to make it on my own. So my friend got me a job at the Merc. Then I took it from there.

IN THE WORKFORCE

I'ma tell you this about my friends around here. Outta me, Vince, who else? Ricky Hughes, Pat. Okay, I work at the Park District and at the Merc. Vince work at the park. Ricky Hughes, he work construction somewhere. Mitch Adams, who live right down there, he a butcher and he work at some factory. And my boy Pat—'cause his cousin Clifton Tiller was like my brother—Pat a Chicago Police [officer]. Outta all the people that graduated from Groveland [Grammar School], we the only five people that I could count that graduated. Well, Vince ain't graduated with us. Really, he just moved into the neighborhood. Outta us four guys, we the only four people with legitimate jobs and ain't strung out on drugs. Everybody else in our neighborhood, all my other friends that grew up around Groveland when we was kids growin' on up till now, they either dead, in jail for murder—I'm talkin' about with life sentences, never seein' this side of daylight. And it's some people now that I see when I drive to the Merc. I park on Greene Street and that's some kinda Christian League over there, and it's a halfway house for drug addicts. And it's a lotta people over there that I know, but they don't remember me.

And Big Jimmy live down [the street from me]. His mother worked in the personnel department at General Motors. And I asked, "Man, Big Jimmy, why don't you get me a job?"

"Man, you'on wanna work."

And then like Mr. Albright, I asked him, "Yeah, can I have a job?"

And he was like, "Man, you'on wanna work. You runnin' around with the gangs and shit."

It would dawn on me. I be like, "Damn, this shit amazes me how so many mufuckas know what I want."

And that's what really motivated me to work. So I said,

fuck it. My father's friend Fred called me. He was like, "Man, I can't get you no job, but I can get you on the [trading] flo'." And basically I sold myself. I worked from '79 to '80 for Woodstock, this company called Woodstock. The guy who owned the company saw me walkin' through the office one day. He said, "What's yo' name?"

I said, "William Waters, Jr."

And he's a' old rich dude. I guess he was lonely. I'on know what the fuck his problem was. He wasn't gay or nothin' 'cause I ain't play that shit. He was like, "You drink beer?"

I said, "Yeah."

"Sit, sit down right here." He'll give me some trading cards: "Here, count this up and sit there. Have a few beers and you watch TV, whatever you want." So I be up there watching TV. Mufuckas down there workin' like slave dogs. Then all the sudden he say, "You got a license."

I go, "Yeah."

"Go get my car." I go across the street to Reuben and get his car. And then I would take him somewhere down Madison [Street] west to some detox place and he's stayin' there. I go to sleep from eight to twelve. Then I take him to some bar. Park in the front. He'll give me a hundred dollars and tell me go home. And I go home. He be like, "Here, catch a cab home."

That's when I worked for Woodstock. 'Cause Rich Graff and Marty Graff owned Woodstock. So when '81 came, they laid me off. Or, naw, Marty and Rich sold the company. They got bought out by Merrill Lynch. I knew I was outta there. So I said, fuck it. I just grabbed a handfulla trading cards, writing my name and number down [and giving them to people at the Merc].

For two weeks I hung around [Groveland] with Vince's brother Slice. And I was like, "Damn these mufuckas." I couldn't stand it. 'Cause I'm so used to wakin' up early in the morning, going to work. I couldn't stand it.

[My neighbors now] be like, "Damn, boy. You sho' be goin' to work, don't you?"

I go, "Yeah."

"Boy, you ain't get home last night till three, but you goin' to work. I admire that in you."

I go, "Well, you can't sit up on your ass and do nothin'.

Ain't nobody gon' give you nothin'." That's what my father said, "Boy, ain't nobody gon' give you nothin'."

So I said, fuck it. I'm going back to the workforce. I went down there [to the Merc] and this Jewish guy name', what was his name? Ah, Harry Rosen or Harry Rosenthal or somethin' like that. Little short Jewish dude with the full beard and the hair. Look like a rabbi. Or he look like a mountain man. So Harry called me one summer. It was hot outside on a Friday, about 10:30. He said, "Man, we busy. I need a phone clerk. I talked to a lotta people down here. They say you come, you do work. You have a' attitude problem."

I go, "Yes, I do. But it's a small one and it's very much in control."

And he goes, "Yeah, I know." He goes, "Alla the people that I talked to, they say you do have a' attitude problem. But as far as your work go, you's a great, good worker." He goes, "When can you get here?"

I said, "Well, when do you need me?"

He goes, "Well, I really need you today."

I think on my feet pretty quick. So I'm lookin' outside. I said [to myself], "Damn, the sun out. I wanna kick it, get some beer, smoke some weed, fuck with the ladies and shit. You know, a nigga wanna kick it and shit. Fuck it." So, I'm thinkin' real fast. I said to myself, "Well, if I'on take this job, he gon' hire somebody else 'cause he gon' figure I ain't enthusiastic to work." I said [to the employer], "Well it's ten, ten o'clock." I said, "I can be down there before twelve."

He said, "Okay, I'll see you at twelve." And he hung up the phone.

I jump in the shower. I'm walkin' down Poplar Street, I see one of my homeys. He's like, "Man, where you goin'?"

I said, "Man, I got a job interview."

He said, "Man, get yo' ass in the car." He drove me all the way to the Dan Ryan [train stop]. Got there, the train was coming. Caught the train and went there to work.

He got me on the [trading] flo'. Got me a coat, got me a badge. I got on the floor with the little pencil protector and shit, pocket protector in your pocket. Got the pen. I'm writing orders. You know, he listenin' on the phone. He seeing how I'm writing orders. He like, "Damn." So after the first order, he ain't listen no more. You just listen and you take whatever the customer tell you, time stamp it, send it out. And you look at the [trading] board, see what his order should be filled. So at the end of the day, I told him too. I said, "You know it was hot outside. It's Friday, it's about 80 [degrees]. I wasn't gon' come in. I was gon' tell you can I come in Monday. But I was thinkin' if I woulda told you I was gon' come in Monday, you woulda figured that I wasn't enthusiastic to work. And I figured you woulda hired somebody else."

He said, "Will, you must be a fuckin' genius or a mind-reader because if you wouldn't have came in today, I most definitely had somebody lined up to take your place."

I worked at Tabor from '81 to '91 and then they laid me off when me and my father bought a house in Hanover Park.[8] 'Cause the white guy came to me. I, you know, I go with my gut feeling. I sensed it. I knew it was coming. 'Cause I'm like this: Me and you can work together, we could get along. I can work for a man. I could work for a woman. But I'ma be me. I'm not gon' kiss nobody's ass. I'ma be the same crazy fool. I'on care. But I'ma do my job to the best of my ability. And he was like, "Close the door."

I said, "Man, I ain't got nothin' to hide from Ruby." Ruby was the keypuncher. I go, "Dude, if you got something to say, say it. Am I laid off, or am I fired?"

He goes, "Well, I'm sorry, Will. We gotta lay you off."

I go, cool, stuck my hand out. I shook his hand. I go, "Harry, you have a nice day." And I left.

And he standin' there scratchin' his head 'cause I was supposed to be this dumb, black, ignorant kid from the South Side. First thing I was supposed to do is start throwin' desks and shit out the window. [If I had done that] Blam! They hit the button, call security up there. The police downtown comin' like that. Nigga go to jail, he lost his job. [Plus,] "Oh, you gotta pay for that window." They gave me, they gave me $5,000, and they paid for my unemployment.

Once I got laid off [from the Merc] in '91, that's when Ms. Charles was up here [at Groveland Park]. She like, "You should go on and get your degree." So me and Vince, we started going to Oliver [sic] Harvey.[9] The park would reimburse you if you passed the class. We passin' the class with As and they never reimbursed. I said, fuck it, I'll pay for the class out my own pocket. So, I'm four hours short of my [associate's] degree in physical fitness. 'Cause I was gon' get a *B* in swimming but I say, "Man, why you givin' me a *B*?" I could swim backwards but I don't like swimming backwards.

He said, " 'Cause you got to learn how."

'Cause I gotta get this plug 'cause too much water go in my nose, and that shit be burnin'. I asked the teacher, I said, "What's my grade?"

He said, "A *B*."

"What the hell you mean a *B*, man? I was one of the best swimmers in this class."

"You ain't swimmin' backwards, Mr. Waters."

So me and Vince went right out there to Sportmart and we got us one of them things for your nose.

Then [in '93], the guy who I worked for at Tabor [called me], Tom Anderson. I trained his little brother when he came. And me and him used to always talk. He go, "Man, one day I'ma have my own business." That's how we used to talk. Yeah, we got people workin' for us. Kick it back, coolin' out. So, me and him stayed in touch when he left and went back to [college] and graduated. 'Cause, you know, he grew up in Arizona. He know all about basketball, 'cause he used to kick my ass every trip. And I was bigger than him. He a little thin white boy. And, you know, his father was in the cattle business, so that's why he knew a lot. So he kept saying, "Man, I'ma get some big customers. Man, I want you to work for me." He said, "I'll take care of you, Will."

I said, "I know you will, Tom." 'Cause to me he like a good friend. He like my brother. Him, his wife, I mean they loaned me, they gave me $700 so I could put a down payment on my truck. And I paid it. Real close.

He called me in November [of '93], naw October. I said I'm not comin' down. He called me in November. I said I'm not comin' back down there. And then November, December passed. And I kept lookin' at my checks from the park. Damn, my shit short. So I went to Ms. C., "Ms. C., this shit ain't right."

She go, "Yes it is."

So I go, "Fuck it."

Then he called me in January. He go, "Will, since I've been callin' you I done fired seven people 'cause they don't know a hole in the ground. Dude don't know where his head or his asshole is." The customer call, want you to read the board. This was up on the board. All you gotta do is give 'em the high, low, and the last. It's easy. The high, 69, ah, 6980. What's the low? 6940. What's the last? 6910. Mark it down 30 or whatever. That's all they wanna hear. So he goes, "You comin' down, Will?" He was like, "Man, I'll start you off with $10 an hour."

I go, "Man, I'll be there Monday." And I been back ever since—7 [A.M.] to 2 [P.M.]. Soon as I leave there, I just come straight [to the park]. Have all my stuff in the truck.

You work hard. I mean, we all do. Everybody wants that American Dream where I want a nice car. I want a nice house. I want a pretty girlfriend. I want to have kids and all this. 'Cause I see myself gettin' married. I would like to have a son, but it would scare the shit outta me. Children would change me. 'Cause see like, what's that little sayin' they have in Africa? It take the whole village to raise a child.

CONCLUSION

The collage of stories just presented is only a fraction of what I learned from Spider over the course of the field work. He conveyed sincere affection for his white friends at work and black friends in the neighborhood, and he sometimes mixed the two. He was proud of working two jobs. He eagerly talked about his daily routine at the Merc.[10] Once, Spider's Groveland friend Lucky challenged his allegiance to the neighborhood because Spider always spoke so highly of his white friends at the Merc. Addressing Spider as a fellow Black Mobster, Lucky asked, "Folks, you like them mufuckas, don't you? You always talkin' about 'em. You like them mufuckas?" Lucky's tone indicated that an affirmative answer may be blasphemous to racial and neighborhood solidarity. Yet Spider replied with confidence, using his best imitation of a proper, highbrow accent. "Some of my best friends are white, Lucky." Spider was able to maintain loyalty to both worlds, continuing his dual identity as Spider in the neighborhood and William (or Will) at the Merc. As a result, Spider displayed a degree of cultural dexterity that some of his neighborhood friends often did not understand.

There are many residents who stand more firmly than Spider in their middle-class status, speaking little or no Black English, having little contact with the characters that Spider described in his story, topping Spider's impressive stock investments, and having to work only one well-paying job to live at the level of comfort that Spider works fourteen-hour days to attain. At the other extreme, there are those who are much less fortunate, with no job—much less two; no family home that is paid for and a getaway house in the suburbs; and no excess cash to quickly recoup after a break-in. Again, Spider's negotiation of his identities as a gang member and an employee on the floor of the Chicago Mercantile Exchange might be extreme, but in its unconventionality it illustrates a number of practices, feelings, and experiences that characterize the lives of less eccentric Groveland residents.

9

Typical Terri Jones

Whereas William "Spider" Waters is remarkable for his idiosyn-
crasies, Terri Jones is most striking in her ordinariness.[1] She and
Spider are nearly the same age, and their neighborhood perspectives
complement one another. They attended the same elementary school,
they both were involved in Groveland Park recreational activities, and,
ironically, both of their mothers worked for telephone communications companies. Both agree that the neighborhood is close-knit, with
families watching each other's children, and keeping updated as the
children grow older. Yet their similarities are overshadowed by the
differences in a few key decisions and involvements. Spider consorted
with the fledgling Black Mobsters in his youth, and participated in
their growing organized drug enterprises off and on through his
young adult years. Terri, on the other hand, was a marginal observer,
familiar with the key players in Groveland's gang and drug scenes
only because her aunt lived across the street from Lance's family's
home. And while Spider went to the local high school, cultivating his
delinquent neighborhood ties, Terri attended a magnet school and a
special college preparatory program, which took her away from neighborhood activities.

These dissimilar exposures even influence the way they told their
stories. Perhaps because he sensed my curiosity, Spider was bent on
being my eye into Groveland's underworld, retelling the violent stories of his youth such that they resembled tales of the Wild, Wild
West. Terri's portrait of Groveland is far more serene, her forecast for
its future brighter. Her language contains almost none of the gritty
descriptions that Spider enjoyed giving, and her grammar slips away
from Standard English mostly when she wants to make a point with
it. And still Terri Jones exemplifies the middling position of the black
middle class in her diverse family connections, her understanding of

racial inequalities, her own shaky lower-middle-class status, and her commitment to monitoring the stability of the neighborhood.

EXTENDED FAMILY BACKGROUND

My mom works for the telephone company. Cyntel, now Sprint. My dad works for the City. My mom went from being a cashier to being a customer service agent. But here is the thing, my mom does not wanna be a manager. I mean, has no aspirations for like career success. She just wants a secure family and home. My dad's been working for the city. He makes like 19, $20 an hour. He may have made more than that. And that's sufficient for them. My mom says all the time that, unlike me and my sister, she's not out to run anything. And she's been offered management positions, but she's not interested in taking on any of that responsibility. I think my mom's ready to quit. She'll probably, she may take the [early retirement] buyout. But my dad got sick like this year. But he came all the way back, so he's back at work.

My parents did not grow up in this community. We're from the South. My father and mother are from Dumas, Arkansas, Little Rock, Pine Bluff. We're from that whole area. And, you know, we go back every year. My family did a very typical migration. My grandmother had twelve children. Yeah, big family. The first son moved to Chicago and they brought [sic] a' apartment building. And then each family member moved to Chicago, lived in the apartment building. They paid the mortgages together and the next family saved for an apartment building. And we actually have four apartment buildings. So that's four, I mean, house twelve families. And then they started buying homes. So, initially we all lived on the West Side. On one block. I think that's really funny because our block party was our family reunion. And that was really really funny when I look back on that. But that's how we got up here.

Okay, so that's where we from. My mother and father weren't together. He was in the service. And my mother came and moved in the basement of one of those homes. Raised us with her sisters. And like one worked outside the home, one did hair inside the home, and my mother worked outside the home. And so the hairdresser was the babysitter. And she kept all the kids, you know, that lived in the house. And when they all came home they split the money evenly and they survived. It was a plan. It was a structure. And we were raised with all my cousins that were the same ages that we were. And it was like one big day care. It was fun. We had a great time. We have great memories, we really do.

We used to go [back to the West Side] once a week. We used to have family rituals—fish fry every Friday, and we played cards. And so we got together every Friday, nonstop. It was come from work, we knew we were going on the West Side. We'd switch houses. We knew we were going to eat fish, play cards, and the kids was gon' play. Now, I try to still visit once a week. You know, just two or three people's house, and interact more with my cousins because I just try to stay in touch; be the person that gets involved with family. They don't wanna come out here. They feel it's a journey to, you know, come to the South Side. So we just have to get up and go over there.

Now we moved to the South Side, my mother married her husband whose family was on the South Side. And that's how we moved to this community. I think we moved here when [me and my twin sister] were four [years old].[2] And I'm so glad we moved over here. You know really. Our family's really stable where they are, but you know environment is a big factor. And the families that live on the West Side, they are victims of their environment, you know. And so we moved here, a good neighborhood. And I think that it changed our lives maybe in terms of who we would be, dramatically. I can still see us being strong people. But like some of my cousins are just lost souls, you know. 'Cause they got into drugs and all that stuff. And my mother always says she's so glad that she didn't buy the house that she thought about buying because she would be right in the middle of it, you know. So, I'm glad we moved to the South Side too. So I always say our stepfather saved us.[3]

THE NEIGHBORHOOD FAMILY

I know a lot of people. I walk to the store. I talk to people. And I visit, like you know, I do have my neighborhood people.

Like the Abduls, Mrs. Abdul, she's sick. I go have coffee with her maybe once a week. And then I spend time with Allie and I know the people in her [part of the] neighborhood that she knows. And just seeing people at the store and talking to people, you know. And the teenagers too. Me and my sister are twins. And so they know us. They know us as "the twins." It's another set of twins, Karen and Sharon, their nicknames are Star and Slick. So either it's Star and Slick, or the other twins. So even if I don't know them, they know that we're one of the twins. And so they even feel comfortable enough when I don't even know their names [to say], "You're one of the twins?" Or, "You were my play leader." Or, [they] know my sister, and so then I know them, or meet them because they feel they know us.

Bristol and Groveland have a lot of homes. So then I would say it's very family-oriented. The areas where we have apartments it's a little less structured, you know, because people movin' in and out. That would be right on the other side of Memphis [Street]. That's where the apartments start in the community. I'm more cautious when I go under the viaduct on Sixth Avenue, from I guess Memphis to Highland. That's a little rough over there. And that part of the community is deteriorating. But it's building back up. They're renovating. But those buildings went to the point of you know drug houses, no one living there.[4] But now that area's coming back a little bit. So, I would say that this community is very stable. What I find interesting is that the people, the children who grew up here are moving back here. I know about four or five of the people who brought [sic] homes in Cedarcove, in this area. And then my sister she didn't move too far. I mean to buy a home I thought she would move somewhere else. But that's interesting. So I see a lot of stability in this neighborhood. And it's a' old neighborhood and people know each other. They know families. And a lot of people live here, you know, people prominent in the city live in this area. Even though it's not that glamorous, [just] bungalow homes. And I don't even know that the emphasis is put on a fancy home like the suburbanites. [In the suburbs], you know, it's your home that's your presentation. You're impressing people with [it]. But I think when you live in this community you just lookin' at a stable community, you know, that people are more comfortable with.

I think that we're definitely going to have some improvements and some changes. I would say first of all with some developments in the neighborhood, like the Bristol Place up there on Eighth Avenue. I actually know five people who brought homes there. And they brought the big houses and I was shocked. I was like you wanna live here? You know, because even my mom went over there and all her friends, and they went in and they was like, "Oh, they are asking too much for those houses." And I think I know a couple people who considered selling their houses and moving into the new development. But when I found out that people I knew, young people, you know, were buying those houses I was a little shocked. But it was reassuring that this neighborhood would continue to grow towards a positive growth.[5]

And I also think that the government is encouraging banks to loan to black communities. I mean there was a' issue probably about two or three years ago. Gentleman lived a couple blocks down, had a big write-up in the [newspaper], couldn't get a loan. He, you know, had great demographics in terms of how much money he made, how much his wife made, his credit rating. But he still was refused. And I think that's a big issue why our communities don't develop. 'Cause we can't get money, you know, to reinvest. To make our homes beautiful. To remodel. And then just have those great big loans pouring over. 'Cause we get a loan, it's really close to what our needs are. And we're still in a needy situation. So I think that refinance is gonna be made available. I think people are becoming more aware of refinancing and banks are offering loans. And I think that, you know, the system is recognizing that home-ownership is the key to stability, and especially to black families. So I think all those factors are gonna help our neighborhood improve.

I think because of the consistency of our neighborhood that it's going to stay that way. People, you know, look through this area to move into. When a home is for sale, like I said it's rare, but it isn't on the market long, you know. When somebody sells their house it's a big deal, you know. You wanna know why are they selling their house. So you rarely see a house for sale. So I see this community being really stable. I'm getting ready to move. I'm looking for a place now. And I haven't really left this area. And I wanna live close to my mother. And I keep saying, "Is this [my] comfort zone? Why am I staying over here?" I definitely do not wanna move north. Wanna stay south. I wanna live in a black community. I wouldn't even mind living in a mixed community, but I'm very comfortable here.

I know my neighbors on this side, on this side, [and] across the street. Our neighbors across the street they moved, the Thomases. And we have some new neighbors, two gentlemen. And we don't know them, but these neighbors know them, the Ryans. And then scattered along the houses, even down on the opposite end, the Carters. It depends on if they had children our age whether we know them or not. We used to interact quite a bit and we still interact, you know. But it's vary with degrees. We've just had personal conflicts, you know. But all the men get along. We really interacted quite a bit. The Gills would take us to school when we were little. We still, we barbecue together. Let's see, my mom and dad used to go out with the Ryans. They would go out all the time. We have card parties, they come over. And we get together still but it's not as much. So these two neighbors we do interact with quite a bit. I'm sure it's more than enough. They used to be really tight.

The Gills, their daughters all moved into different areas. But I do see them out. And they're in this neighborhood in some areas. So we see them out. And we do, you know, when they're home or when they come visit, they'll come over here and we'll all catch up like that. We sit outside a lot during the summer. Everybody's in the backyard. So there's a lot of fence-talking, and "You got the grill started? Will you put these pork chops on there for me?"

Mr. Ryan, he's pretty much, you know you have the neighborhood watchers. He sits out on his porch all day and so he knows everything that goes on. He keeps you updated. There's no block club but, you know, Mr. Ryan knows everything that's going on. He talks to everybody. He walks. My dad walks like in the mornings. They walk, they walk to the barber. They go to the barber right here. So there's a lot of [what] I call newsletters, or systems of communicating what's happening. And Mr. Dudley, who lives across the street, when you go to the grocery store, he'll bring you back and forth. So you can always get a ride with him. If he sees you on the street, he picks you up and he tells you everything that's happening in the community. Yeah, there's a lotta communication. The men are out.

THE EVOLUTION OF GROVELAND GANGS

I would always say if I had to get in a police car and drive around I could show him where all the gangbangers are. Who they are. I know them. There're certain families, you know. And Lucky's family, you know, all his brothers are, they've been killed. One brother, oldest brother killed, the next one is in jail. And Lucky, he'll be next. He's runnin' hot. Because my father's sister lives directly across the street [from them]. And we used to play with them.

I would say the worst criminals we have in this neighborhood are the Taylors. I don't know if his brother's in the [police] sweep, but he's horrible. But he's real soft. I think he's just more intelligent, you know. Or more intelligent and probably just more fierce with people. They live, is it Second Avenue? Yeah, Second and Meridian. I don't know his name because he's one of the younger brothers. But I remember him from a little guy. And I've seen them have their gang meetings. You see them all going to the same place. You know what they're doing. But I know those two are actively involved. And then I know some people who sell drugs.

But I think the gang activity and the drug activity, even though they're related, are definitely two separate entities. Because with the gang activity there's violence. And violence has a direct effect on the community 'cause it's random. And the drug activity, even though they're selling drugs, it's not necessarily that they're being sold in the community. I can think of it as a' incubator, it's a' incubator there. But it's not directly going into the community.

The gang activity, even though it's present, it's been kept to [a] minimum. Now, some of the young people I know in this neighborhood have told me that whoever is the gang [leader] has said no drug-selling in Groveland. And that's the law. And I haven't seen any really. You know, gang activity is more organized now. It's more organized crime. I don't know of any drug houses. I couldn't tell you that's a drug

house. Not in this particular area. Like I said if you go back
on Sixth [Avenue] under the viaduct, there're definitely drug
houses. But not to say that I don't think that people sell. I
think it's [different] when you sell drugs in a house, and a
drug house. A drug house is where people go buy drugs and
use the drugs in the house at the place where they buy them.
There're definitely no drug houses that I can think of. Now
there may be some drug sales out of some people's houses.
But I don't know any in particular. But I definitely know that
somebody has to be. I mean, I think.

You know, even when there's a little cluster of boys on
the corner, it really doesn't look like drug-selling. Looks like
they're just hanging out. When I go across Ridge [Avenue] on
Sixth and Wright, that's a little drug corner. But, you really
don't see anybody standing out here [in this part of the neigh-
borhood] selling drugs. Well, we have a little group of boys
there, but see, I know them. Like Wendell and Shaka. And
they just hang out over there. They're eighteen, maybe nineteen [years old]. So if I drive by and it's a whole bunch of
'em, then I'll call Shaka over to the car and say, "What [are]
y'all doin'? Y'all sellin' drugs?" And he'll say, "Naw, we're just
talkin'." And I just mess with 'em or whatever. And then I'll
tell him I'll tell his mama [Mrs. Abdul] I saw him on the corner. He said, "Don't say that."

I think you have to determine groupings from gangs. You
know? You know like in the summer playing basketball in the
park, if we had a way to get the older boys [away] from the
younger boys, I think we might be able to division some of
that out. But if those are the role models, and if they up there,
they're drinkin' and smokin' and they're playin' ball, and the
boys are exposed to that and all of that, I think they're gonna
be curious about that. And that's their mentoring, you know,
to turn 'em on to those negativities. I think what keeps them
from getting involved in gangs is the family. Because, I mean,
the people that I've seen in gang activity, the mother is aware
but doesn't respond. Or does not really open up to the real-
ism. Or becomes receptive of the benefits. You know who was
selling drugs, who got busted was the Bronsons—Toshi.
Right there on Eighth, right across from Lucky's house. That
house on the corner that's abandoned. Seized, the government
seized their property. Toshi was selling drugs. And not that

he was sellin' 'em out of his mama's house. But I think, you know, it was evident that she was benefiting from the sale of drugs. And so they seized her property.

So, you know, if your kid comes home with new clothes and you didn't give 'em the money, you know they got the money from somewhere. So either you do what some people do. They take those clothes off them kids right there, throw 'em out their house and say, you know, "Whatever you're doin', it's not gon' happen here or you got to go too." Some kind of intervention. But I think that the family unit is strong enough so that even though there may be some temptations to gangs, and probably some activities, that the option of going either way probably may be 70-30, you know. So if they even get out of it when they go to college or go away. Or go to Chicago State or whatever. Or just come into their own thinking. I don't know if the pressure is that great like it might be where there's no parental involvement. Or a structured family.

I think that the family unit is the most important part of that. And even when you have the single [-parent] family. I still consider it the union, unit, but there is a missing factor there. So then there is some potential to stress, to get involved in other things. Because we know these things are happening, we have to take a' active part in getting involved with the youth. Any loose, you know, you can identify where there's not the total surrounding. Where maybe a single parent. Or if you at the park and the kids, they want attention. One thing, they want attention. They need love. That's always been a factor with black people in general, the deficits of self-esteem thing. So I say for anybody who's aware to become actively involved with kids. You can start with your own family. And that will be a direct effect. You can start right in the community with the kids around here. And it will make a difference, you know. They'll even come and, you know, they'll ask you things that they wouldn't ask anybody else. And then it's up to you, you know, to just figure out the best way to handle it. But be truthful, but give 'em sound advice or whatever. So the family union is the unit that keeps all those factors together. And that would be a man and a woman. And if you're lucky, your grandparents.

'Cause I have a problem with [putting them all in jail].[6] They target black men and poor black men. And they're taking all of these black men out of the community when we need them. I mean, they do some bad things, but the attention is biased and unbalanced in that the source of these drugs, the bigger people who are bringing the drugs into the neighborhood, aren't being prosecuted. Like I have cousins who are now in jail for forty years because of crack, whereas cocaine would never get you that much time. They target poor black men and the street-level sellers, and there is not equal time spent looking for and prosecuting the higher-ups.

THE ROAD TO COLLEGE

Grammar school, we went to Groveland [public school] here. That was just the school in the community. And it was a good school basically. We had great teachers. The teachers are still good. Lot of the teachers still teach there. And any time I see those teachers out, they know the kids. I don't know if that's not a strange thing, you know. But they know the children that went to that school. So I think we have a good grade of teachers there. And I cater for some of the teachers now. You know and I go into their homes and it's a totally different concept.

High school, I went to Newton [which was a magnet school]. I didn't know where I wanted to go [so I] went to Newton. And that was a big trip for me. But I think I was trying to get out of my environment. Get away from home. And I did that. I met new people. And it was a good experience. I participated in a program at the University of Chicago, Upward Bound. And I met Ms. Collins there. She was one of the teachers. And I didn't really plan on going to college. And not that I was not going to college, but I hadn't had a plan to go to college. I hadn't discussed college with my mother. We're first-generation college people. Some of my other family members have college. But my parents, I think they were gearing us for college, but not forcing college on us. And, you know, it wasn't even factors of money. It was just, you know, if you wanna go to college, then go ahead and go. But you had to prepare. They weren't doing the things necessary for us to go.

I don't think I even applied. I hadn't really applied anywhere. I don't know what I was really going to do. You know, I think I was just caught up in the graduation of high school and not really planning. But Ms. Collins just wrote me a letter and I took it down to New Orleans. And I think I went and brought [sic] a suitcase. Because I was smart but not really dedicated at all. But any time I took a standardized test, I did very well, you know. And so I went and brought me a suitcase, packed my bags and said Mom, I'm going to college. And I went to Xavier.[7] I didn't even apply. And then my mom said I think we have some relatives down there. And my mom called my relatives down there and they told me I could stay at their home till I got a place, or got into the dorms. And these are like second-generation relatives. And I went there. They were very nice people. And I didn't even move into the dorm, because, you know, I was in the community of New Orleans. And I didn't even know where New Orleans was.

But I went to school and at first I was real resistant. You know, because everybody knew each other already, and I was new. You know Xavier has the [summer] pre-prep program. So I didn't know anybody. And then Allie was there who was from my neighborhood. I got to know her and then moved in a little bit. So then I started meeting some people there. And I really fell in love with New Orleans. I mean, as opposed to going to school. You know, after school I really looked forward to going back to my newfound relatives' home. And the kind of activities they had, and their family environment I loved, you know.

I was in pharmacy school, but I really wasn't dedicated 'cause I was hangin' out. Basically I wasn't ready yet. You know, I had found this newfound independence and all of that. And got caught up into that. But I did well in school. Like one semester I wouldn't do good, and then the next semester I would do extremely well. My parents stopped sending me money for college two years into college. That was it. My mother said if I didn't make good grades she was not gon' give me any money. And I said okay, I'm fine with that, but I'm gonna stay in New Orleans 'cause I really like it down here. And then I supported myself for the next year and a half. But then when I was ready to graduate from school, I thought that New Orleans was not providing me the environment to do that in. 'Cause I was definitely hanging out! I decided to come back home and finish school. When I was ready, you know, I breezed through college. And it wasn't difficult. But while I was not ready, while I was developing *me*, I couldn't focus on school.

I applied to pharmacy school up here and I had got accepted and all of that. But while I was in New Orleans I was working at hotels. And I was doing very well. You know, I went in as a waiter and left out as a manager. And I was interested. I said, well, I'm gonna see if I can get in a hotel program. And on the very last day I decided to go into the hotel [program]. Chicago State, they had a new program. And it was a great program. I loved it. And I got lots of exposure, did lots of traveling, had lots of internships. 'Cause it was new and there were no, you know, nothing defined. And it was a great decision. It's working very well for me. Because I cater I have been exposed to all levels of black people. And it's amazing. Because I'm really never at home. All I do is come home and do paperwork, make phone calls, type out contracts, and plan menus. Probably with pharmacy, I probably would be bored. I'd probably be a drug user by now. Being there makin' up some drugs, takin' some home, sellin' some on the side.

And I think it's the learning college experience that established friendships. Really all my friends are out of town. Terrance is one of my good friends. Sherry, you may know her, Sherry Robertson, yeah, Sherry is my good friend. Corey Copper, he's my good friend. And then my good friend here in Chicago is Allie, lives on Delta [Street, in Groveland]. And then Andre. And all of those people I met through college. Ah, they're all professional people—teachers, doctors, lawyers, accountants. We plan a vacation together once a year. We used to do New Year's every year. And that was until I think the life stories has prevented that from happening. This is the first year we did not spend New Year's together because Terrance got married. So now we have to meet Terrance's needs and his wife's needs. And Allie's pregnant. And then Corey's thinking about getting married. So, we're gonna have to develop a new strategy. I think since New Year's is an important date to the family that we'll probably have to plan like meeting in the summer now. So we can incorporate something that the family can all come out and we can still get together. But we used the New Year's as a nice motivational time. We'd spend a whole week together. And we would go somewhere different every year. And I would really be energized. And I would invite my other friends. I'm like look, we get together, we have fun, we relax, and we motivate each other. And when I come back from that vacation with them, I am ready to get busy.

HAVES AND HAVE-NOTS

I would describe this neighborhood as poorer. [There's] rich, poor, poorer, and po'est. Okay? There is no middle class. And I think the economics is gonna be more important than anything, you know. I think economics is gonna be the greatest. And then the second thing is gon' be technology. Or basically education. And even now, it's not about education. It's about technology. Because I figure that we skip all the reading and writing and take our kids right to, you know, different programs, and computer programming, and computer language, and get in on the Web. So, you know, I think that you're just gonna be technically inclined to communicate.

If you have the money, you can participate. The richer are looking out for the rich only, and getting richer. And the elimination of the poorest guy, the least survivor, you know, you just gonna be out of the picture and not really a concern. Because the po' folks are gonna try to survive and forget the poorer people. I see people separating themselves already. Just think about the welfare reform and how many people probably think that that doesn't even apply to them. Those people are gonna have to find some way of surviving. Maybe the poor black class—meaning upper black class—is going to have to intervene. Because, I hear people and they say what the effects of welfare reform will be. They're actually afraid, you know. You know, it's just gonna be horrible. So, I think that there's gonna have to be some intervention on black middle class, or people who feel they don't fit into categories of welfare reform to make that transition smoothest. 'Cause I think we'll be the first victims of welfare reform. And then white society will feel it. But just think about your family. You know, those people that are gonna be hurt by it, they're gonna come to their family first for support. And you're tryin' to support your family. And how much support can you give? And then when it's not there, then the next act will be violence in some form. And I think that the violence is gonna be first black on black. And then eventually will spread into the white community. You know, so I think that people're gonna have to wake up to that—black people especially—and the effects of that. And just get involved.

I think that the value of money has grown now, even though this still is a good neighborhood. I would think you're lookin' at combined incomes of maybe $100,000 to maybe at the max $150,000. Where people are making 75-75. There may be some with more, [with] maybe an adult child, which is very likely in this neighborhood. Which is 30 [thousand], maybe lookin' at 180. I had to fill out a form when me, my sister, my mom and dad were living [here]. They had the question "Combined Income?" and I put on there like $120,000. And the lady was like—[mimics astonishment]. And I was like well wait, you know, we have four adults in the house. Four professional people. I know my mom's makin' 50, my dad's makin' 50, I'm makin' 15, my sister's makin' 30, you know, or whatever.[8]

But to me, that's not really a lot of money. You know that's still struggling. That's still that if somebody loses their job, you still trying to meet your expenses. Now once your home is paid for, then you start, you can get well-off and start to save some of that money and build a retirement. I mean if all those safety nets are there, then that's okay. And I think that these families probably have that established. But still that's not a lot of money. I say if you can spend it—if I gave you a million dollars and you can tell me how you can spend it, that's not enough money. 'Cause you won't have any left. You'll be broke. So, but poorer would describe this neighborhood. But, in terms of stability, where there're retirement funds, where they have invested their monies in the companies that they work for, where that if there is a trauma in the family that there is a nest egg and they still will be able to exist and survive. I would say, you know, they may be, well, more well-off.

I'm poorer. Not poorest, but poorer. Not that I'm gonna stay there, you know. But, I'm working my way out. But only if it's in terms of economics. Because there's real money out there. I know that I'ma be a millionaire. Not to brag but I'm gonna make me some money, okay. And I know that first of all to make some money you have to get out of the frame that you can only make this amount. So, as long as you work for somebody else, you're only capable of making what they allow you to make. So, the first step is to figure out, if I work for somebody else, how can I make more money doing whatever it is I do? Or, what can I do that's gonna allow me to make more money? So, I just say I'm poorer because, you know, all my money's tied up. My expenses are great. You wouldn't even believe it. And, you know, my money's grown quite a bit. My income's grown year to year to year. And I just see it growing. I'ma make it grow. And I don't wanna be rich, just wanna be comfortable. But I do wanna have money to do whatever I wanna do. If I wanna give it away. And so, you know, I wanna strive to be a millionaire. How 'bout that.

CONCLUSION

There are always features in case studies that make them less than generalizable. In Terri Jones's case, she is one of the 20 percent of Groveland residents with a college degree, which means more than just a higher education; it also suggests a range of experiences outside of the neighborhood and with a diverse group of peers. William "Spider" Waters displayed this breadth of associations as a result of his job at the Chicago Mercantile Exchange. But life is more provincial and insular for many other Grovelandites. One of Neisha Morris's aspirations, for example, was to see a world beyond the streets of Groveland. Terri gained such exposure when she went off to college and met friends from places around the country, and now continues to make travel a part of her routine. Terri is afforded such freedom because she is single and childless, another characteristic that even she is beginning to feel is unique among her own group of "thirty-something" friends. Terri's Groveland peers who have families have more immediate concerns, such as the quality of schools, the availability and safety of recreational activities, or the manners and upbringing of the playmates on their block. Terri, on the other hand, can concentrate on building her catering business and striking it rich. Despite these details, Terri's embeddedness in neighborhood networks and her attention to the importance of the environment pick up on key themes expressed by other residents. She may be more solidly middle class than other Groveland residents, but her family's journey to that position highlights the importance of packaging kin and community resources in order to ensure the stability of the next generation.

CONCLUSION

On a tour of Chicago's neighborhoods, our jumbo coach bus drove through a predominantly African American neighborhood not too far from Groveland, and just about as middle class. It was a cold autumn morning, and the tree-lined streets were completely empty. Yet there were conspicuous clues that somebody cared deeply about this neighborhood. Matching lampposts stood like sentries at the edge of each home's neat lot. Welcoming block-club placards on the corners— "Please Drive Slowly"—conveyed a concern for children who might be too engrossed in play to mind the traffic. The occasional candy wrapper or grocery bag on a few lawns did not ruin the overall tidiness. The homes with fresh paint, edged grasses, and decorative screen doors outnumbered the properties of loafers who had ceded victory to the weeds, or refused to sweep the sidewalk. As we took in the pleasant sights, our learned Chicago tour guide, who was white, reported to our group of sightseers, most of whom were also white, "From looking at it, some of you all might think this is a predominantly white neighborhood, but actually this neighborhood is all black." He spoke as if he had let us in on a little secret.

The guide's comment, dressed in its disclosing tone, initially struck me as narrow-minded, since I had, after all, grown up in a like neighborhood, and was not at all surprised by this find in Chicago. Yet with the near completeness of racial segregation in many large American cities, it would indeed be difficult for many whites to just happen upon a place like Groveland. For the most part—and especially in cities like Chicago, Milwaukee, St. Louis, Detroit, Newark, Buffalo, Philadelphia, and so on—African Americans live on the "black side of town," and whites on the "white side of town."[1] To a somewhat lesser extent and depending on the city, Hispanic and Asian American groups each have their "side of town," too. People's routine patterns ensure that they have little reason or opportunity to see Groveland

201

and neighborhoods like it. The average nonblack citizen's ignorance of these enclaves is bolstered by the common belief in academia that the black middle class actually moved away from black neighborhoods after the 1960s, leaving behind their poorer former neighbors. (I challenged this argument in chapter 1.) Recognizing all this, perhaps black middle-class neighborhoods *are* a secret. And the black middle class, while far from a secret, is shrouded in misperception.

Groveland's first generation of residents who entered adulthood in the immediate post–World War II era remember a time of largesse. With their stable jobs and in search of better housing, African American college-educated professionals moved to Groveland. Along with them came customer service representatives, hairdressers, transit employees, and railroad workers. All earned enough to buy a home and perhaps send the children to Catholic school, or take a yearly trip back Down South. They replaced the white residents who were also benefiting from postwar prosperity, and were looking to move to the growing suburbs. Far from integration, the change in Groveland was complete racial turnover. As Groveland's African American residents established their stake in the neighborhood, the statues of Jesus in the old neighborhood churches were painted darker, the restaurants started serving soul food, and the drugstores stocked black hair-care products. In their new, attractive neighborhood, Groveland's first generation began to reap the benefits of the civil rights movement.

The expansion of the black middle class in the 1950s, 1960s, and very early 1970s came to a halt in the last two-and-a-half decades of the twentieth century. The generations that followed Groveland's African American pioneer settlers have found it progressively more difficult to match what their parents amassed in those days of plenty. Executive profit-hoarding, corporate and government downsizing, and global labor markets have pillaged the wallets of the American middle class, both white and black. But with lower incomes and a flimsier financial cushion, African Americans are more susceptible than whites to slipping back down the class ladder. A contemporary profile of the black middle class reveals that higher-paid professionals and executives do not predominate as they do among the white middle class. Instead, office workers, salespeople, and technical consultants—all lower-middle-class jobs—make up the majority of black middle-class workers. Working-class African Americans, who have been even harder hit by production shifts, are also an integral part of neighborhoods like Groveland. Linda Brewer, a Groveland resident in her mid-thirties, listed the jobs that anchored her parents' genera-

tion. "A lot of these people around here, you know, post office workers, steel mills. They father had two jobs," she reflected. "But them
jobs are no longer here. So now they kids are poor." The second generation, of which Linda is a member, struggles to buy homes, or maintain the houses their parents purchased. Along with the third generation of teenagers and young adults, they are somewhat bewildered by
the fact that without a college degree, they often have to live with
their parents in order to get full consumption and leisure mileage
out of their lower-middle-class paychecks. The black middle class is
particularly fragile. As Anna Morris summarized, "I get enough to get
by. I don't get any more. I take care of my children. I think we're sort
of well-to-do, but who could say. You could go any way any day."

In addition to being acutely affected by economic changes in production and the distribution of incomes, members of the black middle
class are also unique in the kinds of neighborhoods in which they
live. Racial segregation and disproportionate black poverty operate to
cordon off black communities with higher poverty rates than equally
segregated white communities. As the geographic span of high-
poverty areas has expanded since the 1970s (Jargowsky 1997), they
continue to push into nearby black middle-class neighborhoods.
Groveland's unemployment and poverty rates have risen consistently
since the 1970s. Black middle-class neighborhoods like Groveland
subsequently have more crime, fewer services and resources, less political clout, and less adequate schools than most white neighborhoods. In the case of crime, the homicides that fill the evening news
occur only a few blocks from the quiet streets of Groveland. Too often
they happen in the neighborhood, challenging residents to devise
strategies to keep their own children safe.

Parents, block-club leaders, church members, and all others who
work toward keeping control of crime and disorder in Groveland
make much use of the strong family and friendship ties that have
developed since blacks first moved into the neighborhood. Instead
of being despised aliens, the gang members and drug dealers in the
neighborhood are recognized as someone's cousins, someone's grandchildren. This familiarity does not necessarily mean that residents are
soft on the general problems of crime and violence. The landlord of
a three-flat building in Groveland angrily addressed the police at a
beat meeting. "I don't want no drug dealin' in or around my buildin',"
the woman said out of frustration with the young men who had set
up their illegal business in her rental property. "I got good tenants in
that building and I want to keep them. If you need me, I'll go press

charges. I want them in jail. I want 'em locked up." Yet despite these frequent and impassioned demands for beefed-up police protection, the simple fact that many residents have known each other for years often works to make Grovelandites feel more comfortable than would a squad car on every corner. At the same police beat meeting, Mr. McArthur, who was a youthful seventy years old, shared with his fellow residents how safe he felt on the streets of Groveland because the neighborhood youth involved in the drug trade are in fact the same kids he had watched as children.

> On my block I can walk up and down the street at any time of day or night. And my wife and daughter can too. I can walk down my street any time. And it's like a' inner fear they have. The kids that are out there doin' wrong, they know they doin' wrong and know they better not do nothin' in front of me. But I can walk down my street anytime because I feel safe walkin' in my community, 'cause I've known these little kids since they was growin' up. And I tell you, I feel safe anytime out there because they're out there twenty-four hours a day. I feel bad callin' the police on these little kids 'cause every time I walk past, they are so nice [asking], "How you doin', Mr. McArthur? How you been?"

The dense networks across the lines of legitimacy, and fostered by residential stability, present a double-edged sword. Grovelandites, while not apathetic, make compromises on the destruction that gangs and drugs can bring because they also find certain comfort in their protective reach.

For Groveland youth, close-knit neighborhood life translates into a diverse group of role models. In their families, among their peer group, at school, and on their block, they have within their reach the ingredients for success, as well as the easy opportunity to join the wrong crowd. Again, it is the composition of black middle-class neighborhoods and the communities within which they are embedded that produces such a range of choices. While black middle-class families are indeed important "social buffers" (Wilson 1987) in the African American community,[2] their health is simultaneously under strain, because living with and near poverty exerts negative pressures on youth. Higher poverty rates mean that a sizable minority of the youth in black middle-class neighborhoods will be attracted to the financial perks of crime. With the opportunities in place, middle-class youth are also drawn to the fast money. White middle-class families and their children, who generally live in much more class-homogeneous neighborhoods, do not experience these same pressures.

Yet the *opportunity* to experiment in crime is not enough to account for the decision to sell drugs or join gangs by youth like Tyson Reed, whose mother sent him to the best schools and was herself a successful educator. Like other youth, black and white, Tyson and his peers revere popular-culture styles that valorize the excitement of deviance. Tyson Reed was attracted to the flair of the underworld, despite his extensive middle-class exposures. He was quite cognizant of his mediating perch.

> 'Cause it's good to be educated and it's good to have the street sense. But sometimes it's bad just to be a hoodlum [who] don't know no better. Then sometimes it's real bad to be a damn nerd. You can have all the book smarts in the world, you ain't gon' make it in the real world. But then again, you could be the biggest hoodlum in the world and if you ain't got book sense, you know, law sense, you ain't gon' make it either. So, that's why I always felt it was best to have both of 'em.

Like Tyson, Spider also enjoyed straddling different worlds. Spider's father moved from Groveland into a predominantly white suburb. "It's quiet out there," he said about the suburbs. "Then, when it got too quiet, I come back out South for some good ol' South Side violence. Hear some guns shootin' off in the alley behind the crib [house]. Damn, I feel at home!" Liking the quiet of the suburbs, but simultaneously getting a thrill from the sound of gunshots, Spider melds "decent" and "street" orientations (Anderson 1991, 1994).

Despite their middle-class background, some youth are "seduced" by the criminal lifestyle (Katz 1988). They see Lance—the neighborhood's top-ranking Black Mobster—with a new Cadillac every few months, a mink coat, designer outfits, matching gym shoes, and the attentions of both women and men. The undecorated life of the teacher next door never inspires such awe. Groveland's teenage boys learn that money and power—no matter how they are earned—boost their status in the games of adolescent courtship. A young, overweight local kid named Kareem had no chance of winning a neighborhood beauty like Neisha Morris with either his looks or his sincere affections. But after Kareem moved up in the gang and began to profit from its drug business, Neisha grew fonder of him. For these reasons, some youth and young adults find the fast life more appealing than a safe middle-class existence.

Their attraction to the flashy lifestyle of the "gangsta" is nurtured by mass cultural productions. Black youth are an important target audience for marketers like Nike, whose shoes are ubiquitous in Groveland. Mass-culture industries employ black entertainers and athletes to endorse their products, and include black cultural themes in their advertising. More important, commercials, television shows, music, and the movies market more than just consumer goods. They market lifestyles. Gangster movies (black or otherwise), violent video games, fashion magazines, and rap music all supply the lifestyle images that young people in Groveland enjoy. Some of the behavior in Groveland clearly imitates this fantasy-world of the mass media.

White youth, of course, also contribute to Nike's multi-billion-dollar revenues. They also bomb each other playing Sega video games, line up to see the latest repackaging of *Scarface*, and try to walk with the bold swagger of gangsta rappers. Adolescence is color-blind in its demands for excitement and its propensity to test the boundaries. Groveland's young people are not alone in their attractions to the fast life. But the stakes are higher for Groveland youth. Gun violence is a more serious reality in black communities. When Ray Gibbs got involved with the gang in Groveland, he wound up getting shot as he walked through a nearby rival neighborhood. Ray survived the wound and his delinquent ventures into selling drugs, but fifteen-year-old Brandon Johnson—church youth-group member, YMCA participant, and young Black Mobster—did not. Even the youth who do not officially join the gang, and never commit a delinquent act, but who mimic media gangstas in their fashions, language, walk, and general disposition, are at risk of being misread by the more devoted badmen, or by the official agents of social control, like the police. Because of the mix of residents that poverty and segregation produce, the penalties for following the typical adolescent urge for excitement can be severe in a neighborhood like Groveland, even for black middle-class youth.

BEYOND URBAN POVERTY

"Rediscovering" the black middle class necessitates a rethinking of central contentions in the urban poverty literature—especially social isolation and black middle-class out-migration. Both of these hypotheses downplay the diversity within the African American ghetto. Even the term *ghetto* has lost its original use as a referent for segregation, and has become more widely used as a synonym for poverty neighborhoods. Yet Groveland's residents, especially the youth, are aware of their connection to the neighborhoods that other people call ghettos. Tenasha Graham jokingly called Groveland Elementary School "mini-ghetto university" because of its developing reputation for fights and poor student performance. And other Groveland residents explicitly referred to their neighborhood as "the ghetto," especially when comparing it to predominantly white parts of Chicago. Indeed, many families moved to Groveland to get away from such disorder, and some are still adamant about differentiating their neighborhood from "the real ghetto." Yet when evaluating the full range of neighborhoods in the metropolis, most Grovelandites clearly see the spatial separation of racial groups, and they express a keen understanding of how such racial segregation in space translates into inequalities in municipal services, political power, crime rates, and financial investments, to name a few. Urban poverty research could be strengthened by paying attention to the long reach of the ghetto outside of high-poverty neighborhoods and into places like Groveland, where the balance of poor and nonpoor residents is particularly tenuous. I do not at all intend to dismiss the despair that, for example, Alex Kotlowitz (1991) conveyed through the stories of two young boys who could not be boys because of the very adult pressures they faced growing up in a Chicago housing project. But I do intend to widen the geographic and social lens that is used to analyze the ghetto to include areas like Groveland that are equally racially ghettoized, but differently composed.

Paul Jargowsky (1997) has carefully documented the demographic distribution of neighborhoods and the residents within them. Although his analysis is most concerned with high-poverty neighborhoods, his findings (especially his chapter 4) say much about the range of neighborhood types. About half of the residents in the average high-poverty neighborhood are in fact not poor; most poor blacks do not live in high-poverty neighborhoods; and most majority-black neighborhoods are not poverty neighborhoods. Focusing on the expanses of privation that comprise high-poverty areas and the oppressive preponderance of antisocial behavior within them renders invisible the church members who work diligently to salvage the corners of their block, or the parents who take weekly trips to other parts of the Black Belt where the parks are a bit safer and the grocery stores carry fresher vegetables. At least from a spatial perspective, there are opportunities for poor African Americans to interact with nonpoor blacks at the neighborhood and community levels. But this impression is rarely conveyed in the urban poverty literature, where poor African Americans are portrayed as being nearly completely cut off from working role models.[3] Recognizing the presence of working residents in poor neighborhoods and documenting the relationships across lifestyles, ages, and classes could in fact *strengthen* the argument made by many liberal social scientists that the solution to urban poverty lies in *radical systemic changes,* not in the reorganization of poor people's cultural beliefs, or a boost to community capitalism. If we pay attention to the working role models that already exist within the inner city, as well as the institutions that support positive activities, we would be more sure that such indigenous resources make a difference, but are wholly insufficient for the crucial task of eradicating the disproportionate poverty among African Americans. The ghetto, which includes Groveland and the other black middle-class neighborhoods nearby, is not bereft of role models and institutions. What is missing are jobs that pay a decent wage, health care, decent affordable housing, and effective educations. These issues are raised in the urban poverty literature, but within a discussion of the social isolation of the black poor.

The proffered remedies to social isolation include moving inner-city blacks to the suburbs or promoting integration generally, creating jobs in the city, and encouraging housing and business investments in poor neighborhoods. But none of these tactics recognizes the fact that creating more of the kinds of jobs that are currently available to low-skilled groups will not go far enough in improving the socioeconomic conditions of poor African Americans. And stemming continuous patterns of black middle-class migration out of core ghetto areas might make a few houses on the block look nicer, but it will not provide decent physical infrastructure or essential social services, which have been systematically strangled in the last few decades. A more radical agenda is needed than that of simply lessening the social isolation of poor blacks. Acknowledging the *existing* diversity in the ghetto, and the presence of friendship, kin, and neighborly networks between poor and nonpoor African Americans, would underscore the limited impact that such connections can have when they are not accompanied by simultaneous changes in the way in which profits, incomes, and resources are distributed.

The social isolation model is also challenged by the comprehensive geography of the inner city. New and sophisticated demographic mapping techniques illustrate the spatial concentration of poor African Americans. They also show the heterogeneity that exists in the larger black community as the black working and middle classes filter out of poor neighborhoods and into adjoining areas on the periphery. There is reason to focus on the most impoverished areas of the ghetto, which are most in need of immediate attention, but broadening the analytic framework suggests that poverty neighborhoods are in fact one part of a segregated black community that also consists of moderate-, middle-, and sometimes high-income neighborhoods. Groveland's location within the "South Side" symbolizes the understanding that residents have of their neighborhood being connected to other areas in the black community. Within the South Side are the Robert Taylor Homes (public housing projects); the high-density rental housing along the lakefront; the stately mansions owned by people like Jesse Jackson, Muhammad Ali, and Louis Farrakhan; and the bungalows that Grovelandites call home. A spatial pattern of class stratification has existed in Chicago's black community at least since the 1920s, when the tiny black elite of that era out-migrated to the "best" areas, where health indicators were better, educational attainment and employment were higher, and reliance on public relief was less common.

For today's residents of Groveland, the high-poverty areas that receive so much attention in the popular and scholarly literature are never so far off. The social workers in Groveland have their clients there. The teachers in Groveland instruct the students there. The sanitation workers pick up the garbage there, and the family members who are still climbing the class ladder live there. Grovelandites know full well that their neighborhood is different from the poorer parts of the Black Belt, and they hold their share of stereotypes about the residents who live there. Class, status, and lifestyle are real axes of distinction in the black community that are perhaps heightened by the spatial proximity of, and interactional networks that exist between, blacks of varying classes. The compact geography of the Black Belt does not suggest a homogeneity of outlook or practice among its residents (Gregory 1998). It does represent an ecology that, because of extreme segregation and disproportionate poverty, is unique to African Americans, and thus has a particular impact on processes of neighborhood maintenance, raising children, and organizing social and cultural life. These realities teach us something about the simultaneity of mobility and marginalization in American society.

RACE, CLASS, AND PLACE

African Americans have made impressive socioeconomic gains in this country, especially since World War II. Educational attainment has increased and performance has improved. The poverty rate for blacks, while still alarmingly high, is well below the 80 percent black poverty rate in 1950 (Jaynes and Williams 1989). Blacks have a visible presence in politics, business, and entertainment. And the black middle class has grown in terms of both absolute numbers and its proportion in the black community overall.

The status of the black middle class should be of paramount importance to those interested in the future of African Americans as a group. These are families and individuals who have invested in education and hard work in order to climb the occupational hierarchy into white-collar professional, sales, clerical, managerial, and entrepreneurial occupations. The older generation, born in the South, battled racist laws and practices and accepted the risks of northern migration to attain their present positions. Now they hold stable middle-class occupations as nurses, insurance brokers, phone operators, and managers. They have captured the American Dream of a single-family home with a backyard and a two-car garage. Some can afford elite private schools for their children, and many are able to retire with a solid pension, equity in their homes, and successful children to look after them. Yet despite these middle-class characteristics, African American families like the ones in Groveland still face unique economic, sociospatial, and cultural perils. The experience of middle-class status is not uniform across groups. Instead, it is colored by the crosscutting reality of race.

There are many manifestations of simultaneous racial and class stratification. As an example, the black middle class is disproportionately dependent on public-sector employment (Collins 1983, 1989; Freeman 1976; Grant et al. 1996; Steinberg 1995; Owens 1998). Government jobs have been the most positively affected by affirmative action policies (Leonard 1984, 1991), and the system of government-provided professional and social services that grew after the 1960s has been heavily staffed by black employees. Therefore, blacks are clustered in local, state, and federal jobs that interface with the black community. Even in the private sector, black workers and black businesses perform segregated functions that cater to a black clientele (Collins 1983, 1993). This stratified labor-market arrangement makes middle-class black occupations particularly vulnerable to waning public support for affirmative action and the fiscal support of welfare and social services.

Other examples of the intersection of race and class are the disparities in wealth (Jaynes and Williams 1989; Oliver and Shapiro 1995) and the daily experiences of racism (Cose 1993; Feagin and Sikes 1994). Regarding the latter, Harvard University professor Cornel West was reminded that neither money, nor education, nor prestige negated the fact that he was black. One empty cab after the next passed him as he attempted to get to a photo session to take pictures for the cover of his book. Middle-class blacks continue to face racial obstacles, and have yet to attain parity with whites.

The stories of Groveland families add the importance of *place* to this evidence of racial and class stratification. The lives of Grovelandites cannot, of course, speak for those of black middle-class Americans across the country. There are substantial regional differences; African Americans in some western and southern cities experience less racial segregation than those in the Rust Belt cities of the North and Northeast. Southern African Americans who stayed South while their relatives flocked to the North have yet another story to tell. Black immigrants from Africa or from the Caribbean islands bring another history and lifestyle to what it means to be black and middle class. No research of the kind conducted in Groveland could characterize the diversity of black middle-class experiences. However, we do know that a slight majority of African Americans nationwide (53 percent) live in census tracts where over half of their neighbors are also African American, and the majority of these areas are not low-income neighborhoods (Urban Studies Group 1997). If only in terms of their residence in predominantly black, nonpoor neighborhoods, Groveland's residents share much in common with other black families across the country. The ecological context of black middle-class families is a basic feature of difference between the white and black middle class. The location of black middle-class neighborhoods dictates the experiences to which black middle-class youth will be exposed. Living near blighted, poor neighborhoods with substandard schools, crumbling institutions, and few businesses presents an extra challenge to managing the negative influences on black middle-class children.

Groveland parents try to curtail their children's negative involvements. They set limits on where their children can travel. They choose activities—church youth groups, magnet schools or accelerated programs in the local school, and the Boy Scouts and Girl Scouts—to increase the likelihood that their children will learn positive values and associate with youth from similar families. Still, many parents are working long hours to maintain their middle-class incomes. They cannot be with their children at all times. On their way to the grocery store or to school or to music lessons, Groveland's youth pass other young people whose parents are not as strict, who stay outside later, who have joined the local gang, or who earn enough money being a lookout at a drug house to buy new gym shoes. They also meet these peers in school and at the park, and in their music lessons as well. For some teenagers, the fast life looks much more exciting than what their parents have to offer them, and they are drawn to it. The simple fact of living in a neighborhood where not all families have sufficient resources to direct their children away from deviance makes it difficult for parents to ensure positive outcomes for their children and their neighborhood. For African Americans, then, there is a unique middle-class experience.

Middle class is a loaded term. As an economic term it is the most straightforward. It is relatively easy to look at the full distribution of incomes in the nation and slice out some "middle" proportion. Everyone captured in this range falls in the middle class by economic standards. But does that really jibe with what people think of when they say "middle class"? In casual or popular usage, the label "middle class" is often closer to the non-economic notion of "mainstream." When that comparison is explicitly recognized, the normative nature of the term becomes clear. "Mainstream" compared to whose "stream"? "Mainstream" in all realms, or only in key arenas like family and work, and who decides? "Mainstream" by today's standards or in a nostalgic sense? Can nonwhites even *be* "mainstream"?

The answers to these questions indicate that while "mainstream" and "middle class" may both be normative judgments in their lay use, the road to reaching middle-class status is structured by economic, political, and social forces that are larger than any one individual's efforts. If the spatial incarnation of "middle class" is actually "suburban," then African Americans are less able to be middle class by virtue of a history and present of racist lending, rental, and selling practices. If the cultural manifestation of "middle class" includes only those who almost always speak Standard English, then African Americans—along with immigrant groups and some rural whites—are disadvantaged because segregation affects the degree of exposure to those who decide what English vernacular is acceptable. If going to a good school is an educational component of being "mainstream," then fewer blacks can be so labeled because of how their poorer neighborhoods undergird the discrepancies in school funding. And if "mainstream" means growing up with two biological parents, then a goodly proportion of both blacks and whites fall short of the bar. Black marriages may be especially at risk because of financial strains, but ever fewer Americans of all races can sustain the mainstream two-parent goal. The point in wading through this list of "mainstream-isms" is to illustrate that if African Americans are less likely to measure up to the normative notion of "middle class," it has much to do with the barriers that they face to reaching such a status.

Yet African American families make do with what they have, as the residents of Groveland illustrate. They mix strong cultural traditions with their economic resources to come up with their own "mainstream" practices. The role of the extended family is perhaps the best illustration of how black middle-class families adapt to an increasingly precarious economic context, following in the tradition of how poor African American families have coped with poverty. There were countless families in Groveland that flourished only because of the combined time and money resources and emotional help of many family members, sometimes all in one house and sometimes spread across the neighborhood and city. The family is the basis for upward mobility, as Terri Jones's family exemplified. Her mother's and aunts' strategy of having two sisters work outside the home and one work inside the home while watching the children allowed each to prosper. And Mr. Graham's four-generation family rests on his hard work and the constant help he gives, especially in the forms of babysitting and providing the home that his daughters can always come back to. The extended family is also the unit that is supportive in times of financial crisis. Mrs. French's daughter was solidly middle class until she split up with her husband, and then had to move with her son back to her parents' house. "Mainstream" might privilege the nuclear family model, but in reaction to their mostly lower-middle-class incomes, Groveland families keep alive a culturally based emphasis on the extended family in order to maintain an economically middle-class standard of living.

To manage the neighborhood context, Groveland families utilize the existing relationships between the do-gooders and the lawbreakers. A narrow definition of "middle class" might not include being friends with or a relative to a gang member or a drug dealer. But such a definition does not recognize the contingencies of being black and middle class. In order to achieve the "quiet neighborhood" that many Grovelandites agree that they have, the park supervisor allows the

Black Mobsters to play dominoes in the field house, and the activists work with Lance despite his criminal position to vote the neighborhood dry. These are the mainstream behaviors that Grovelandites enact in light of their unique ecological situation.

Finally, Groveland youth adapt to the cultural context by balancing the mass-media imperatives of being a gangsta with "decent" aspirations, activities, and involvements. White middle-class youth are also attracted to the same "street" characters that are widespread in popular-culture productions. But young Grovelandites must be more vigilant in separating style from behavior, and particularly aware of who is reading their styles, and how those styles might be interpreted. In its conventional usage, "middle class" might exclude wearing baggy jeans or rapping along to an explicit song about rough sex and gunplay, but Groveland youth perform these styles simultaneously with participating in the church youth group, or going off to college.

The black middle class challenges the definition of middle class and mainstream, which follows a kind of majority-rule logic. Middle class and mainstream are both based on a white American model, which does not allow for the structurally and culturally determined adjustments that nonwhite groups must make to being middle class. Moreover, if there were a more developed literature on the lifestyles of the white middle class, the entire construct might buckle under the evidence that not even white families measure up. The findings might expose the pretense that the white middle class uniformly ascribes to and follows "mainstream" standards. Gangs, drugs, teenage sex, family dissolution, economic hardship, and generational cultural cleavages all exist among the white middle class. While there are fundamental axes upon which the black middle class differs, the white middle class may also exhibit behavioral adaptations that diverge from the sanitized notions of middle class and mainstream. Whatever the scenario among whites, the "mainstream" families in Groveland broaden the definition to include African Americans who speak both Black English and Standard English, who are single mothers, and who live next door to a drug dealer.

MAKING A DIFFERENCE FOR THE BLACK MIDDLE CLASS

The continued obstacles faced by middle-class African Americans speak to three interrelated policy issues: affirmative action, residential segregation, and race-targeted antipoverty programs. I am neither a policy maker nor a student of government, and so I do not intend to put forth any particularly ingenious proposals. Each of the issues that my research addresses sits rather permanently on the policy table, inciting years of debate and interest, with incomplete results. My goal is rather to add the concerns of the black middle class to the debate, and illustrate how some proposals can have positive results for this group, even if they are not so aimed.

Race-based affirmative action is the policy most relevant to the well-being of the black middle class, and it has been under attack almost since its inception. A frequent criticism is that under affirmative action, middle-class African Americans benefit from race-based policies while disadvantaged whites have no legal recourse. Affirmative action opponents argue that it is unfair that the daughter of a black doctor should be preferred (in college admissions, say) over the son of a white coal miner. I contend, however, that race-based policies continue to be necessary, even for middle-class African Americans. The assumption behind such attacks on race-based policies is that the higher class status of the black doctor bestows more benefits on his/ her family than does the privileged racial status of the white coal miner. As Ellis Cose (1997) argues, such an argument suggests that "class trumps race." It is of course difficult to weigh the specific benefits that accrue to either racial or class privilege. Yet the finding that "even the most affluent blacks are not able to escape from crime, for they reside in communities as crime-prone as those housing the poorest whites" (Alba, Logan, and Bellair 1994, 427) is one indication that being African American occasions a downward tug, even on an upper-middle-class family. A black doctor, or factory worker for that matter, by the nature of his or her community surroundings alone, faces particular roadblocks that a similar white person does not. As William Julius Wilson (1996, 198) notes, class-based affirmative action policies ignore the "long-term intergenerational effects of having one's life choices limited by race, regardless of class."

The stories in this book caution against seeing blacks who have achieved middle-class status as being unaffected by the simultaneous system of racial stratification. White middle-class families have been able to physically and socially distance themselves from the concentrated urban poverty of America's large cities, while the black middle class continues to struggle to maintain predominance in their neighborhoods, which border these areas. The *Chicago Tribune* devoted a front-page story (Grossman and White 1997) to these residential differences. The article noted:

To a certain degree, many city dwellers—regardless of where they reside—live with a measure of insecurity. And there are predominantly white middle-class communities, particularly along the lake shore, that also collide with poverty and violence. . . . But those are the exceptions. On Chicago's predominantly white Northwest Side, pockets of poverty are separated by spacious areas where the middle-class life predominates. On the Southwest Side, the black middle class acts as a buffer between poverty zones and white neighborhoods.

The *Tribune* article found that 79 percent of black middle-class households in Chicago live within four blocks of census tracts where a third or more of the population is poor, compared to only 36 percent of white middle-class households. The divergence is likely to be more stark when including the suburbs, which the *Tribune* article did not. These differences illustrate that the majority of middle-class whites have absolutely no experience with the kinds of residential contexts in which black middle-class families reside.

As neighborhoods are more segregated, and poverty is more concentrated on "the black side of town," the quality of the schools declines. Douglas Massey (1987) and his colleagues show that high-status blacks are the first to "invade" stable white neighborhoods, but these neighborhoods ultimately undergo racial transition and become predominantly black, just as Groveland did in the 1960s. Over the course of neighborhood change, the percentage of students testing below the 15th percentile in the local schools rises from 19 percent in "black entry" census tracts, to 32 percent in tracts under rapid transition, to nearly 40 percent in established black tracts. These changes are the result of the concentration of both racial and economic disadvantage in black neighborhoods. Middle-income African American students who attend these schools suffer from the schools' overall poor performance, and are affected by the consequent realities of low teacher expectations and a slower pace of instruction.

This scenario plays out in Groveland, especially at the high school level. In Groveland, where graduating from the area high school is only about a fifty-fifty proposition, middle-income students must resist the trend set within the school. To raise the chances of their children's success, a number of families pay for Catholic high schools, where graduation rates are much higher and a large proportion of the graduates go on to college. For instance, not one of the four children in the French family went to the local public elementary schools, and only one attended a nearby public high school. Mrs. French used her personal connections to secure spots for two of her children at a top-ranked magnet high school, and she and her husband paid the hefty tuition costs for their youngest son to attend an elite Catholic high school. (The French children were still influenced by the neighborhood context outside of school.) For those families who cannot afford the rising costs of private school (or choose not to make the financial sacrifice), or who are not chosen from the long waiting lists for the magnet schools and do not have influential friends, the area high schools—with their lower graduation rates and less rigorous curriculum—are their only option. Under a system of class-based affirmative action that disregards the racial disadvantages that middle-class African Americans face, these students would be expected to compete for college admission or jobs with middle-class white students who have not been disadvantaged by the composition of their neighborhoods. The example of vastly different school experiences illustrates the continuing importance of racial stratification for performance and achievement, and the need to affirmatively recognize such differences (as well as to actively rectify them) in hiring and admissions decisions.

In addition to the continuing need for affirmative action, attention must be given to lessening racial segregation, and to improving the lot of the black poor. Without residential segregation—and the social segregation that it engenders—African American communities would not, as they do now, bear nearly the full burden of disproportionate black poverty. The black poor would be more evenly spread out across racial neighborhoods. This would have positive benefits for low-income families, who would have access to suburbanized jobs, better schools, and safer streets. It would also improve the circumstances of the black middle class by lowering the poverty rates in their neighborhoods and surrounding communities. African Americans would then reap more of the benefits of what are now unequally distributed resources. As a long-term result, black poverty should decline.

On the other hand, another strategy might focus on the need for extensive education, jobs, and training programs to change the socioeconomic condition of poor blacks *where they currently are*. The only rising tide that will lift all boats in the black community is the rising tide of the black poor. Improving the lives of poor blacks would result in a different kind of black community, with a lower overall poverty rate. Less poverty would lower crime rates and reduce social disorder. Blacks who are already middle class would be less likely to want to leave these more stable communities. With more stability, the amenities of black neighborhoods, such as the proximity to downtown financial and business districts—or Lake Michigan in Chicago—would make them once again attractive to investors and home buyers, both black and white. And, perhaps, after a time, racial segregation will subside.

Eradicating residential segregation and improving the economic situation of the black poor both move toward lessening racial inequality. Unfortunately, each is a far cry from garnering the support of many white Americans who see these goals as threats to their own status and standard of living. Complicating matters further, Wilson (1996, 200) points out that, with respect to integration, "As long as there are areas to which whites can retreat, it will be difficult to reduce the overall level of segregation. Blacks move in, whites move out." Blacks, like whites, also indicate preferences for residential situations in which they are the majority. While this preference is definitely related to past negative *inter*racial experiences, there are also social, cultural, and psychological rewards to living in a neighborhood that celebrates black culture and history, and fosters positive *intra*racial interaction. Hence, complete residential integration is stifled not only by white resistance, but also by black and white preferences.

These facts bring me to conclude that improving the condition of the black poor within black communities would have a strong positive impact on the black middle class, and is a more feasible (but definitely not simple) policy option than residential racial integration. If the black poverty rate were comparable to that for whites, black communities would not be disproportionately burdened by poverty. The residential context of the black middle class, then, would be more similar to that of the white middle class. We know that separate has never been equal, and maintaining segregated neighborhoods (and thus segregated social lives) will continue to thwart the sufficient preparation of African Americans for mainstream, predominantly white institutions. The success of a determined effort to improve the lives of poor African Americans, therefore, hinges on the notion that such improvements will encourage integration.

The positive reverberations of interventions aimed at alleviating black poverty illustrate why such policies should take priority. Whatever the combination or order of approaches, they must be sensitive to the distinctive experiences of the black middle class, who currently nibble on this country's prosperity, but are beset by the legacy and continuance of racist inequalities.

APPENDIX A
Research Method

This research was conducted in the tradition of urban sociological field methods formalized by the Chicago School in the early part of the twentieth century. Robert Park at the University of Chicago charged his students with investigating the empirical world through the use of humanistic and participatory methods. This focus has had an indelible impact on successive generations of Chicago graduate students. Joseph Gusfield (1995, xii), who trained during the era of the "Second Chicago School," remembers the continuing emphasis on qualitative methods.

> What stands out for me is the intensive focus on the empirical world; on seeing and understanding behavior in its particular and situated forms. Data that do not stay close to the events, actions, or texts being studied are always suspect. There is a hostility to generalizations at any level that are not connected to description, to immersion in substantive matter.

These principles of descriptive and grounded research have informed much of the classic research on African Americans. Under the direction and training of early Chicago School scholars, an ethnographic research agenda was initiated in black communities. My own research draws from the intellectual and methodological contributions of Robert Park's students—from Frazier's (1939; 1957) studies of the black family and the black middle class to St. Clair Drake's and Horace Cayton's ([1945] 1993) massive social survey of Chicago's South Side black community. These works, along with the insightful and thorough research of Du Bois ([1899] 1996), form the foundation for investigations into the black community to this day.

CONDUCTING THE PRESENT RESEARCH

This research began in January of 1993 under the auspices of the Comparative Neighborhood Study (CNS), which included four Chicago neighborhoods—one white, one African American, one Mexican American, and one mixed white and Mexican American. The aim of the larger study was to compare these neighborhoods with respect to processes of social organization and unique aspects of culture, and to investigate racial discourse and prejudice within and among the various ethnic groups.

The Groveland neighborhood was the first site chosen for the study. The principal investigators for the CNS specified seven black community areas on the South Side of Chicago to be surveyed as possible sites for the research. These seven community areas (along with a few other census tracts and one community area that was not considered) make up a contiguous band of middle-class black neighborhoods on Chicago's South Side (see chapter 1). The 1990 median family income for six of the seven community areas was above $30,000 (the 1990 median family income in Chicago as a whole was $30,707). Because the study was to focus on working- to middle-class neighborhoods, these community areas comprised the target area from which to select the research site.

With a research partner, I surveyed all seven community areas. We paid close attention to the physical health of the community, evaluating such aspects as upkeep of the business district, presence of trash and graffiti, and repair of homes. We also noted the presence or absence of social institutions, such as churches, community centers, and parks. We talked to people in the local institutions and businesses to gauge the extent to which residents and people who worked in the neighborhood used the official name of the community area and saw it as a unified whole: we wanted a neighborhood that had a degree of legitimacy among the residents. Finally, the geographic size and population of the community area were taken into consideration. An ethnographic study can better penetrate the diversity of local activities and people if the neighborhood is small and manageable, rather than populous and expansive. A report was written on each of the community areas. In consultation with the principal investigators, Groveland was chosen out of the seven middle-class areas because it best satisfied the above criteria.

Socioeconomically, Groveland falls on the high end of the community areas surveyed. Only one community area had a median family income above that in Groveland, and only that same community area had a lower poverty rate. Because this book emphasizes the effects of poverty within and around black middle-class neighborhoods, the fact that Groveland is more economically prosperous than the adjacent community areas means that the findings in this study will be *understated*. In black middle-class areas with even higher poverty rates, the choices and options that middle-class adolescents have are even more varied and salient.

Under the direction of the CNS, the first few months of field work were spent mapping the physical area, taking pictures of housing structures and businesses, describing the housing stock, detailing the decorations of churches, the park, and the public library, and noting casual interactions in public spaces. These rudimentary observations were followed by a period of locating knowledgeable informants, including political figures, directors of community centers or parks, presidents of local community or business organizations, heads of churches and church organizations, local librarians, local newspaper reporters, real estate agents, lay and professional school officials, directors of social welfare agencies, and the police. The third and final stage of the project involved establishing close personal contacts with neighborhood residents.

These three stages of the CNS resulted in intensive participant observation in numerous settings in Groveland, interviews with key leaders as well as lay residents, and attendance at meetings of the Chicago Area Policing Strategy program, the Chicago Park District, the Ward Regular Democratic Organization, local church meetings, and the Chamber of Commerce. My research partner attended meetings of the Local School Council and the Groveland block clubs, and also spent much time at Groveland Park. My research partner and I read all of each other's notes, and met almost daily throughout the study. The interactions and events that he recorded at Local School Council or block-club meetings were similar to the ones I documented in meetings of the police beats, or the school board of the Catholic school. I collected the vast majority of data presented in this book, but I do occasionally use excerpts from his field notes with his permission.

There were conscious attempts to minimize the problem of selectivity by getting involved in a wide range of activities and social networks. These efforts yielded substantive conversations with gang leaders, social service providers, grandparents, and toddlers. Although limited to those people who did actually leave their own homes, the participant-observation component of this project tapped a rich cross-section of Groveland residents. Demographic information, newspaper clippings, photographs, neighborhood flyers, and other supportive data were collected throughout the study. The CNS officially ended field work in September of 1995, after nearly two and a half years of data collection in four Chicago neighborhoods.

After the completion of the CNS, I moved to Groveland, continued the participant observation, and conducted thirty-one taped, in-depth interviews (including three pilot interviews). The interview sample was chosen to represent various age groups—youth (13–21), young adult (22–45), and mature adult (46+)—and socioeconomic statuses—lower, working to middle, and upper-middle class. The literature on the black class structure guided my placement of residents in class groupings (Blackwell 1985; Landry 1987; Vanneman and Canon 1987; Wilson 1978). Youth who were still in school were classified by the position of their parents.

Interviewees were identified using three strategies. First, I began by interviewing residents that I had come to know quite well. Their taped responses to my interview questions were useful checks of the experiential data that I had collected in various casual settings. The participant-observation field notes were frequently my reconstructions of conversations or events, but the interviews were transcribed verbatim, providing me with the respondents' thoughts in their own words. Next, I interviewed Groveland residents referred to me by my close contacts. I did not have participant-observation data on these interviewees to augment their more formal testimonies. I did, however, have some stories provided by the person who recommended them. The first set of interviews with close contacts provided background and introductory information on the friends and relatives that they recommended. Finally, the third set of interviewees were neither close contacts nor recommended by close contacts. Some residents in this third group were people that I met at community meetings, or saw participating in community activities. I had little observational data on these interviewees, and no contextual information provided by a close contact, yet these interviews still elicited useful information. Because the goal of interviewing was to get a variety of residents' opinions, not to have quantifiable data, this relaxed sampling method was sufficient.

There is a bias in the interview sample, however, that warrants special mention. The older youth and young adults who have left Groveland for college or for careers outside of the area might represent the most upwardly mobile segment of their age group. Many of the young adults who remain with their parents in the neighborhood do so out of financial necessity. As a result, interviewees who grew up and continue to reside in the neighborhood may be less upwardly mobile than the overall population of young people who have grown up in Groveland. Some of this bias was minimized because I met many college students before they went off to college. I interviewed these youth when they came home for vacations, and through their stories I could get a partial handle on the processes of growing up in, and then moving out of, Groveland. Nevertheless, it was difficult for me to meet and interview young adults who had been raised in the neighborhood, went off to college, and subsequently obtained well-paying jobs across the country, although some of these stories emerged in interviews with parents. As a result of this bias, this study gives minor attention to the stories of youth and adults who have experienced considerable upward mobility. Instead, I focus on the obstacles that have complicated the forward progress of their peers who remain in the neighborhood, or the neighborhood ties that have prompted those who have achieved middle-class status to stay in Groveland. My portrait of Groveland might be unfairly gloomy in this respect, but it serves to underscore the unique perils of living and raising children in a black middle-class neighborhood.

All of the interview and participant-observation data were coded into over thirty general themes of interest, some of which were driven by extant theories (e.g., intergenerational interaction, density of networks) and some of which emerged in the process of the research (e.g., discussions of guns or gun violence, role of the church). The participant-observation field notes, along with the interviews conducted for the CNS, were coded by hand. This entailed reading the field notes and creating a running list of major themes. The date, field-note page number, and summary identification were listed under the major code for each relevant field interaction. The thirty-one taped interviews were coded using FolioViews, a qualitative data analysis package. The computer coding was not much different from the manual method, although the computer program stored the entire field experience into a folder that contained all relevant field notes for that code. The coding process substantially increased my familiarity with the material by guaranteeing at least three layers of experience with the data: (1) the social interaction itself (interview or participant observation), (2) writing field notes or transcribing an interview, and (3) rereading the notes for coding purposes.

The arguments in this book should be read as a conversation between the specificity of people's words and actions in Groveland and the grand declarations of sociological theory. Following the methods of grounded theory (Glaser and Strauss 1967), I used existing sociological theories and categories as "sensitizing concepts" (Schwartz and Jacobs 1979). I had knowledge of such theories as social (dis)organization and social control theory as laid out by early Chicago School theorists, and cultural theory as discussed in the work of the Centre for Contemporary Culture Studies in England. This preparation guided me to take note of the informal ways in which adults controlled the behavior of youth, which is key to social organization theory and to keep in mind the meaningful uses of consumer artifacts in order to better understand the role and function of expressive culture. Hence, some of the codes used to analyze the data—such as intergenerational interaction, social networks, or consumption styles—reflect particular concerns raised by the literature.

Yet so much emerges from the process of field work itself that cannot be anticipated by existing theories. As Lofland and Lofland (1984, 46) point out:

The researcher does not only (or mainly) wait for "significant" (sociologically or otherwise) events to occur or words to be said and then write them down. An enormous amount of information about the settings under observation or the interview in process can be apprehended in apparently trivial happenings or utterances, and these are indispensable grist for the logging mill.

Hence, analytic codes like "discussions of guns" or "the role of churches" became particularly salient only after I had been in the field and logged the minutiae of everyday interactions. And because neither I nor the principal investigators of the CNS took a narrow approach to studying neighborhood life, the strategy for taking field notes was to be as exhaustive as possible. It was only through the constant reinspection of the notes that significant themes grew out of mundane and unrelated interactions. The conclusions in this book were reached through the simultaneous processes of collecting data and coding it, and then going back to the field to further explore those codes; that is, the ideas were reached inductively through theoretical sampling (Glaser and Strauss 1967).

WRITING

Since the 1970s, the project of ethnographic writing has come under much scrutiny (Clifford and Marcus 1986; Geertz 1973; Fernandez

1974). The ability of ethnographers to authoritatively speak for the communities they study is no longer uncritically assumed. Ethnographic writing has begun to explicitly address the unique subjectivity of the method. Experimental projects—especially in anthropology—that straddle the lines between science and biography, nonfiction and art, have pushed the limits of what is acceptable ethnography (for an early example, see Bowen 1954).

Variations in expository style can work to make a point more compelling. Ethnography can be heavily descriptive, which allows readers to get a detailed look at the social and cultural life of a certain group, and bring their own informed interpretations to interactions (Liebow 1967; Shaw 1966). On the other hand, highly theoretical ethnographies draw connections between a particular site and larger social scientific questions (e.g., chapter 9 in Hannerz 1969; Bourdieu 1977). Theoretically inclined ethnographers "use descriptive data to illustrate their theories and to convince readers that what they say is true" (Taylor and Bogdan 1984, 125), while descriptive ethnographies leave more interpretation to the informed reader.

In writing the stories of Groveland residents, I tried to fall somewhere between these two poles. I do not stray into the realm of fiction or art, but I do take advantage of the creative leeway called for in recent challenges to ethnographic authority. Some chapters are written so that the data fit neatly within explicit theoretical assertions. Pieces of data are used to illustrate the theoretical story I want to tell. Other chapters allow the reader more freedom of interpretation by presenting longer and more descriptive stories from the field (e.g., chapter 7). Even in chapters 8 and 9, which contain extended first-person narratives, I provide an opening, grounding discussion and a conclusion. My goal for writing, then, is that readers find some commonality between themselves and Groveland's residents, while also recognizing the peculiarities of being black and middle class.

APPENDIX B
Groveland Neighborhood Characteristics

Table 1   Groveland Demographic Trends, 1960–90

	1960	1970	1980	1990
Total population[a]	12,700	14,400	13,800	11,700
Percent white	100	16	3	1
Percent black	0	83	96	98
Percent owner-occupied homes	74	70	71	75
Percent poor[b]	6[c]	5	10	12
Educational attainment	12.1 years	12.4 years	12.6 years	na[d]

[a] Rounded to the nearest hundred.
[b] This refers to the percentage of *families* below the poverty line, not individuals.
[c] The official poverty line had not been established at the time of the 1960 census. The figure here refers to the percentage of the population with family incomes below $3,000.
[d] The 1990 census did not compute median years of schooling. Instead, it reported proportions of residents having completed various years of schooling. That index showed little change for Groveland between 1980 and 1990.

Figure 1   Median Family Income, Family Poverty Rate, and Homicide Rate per 10,000 Residents, Groveland and Surrounding Neighborhoods, 1990

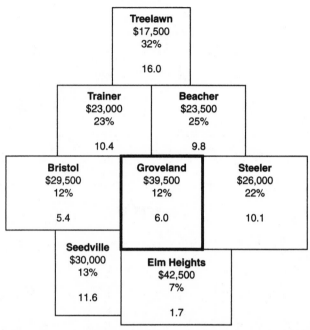

Sources: Local Community Factbook, Chicago Metropolitan Area, 1990, and Illinois Criminal Justice Information Authority 1994. Jeffrey Morenoff provided the homicide statistics.

Figure 2   Income Distributions in Groveland and Beltway, 1990

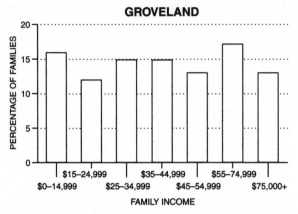

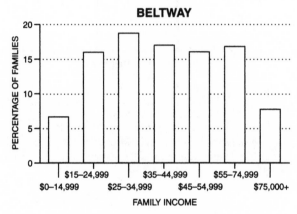

Source: Local Community Factbook, Chicago Metropolitan Area, 1990.

EPILOGUE

Black Picket Fences (*BPF*) was published in the last century. That might sound overly dramatic, but considering the changes that have taken place since 1999, when the first edition was published, it is not hyperbole. The research for *BPF* began in 1993. Very few people had heard of the World Wide Web, which young people today might only recognize as the abbreviated "www." Computers were mainly for word processing, and telephones—land lines, that is—were the primary method of communication. President Bill Clinton was overseeing major overhauls of welfare, immigration, and crime policy, but the international scene was relatively quiet. That is, *BPF* was pre-September 11th, and thus before Iraq, Afghanistan, and the War on Terror. On the economic front, it was a time of growing employment, falling poverty rates, and budget surpluses, although financial deregulation and, in particular, subprime mortgage lending were setting the stage for the near total collapse of the banking sector, the housing crisis, the recession, and the current slow recovery. In the early 1990s, "gangsta rap" was a hot topic, crack was an epidemic, *The Cosby Show* aired its last season, and Barack Obama was just a law professor at the University of Chicago. In other words, much has changed.

Amid these momentous societal shifts, Groveland looks pretty much the same in 2013 as it did twenty years ago when I made my first visit. There are still blocks and blocks of neat brick bungalow houses with landscaped yards, nice cars, and litter-free streets. The main commercial area has more chain stores and fewer mom-and-pop businesses, which coincides with national trends (Jarmin, Klimek, and Miranda 2009). This may be good for Groveland families' budgets when it comes to new supermarkets and drugstores (Chung and Myers 1999), but bad for their waistlines when it comes to fast-food chains (Larson, Story, and Nelson 2009), and bad for maintaining a distinct community identity (Zukin et al. 2009). Gone are the Soul Seas restaurant and the black-owned gas station at the major intersection, replaced by a fast-food joint and a chain pharmacy. Off the commercial streets, Groveland Park still offers dozens of activities, and a new Chicago Public Library branch recently opened in the neighborhood. The people look pretty much the same too. This is true not simply because the racial and, to a lesser extent, class composition have barely changed, but because they are literally the same people. Over 60 percent of the families that lived in Groveland in 2010 had moved into their houses before 1999. So, when I went looking for some of the people whom I interviewed in the first edition of *BPF*, I easily found them using the same addresses and phone numbers.

If so little has changed in Groveland, then what is the purpose of a second edition? What can be learned by reconsidering the research? There are two important answers to that question. First, taking a fresh look at Groveland offers a long-run assessment of social and urban processes that is rare in the social sciences. While there are several important longitudinal surveys that can study change and stability, they are mostly quantitative datasets that follow *individuals*. Reexamining the ethnography of Groveland requires looking at both the people in the neighborhood *and the neighborhood itself*, yielding life histories and a neighborhood history. While I did not conduct a full-blown repeat ethnography, or ethnographic *revisit* (Burawoy 2003), the facts that I still live on the South Side of Chicago, have kept in touch with many of the people in the book, and have had several occasions over the years to be back in Groveland mean that this is more than simply an update. This recurring familiarization with a field site is useful not only for studying change, but also for studying "what stay[s] the same, despite change and through change" (Burawoy 2003, 670). In this tradition, this epilogue allows for thinking about the trajectories, processes, and outcomes of both neighborhoods and the people who live (or lived) there.

Another contribution of a second edition is to resituate Groveland in the array of urban neighborhoods in the US and to reconsider the residential situation of the black middle class in light of newer research. It is gratifying to know that the book has been read from coast to coast in the US, and even overseas, but how representative is life in Groveland of the experience of other African Americans? How does that compare with whites? And how does Groveland compare with neighborhoods in Los Angeles, or Houston, or Cleveland, or Memphis, just to name a few cities? The literature on the black middle class and black middle-class neighborhoods has grown substantially since the publication of *BPF* (Landry and Marsh 2011; Pattillo 2005), which has also provided some comparison for new research on the Latino middle class (Agius Vallejo 2012). It is important to interrogate the book's utility given the availability of more recent contributions.

To address these goals, this epilogue has four sections. First, I describe my approach to "reentering" Groveland, and I give some updates on the lives of the young people (who are now all grown up) featured in the first edition. In the second section, I elaborate on the insights that can be gained by returning to Groveland, paying particular attention to what we learn about class mobility and reproduction at the individual and neighborhood levels. In the third section I review the broad topics that were discussed in the first edition, namely the economy, crime, and housing. It presents the Groveland of today through both statistics and the observations of current and former residents, with an eye toward how Groveland helps us to understand urban patterns of stratification more generally. The fourth and final section puts BPF in dialogue with the social science research done since the first edition. While the universe of literature relevant to the topics of race, class, and place is extremely vast, I focus on studies of the residential situation and experience of the black middle class. I argue that the recent research substantiates and bolsters the stories told in BPF, pointing to the continuing relevance of the kinds of privileges and perils portrayed in this book.

GOING BACK TO GROVELAND

In the first edition of the book I described my field experience in Groveland as "close-to-home ethnography" because the neighborhood so much resembled the place where I grew up in Milwaukee. However, at the time I began my research in 1993, I had lived in Chicago for only a few months and it really wasn't "home." In contrast, by 2012 when the research for this second edition was conducted, Chicago had been my home for over twenty years, and to say that I had to go "back" to Groveland to do the research is somewhat misleading. In the early years after completing BPF, I went to the neighborhood often to go to church. Then I went to get my favorite Jamaican food. Then I ended up tutoring a middle schooler who lived near Groveland, and that took me back. And sometimes driving through Groveland was just the quickest route from my new neighborhood to Target or to the movie theater or further afield on a road trip.

Over the years I have also bumped into Groveland residents *outside* of the neighborhood: downtown, at music festivals, near my job in a Chicago suburb, or walking along the lakefront. By far the most lively, enjoyable, and unpredictable of those encounters were with the most lively, enjoyable, and unpredictable character in the book, William "Spider" Waters, Jr. One time I was herding my niece and nephews through the crowd at the Sears Tower when I looked up, and there was Spider, working as a security guard. I squealed in surprise. He yelled my name too, we hugged, and we both started telling his coworkers about his starring role in my book. He let my whole family and me up to the top of the Sears Tower for free and we spent another fifteen minutes talking after our visit. Then, years later, it turned out that the security company that Spider had been working for at the Sears Tower lost their contract, and Spider got transferred to the University of Chicago. In the eeriest of ironies, when I went to interview Spider for this edition, I met him at his job, and we sat in nearly the exact place in the exact building where my graduate student office had been twenty years earlier, where I would write my field notes about Groveland.

While the fact that Spider worked at the University of Chicago is a particularly uncanny twist, I tell this story because there is nothing otherwise odd about how Spider's and my worlds frequently intersected. *BPF* is about the black middle class. These are the folks who work in universities and in schools and in police departments and in office buildings downtown. The most important contribution that I think this book makes is that it studies very regular folks. They're not rich or poor, fancy or uncouth, CEOs or chronically unemployed. These are truly the stories of Middle America, albeit an America that is deeply stratified by race.

In addition to Spider, I reinterviewed Neisha Morris, Rashaad Lincoln, and Tyson Reed, all of whose stories were central to the book's arguments. All have good, solid jobs. Rashaad has the most education, having earned a graduate degree from a good school. His career ultimately took him out of Illinois, but I was able to catch up with him on a trip home with his wife and children. Tyson finished college, has a high-ranking position in the public sector, and lives with his wife and child in his childhood home in Groveland, which he bought from his mother when she moved to the Chicago suburbs. Despite being truly thrilled with gangs and guns as a teenager, he shared with me his retrospective explanation for his success: "Well, I wanted it [success] more, where other people were satisfied with being on the block for the rest of their life." While he emphasized a "hard work" narrative, both Tyson's mother and Rashaad's parents were college graduates, and Tyson's mother was completing her PhD when I first interviewed him in 1996. In many respects, both of them took advantage of the privileges and avoided the perils of their family and neighborhood contexts.

Neisha had her first child and was pregnant with her second when I was completing the research for the first edition. She was then just out of high school and her boyfriend was killed during her second pregnancy. She did not go to college, but she did follow the model of her family and began working at the Chicago Park District, where her father had worked for many years. Talented, energetic, and mature, she became a park supervisor quickly and made a good living with good benefits. However, the always tight budgets in the city's park system made creating more programming with fewer resources unbearably stressful, so she left the park district and is currently working in a private childcare center. She lives next door to her mother in Groveland, with her new long-term partner and their blended family. Both she and her boyfriend have cousins, aunts, uncles, and grandparents all throughout Groveland.

Charisse Baker, another young person spotlighted in *BPF*, and I kept playing e-mail tag, and I was not able to reinterview her, but through frequent contact over the years I know that she graduated from college and works at the same large nonprofit organization where her mother has worked for decades, and lives in her childhood home in Groveland. I did get together with her sister Deanne, also a college graduate, who has worked for several large Chicago private and nonprofit organizations, and was living in the south suburbs with her husband.

I also reconnected with people who were not as central in the first book, but whose stories are relevant because of their continued ties to the neighborhood. In all, I did nine audio-recorded interviews, ranging in length from an hour to three hours. There is not space in this short conclusion to share all of the rich stories of how their lives have unfolded, yet I hope to capture a few highlights in the following pages.

In addition to the interviews and frequent visits to Groveland, I reviewed a substantial amount of quantitative data for the city of Chicago and each of its neighborhoods. I collected crime data, child poverty indexes, housing affordability measures, mortgage lending patterns, business surveys, and a wide range of social and economic indicators from the US Census and American Community Survey. While there is too much information to present in this epilogue, these data have significantly informed the characterizations of the neighborhood that I present below. I employ these two kinds of data—the qualitative experiences of current and former residents and the statistical portrait provided by the census and other sources—to examine how Groveland sits within larger debates about the housing crisis, urban crime, national public housing debates, public sector employment, and many other pressing issues of the day.

SOCIAL MOBILITY AND SOCIAL REPRODUCTION

"It's funny you bring that up," responded Cynthia Keys to my question about if she thought she had outpaced her parents in terms of her own career development. She continued,

> I was going through some old paperwork and I found when my mom filled out my financial aid paper my freshman year in college. And I saw how much money she made. And I cried. I picked up the phone [and called her] and said, "And you put me through college [with that salary]?" To know that she was making that much having two kids [in college] and I am, you know, considerably above where she was around the same age.

This was Cynthia's American Dream moment, when she realized that she was better off than her parents. It is not a rags-to-riches story. Cynthia's mother worked for a utility company and her father was a salesman (no rags), and Cynthia had a well-paid but mid-level position in corporate America (not riches). Still, Cynthia's epiphany is about the climb *up* the class ladder, which is a core value and expectation of most Americans. Going back to Groveland and to the young people who grew up there allows for a conversation about this core concern of American culture and politics: social mobility, or the lack thereof.

In the mid-2000s, the Pew Charitable Trusts launched the Economic Mobility Project (EMP), which is an ongoing study of how people's economic circumstances change over the course of their own lifetimes (intragenerational mobility), and how they do relative to their parents (intergenerational mobility). Even though the word "mobility" often connotes a positive change, there is always the possibility of *downward* mobility instead of *upward* mobility. Moreover, some people hold pretty constant across their lifetimes and others grow up to be not too unlike their parents; these are cases of social *reproduction*.

The EMP shows that social reproduction is much more common in the US than our national myths might suggest. Taking a stab at the core ideal of upward mobility, one news story characterized the EMP findings as follows: "While many believe it's easier to move up the economic ladder in America than anywhere else in the world, the United States simply does not do very well on that score" (Ydstie 2012). EMP (2011) research shows that the ability to do better than one's parents (or to do worse, as the case may be) is not exceptionally American, and exiting poverty is particularly hard in the US. More specifically, a person's family

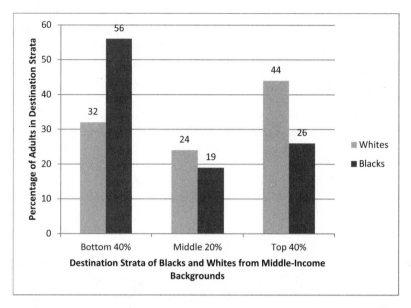

Figure E.1   Adult outcomes for blacks and whites from middle-income backgrounds.*

*Data are from the Economic Mobility Project (2012, fig. 15) for the middle-income quintile only.

background predicts their own social class better in the US than in any of the other sixteen peer countries studied. That means that in the US there is more social reproduction across generations than movement up or down the class ladder (see also Ermisch, Jäntii, and Smeeding2012). "Low income, low outcome" is how Jay MacLeod (1995; 2009) cleverly characterized this stickiness of class in the US in his book *Ain't No Makin' It*, one of the most celebrated ethnographic revisits in sociology. Given this backdrop, my expectations for going back to Groveland were that a good proportion of the young people in Groveland had probably reproduced the lower-middle-class standing of their parents as adults.

However, another EMP (2012) report shows that mobility and repro- duction processes do not work the same for blacks and whites in the US. The first edition reviewed the evidence that African Americans were less likely to experience upward intergenerational mobility and more likely to experience downward mobility than similar whites (see p. 21). But these data were from the 1980s. The EMP shows that these disparities continue to exist. Figure E.1 reports national data on the proportion of blacks and whites who grew up in middle-income families as children and who ended up in various strata of the income distribution as adults. For African Americans, 56 percent of those who came from middle-income family backgrounds ended up in a lower quintile of the income distribution as adults, compared to 32 percent of comparable whites. (Figure E.1 combines the bottom two and top two quintiles.) Whites show slightly more social reproduction than blacks, with 24 percent of them ending up back in the middle of the income distribution, compared to 19 percent of blacks. At the upper end of the distribution, whites show considerably more upward mobility than blacks; 44 percent of whites from middle-class families end up in a higher quintile, compared to 26 percent of blacks. Many of the young people growing up in Groveland share the middle-income backgrounds of the people represented in these national data. These findings show that they will have a harder time than similarly situated whites to better their parents' relative economic situation.

The first edition of *BPF* contains many stories that give life to these numbers. The "peril" of the book's subtitle captures the ever-present specter of downward mobility, as illustrated in the experience of Tracy Harris, for example, who, despite having two gainfully employed college-educated parents, dropped out of college and was "alternately employed with the state unemployment office, or collecting her unemployment benefits from the same office" (48). Another example was the four-generation Graham family (see pp. 46–47). While James Graham, the family's patriarch, earned enough to buy his house in Groveland and ensure that his wife never had to work outside the home, neither his daughter Renee nor his granddaughter Tenasha achieved financial independence as adults. The most unfortunate cases of downward mobility were the young people who were killed or in jail because of their forays into the world of drugs and gangs. "Oh, you so lucky," Lucille Arthur recalled her friends telling her about her daughter who she actually thought was somewhat of a disappointment. "You don't know! Your child ain't on drugs. Your child ain't callin' you every week for money. She supportin' herself" (54). This positive spin only illustrated the possible depths of some falls down the class ladder.

As in most social science research, it is always hardest to find the people who have "fallen from grace" (Newman 1989). This was my experience in going back to Groveland. The most disadvantaged people are not likely to be homeowners, they may not have home phone numbers, and they are not on professional social networking sites like LinkedIn. Even Facebook requires a computer and Internet access, which are definitely stratified by social class. Given all of this, and especially the fact that the split in mobility trajectories likely began as early as high school, I expected that the people I would find in Groveland were likely to be the more successful of their cohorts.

Neisha Morris, now in her thirties, reported positively on the current situation of the friends she grew up with. She told me: "All of my friends, that I can say, if they haven't tried to do something, they trying to do it now. Like Tamara, she just got her doctorate.... Everybody that I know is in school, graduated from school, working on school. If they didn't graduate from school, they still have a job, a good job, and still maintaining cars and taking care of they kids." I heard a similar line from Deanne Baker. When I probed, asking, "There must be disappointing stories? Downward folks who dropped off the radar screen, didn't do as well as their parents?" Deanne paused, and then responded, "I have no idea who those people are."

Yet digging deeper with Neisha Morris showed that she did know who those people were, and she knew them very well. Neisha's cousin, who also grew up in Groveland, has struggled financially and does not have a steady or a good job. Neisha was sympathetic, saying, "She's done a few things [wrong], but it's hard to find a job. It's hard for a person with a bachelors and a masters to find a job, let alone somebody that don't have one at all." Similarly, Neisha's younger brother is in his late twenties, didn't go to college, lives with their mother, and more often than not he has a job, but not one that pays a lot. His income would definitely put him in a lower stratum than his family of origin, and also lower than his sister.

Many Americans, no matter their race or neighborhood, can relate to these stories. These are the common stories of middle-class fragility. Figure E.1 showed that even a third of middle-income white adults end up in an income stratum below the one in which they were raised. However, the racial disparities cannot be discounted since such downward movement is significantly more common for blacks. Neighborhood disparities by race also cannot be discarded. Sharkey (2009) shows that nearly half of middle- and upper-income black people born between 1955 and 1970 were raised in poor neighborhoods, compared to only 1 percent of similar whites, and these neighborhood differences explain a sizable proportion of the black-white gap in later adult outcomes. Beyond the neighborhood, black and white families also look very different. Heflin and Pattillo (2006) find that 41 percent of middle-income blacks have a sibling whose income is below the poverty line, compared to only 16 percent of middle-income whites. These findings based on nationally representative data illustrate the multiple contexts of disadvantage that middle-class blacks face compared to their white peers. Hence, despite initial declarations that everyone is doing well, looking a little closer at the interview and the survey data shows otherwise.

Turning the focus away from individuals, the concepts of social mobility and reproduction can also be useful for discussing the life course of neighborhoods in general and Groveland in particular. Groveland has remained a predominately black, lower-middle-class neighborhood over the twenty years that this study covers. Surely people have moved in and out, businesses have come and gone, and the political leadership has changed. Yet, as sociologist Robert Sampson notes in his epic study of Chicago, *Great American City*, "Mechanisms of social reproduction are fairly general in their operation: communities constantly change, but in ways that regularly follow social and spatial logics" (2012, 409). The logics that Sampson and others have uncovered are driven primarily by race and class. As Sampson and Sharkey (2008, 27) write in a more detailed investigation of residential mobility in Chicago, "No matter where individuals choose to live, and no matter what their background or reasons behind their decisions, the racial income hierarchy of neighborhoods is rendered durable." In other words, while over the last sixty years, somewhere between 12 and 20 percent of Americans moved *every year* (US Census 2011), people seem to end up in neighborhoods that are not too unlike the places they left. Hence, neighborhood "change" is better described as a kind of churning pattern that maintains the advantages of advantaged places and keeps disadvantaged places at the bottom.

Of course, there are some examples of radical changes in who lives where and what neighborhoods look like. Changes in land use from industrial warehouses to upscale lofts or from college dorms to faculty housing will obviously change the socioeconomic profile of a neighborhood, but these are often the result of massive public and private interventions. By contrast, the maintenance and reproduction of racial and class segregation happens more slowly, steadily, and subtly. Real estate agents nudge black clients toward black neighborhoods and white clients toward white neighborhoods (Ross and Turner 2005); college graduates consult their fellow college graduates about the best school districts and rely on their parents' help with the down payment if those good places are a bit pricey (Johnson 2006; Shapiro 2004); or unconscious bias makes people avoid black neighborhoods even when they feature good housing, low crime, or other positive attributes (Krysan et al. 2009; Lewis, Emerson, and Klineberg 2011). The big picture stratification of places endures because of these often small and subtle practices of reproduction. In this way, Groveland remains more advantaged than other predominately black neighborhoods in Chicago, but less advantaged than predominately white neighborhoods in the city and suburbs.[1] This position of privilege and peril is explored more fully in the following sections.

THE ECONOMY, CRIME, AND HOUSING IN GROVELAND

Groveland and the Economy

"What are the needs in the community right now?" I asked the youth pastor of a local church. "Jobs!" was his simple answer, and then he elaborated:

> The number one thing they talk about in that community is the jobs. [There aren't jobs], not for the youth, not for nobody. You know how they used to have summer programs and stuff. The mayor done cut all that out. So the kids don't have nothin' to do. When I lived there it was middle class, but it's kinda hard to say now. But they got the same people there, but they don't have no jobs now. People want to work but can't find any job. But then I was talking to this one guy, he had to get a McDonald's job so he could support his family. But he had to work there so that the Lord would open up an opportunity to get a better job. He grew up there all his life.

These words show that Groveland residents have the same concerns as most Americans. In 2012, the national unemployment rate hovered above 8 percent, and Illinois was slightly worse off. Yet, as has been the case for decades, the nation's black unemployment rate is double the rate for whites, and in May 2012, the unemployment rate for black youth aged sixteen to nineteen stood at 37 percent. These stark and persistent racial inequalities in unemployment have been cause for intense debate given the election of Barack Obama, with many leaders in the black community calling on the nation's first black president to consider race-targeted solutions (Boles 2011; Kennedy 2012; New York Times 2011).

While youth unemployment is a real problem for Groveland families, especially for those on tight budgets who want to keep their kids engaged in something positive, the situation is even more dire for Groveland adults. Table E.1 updates the demographic portrait of the neighborhood with data from 1990 to 2010 (see appendix B for data from 1960 to 1990). The economic crisis of 2008 is reflected in the downward trend of the neighborhood economic indicators. The unemployment rate more than doubled from 8 percent in 2000 to 17 percent in 2010. The

Table E.1   Groveland neighborhood characteristics, 1990–2010

	1990	2000	2010
Total population	11,700	11,100	10,200
Percent black	98	97	96
Percent owner-occupied homes	75	71	70*
Percent of families below poverty line	12	8	19*
Percent with bachelors degree or higher	20	22	26*
Median household income (in 2010 dollars)	$56,900	$56,200	$46,900*
Median house value (in 2010 dollars)	$106,800	$121,800	$170,000*
Unemployment rate (%)	12	8	17*
Housing vacancy rate (%)	5	4	8*

*These 2010 figures are five-year estimates (2006–2010) from the American Community Survey, as opposed to the full population count from the 2010 census. Some caution should be taken when interpreting these numbers. However, while the margins of error in these estimates are sometimes quite wide, even the lowest bound estimates of most of these measures indicate increasing disadvantage when compared to 2000.

median household income declined significantly over the same period, although part of this can be explained by the fact that the population is aging, with nearly 20 percent of residents over 65 years old, and with 35 percent of residents receiving income from Social Security. While the unemployment rate in Groveland exceeds that of the city of Chicago, the median household income at $46,903 is higher than the city median, and is almost exactly the national figure.

The percentage of families with incomes below the poverty line also more than doubled, reaching 19 percent in 2010. Even with a very wide margin of error of 9 percentage points, this neighborhood poverty rate puts Groveland very close to qualifying as a "poor" neighborhood by the standards used by demographers (Jargowsky 1997; Kneebone, Nadeau, and Berube 2011), and surely exceeds the point at which negative neighborhood effects are empirically measurable (see esp. Galster, Cutsinger, and Malega 2008). Moreover, a minority of whites live in neighborhoods with poverty rates as high as that observed in Groveland. Indeed, considering all US metropolitan areas, the poverty rate of the average white person's neighborhood in 2009 was 10.7 percent, whereas the average black person lived in a neighborhood where 19 percent of their neighbors was poor (equivalent to the Groveland poverty rate) (Logan and Stults 2011). Overall, African Americans in Groveland are still better off than many blacks in Chicago, with lower neighborhood poverty and unemployment rates, a higher proportion of college graduates, and a higher median household income, all of which support the claim that Groveland is still a (lower-) middle-class neighborhood, despite increasing poverty rates. This position of being "more advantaged than other predominately black neighborhoods but less advantaged than white neighborhoods" is the recurring theme of this book.

One final point about Groveland and the economy concerns the kinds of jobs in which Groveland's residents work. After analyzing contemporary national employment and occupation data by race, Pitts (2011, 6) reports the following findings:

> The public sector is the largest employer of Black workers; there is a greater likelihood that a Black worker will be employed in the public sector compared to a non-Black worker; wages earned by Blacks in that industry are higher than those earned by Blacks in other sectors; and inequality within an industry is less in the public sector compared to other industries. . . . Consequently, any analysis of the impact to society of additional layoffs in the public sector as a strategy to address the fiscal crisis should take into account the disproportionate impact that reductions in government employment have on the Black community.

These findings are not news to scholars who study African American employment patterns, and they put into perspective some of the stress that Groveland residents are now facing as city, state, and federal budgets are all in severe deficit, putting government jobs and the value of public goods from public education to the postal service under scrutiny, and even attack. In analyzing the successful efforts of Wisconsin's governor to dismantle state employee unions, one editorial proclaimed that this was "the dirty secret of public-sector union busting. Look a little closer at who really stands to lose if [Wisconsin Governor] Scott Walker gets his way: Women and minorities" (Battistoni 2011). These efforts will have grave impacts on Groveland as well where, in 2010, over 25 percent of employed residents were government workers, most in the fields of education, health, and social services.

A shrinking public sector will no doubt shrink Groveland residents' ability to hold on to middle-class status. Yet this is only half the story. The other blow to middle-class blacks comes from the fact that they are disproportionate *consumers* of public sector goods. For example, at every level of income, black children are less likely than white children to be enrolled in private schools. The gap is largest for the lower-middle class. According to the 2000 census, among families making $25,000 to $35,000 a year, 12 percent of white children were in private schools, compared to 7 percent of black children. When state and local education budgets are slashed and teachers are laid off, the children of lower-middle-class black families—whose prospects define the future of the black middle class—are disproportionately hurt. This story is repeated across the various services that public sector workers provide. In health care, blacks are more likely than whites to utilize public hospitals, no matter their income (Gaskin 1999). In public safety, according to the National Crime Victimization Survey, higher-earning blacks have victimization rates comparable to lower-income whites. For example, blacks with family earnings over $75,000 are more likely to get their cars stolen than whites in families earning less than $7,500. Cuts to public budgets will mean fewer police and fewer jobs programs that provide alternatives to crime. Middle-class blacks will feel all of these things more acutely than middle-class whites. There is no doubt that the loss of public-sector jobs will disproportionately hurt black workers, many of whom earn a middle-class living, but we haven't yet begun to imagine the collateral consequences for the black middle class as the goods that those public sector workers provide begin to disappear.

Groveland and Crime

When I asked Spider Waters if crime rates had changed in the neighborhood from the time when I was hanging out with him at Groveland Park he answered without hesitation, "Just skyrocketed!" I got pretty much the same answer from Tyson Reed. "Crime, do you think it's gotten better or worse?" I asked him. "Crime? Crime is definitely harder in Groveland, in my mind." And when I met up for coffee with some of the people who had been involved with the St. Mary's youth group, I listened to them also talk about how the neighborhood had gotten worse in terms of crime and safety. While none of them lived in Groveland anymore, their parents all did, so they visited regularly. Cynthia's description characterizes the common narrative around crime: "In my opinion we were in a very nice neighborhood but I don't know what's changed over the years. The crime is so high and it's really not safe. Today, if I go there, I'm kinda nervous because you never know what's gonna happen 'cause so much has happened throughout the years." Rashaad talked about being concerned for his mother, who still takes a daily walk through the neighborhood. "My parents have verbally said that they feel like the community's gone down over the years," he said, "but my mom's still like, in the summer time, going on her walk and she'll do it as the sun is going down. So I'm like, okay, you must not feel too threatened if you still taking that walk." Cynthia jumped in regarding her mother's walks through the neighborhood: "I wish she *would* feel unsafe, but she doesn't."

After nearly an hour of hearing how bad the neighborhood had gotten and how the kids in the neighborhood had changed, I decided to put out a challenge by sharing the statistics that crime in Chicago (and in many big cities across the country) had shown a steady decline since the early 1990s. "So there were probably more shootings when you all were growing up in the neighborhood than there are now," I said. "No way!" Cynthia responded incredulously. "Then I think we need to write WGN on what news to report on because they make it seem like that's all that happens all day every day."

Compared to other African American neighborhoods in the city, and even compared to the neighborhoods that surround it (see appendix B; fig. 1), Groveland was never a high-crime neighborhood, and most residents recognize that fact. Nonetheless, the crime rate in Groveland is not negligible; it is higher than the crime rate in most white neighborhoods; and it is nearly impossible to live in a major American city and not express concern about crime. All of these things explain the responses I got to my question about changes in crime over time. But what do the statistics say?

Looking at the police district within which Groveland is located shows that from 1993 to 2011, the overall crime rate in the district for all index crimes declined by 22 percent,[2] violent crime went down by 42 percent, and the murder rate declined by 68 percent. In 1998, the Chicago police department began reporting crime statistics by community area. Groveland-specific statistics show overall crime went down by 15 percent and violent crime went down 17 percent between 1998 and 2011. In 1998 there was one murder in Groveland and in 2011 there were two; throughout this fourteen-year time period, the murder rate fluctuated between one and three, with occasional bad years when there were six or seven homicides. Given that the crime data show clear trends that things overall have improved (with homicides holding relatively steady), why do people feel like crime is worse in the 2010s than it was in the 1990s?

Interrogating this very salient perception of increased crime despite the crime statistics is helpful for putting Groveland in a broader research context. I see four explanations as particularly fruitful for understanding how current and former Groveland residents read the crime changes over the years. The first is simply that perhaps my question was unclear and people were responding about a time period much shorter than the fifteen-to-twenty-year window I wanted them to ponder, which in retrospect was an unfair question. Indeed, the first six months of 2012 witnessed a nearly 40 percent increase in the number of murders in the city of Chicago as compared to the first six months of 2011. The district in which Groveland is located saw a 33 percent increase in homicides, but a 10 percent reduction in overall index crimes. So the first explanation is simply that the most recent bad news was the most top-of-mind when I asked about crime.

The second explanation is the one that Cynthia herself gave in the previous quote. The news media is obsessed with crime reporting. The first story on the *Chicago Tribune* website nearly every day is a tally of the number of people shot and/or killed the previous day. More specifically to Groveland, despite the array of activities and events in the neighborhood—from reunions of the local grammar school to weekend farmer's markets to book clubs to seminars on understanding Medicare—a search of the neighborhood's (real) name on the *Chicago Tribune* website yields a first page with ten results, seven of which are about local crimes or crime rates. Television news goes beyond newspapers to provide graphic images and heart-wrenching interviews of families mourning the loss of their loved ones. While a generous reading is that news organizations hope that their chronicles of violence in mostly black and Latino neighborhoods will create empathy (Höijer 2004), the evidence is stronger that it contributes to the stigmatization and avoidance of black people and black neighborhoods (Charles 2006; Correll et al. 2002; Crowder 2000; Crowder, Hall, and Tolnay 2011; Entman and Rojecki 2000; Greenwald, Oakes, and Hoffman 2003; Krysan, Farley, and Couper 2008; Krysan et al. 2009; Emerson, Yancey, and Chai 2001; Quillian 2002; Quillian and Pager 2001; Sampson 2012). In analyzing the impact of the news media on perceptions of the city, Dreier (2004, 194) writes: "It comes as no surprise that even people who live in communities with little crime or drug problems think that they are the middle of a crime wave perpetrated primarily by black males."

The third explanation is also about stigma. However, instead of blacks being the objects of stigmatization, this third explanation stresses intraracial stigma by class. That is, within the black community there is a salient narrative of blaming poor people for community problems. Even in the 1990s, Groveland residents voiced a narrative of decline that focused on increasing numbers of poor families, especially through the Section 8 program, which provides rent subsidies to low-income families in the private housing market. Tommy Smith said the following back in 1996:

There may be five houses on the block—no six—six houses on the block that once upon a time was full with residents that grew up and started at the same time as me. They either died or moved away. Out of that, one of those houses is knocked down, one is vacant, one is burned down, and one is empty on a Section 8 listing, and one is, two are empty. And, the people who did move in two of the vacant houses were low-income-housed people. And in that, again, they just did not take care of their property. And did not care much about the individuals surrounding them. And, no, I did not know them very well. (37)

Residents today voice a nearly identical narrative. Tyson Reed talked about the influx of public housing families. "When they moved into some of those communities," he said referring to Groveland and the areas that surround it, "you almost had a version of black flight. Not white flight, but black flight. So now you take out people who care about their cars and now you got people walking down the street busting windows. You got people who, you know, kick in people's doors. All that type of thing. So what's going to happen to that community? It's gonna go in the toilet. At least that's the way I feel." Whether discussed as Section 8 families or people from the projects or just simply "renters," the association of lower-income people with an increase in crime in the neighborhood (and definitely with a decline in property upkeep) was shared by many of the people I reinterviewed. People perceived hanging out to be more of a problem and thought that respect for elders had all but disappeared. The organized control that was once levied by Lance and the Black Mobsters was no longer in operation, and instead "cliques" and "mobs" of young, low-income, recent arrivals showed no shared or stable allegiances. However, while the data support the observation that there are a greater proportion of poor families and renters in the neighborhood (see table E.1), it has not lead to an increase in neighborhood crime, but rather crime has gone down. Nonetheless, these are important narratives about the stigmatization of poverty and poor people that are much bigger than Groveland, a point to which I will return (Katz 1989; Pattillo 2007; Soss, Fording, and Schram 2011).

The final explanation for the disjuncture between the reality and perceptions of crime in Groveland comes from Neisha Morris and her mother, Anna, who were the only people who did not sense that crime had gone up in the neighborhood. In their complaints about fights at the local school or unfamiliar youth hanging out in front of their homes, it was as if they could not completely ignore the narrative of a crime surge that was heard so often in the neighborhood, but they also took time to think about how it used to be. Anna told me, "Well the crime back then was way worse to me 'cause you remember how Neisha and them was losing friends every time you turn around. It's not that bad. It's not hardly no crime. It's just the stupid little things these kids do." Neisha later echoed her mother's sentiment, remembering all that she had been through as a teenager.

> As far as the crime goes, it's a lot. But to me it was a lot when I was little. I guess I can say that because I went through a lot of my friends dying when I was young. So it's the same to me. So, another person might not feel that way 'cause a lot of people didn't go through what I went through. So to me, it's not a big difference. It's the same. I know 6 or 7 people who got killed in '95, in '94, right over here.

In this quote, we hear Neisha making comparative statements based on experience that rationally brought her to the conclusion that crime had not changed much in the neighborhood. Yet, she did not feel fully rational about crime in general. She could not shake the fact that she still felt much more vigilant and concerned about crime, despite her assertions that there was no need to be any more concerned. She pondered aloud about this discordance:

> It's just that the older we get we just look at it differently. I think that's what the main thing is. This stuff has been going on forever, nothing is changing, it's just that we view it differently and we take it more seriously. Somebody getting shot over there when I was younger probably didn't mean as much to me as now me looking and knowing my children are out here and somebody just got shot over there. Not to say that it didn't mean anything that somebody got shot. But it didn't register to me as much because I was younger. But now that I'm older you see things differently.

Neisha's perspective helps to understand why Tyson, Cynthia, Rashaad, and Spider all thought that things were worse. They are at a different point in their lives, older now, some homeowners, and many of them parents themselves. For example, Spider had worked for years at Groveland Park, keeping order and peace, overseeing basketball tournaments and managing the summer camp. And yet when I asked about him taking his eleven-year-old son to the park now he answered:

I like taking Payton to the park in my father's neighborhood [in the suburbs]. 'Cause, say, if I see you and your boyfriend get out the car. If y'all got kids, y'all family. If I see the Mexicans pull up. It's him and his wife getting out to play. [But] when I go up to Groveland Park and play with my son, it's always three niggahs that get out the car, all three of 'em got a fifth of Grey Goose with they pants saggin'. So you already know one thing that's going to happen. I know they got guns. . . . Next thing you know, they gon' start shooting each other. And it's always an innocent person that gets shot. 'Cause I say if they shoot my son, I'm killing everything that's moving. So when I go to the park out in the suburb, people pull up, they wave at you, they see you running around. We run up a big mountain and he climb on everything. And then before you know it, it's 7:00, then we going somewhere to go get dinner. And then Sunday morning, I'll wake up and cook breakfast.

There is no clearer and simpler statement of parental responsibility than Spider making a decision to take his son to a park where he perceives the likelihood of random violence to be close to zero. The irony is that sixteen years ago in my interview with him, Spider had the following to say when comparing his father's suburban neighborhood with Groveland: "It's quiet out there. Then, when it got too quiet I come back out South for some good ol' South Side violence. Hear some guns shootin' off in the alley behind the crib. Damn, I feel at home!" Whatever risky business might have excited him as a young man is all behind him now, and the most important thing is the safety of his son. From his current vantage point, Groveland does not seem to provide that kind of safety. That is not to say that there are no children playing on Groveland streets or going to Groveland Park. There are plenty. And even Neisha lets her daughter ride her bicycle on the block, and her teenage son was off at Open Gym at Groveland Park on the night that I visited her. Still, she is always worried, as a parent always is, especially parents in places where there are real safety risks, even if they are fewer than in past years.

Groveland and Housing

To say that the US housing market in 2012 was volatile with an uncertain future is an understatement. Groveland allows us to consider how housing trends and policies that are impacting metropolitan areas across the country are experienced at the neighborhood level. I discuss three pressing housing market issues that are particularly apparent in Groveland—the subprime lending and foreclosure crises, changes in public housing policy, and the swell of black suburbanization—with particular elaboration of the first point.

In December of 2011, the US Department of Justice put out a press release with the headline, "Justice Department Reaches $335 Million Settlement to Resolve Allegations of Lending Discrimination by Country-wide Financial Corporation; More than 200,000 African-American and Hispanic Borrowers Who Qualified for Loans Were Charged Higher Fees or Placed into Subprime Loans." The government lawsuit alleged that Countrywide had discriminated against African Americans and Hispanics by charging them higher interest rates than they charged similar whites, and by steering them into high-cost loans even when they qualified for conventional ones. The press release read: "Countrywide's actions contributed to the housing crisis, hurt entire communities, and denied families access to the American dream. . . . We are using every tool in our law enforcement arsenal, including some that were dormant for years, to go after institutions of all sizes that discriminated against families solely because of their race or national origin" (US Department of Justice 2011).

The Countrywide settlement supports what considerable research has shown, which is that blacks and Latinos experience significant discrimination in the mortgage market (Jackson 1985; Kuebler 2012; Squires 1994; Yinger 1995), and that they were disproportionately targeted by lenders and banks to receive subprime loans (Aalbers 2012). These loans can be characterized by higher interest rates, payment plans that only work if the value of the house increases, large deferred payments, prepayment penalties, and other complicated and disadvantageous arrangements that are often not fully disclosed or explained to the homebuyer. The research is clear that black neighborhoods and mortgage seekers were targeted for subprime loans no matter their socioeconomic status and despite other indicators of credit worthiness. For example, a study by the Institute on Race and Poverty (2009) at the University of Minnesota showed that African Americans in the Minneapolis metropolitan area earning over $150,000 a year were more than two-and-a-half times as likely to be denied a home loan as whites who were earning below $40,000 (and four times as likely to be denied a loan as whites in the same income group). For people who actually got loans, high-income blacks were three-and-a-half times more likely to be in a subprime loan than whites in the low-income group (and six times more likely than high-income whites).

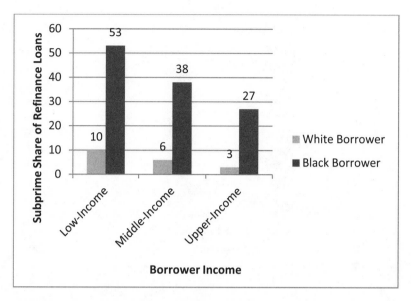

Figure E.2 Subprime share of 1998 refinance mortgages by borrower race and income* (Chicago metropolitan area).

*Low-income borrower: income not more than 80 percent of the metropolitan area median income (AMI); middle-income borrower: 80–120 percent AMI; upper-income borrower: 120 percent AMI. Source: US Department of Housing and Urban Development (2000b).

These are the stark realities of discrimination in mortgage markets, which were repeated in cities across America, including Chicago. Figures E.2 and E.3 show data from a report of the US Department of Housing and Urban Development (2000b) on the disparities in subprime lending in the home refinance market in the Chicago metropolitan area in 1998 (for the national situation, see US Department of Housing and Urban Development 2000a). Figure E.2 presents data for individual black and white borrowers in Chicago. More than a quarter (27 percent) of upper-income blacks were in subprime refinance mortgages, compared to only 10 percent of *low-income* whites and 3 percent of comparable upper-income whites. As the Department of Justice investigation revealed, this is in large part due to mortgage brokers steering blacks into loans that are ultimately more profitable for the lender and riskier for the borrower. Figure E.3 looks at refinance lending at the neighborhood level and illustrates that the proportion of all refinance loans that were subprime was six to seven times as high in predominately African American

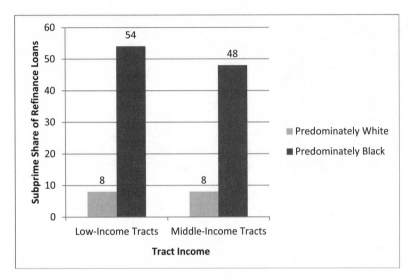

Figure E.3   Subprime share of 1998 refinance mortgages by race and income of neighborhood* (Chicago metropolitan area).

*Predominately white tract: at least 85 percent white; predominately black tract: at least 75 percent black; low-income tract: not more than 80 percent AMI; middle-income tract: 80–120 percent AMI. Source: US Department of Housing and Urban Development (2000b).

neighborhoods as compared to predominately white neighborhoods. The income composition of the neighborhood—that is, whether it was low- or middle-income—hardly mattered at all; middle-income black neighborhoods received six times the proportion of subprime refinancing loans as low-income white neighborhoods. This means that above and beyond the targeting of individuals, lenders targeted whole black neighborhoods (and avoided white ones), which constituted a sort of "double whammy" for African Americans living in predominately black neighborhoods and double protection for whites in mostly white neighborhoods. The US Department of Housing and Urban Development (HUD) studied these patterns in Los Angeles, Atlanta, Baltimore, and New York, and the magnitude was the same across them all.

The rash of subprime lending—which was heating up, but was not apparent in the initial research for *BPF*—eventually led to the foreclosure crisis, which also has decidedly racial contours. A 2011 report by the Center for Responsible Lending concluded the following:

Although the majority of [foreclosure-]affected borrowers have been white, African-American and Latino borrowers are almost twice as likely to have been impacted by the crisis. Approximately one quarter of all Latino and African-American borrowers have lost their home to foreclosure or are seriously delinquent, compared to just under 12 percent for white borrowers. (Bocian et al. 2011, 4)

The report goes on to reiterate that race was more important than income for explaining patterns of foreclosures, stating: "Racial and ethnic disparities in foreclosure rates cannot be explained by income, since disparities persist even among higher-income groups. For example, approximately 10 percent of higher-income African-American borrowers and 15 percent of higher-income Latino borrowers have lost their home to foreclosure, compared with 4.6 percent of higher-income non-Hispanic white borrowers" (Bocian et al. 2011, 5).

Rugh and Massey (2010) compellingly show that racial residential segregation has fueled and exacerbated the housing foreclosure crisis. Using data from the one hundred largest metropolitan areas, the authors study the link between measures of racial segregation in a city and its foreclosure rate. The authors find clearly that metropolitan racial segregation created the opportunity for the kind of subprime mortgage targeting discussed above, which increased rates of foreclosure. As the authors conclude: "Segregation therefore racialized and intensified the consequences of the American housing bubble. Hispanic and black home owners, not to mention entire Hispanic and black neighborhoods, bore the brunt of the foreclosure crisis. This outcome was not simply a result of neutral market forces but was structured on the basis of race and ethnicity through the social fact of residential segregation" (645).

And if all of that weren't enough, the final blow is what the housing crisis has meant for racial disparities in wealth. Since for most people their homes represent their most substantial nest egg, the decline in housing prices and racial disparities in foreclosures have blown open a gap in black/white wealth that was already wide. The median net worth of African Americans in the US declined by 53 percent from 2005 to 2009 (and by an even larger 66 percent for Latinos), but declined by only 16 percent for whites. This translates into a doubling of the wealth gap: In 2009, for nearly every $19 in wealth that whites possessed blacks owned about $1, up from a ratio of about $9 to $1 in 2004 (Pew Research Center 2011). In Groveland, the cumulative loss in property values due to foreclosures in 1997–98 alone totaled over $1 million (Immergluck and Smith 2006, fig. 4).

Groveland's experience of the subprime and foreclosure crises is similar to its middling position on so many other dimensions. As the above data suggest, as a black neighborhood it was definitely targeted for subprime loans, and its middle-income status did not buffer it from such predation. However, Groveland does not rank at the top of the list of neighborhoods with the highest proportion of subprime loans or highest foreclosure rates in Chicago. Keeping in mind the fact that the foreclosure wave began well before the housing crisis of 2008 (Immergluck and Smith 2006), and thus more recent figures cannot capture cumulative disparities over time, in 2009, Groveland had thirty-seven foreclosure filings per ten thousand mortgageable properties, which was just below the rate for the city of Chicago. However, foreclosure rates in Chicago were considerably higher than the foreclosure rates in the predominately white counties that ring Chicago. That is, in order to understand Groveland's place in the stratification of places, the comparison needs to include the entire metropolitan area, not just the city, which is generally more disadvantaged.

When I asked people in Groveland about the foreclosure crisis, they did not share stories of friends or family members who had lost their homes. Instead, they referenced the aftermath: boarded up, vacant houses. Table E.1 shows the increase in vacancy rates in Groveland between 2000 and 2010, and these are the eyesores to which order-minded Groveland residents are most attentive. They also worry that vacant and foreclosed houses will eventually be bought by investors who will use the houses as rental property.

Who are the likely tenants of this newly available rental housing in Groveland? When I asked Sheila Boone, "Who is moving into this neighborhood?" she began with a simple answer that then grew into a winding but rich elaboration of the history of a house on her block and its residents. She told me:

> Section 8. Which can be, you know, we know our families are constructed in any number of ways. So, for example, next door to me, after the family that had originally been there for so many years, the father got senile, the daughter got a second mortgage, prostitution, drugs, went to hell. Developer got it. Then a young family did move in. Mother, father, little boy, little girl. By the time they moved out last year, he was in high school. And he was a tiny little guy, maybe five [years old] when they first moved in. So they had been here for some period of time as well. So they have now bought another home, I'm told in Bronzeville, and they're renting their home [next door] to Section 8. And we believe that that is the most frequent thing that's happening in terms of how people are

now moving into this area. Because we have a lot of foreclosures. We have a lot of just lost homes.

Sheila touches on so many salient points in the life course of the house next door to her own. It begins with a family that was likely the first black occupant of the house in the 1960s, when the neighborhood was experiencing its racial transition from white to black. A wayward, downwardly mobile second generation squandered their parents' legacy and lost the house. After the intermediacy of a developer, a new young black family moved in and raised another family, and then moved to the gentrifying new mecca of black middle- and upper-class Chicago, Bronzeville (see Boyd 2008; Hyra 2008; Pattillo 2007). A bad housing market made it unwise to sell the house, so they rented it instead. Changes in national housing policy (discussed below) created a growing demand for apartments by people with Housing Choice Vouchers—which most people still refer to by the old designation of "Section 8." The result: in moved Sheila's new neighbors, a new family being subsidized through Section 8.

The federal government has moved significantly more resources into vouchers and is moving away from building and managing actual housing in developments like public housing projects. In 1993, 1.2 million families received vouchers nationally; this number grew to nearly 2.2 million families by 2011. With vouchers, families can look for an apartment in any neighborhood and rent any reasonably priced apartment that passes a safety inspection. So, Sheila's former neighbors (who are now landlords) receive a monthly rent check from both their tenant and from the local housing authority that administers the voucher program.

Many Groveland residents see these new federal and local housing policies as likely to destabilize their neighborhood. The City of Chicago has demolished nearly all of its high-rise public housing, totaling nearly 20,000 public housing apartments. In the early 1990s, there were about 20,000 people who lived in the Robert Taylor Homes alone (Venkatesh 2000). All of the families who lived there—and in Stateway Gardens, the Ida B. Wells Homes, Rockwell Gardens, and many other developments that have been demolished—were pushed into the private rental market and had to search for apartments where the rents were low enough that the voucher would cover them (roughly 40 percent of the average rent in the city) (Chicago Housing Authority 2011; Joseph and Chaskin 2012). Not only has this transformation indelibly altered the physical vistas within the city, but it also represents tremendous residential flux within black neighborhoods where rents are generally more affordable. Groveland residents have watched the demolition of public housing in other parts of the city with particular angst. Neisha Morris told me, "It's not even really the foreclosures. 'Cause now it's so many houses available. And I just, I think about the Section 8 stuff and it's mixing the lower income with the middle income and it's like: what you did over there was okay, but now you bringing it over here, and it's just bringing the area down."

Data from HUD confirm Groveland residents' perception that the number of families using vouchers has increased. In 1998, there were fifty-eight voucher-supported households, and by 2009 there were 200. This represents a change in the proportion of the total households in the community that are receiving voucher subsidies from less than 2 percent in 1998, to nearly 5 percent in 2009. The perception of an increase in the number of subsidized families is correct, but voucher families are still a small minority of the population. Furthermore, most of these new low-income families are not ones that have been displaced from the demolished public housing projects. As with the moral panic around crime in the neighborhood, the fear of displaced public housing residents is similarly overblown. The Chicago Housing Authority reports that there are thirty-four families (or 0.8 percent of all housing units) in Groveland who were displaced from the projects. That did not stop Tyson Reed from predicting that this "influx" of displaced poor people will mean that the neighborhood is "gonna go in the toilet."

This topic, felt keenly on the streets of Groveland, is also a matter of national debate. A 2008 article in the *Atlantic* magazine fingered displaced public housing residents and new voucher residents as the cause of rising crime in the suburbs of Memphis (Rosin 2008). Scores of opinion pieces and comments were written in response, and a group of very prominent scholars from across the country strongly criticized the article, writing:

> Rosin paints a lurid, stark picture, using Memphis as a case study, to indict a number of national efforts begun in the early 1990s to tackle the thorny problem of geographically concentrated "ghetto" poverty. . . . But Rosin gets key facts wrong and uses others in misleading ways. She provides no evidence that the low-income families who moved to neighborhoods outside the traditional ghetto contributed significantly to the growth of poverty in those areas, let alone that they were responsible for the uptick in crime. . . . We've learned a great deal, over the past decade, about the role that low-income housing policy—the successes and failures alike—can play. It's a shame the sensationalized "murder mystery" didn't find a story there. (Briggs and Dreier 2008, 1, 2–3, 14)

Rigorous research followed these early editorial opinions. Using national data, Ellen et al. (2011), for example, found that indeed there was a positive correlation between an increase in voucher households and crime in a neighborhood, *but* (an important "but") more detailed, time-sequenced analyses pointed to the possibility that voucher householders were moving to areas where crime was already increasing, rather than being the cause of it.

In Chicago and Atlanta, Popkin and colleagues (2012) asked the same question: Are neighborhoods that were the destinations for families relocated from demolished projects in Chicago and Atlanta experiencing increased crime? What they found was more complicated than a simple yes or no answer. Crime went down in most of the destination neighborhoods of displaced public housing residents, but (another important "but") the authors estimated that crime would have gone down *even more* if those relocated public housing families had not moved in. In other words, relocation stunted the crime decline in neighborhoods that received large numbers of public housing residents. For example, the authors report that gun crime would have been 4.3 percent lower in destination neighborhoods in Chicago (lower, that is, than it had already declined) had relocation not occurred. The greater the proportion of relocated families within the neighborhood, the greater was the impact on crime. However, in both Chicago and Atlanta, only a few neighborhoods reached sufficient density of relocated families to really make an impact on crime rates. Overall, the authors come to a conclusion not too unlike that reached by Ellen et al.: "Our story is not the popular version of previously stable communities spiraling into decline because of public housing residents moving in, but rather a story of poor families moving into areas that were already struggling" (7). Furthermore, while they found a correlation between dense concentrations of relocated families and crime increases, they found no association between crime rates and families using vouchers who were not being relocated from public housing.

How does all of this apply to Groveland? What is happening in Groveland is that the full, complex story about federal and local housing policies and widespread racial discrimination in the mortgage market is reduced to a much more simple and visible target: former public housing families and low-income voucher holders. Surely people in Groveland recognize that even middle-class people are losing their jobs and becoming poor, and that many of the low-income families in the neighborhood are not newcomers at all, but rather downwardly mobile children of previous generations. Yet, just as anxieties about unemployment at the national level get directed at immigrants, the local experience of neighborhood fragility obscures the macroeconomic context, and instead gets boiled down to the slightest increase in subsidized residents. This exercise highlights the importance of placing phenomena that at first glance seem to be about the undesirable behavior of people from stigmatized groups back into national (and international) contexts, uncovering the proverbial forest instead of just blaming the trees.

Feelings of threat and decline in Groveland make people want to leave. Chicago's black population declined by nearly 200,000 residents between 2000 and 2010, and Chicago was not unique. Detroit also lost nearly 200,000 African Americans, and New York, LA, DC, Oakland, and Cleveland (among others) all saw black population declines of more than 30,000 people. Even the city of Atlanta, the much-touted new center of black life and culture, lost black population. However, in the case of Atlanta, the black population of the suburbs *grew* by nearly a half-million people, whereas the gain in black population in Chicago's suburbs did not offset the decline of the black population in the city proper (Frey 2011). "Black flight" is how some observers are referring to this phenomenon of the exodus of African Americans from the city proper to the suburbs (Woldoff 2011), especially the distant suburbs (Pfeiffer 2012a; 2012b), even though black suburban movement is often to areas that are not strong economically (Adelman 2004; Holliday and Dwyer 2009; Orfield and Ashkinaze 1991; Stoll 2005).

Tyson Reed shocked me with the news that he was actively looking to leave Groveland, and some of his neighbors were too:

> So my immediate neighbor, one to the south, has one son who is about 18 [or] 19 now [that] got shot. [He has] one son that's about 17 that's on the border. And a daughter that's probably about 12 or 13. He's already said he's moving. And they didn't grow up in Groveland. He actually grew up on the west side and was like, "Naw, dude, we goin' further. We goin' to Indiana." My neighbor on the north of me, they're not married, but they've been together for the last 12 years or so. She had a son who is now 24, 25 who is an idiot. And she wants to move to a South Loop type area. He's kind of drawing a line in the sand. I think the difference between me and them talking about it is they don't have young kids. And even though there's a playground right there, I'll never take my daughter to that playground. I have a niece and nephew and my niece is 8. My nephew is 3 [or] 4. I'm never taking them across the street to the playground. Ever. Ever. Ever. Ever.

Tyson makes a number of crucial points in his telling of the calculus that he and his two neighbors are making about their futures in the neighborhood. First, it is no surprise that having children is a major life course transition that motivates residential mobility (Clark and Dieleman 1996), and Tyson's focus on his new fatherhood illustrates this point. Second, one of his neighbors desires to "draw the line in the sand," referring to a decision to stay put and not succumb to whatever signals of decline might be evident, echoing the sentiment that some whites felt and feel in situations of neighborhood racial change (Cummings 1998; Kefalas 2003; Woldoff 2011). After all, fleeing could create a self-fulfilling prophecy by depleting the neighborhood of the most capable residents. This neighbor's partner, however, is not so determined to stay. She wants to move to the South Loop, illustrating a third important point in this vignette: the gentrification of (near-) downtown areas as another attractive destination for professional black families (Moore 2009; Pattillo 2007). Finally, the third couple exemplifies what is most apparent in the demographic data—the exodus to places far away from the city, in this case in an entirely different state, Indiana. Along with this suburban exodus is the migration of African Americans to the south and west (Frey 2004). So, here we have three couples, each looking to leave Groveland, and each with different possible destinations that are illustrative of major migration patterns uncovered in the literature, leaving the prospects for neighborhoods at the edges of cities, like Groveland, and in the inner-ring suburbs in a precarious state.

RESEARCH ON THE BLACK MIDDLE-CLASS RESIDENTIAL EXPERIENCE

When *BPF* was published, the 1990 data showed that a majority of African Americans in the US lived in majority-black neighborhoods. In 2000 that was still the case, but 2010 marked the end of the era when a majority of blacks lived in neighborhoods where more than 50 percent of their neighbors were black. Similarly, the average white person today lives in a neighborhood that is 70 percent white, whereas in 1980 they lived in a neighborhood that was 88 percent white. So, whites too are becoming less racially isolated and interacting with a greater proportion of nonwhites. Furthermore, the average level of racial segregation of whites and blacks across all US metropolitan areas dipped below the levels that sociologists have determined to be "high segregation," and has moved into the moderate range. Finally, the number and proportion of neighborhoods that are racially integrated—either defined by the absence of a predominant racial group or through the significant presence of two or more groups—continues to grow (Iceland 2009; see also Ellen 2000). All of these indicators have caused one set of observers to claim that we are at "the end of the segregated century"; that is, whereas the 1900s marked the age of segregation the 2000s ushered in an era of diversity and integration (Glaeser and Vigdor 2012).

While these trends are undeniable, stark racial disparities in residential experiences persist. Black-white segregation remains stubbornly high in the country's largest cities like Washington, DC, Philadelphia, Miami, Los Angeles, and Chicago. For example, in the New York metropolitan area, the segregation index in 2010 was 79, which means that nearly 80 percent of the white (or black) population would have to move to a different neighborhood in order for every neighborhood in the New York area to mirror the racial composition of the metropolis overall (Logan and Stults 2011). Moreover, racial segregation continues to concentrate poverty in majority black and Hispanic neighborhoods, making whites much more likely to live in areas with low poverty rates. For example, the typical affluent black person in the US lives in a neighborhood with more poverty, fewer college graduates, and more boarded-up houses than the typical *poor* white person (Logan and Stults 2011; Adelman 2004). These kinds of data lead observers to highlight the continuing significance of race as a criterion upon which people are residentially segregated (Cashin 2004), thereby unevenly distributing all kinds of resources that are important for upward mobility, from good schools to health care to access to healthy food. It is important to emphasize that these two realities exist *simultaneously*. Progress has been made but equality is still far off.

Aside from the broad descriptions of inequalities, there has been growth in the literature on the qualitative experience of middle-class blacks in their neighborhoods. This research explores the question: What does racial residential segregation (even with class sorting) mean for the neighborhood experience of middle-class African Americans? Several ethnographies expound on how high poverty rates within black middle-class areas negatively impact neighborhood social and political cohesion. For example, Valerie Johnson's (2002) study of Prince Georges (PG) County, Maryland—the poster suburb for black middle-class America—investigates the reasons why, despite their numerical majority, blacks do not control many of the important positions of power in PG County. She argues that socioeconomic diversity among black Prince Georgians means that they have been unable to coalesce around particular interests in order to advance policy initiatives or elect representatives in large numbers (also, on class in PG County and Washington, DC, see Hopkinson 2012). Ginwright (2002) finds similar ideological disputes between poor and middle-class blacks in an Oakland school setting, where the social and human capital of middle-class black school activists overpowered the working-class parents in the schools. Research in this vein highlights the particular organizational challenges that confront middle-class blacks and poor blacks in shared residential environments.

Bruce Haynes's *Red Lines, Black Spaces* (2001) is a study of Runyon Heights, a predominately black suburb outside of New York City. Like *BPF*, his study illustrates the vulnerability of black middle-class neighborhoods to increasing poverty, and the efforts of middle-class black residents to hold the class line (see also Gregory 1998). John Jackson's book *Harlemworld* (2001) directs attention to the class diversity of identities in black Harlem, which he shows is erroneously assumed to be overwhelmingly poor, but is in fact rife with distinctions along class (and gender and ethnic) lines (see also Prince 2004; Taylor 2002; Hyra 2008). On the issue of gender, Marsh et al. (2007; Dickson and Marsh 2008) document the increase in living alone among middle-class blacks, especially black women. The authors term this group the "Love Jones Cohort," after a popular film of the 1990s. Several other studies that are not specifically about neighborhoods focus on the "performance" of black middle-class status in literature and film, and through particular cultural tastes and consumption practices (Daniels 2004; Banks 2010; Young and Tsemo 2011), and a number of books have investigated differences in cultural capital along race and class lines (Lareau 2003; Pugh 2009).

Karyn Lacy's *Blue Chip Black* (2007) represents a crucial new intervention in the study of the black middle class and their residential environs. The US Census shows that 2010 marked the first decade in which a majority of African Americans lived in the suburbs of the hundred largest metropolitan areas, rather than within the city proper (Frey 2011), whereas the majority of whites became suburban by 1970. While several of the books discussed above study black suburbs (see also Wiese 2004), Lacy's ethnography goes a step further to show the diversity of the black suburban experience, comparing blacks living in a majority-black suburb to those living in two different kinds of majority-white suburbs. Moreover, whereas *BPF* is a study of lower-middle-class African Americans in a lower-middle-class city neighborhood, Lacy divides the black middle class into the "core" black middle class and the "elite" black middle class, and focuses more on the latter group.[3] While going in the direction of studying more affluent blacks should in no way overshadow the fact that over 25 percent of African Americans are poor (double the white poverty rate), and that 66 percent of African Americans born between 1985 and 2000 grew up in a poor neighborhood, compared to only 6 percent of whites from the same cohort (Sharkey 2009), Lacy's study is still crucial for portraying the variety of black experiences in the US.

Drawing from *BPF* and *Blue-Chip Black*, Sharkey (2011) offers the most comprehensive current demographic appraisal of black middle-class neighborhoods and middle-class blacks' residential attainment. Three findings are worth highlighting. First, Sharkey finds strong evidence for the claim in *BPF* that not only are black middle-class neighborhoods more disadvantaged than white middle-class neighborhoods *internally*, but they also exist within a more disadvantaged geographic context. For example, half of all "advantaged" majority-black neighborhoods in the US are surrounded by disadvantaged neighborhoods, compared to only 12 percent of advantaged majority-white neighborhoods. Sampson (2012) refers to this concept as "spatial interdependence" and finds for Chicago that "even white working-class areas do better than the highest-income black neighborhoods when it comes to the economic status of near neighbors" (249). Even when predominately black neighborhoods score highly on various factors that are *protective* (what Sampson calls "collective efficacy"), they are more likely to be surrounded by neighborhoods that score poorly on that measure, whereas well-organized white neighborhoods are surrounded by similarly well-organized places. Sharkey finds that the spatial connection of black advantaged neighborhoods to disadvantaged neighborhoods has changed very little over time.

Second, 52 percent of middle- and upper-income African Americans live in disadvantaged neighborhoods *that themselves are surrounded by disadvantaged neighborhoods*, compared to only 11 percent of middle-income and affluent whites. While for blacks this proportion declined from 74 percent in 1970, the modal experience for nonpoor blacks in 2000 was still one of residential precariousness. How can decreasing black-white racial segregation coexist with continuing neighborhood disadvantage for middle-income blacks? Part of the answer is that the white neighbors of African Americans in integrated neighborhoods are often poorer than the black families themselves (Alba, Logan, and Stults 2000). This fact calls into question the usefulness of "living with whites" as a straightforward measure of advantage (Wright, Ellis, and Parks 2005).

Following Lacy's provocation, Sharkey's third important finding points to the growth of a new residential experience, especially for elite blacks. Sharkey reports that "from 1970 to 2000, the proportion of middle- and upper-income African American households that live in advantaged neighborhoods surrounded by spatial advantage grew from 12 percent to 31 percent." That is, nearly a third of nonpoor African Americans are living in very comfortable neighborhoods that are a "comfortable" distance away from areas of disadvantage. While some of these areas are predominately black, many are racially integrated or predominately white suburban neighborhoods like the ones Lacy studied. These data offer the most up-to-date accounting of black middle-class residential attainment. Just as this section began, they demonstrate the tenacity of racial residential stratification, while simultaneously pointing to areas of progress, albeit mostly for the most advantaged segments of the African American population.

CONCLUSION

Over the years, I have received various notes and e-mails from students who were reading BPF in their college classes. Additionally, with Google alerts I know when someone mentions the book in a blog or an op-ed or some other kind of website posting. Mostly the communications and mentions have been very complimentary, but surely there has been criticism. For example, the reviewer in the *Journal of Negro Education* wrote that "the presumed comparison between the experiences of the residents of the neighborhood and their White middle-class counterparts remains unsubstantiated due to the lack of specific data from a comparable White neighborhood" (Gregory 1999, 590). This is a good point, although the demographic studies about how white and black neighborhoods differ are pretty powerful in and of themselves. Still, I would direct readers especially to Maria Kefalas's book *Working Class Heroes* (2003), William Julius Wilson and Richard Taub's book *There Goes the Neighborhood* (2006), and Michèle Lamont's books *Money, Morals and Manners* (1992) and *The Dignity of Working Men* (2000) for primary data on various segments of the white (lower) middle class.[4]

Other critics read BPF as blaming black poor people for the problems of the black middle class. I see how that reading is possible, and it is true that a greater proportion of poor families in a neighborhood will mean more people who do not have the disposable income to plant flowers or afford extracurricular activities for children or fix a broken gate or pay dues to a block club. Given these facts, I concluded BPF by arguing that "improving the condition of the black poor within black communities would have a strong positive impact on the black middle class" (218). Still, what I really mean to convey is more structural than individual, or interactional. The greater neighborhood poverty with which middle-class (and poor) blacks live compared to middle-class (and poor) whites, added to continued antiblack stigma, has significant consequences for access to important mobility-enhancing *resources*, since many public and private investments are unfortunately based on the political, economic, or sociocultural clout of the people who live there, and poor people have less such clout (see also Pattillo 2009).

These important critiques notwithstanding, the overall response to the book has been overwhelmingly positive. It is especially rewarding when the stories and arguments in the book echo with readers because the goal of research is, of course, to get it right. Simi Olusola-Ajayi was a freshman at Pennsylvania State University in spring of 2011, when she read *BPF* in a seminar. I do not know her, but I found her paper on her blog, and it illustrates that *BPF* continues to capture an important social reality for the current generation of college students. Simi writes (2011): "This paper is going to begin with an examination of the similarities and differences existing between Groveland adolescents and the adolescents in the neighborhood I grew up in." Then, she notes for clarity: "It is important to state in context of this paper that I grew up in Nigeria." Although raised in a very different national and cultural context, Simi describes her neighborhood as middle class with a similar kind of economic mix as Groveland and with the same kind of long-term family and neighborly ties that characterize Groveland. Furthermore, she especially identifies with the practice of code switching as she too moved between Yoruba, Pidgin English, and British English, depending on her audience. Simi concludes by beautifully conveying how the characters in *BPF* have a reach and resonance far beyond the few square blocks of Groveland. She writes:

There are so many similarities existing between Groveland and my neighborhood but in respect to this paper, I will conclude by stating that just like Groveland, we have our Neisha Morris and Tyson Reed, whose parents tried to equip them for a better life but still ended up at the bottom (Tyson was however fortunate to rise later). We also have our Terri Jones who have college degrees, and Charisse Bakers who have lived sheltered lives but still get a frequent feel of the environment.

From Lagos to Chicago to Happy Valley, Pennsylvania, the concerns raised in *BPF* continue to capture the realities of an important part of American society, of the processes of race and class stratification, and of first-person experiences beyond the US. So, while I welcome the next generation of rich ethnographies to explore important new frontiers of research into topics like black suburbanization, blacks in predominately white neighborhoods, black/Latino political coalitions, black ethnic diversity, and blacks in southern and western cities, Groveland remains relevant as a faithful depiction of life in lower-middle-class black neighborhoods across the country, as a reminder of the unequal racial geography of cities and suburbs, and as a case for exploring social-class reproduction and mobility for individuals, families, and neighborhoods.

NOTES

INTRODUCTION

1. "Groveland" and most of the names of people and places in this book are pseudonyms. Also, I have made small factual substitutions in cases where a particular description would make an informant more identifiable. For example, if a person attended Olive Harvey Community College in Chicago, I may instead say that he or she attended Malcolm X Community College. Both are predominantly black and in or near black neighborhoods.

2. See Oliver and Shapiro (1995, table 4.4). The ratio for net financial assets (which excludes homes and cars) is even more unequal. The median net value of the financial assets owned by African American households is zero. Figuring wealth by occupation (Oliver and Shapiro 1995, table 5.7), only African Americans employed in upper white-collar jobs average a positive figure for net financial assets, "and their average nest egg [$5] won't purchase a ticket at the movies" (Oliver and Shapiro 1995, 119).

3. On standardized tests and high school dropout rates by family background, see Jencks (1992, tables 4.3 and 5.8). Also, using the General Social Survey, Nash (1991) shows that within social classes, African Americans score lower than whites on tests of mainstream vocabulary. On differentials of drug incarceration by educational attainment, see Meares (1997, chart 1). On social class differences in out-of-wedlock childbearing, see Jencks (1992, table 5.15). On employment and labor force participation differences, see Smith and Welch (1989, table 22). Whereas labor force participation rates declined for black men in all educational categories—and are below the rates for whites—employment for black women who completed high school has remained relatively steady since 1974. However, because employment increased for white women with a high school diploma or more, black women work less than white women within some of the post–high school educational categories (Corcoran and Parrott 1998).

4. The Urban Studies Group (1997) at the Rockefeller Institute of Government has mapped out the racial and class geography of nine metropolitan

areas—Atlanta, Baltimore, Chicago, Detroit, Houston, Los Angeles, New York, Philadelphia, and Washington, DC. Their data graphically illustrate the peripheral positioning of black middle-class areas (relative to core ghetto areas), which has been discussed by Jargowsky and Bane (1991) and Morenoff and Sampson (1997).

5. In their classification of Chicago neighborhoods, Sampson, Raudenbush, and Earls (1997, table 1) find *no* neighborhoods that could be characterized as of low socioeconomic status *and* that are predominantly white.

6. See Brewer (1986), Ladner (1971), and Merton (1972) for discussions of "insider research." Also see chap. 1 of Bourgois (1996) for a discussion of breaking the racial taboo through cross-racial ethnography.

7. Dillard (1972, 229) claims that 80 percent of African Americans speak Black English. Wofford (1979, 368) asserts that 19 percent speak mainstream English "except for slight differences in pronunciation and vocal quality," leaving only 1 percent of the black population as nonspeakers of Black English.

Prior to the 1960s, the prevailing belief was that Black English represented an inferior language that illustrated the intellectual deficiencies of African Americans. The first major scholarly refutations of that notion came in the early 1970s (Labov 1972; Dillard 1972; Baugh 1983). Resulting from intensive participation in black settings, and taping of informal conversations, these studies contended that Black English was not a crude derivative of mainstream English, but instead possessed patterned rules and an internal logic. What this new perspective offered was an affirmation of Black English as different, but not deficient.

The early studies of Black English were conducted primarily in poor communities and among adolescent boys, and presented Black English as the possession of only this small segment of the population. Since then, scholars have broadened their research to take the axes of gender and class into account in the use of Black English. These studies agree that middle-class status does not preclude Black English proficiency (Botan and Smitherman 1991). Terrell (1975) finds that middle-class black boys who had no contact with lower-class black boys still exhibited greater familiarity with Black English than their white middle-class counterparts; this illustrates the importance of family in the transmission of black language.

There are, however, differences in the intensity of vernacular use. Garner and Rubin (1986) interviewed twenty black lawyers in the South about their attitudes toward Black English. All of the interviewees except for one said that they code-switched depending on the context, using Black English in more familiar or comfortable settings. Because the interviews with the lawyers were taped, the authors were able to notice that the one woman who claimed to use only Standard English actually used Black English in her interview. The authors concluded that there are gradations of Black English use, ranging from the most heavy vernacular and slang to what they called "standard Black English," characterized by "largely Standard English syntax delivered in typically Black English phonology, intonation, and cadence" (Garner and Rubin 1986, 33). This variant would be characteristic of the 19 percent of Black English speakers referred to in Wofford (1979).

Stanback (1985) studied black women college graduates and found similar code-switching. Stanback's interest, however, was more in the stylistic components of Black English, such as "signifying," talking loudly, and following a call-and-response pattern. She found that black middle-class women used these styles, and white middle-class women did not (see also Abrahams 1975). In gender-segregated conversations, Nelson's (1990) investigation of black women's oral life narratives underscored the importance of Black English for conveying both cognitive and affective content.

On the other hand, some studies suggest that middle-class African Americans see Black English as a negative component of black culture. In a pair of studies at a predominantly white southern university, Doss and Gross (1992; 1994) found that black students consistently chose speakers of Standard English as people that they would like to get to know, and people with whom they would like to work on a committee. In the first study, black students rated mainstream English speakers more favorably than Black English speakers, while in the second study they again preferred mainstream English speakers, this time over both Black English speakers and models that code-switched. The authors were tentative in their conclusions, however. They reasoned that perhaps the students were rejecting *stereotypes* of blacks that the Black English speakers represented, not the actual speech itself. Also, different results may have been obtained had the audio stimuli been of a conversation rather than of a monologue, thereby signaling contextual uses of Black English, mainstream English, or code-switching. Speicher and McMahon (1992) also found some aversion to Black English among university students, professors, and staff. The middle-class informants in Bell's (1983) study of a neighborhood bar were unsupportive of efforts to use Black English as a teaching tool in schools, but they frequently spoke Black English among themselves in the informal bar setting. Finally, the lawyers studied by Garner and Rubin (1986) did hold in low regard those blacks who did not know when to use Black English or Standard English in the appropriate contexts. The fact that inclusion in the black community can mean exclusion from mainstream society, and vice versa (Baugh 1983; Murray 1991), possibly underlies the ambivalence toward Black English shown by the black middle class.

8. See Massey and Denton (1993, 162–81), for a longer discussion of the relationship between segregation and Black English, and other cultural practices.

CHAPTER ONE

1. There is less agreement on the upper bound of the income-to-needs ratio that distinguishes the middle from the upper class (Danziger and Gottschalk 1995; Duncan, Boisjoly, and Smeeding 1996). Other income-based class definitions include persons living in families with incomes that fall between the 20th and 80th or 90th percentiles of all family incomes (Duncan, Smeeding, and Rogers 1993), or those whose family incomes fall within a fixed income range, such as $25,000–$50,000 (Oliver and Shapiro 1995). The advantage of an income-based definition is that it provides mutually exclusive categories of "middle class" and "poor." Defining someone as middle class based on occupation or education does not rule out the possibility that the person is poor.

2. For other chartings of occupational changes among African Americans, see Blackwell (1985); Farley (1985); Farley and Allen (1987); and Jaynes and Williams (1989).

3. Both Freeman (1976) and Wilson (1978) present data that indicate the premium placed on African American college graduates in the 1960s. Wilson (1978, 101), for example, charts the increase in corporate recruiting visits to black colleges and universities. Autobiographical accounts, such as Lorene Cary's *Black Ice* (1991) and Jake Lamar's *Bourgeois Blues* (1991), give personal renderings of experiences with integrated institutions during this time, while Zweigenhaft and Domhoff (1991) provide an analysis of the early graduates of a special program that placed African Americans in elite private schools.

On unions, Bracey, Meier, and Rudwick (1971) give a general overview of the incorporation of blacks into unions, while Dickerson (1986) offers a more focused discussion of this process in the steel mills in Pennsylvania. Although the beginnings of black unionization predated the postwar period, greater strides were made during the 1950s and 1960s.

4. There are two important caveats to Wilson's focus on class. First, Wilson noted in both his first book, *Power, Racism, and Privilege* (1973), and in *The Declining Significance of Race* (1978) that "any sudden shift in the nation's economy that would throw whites into greater competition with blacks for, say, housing and jobs could create and intensify racial tension and, at least for the whites who feel threatened by black advancement, reverse the trend toward increasing racial tolerance" (1973, 141). Therefore, he did not see the fluid competitive race relations of the postwar period as a static state, and allowed for the possibility that trends could be reversed. Second, Wilson (1978, 2) specified that race continued to be a structuring category in the social and political arenas. Wilson's point was that race was declining in significance with regard to the occupational and economic life chances of blacks, not that it was less important in the realm of housing, or education, or interracial interaction.

5. In their fourth year of conducting citation analysis to determine the most often cited African American social scientists, the *Journal of Blacks in Higher Education* (1997, 18) reported, "The winner and still champion is William Julius Wilson." Wilson was the only African American scholar on a list of the fifty top-selling books in sociology (Gans 1997). *The Declining Significance of Race* was named by *Contemporary Sociology* (1996) as one of the "Ten Most Influential Books of the Past Twenty-Five Years." In a footnote to his most recent book, Wilson himself noted (1996, 276): "Following the publication of *The Truly Disadvantaged* in 1987, an unprecedented number of social scientists began to conduct research on various aspects of ghetto poverty—many of them devoted to testing the theoretical assumptions I had raised in the book."

6. Companion papers by Bound and Dresser (1998) and Bound and Freeman (1992) investigate racial earnings gaps for men and women separately. Black college graduates and midwesterners lost the most ground toward earnings equality with similar whites. These findings are similar to those of other studies that highlight the impact of the 1970s economic downturn on those who had most benefited from the economic growth of the 1950s and 1960s (Blau and Beller 1992, Cancio, Evans, and Maume 1996; Corcoran and Parrott 1998; Harrison and Gorham 1992; Smith and Welch 1989).

7. Wilson (1987) made intermittent references to "higher-income neighborhoods" and "the suburbs" as the destinations of nonpoor blacks. He writes (143): "The exodus of black middle-class professionals from the inner city has been increasingly accompanied by a movement of stable working-class blacks to higher-income neighborhoods in other parts of the city and to the suburbs." Although this thesis is associated with Wilson in the academic world, it shares wide popularity outside of the academy.

8. On black suburbanization see Clay (1979); Massey and Denton (1988); Galster (1991); Taeuber and Taeuber (1965); Logan and Alba (1995); Logan, Alba, and Leung (1996); Schnore, Andre, and Sharp (1976).

9. Since *The Truly Disadvantaged*, Wilson has recognized that the black middle class remains a part of the segregated ghetto. In an appendix to his later book *When Work Disappears*, Wilson reviews some of the studies on racial segregation. He concludes (1996, 242):

> Thus, the black middle-class out-migration from mixed-income areas that then became ghettos did not result in a significant decrease in black migrants' contact with poorer blacks, for the areas to which they relocated were at the same time being abandoned by nonpoor whites, a process that increased the spread of segregation and poverty during the 1970s.

This reality remains obscured, however, by continuing emphasis on the isolation of the black poor.

10. Seventy-five "community areas" were defined in the 1930s by social scientists at the University of Chicago. They attempted to take into account an area's history, local definitions, natural boundaries, and trade and institutional membership patterns. The census tract grid for Chicago was created such that community areas fully contained a collection of census tracts, making census data easily aggregated to the community area level (Chicago Fact Book Consortium 1995). The black middle-class area discussed here refers to eight neighboring community areas.

11. Jargowsky (1997, chap. 2) defines census tracts with poverty rates from 20 to 40 percent as "borderline neighborhoods," noting their propensity to tip into being high-poverty areas by the subsequent census year. He also finds that previously nonpoor tracts became borderline in the 1980s.

12. The patterns described in Chicago inform the finding of increasing class segregation among African Americans (Massey and Eggers 1990; Jargowsky 1996). Class segregation is commonly measured at the census tract level. The index of dissimilarity (D) describes the extent to which census tracts mirror the metropolitan distribution of black incomes. It is practically interpreted as the percentage of blacks of a certain class who would have to move to a different census tract in order to reproduce the black income distribution of the urban area (James and Taeuber 1985). The proximity measure (P*) is another segregation indicator. P* tells the probability that a middle-class black person, for example, will live in a census tract with someone of a different class group (e.g., someone on welfare). Both D and P* are tract-level measurements.

If by its sheer *numbers* the black middle class is more able to predominate in certain census tracts (and those tracts combine into neighborhoods, and those neighborhoods aggregate into communities), then interclass segregation indices will reflect these tract-level changes. A higher proportion of blacks of a specified class would have to move to a different census tract in order to replicate the metropolitan black income distribution (D). Also, middle-class blacks will be less likely to come in contact with poor blacks in their census tract, and more likely to live with other middle-class blacks (P*). The increased size of the black middle-class population, then, improves its ability to establish homogeneous tracts, and results in the finding of increased class segregation among African Americans.

The fact that blacks of different classes are more likely to live in different census tracts does not, however, take account of space. Neither D nor P* says anything about the proximity of black middle-class tracts to black poor tracts. These measures do not capture processes of clustering, or "the tendency for black areas to adhere together within one large agglomeration" (Massey and Denton 1993, 75). Sixteen of the thirty cities studied by Massey and Denton (1993) exhibited notable clustering patterns. Therefore, while the black middle class has created somewhat separate census tracts, these areas are clustered with low-income black tracts in the same way described by Drake and Cayton in the 1930s.

Finally, class segregation measures are based on the overall distribution of incomes. The higher overall poverty rate among blacks translates into more poverty in the neighborhoods inhabited by the black middle class (Erbe 1975; Farley 1991). Consider, for example, a metropolitan area with a black poverty rate of 30 percent and a white poverty rate of 10 percent, which is quite a realistic hypothetical. If there were no class segregation for either race and complete racial segregation, all African Americans (including the middle class) would live in census tracts with a 30 percent poverty rate, while whites would live in tracts that are only 10 percent poor. This simulation is similar to those done by Massey and Denton (1993), except here the focus is on the impact on the black middle class, rather than on how segregation disadvantages the black poor. Because the index of dissimilarity is based on the metropolitan distribution of black incomes, the low overall socioeconomic status of African Americans is replicated in each census tract in a situation of no class segregation. The reality is that there is moderate class segregation among blacks and high racial segregation between blacks and whites. Therefore, segregated black communities bear almost all the full burden of disproportionate poverty among blacks. The black middle class alleviates some of this burden by establishing black middle-class neighborhoods, but its residential situation continues to differ from that of the white middle class. See Pattillo-McCoy (1998) for a fuller discussion of these issues.

13. These disparities have been documented in numerous other studies (Darden 1987; Erbe 1975; Fainstein and Nesbitt 1996; Farley 1991; Landry 1987; Massey, Gross, and Shibuya 1994; Villemez 1980).

14. Farley et al. (1994) investigate the residential preferences of African Americans and whites in Detroit. They find, "Most African-Americans preferred areas where there already was a substantial representation of blacks. The ideal neighborhood was one in which blacks comprised at least one-half the residents" (762). Racial residential instability arises because a majority of whites say they would not feel comfortable in such a neighborhood. Whites report that they would try to move out of a neighborhood where half the residents were black, and they would not be willing to move in. Thus the compositional thresholds vary by racial group and inhibit the formation of stable, mixed areas.

CHAPTER TWO

1. Taken verbatim from Trotter and Lewis (1996, 36). In addition to personal documents, the editors include excerpts from studies and articles on the black migration by such groups as the Urban League and the NAACP.

2. Taub, Taylor, and Dunham (1984) give the history of eight Chicago neigh-

borhoods that confronted the prospect of racial change in the 1960s. They illuminate the difficulties neighborhoods face in achieving racial integration. See
also Molotch (1972) and Hirsch (1983).

3. Census data give some sense of the prevalence of extended-family networks. Nearly 30 percent of the children living in households in Groveland are
relatives of the household head, but not the householder's own children. This
often refers to a three-generation household where the head is actually the child's
grandparent (City of Chicago 1994).

4. Jargowsky (1997) documents the spreading of poverty areas in a number of
cities. Many census tracts that were not poverty areas in 1980, but that bordered
poor tracts, became poor by 1990. Core poverty areas are becoming less densely
populated, but more expansive, as entire metropolitan areas spread. Groveland
has not reached the designation of a poverty area, although neighborhoods to
the north have already gone through this transformation.

5. Although it is a part of the official community area, few Groveland residents
include the area where Tommy grew up as part of Groveland proper. Even when I
asked Tommy to give me the boundaries of what he considered his neighborhood
(which he himself called Groveland), he delineated an area that did not include
his own house, but corresponded to what most people gave as Groveland's
boundaries. Most Grovelandites do not have much business in this physically
and numerically small part of the neighborhood; less than 5 percent of the population lives in this census tract, which is nestled between railroad tracks and a
busy commercial street. Yet this sliver separates Groveland from—or connects
it to—poor neighborhoods to the north, providing an unobstructed corridor to
and from the core of the ghetto, and symbolically alerting Grovelandites to the
possibilities of neighborhood decline. Much of the change that Tommy perceives
is captured in the census figures for the neighborhood. Where Tommy grew up
has always been distinct from the two southern portions of Groveland. In the
1960s, racial change took place most rapidly in the northernmost census tract
because the Black Belt was expanding from the north. By 1990, this section had
declined considerably, with fewer homeowners (42 percent), a higher poverty
rate (26 percent), and more female-headed families with children (64 percent).
The tract-level demographics in Groveland perfectly illustrate the "seeping"
processes discussed in chapter 1, whereby neighborhoods represent a "spatially
arrayed stratification system" (Berry et al. 1976).

6. The study of neighborhood change is dominated by a concern with a
neighborhood's changing racial or ethnic composition (Duncan and Duncan
1957; Merry 1983; Molotch 1972; Rieder 1985; Schelling 1978; Schnore, Andre,
and Sharp 1976; Silver and Melkonian 1995; Suttles 1968; Taub, Taylor, and
Dunham 1984). The association of neighborhood change with racial change
makes sense in light of the massive urban population shifts that took place

after World War II. Racial rhetoric was a convenient and powerful shorthand for residents to summarize their concerns and discontent (Taub, Taylor, and Dunham 1984). But the focus on race has hampered investigations of neighborhood change *within* the black community. There has been a neglect of how black neighborhoods can experience quantitative and qualitative changes while remaining black. Sociological interest jumped from the nature of racially changing neighborhoods directly to the situation of poor black areas, with little attention paid to the local experience of neighborhood change among African Americans. Taub, Taylor, and Dunham (1984, 69–70) allude to this process in their study of South Shore in Chicago. They note:

> Nearly half of South Shore residents report that their neighborhood is changing, an initially puzzling finding for a community that is 90-percent black. That blacks in virtually all black neighborhoods are concerned about stability, however, is explicable in terms of the changing class structure of blacks. . . . For blacks who have achieved middle-class status, a stable neighborhood is one that is perceived as able to hold its middle-class character. An unstable neighborhood is one in which soft-market forces encourage the area to take on increasingly the character of the black underclass. Some middle-class blacks have moved several times in order to stay one step ahead of "the element."

Because their study is primarily concerned with the role of race, crime, and investments in processes of neighborhood change, this seeming anomaly of black concern over neighborhood stability is left unexplored. A number of Groveland residents also have a history of relocating from other areas in attempts to organize a black middle-class residential stronghold.

7. Caskey (1994) provides an overview of the rise of check-cashing outlets (CCOs) across the country, and a profile of their users. He finds that CCOs are disproportionately located in minority and low-income communities. Branch banks in those areas have closed, and the remaining local banks have increased service fees, which make the prices at CCOs seem less exorbitant. See also Dymski and Veitch (1996) for these trends in Los Angeles.

CHAPTER THREE

1. My discussion of generations follows the work of Katherine Newman (1993) on the declining fortunes of middle-class white baby boomers. I explore the nuances of the African American experiences, focusing on neighborhood-specific effects of economic changes over generations, ending with the post–baby boomers, or the group that has been labeled Generation X (Craig and Bennett 1993).

2. Newman (1993) devotes much attention to the prohibitive costs of buying a home for the baby boom generation. While prices in Groveland have not soared as they did in the "Pleasanton" community of Newman's research—median home value in Groveland in 1989 was just over $65,000 (1989 dollars), and on an upward trend (Woodstock Institute 1994)—the particular economic squeeze on African Americans complicates buying and maintaining even a very reasonably priced home.

3. Most neighborhoods, of course, are not primarily repopulated by the children who grew up there, but the economic crunch that Groveland's baby boomers are experiencing is not specific to them. These general economic shifts afflict middle-class African Americans as well as whites across the country. Therefore, if it is difficult for Groveland's children to buy homes in the neighborhood, it is equally difficult for the children of other senior-generation black middle-class families to make such an investment. The pessimistic prognosis is that the patterns of ghetto expansion that marked the 1970s and 1980s will continue, and the area of concentrated black poverty in Chicago will soon reach and possibly envelop Groveland (see Jargowsky 1997 for an analysis of ghetto expansion). On the other hand, if black middle-class families adapt to economic strains by pooling incomes, Groveland's homes may remain secure. Terri Jones's household, for example, is a combination of her income and both of her parents' incomes, allowing each to invest some money. Her parents are preparing for retirement while she is trying to establish her own catering business. With incomes stagnating, it is important to pool earnings to reproduce what used to be the earnings of one person, as was the case for both James Graham's family and Lauren Grant's parents.

4. Demographic studies indicate that "returning home is far more common, and more ordinary, among unmarried adults than many have speculated," and that "a shortage of resources or a need to conserve resources is a major factor leading to a return to co-residence of parents and young adult children" (DaVanzo and Goldscheider 1990, 254). These findings are true across races. African Americans are distinct, however, in the prevalence of multigenerational and extended families (Hofferth 1984), and in their greater likelihood of returning home, even after marriage (DaVanzo and Goldscheider 1990; Goldscheider and DaVanzo 1989).

5. One of the primary points of Wilson's (1996, 216–18) long-term policy agenda is to strengthen school-to-work transition programs. He identifies Germany and Japan as models for how to integrate young workers into the productive economy.

6. Historically black colleges and universities (HBCUs) figure prominently in the college choices of Groveland youth. HBCUs have historically been the route of upward mobility for blacks, but have recently been plagued by dwindling

public financial support and the drain of black students into predominantly white schools (see Jaynes and Williams 1989, 176–79). Still, they are places that nurture students whose high school preparation may have been lacking. According to the United Negro College Fund (http://www.uncf.org), HBCUs "account for only 3 percent of all U.S. institutions of higher learning, [but] enroll 16% of all black students in higher education and graduate nearly 30% of all blacks earning bachelor's degrees in the United States. . . . HBCUs have graduated 75% of black PhDs, 85% of black doctors, 46% of black business executives, 50% of black engineers, 80% of black federal judges, 50% of black attorneys, and 75% of black military officers."

CHAPTER FOUR

1. As further theoretical elaboration, socioeconomic status is negatively related to ethnic heterogeneity and residential instability, both of which are positively related to crime (Shaw and McKay 1942; Byrne and Sampson 1986). Heterogeneity and instability work through their negative impact on informal and formal social control. Informal social control is defined as "the effort of the community to regulate itself and the behavior of residents and visitors to the neighborhood" (Bursik and Grasmick 1993, 15). Both heterogeneity and instability hamper communication, decrease residents' familiarity with one another, and decrease their attachment to the neighborhood and its organizations, all important components of social control. A later reformulation of social organization theory—the systemic model—also stresses the importance of kin and neighborly ties for the social control of crime and disorder (Berry and Kasarda 1977; Bursik and Grasmick 1993; Kasarda and Janowitz 1974; Sampson 1992).

2. I asked interviewees about their "close friends." Respondents were allowed to name as many close friends as they wished. I then asked where these friends lived, about their occupations and races, and how the respondent met them. From these data I was able to determine the mean proportion of close friends who lived in the neighborhood across all interviewees, which was 49.1 percent. This nearly even proportion of local and nonlocal friendship ties is similar to what Oliver (1988) found in his study of three black communities in Los Angeles. However, because I was working from ethnographic field data and the open-ended interviews used in this study, I have limited confidence in the above measure of the spatial dimension of network ties. I am much more convinced of the strong local ties recorded in the participant-observation field notes, and by hearing interviewees elaborate on their friendships and kin. My data are even less amenable to quantitatively analyzing the density of neighborhood ties (Freudenberg 1986).

3. Meares (1997) finds that, although a majority of African Americans support get-tough policies of crime control, more blacks than whites fall into what she

calls the "dual frustration" category. She describes the people who fall into this group as follows: "These mothers want better crime control and law enforcement. Yet, they understand that increased levels of law enforcement potentially saddle their children with a felony conviction—a mark that can ensure economic and social marginalization" (1997, 161).

4. Venkatesh (1997) describes a poor community in which the local gang had essentially taken over, replacing the previous authority of tenants' groups. The middle-class organizational and financial resources in Groveland have inhibited such an absolute displacement of legitimate control.

5. New technology has meant that drug dealers now have their own cellular phones with which to do business, but when this initiative was first undertaken it would have limited the ability to use public phones for illegal business.

6. Both Groveland United Church of Christ and St. Mary's Catholic Church receive the assistance of a nonprofit agency that specializes in organizing churches. Each church invited this agency to work with it, and pays a membership fee. The outside agency provides only training and technical assistance; it does not give specific directions or targets for social action. The proactive efforts on the part of the churches illustrate the independent commitment to getting involved in the neighborhood.

7. "The other side" refers to a physically small but densely populated portion of the Bristol community area (see appendix B, fig. 1). While the overall demographic characteristics of Bristol make it similar to Groveland, this particular census tract has a much lower median family income ($21,000), a higher poverty rate (20 percent), a lower owner-occupancy rate (15 percent), and less residential stability (53 percent moved into the area in the five years preceding the 1990 census). This somewhat marginal enclave is encapsulated by railroad tracks and a busy thoroughfare.

CHAPTER FIVE

1. More white families have wealth—both durable and monetary assets—in addition to income, enabling them to get by for longer periods of time when crises hit. Oliver and Shapiro (1995) report that 78.9 percent of black households, compared to only 38.1 percent of white households, are in "precarious-resource" circumstances, meaning that they do not have sufficient net worth or financial assets to survive for three months at the poverty line if there were a crisis that cut off income. Maintaining a middle-class standard of living (as opposed to survival at the poverty level) is even less feasible for many black households.

2. See Merriwether-de Vries, Burton, and Eggeletion (1996, 239) for a discussion of the "peer context" of young mothers. They state, "Embarking on the role of parent limits an adolescent's access to the social world of nonparents because economic and instrumental responsibilities for their offspring frequently preclude

the expenditure of precious resources on leisure activities."

3. Edin and Lein (1997, 164) briefly discuss the role of men's illegal income in the survival strategies of poor women. They state, "Chronically unemployed fathers who wanted to maintain their claim on their children were powerfully motivated to engage in any kind of work, including work in the underground economy." The Morris family illustrates that such strategies are also used by middle-class families to maintain their standard of living.

4. Tyson's understanding of how delinquency is related to a concentration of single-parent families is supported by empirical evidence. Single-parent families have fewer economic resources and lack the extra pair of eyes important for monitoring youths (McLanahan and Sandefur 1994; Sampson and Groves 1989; Steinberg 1987).

5. Sending children to Catholic school is a common and successful strategy among African Americans to promote upward mobility (Neal 1997).

6. Sullivan's (1989) comparative research on young males illustrates the importance of the neighborhood context for the shape, content, and duration of youth delinquency. He shows how local employment climates affect the maturing-out process from criminal activity. In the white neighborhood Sullivan studied, young men were able to secure union jobs and desist from crime. In the poor black neighborhood, however, no such alternative to crime existed, and young men participated in crime into their young adult years. While this chapter does not examine local employment conditions, it does concentrate on the models for and access to deviant pathways provided by the local milieu.

Of course, not all adolescent socialization takes place within neighborhood boundaries. In addition to geographic neighborhoods, there are "neighborhoods of sociability" that also influence youth (Burton, Price-Spratlen, and Spencer 1997). Parents do attempt to structure children's neighborhoods of sociability so that they further their own positive parenting goals. However, to the extent that young people have control over their circle of friends, Groveland youth are likely to befriend youth from a variety of family backgrounds because of the composition of Groveland and the surrounding neighborhoods. For example, the fact that Neisha went to high school in the Treelawn neighborhood, where the poverty rate is nearly triple that in Groveland, indicates the large sociability catchment area for black middle-class youth.

7. In *There Are No Children Here*, Alex Kotlowitz (1991) depicts the uncertainties of gang affiliation. For example, Lafayette and his friends took to writing "4CH" (for the Four Corner Hustlers gang) on their papers and on the walls, but they did not seem to be participating in any other behaviors explicitly associated with the gang. Primarily, they were posturing. Were they *in* a gang or not? Likewise, vague gang-labeling practices doomed one of Lafayette's older friends, Craig, who was shot and killed by agents from the Bureau of Alcohol,

Tobacco and Firearms. In the newspaper accounts, Craig was identified as a gang member even though no one in the neighborhood knew anything of such an affiliation. Law-enforcement agents may have a separate set of criteria for gang membership than local residents. This is not to say that there are not initiation rites, or organizational meetings, or rules, by-laws, and mottoes that bind together fellow gang members. Indeed, Grovelandites can easily "read" the color or tilt of someone's hat to identify gang allegiances, or recognize a seemingly innocent greeting as reserved for gang insiders. The point is that membership can also be very porous, and sometimes impossible to escape if a young person (especially a male) chooses to have friends in a neighborhood where gangs exist.

8. Cultural theorists such as Hannerz (1969) and, later, Swidler (1986) argue that culture is not composed solely of ultimate values, norms, and beliefs, as Kornhauser (1978) would argue. Instead, culture consists of behaviors that are shared within groups, learned by "precept," and modeled in interaction. Hannerz (1969, 183) writes, "As we have seen there is much verbalization of mainstream ideals in the ghetto, even from those who often act ghetto-specifically in direct contradiction of these ideals." He goes on to argue that the definition of culture must be broadened to include these behaviors, because culture is largely situational and arises in response and resistance to social, ecological, economic, and political constraints.

9. Stack (1974) elaborates on the importance of the kin network for women especially. Setting up a self-contained nuclear family severs the extended kin bond and imperils the stability of the extended network. Because the concept of the nuclear family indicates that familial resources are restricted to mother-father-children, the extended family is effectively disconnected from the possible gains made by the member now in a nuclear-family relationship. Furthermore, the person who cuts herself off jeopardizes her own ability to draw on those resources in uncertain times, although the networks often welcome back strays. Stack (1974, 122) summarizes this dilemma. "The life histories of adults show that the attempts by women to set up separate households with their children and husbands, or boyfriends, are short-lived. Lovers fight, jobs are scarce, houses get condemned, and needs for services among kin arise."

Even more relevant, McAdoo (1978) finds that upward mobility for African Americans does not attenuate kin ties and relationships of reciprocal exchange. Essentially, black middle-class individuals often remain connected to their less fortunate family members and friends. These connections across classes, and often across lifestyles, prompt them to have flexible "street" and "decent" orientations.

CHAPTER SIX

1. Wearing an oversized zoot suit was a transgressive act during World War II

because the rationing system forbade such wasteful use of cloth. In 1943, white servicemen clashed with black and Mexican zoot-suiters over the anti-American message that zoot suits conveyed. At the same time, zoot-suiters also came under scrutiny by other African Americans who read the style as unnecessarily confrontational. As historian Robin Kelley (1996, 200) notes, "Nevertheless, like the folk hero himself, the Stagolee-type rebel was not always admired by other working-class black [bus] passengers. Some were embarrassed by his actions; the more sympathetic feared for his life." The fact that some of those involved in the zoot-suit culture were also parasitic criminals (drug dealers, pimps) made the negative reactions to the style even more pronounced in the black community. See Cosgrove (1984); Kelley (1992; 1996); Tyler (1994).

2. Willis (1993, 368–69) describes how each member of her upper-middle-class family made his or her own stylistic statements, including her son, who stylistically articulated a "modified black rap mode." White middle-class youth, like Susan Willis's son, could just as accurately be described as being in a ghetto trance. Kelley (1997, 39) writes, "Hip hop, particularly gangsta rap, also attracts listeners for whom the 'ghetto' is a place of adventure, unbridled violence, erotic fantasy, and/or an imaginary alternative to suburban boredom."

3. Hagan and Peterson (1995, 24–28) review the evidence on policing in nonwhite communities. Studies find that police view minority youth in general as "hostile and threatening." Also, in high-crime areas, surveillance increases, and officers become more proactive based on their preconceptions, resulting in the "overpolicing of youth and adults from stigmatized areas" (see also Sampson 1986). Poor whites experience surveillance as well (Hebdige 1979), but the empirical evidence discussed above on race and arrests suggests that sanctions against white youth of all classes are less severe.

4. Cultural critic Todd Boyd (1997, 62) discusses the similarities across eras. He writes: "In the parlance of the street, men are praised, with phallic connotations, for their ability to be 'hard'; this is a modern-day variation on what used to be referred to as 'cool.' In order to be hard, one must maintain a state of detached defiance, regardless of the situation." *Hard* fits into the same category of words as *ghetto*. Boyd (1997, 70) also talks about how such dispositions are conveyed through style, or image. "In line with our general infatuation with visual spectacle . . . image, whether real or fictional, is the defining characteristic of contemporary society, especially in gangsta culture."

5. "Gangsta rap" refers to a genre of rap music with roots on the West Coast, but it is enjoying (inter)national and cross-racial popularity. It is distinguished by its often violent and sexist subject matter (see Dyson 1996; Kitwana 1994).

6. I was inspired to explore the plain fun of ghetto styles by historian Robin Kelley's critique of social scientific analyses of poverty culture. He writes (1997, 41), "Black music, creativity and experimentation in language, that walk, that

talk, that style, must also be understood as sources of visceral and psychic pleasure. Though they may also reflect and speak to the political and social world
of inner city communities, expressive cultures are not simply mirrors of social
life or expressions of conflicts, pathos, and anxieties." Also, in rap group 2 Live
Crew's obscenity trial, some academics argued that violent and sexist lyrics were
not meant literally, but existed in a tradition of African American verbal games.
See the debate in *Reconstruction* (1990).

7. See Boyd (1997), esp. chap. 4, for a discussion of what he refers to as the
"cinema of nihilism."

8. Jack Katz (1988) argues that shoplifting is the crime of choice among
suburban youth because the mall is close, accessible, and part of their daily
routine. Likewise, white-collar professionals perpetrate white-collar crimes. They
embezzle, conduct insider trades, illegally pollute the environment, and steal
office equipment. Poor blacks are involved in more visible street crimes because
of the low opportunity costs. It would be difficult for someone without a job
to embezzle from a company. Katz's argument exposes the existence of crime
across different environments and populations, with various manifestations. The
common denominator is the high that criminals get from breaking the rules.

9. Because I was open about my research intentions, Tuesday-night shows
were sometimes explicitly for my benefit. Offering to help my research, they
boasted that they could get me an interview with a real "OG" or a real "thug."
The members of the youth group knew I was interested in learning about their
lives and the neighborhood, and they were eager to share their knowledge.

CHAPTER SEVEN

1. George Moschis (1987, 128) summarizes the literature on black youth
consumer practices and the relationship between television advertising and
consumption. He writes, "Nearly all studies examining the negative effects of
advertising on children and adolescents have found correlations between the
amount of television viewing and several 'undesirable' consumer orientations
such as materialistic attitudes and social motivations for consumption." He also
found that watching more television decreases consumer skills.

2. Marxist theorists of the Frankfurt School argue that mass marketing is
an insidious capitalist tool to control the social and cultural aspects of people's
lives, buttressing capitalist control in the economic sphere. The mass media are
the vehicles through which capitalists market items that are invented purely to
make a profit, not to satisfy the needs of the consuming public. In perfect cor-
respondence with the assessment of the quoted Nike executive, Frankfurt School
theorists argue that mass culture creates false needs. See Longhurst (1995).

3. While the excerpt that Tommy earnestly read aloud expressed clear an-

ticapitalist sentiments, the book from which this passage comes is actually a neoconservative argument for the possibilities of entrepreneurial capitalism (see Gilder 1981, 7). Tommy quoted a passage in which the author was laying out the radical critique of capitalism, not the author's own arguments. He was clearly selectively reading the book.

4. Pitts et al. (1989) investigate this culturally specific strategy and find that whites and blacks have very different readings of advertisements that contain cultural messages. Black experimental subjects rated commercials that were produced by a black advertising agency with all-black casts and portraying various scenes of black life more positively than similar white subjects. The authors (Pitts et al. 1989, 322–23) conclude: "We found that when marketing communication utilizes a strong cultural orientation . . . [they] elicit not only a stronger, more positive response to the brand and the commercial itself from the targeted audience (compared with the nontargeted white audience), but they generate a markedly different response in terms of perception of the value message."

5. Mass-produced styles and lifestyles can be transformed into vehicles for protest. The tattered clothes of 1960s hippies and the black leather jackets and berets of the Black Panthers were the uniforms of racial and class resistance. English scholars have most fully developed the idea of style as rebellion. Youthful rebellion, however, exists primarily at the "imaginary level"; it does not often alter the material relationship between classes (Hall and Jefferson 1976; Hebdige 1979; Brake 1985).

6. I say the "crime" of gang-style posturing because school districts across the country have instituted dress codes to ensure that gangs do not wear their colors or emblems in school (Gursky 1996; LaPoint, Holloman, and Alleyne 1993). From particular clothing items to shoelace colors, schools have restricted what students can wear. To add a twist to this fashion crackdown, shopping malls have also made rules against certain clothing, especially hats. Thus, the ironic reality is that even shopping malls—the ultimate sites and profiteers of consumerism and style—are actually stifling their patrons' ability to showcase their purchases.

CHAPTER EIGHT

1. There were equally key female participants in this research as well, such as Neisha Morris and Charisse Baker.

2. This narrative is far from a verbatim transcript; it is, at most, a third of the entire interview. Also, I have grouped Spider's comments under themes where they were not so organized in the interview. I have deleted many of the false starts and repeated words, and added some words for clarification or transition. Such additions are in square brackets. I have tried to order the stories chronologically, whereas in the interview Spider would often switch from talking about

his boyhood experiences to relaying a more recent event. Without denying the merits of the nonchronological manner in which Spider remembered his life, this rearranged version is much more reader-friendly. I have not corrected grammar or pronunciation, and I have not deleted the profanity.

3. The date here does not coincide with that given in previous conversations I had with Spider. When I first met Spider in 1993, he told me, "Me and my pops just bought a crib in the suburbs. But my mom got a house right over here and so I use that address for everything. The parks don't like to pay you if you don't live in the city." So I think he meant the date to be 1991 or 1992, not 1981 or 1982, as he said in this interview. This would make his father's 1979 LeSabre in greater need of a new engine.

4. The neighborhood that Spider's family moved from is north of Groveland. His family's migration followed the typical southward push of blacks from the core of the Black Belt.

5. Spider was successful in playing it dumb to his mother, who did not know about his affiliation with the Black Mobsters. When I asked Spider's mother about gangs in the neighborhood, she said this: "No, I haven't seen any gangs. I'm sure they around here, but they don't bother me. They had the Mobsters and all them. But like I said, they never bothered my kids. We had some Mobsters lived across the street. But they was grown, got grown and gone now."

6. Spider was clearly using the "two plus two is eight" technique on me, being very vague and unclear when talking about Lance's role and history with the Black Mobsters.

7. Frank White is the main character in the movie *The King of New York*. White is an imprisoned drug dealer who, upon his release and after trying to go straight, goes back to dealing drugs and reclaims his kingpin position in the New York drug trade. Spider's casual reference to Frank White illustrates the incorporation of popular-culture personae into everyday parlance. Just as Spider made the parallel between Frank White and the Black Mobsters' drug-selling organization, rapper Notorious B.I.G. also equated himself with the Hollywood character, rhyming that "the Black Frank White is here to excite."

8. Hanover Park, a northern suburb of Chicago, is 86 percent white, 4 percent black, and 10 percent Hispanic, with a median family income of $45,475. The median income is not much more than Groveland's, but the poverty rate of 2 percent (compared to 12 percent for Groveland) differentiates the two environments.

9. Olive Harvey is a two-year college on the South Side that is a part of Chicago's public community college system.

10. My research partner and I speculated that Spider sometimes shared Merc stories for our benefit. We thought that perhaps Spider believed we could better understand and empathize with his experiences at the Merc because, unlike many of his friends who hung out at Groveland Park, my research partner

and I interacted daily in the predominantly white world of which Spider spoke.

CHAPTER NINE

1. *Ordinary* and *typical* are loaded terms that might say more about me than about Terri Jones. Terri went to college with a very close family friend. I met her when she attended a Christmas party with our mutual friend. When I found out she lived in Groveland, I was excited, surprised, and we exchanged information to schedule an interview. Her biography was not much different from my own, which is perhaps why she struck me as "ordinary." Still, within the range of people with whom I became acquainted in the neighborhood, and in trying to be objective despite my own history, I believe that Terri Jones is more representative of a Groveland upbringing than Spider, although Spider simultaneously captures the wide variety of Groveland possibilities.

2. Terri Jones was born in 1964, which means her family moved to Groveland in either 1968 or 1969. By the 1970 census, Groveland was already over 80 percent black.

3. Other Groveland residents talked about the West Side/South Side distinctions. For example, seventeen-year-old Teresa Walker described Groveland in the following way: "Well, it's not bad. It's not like the West Side or anything. But it's not perfect like the suburbs or whatever. So, I don't know, it's in between. You don't see like drive-bys every day, but then again you don't see the president walking down the street every day. So it's just normal. It's quiet." In fact, Teresa Walker's parents also moved to Groveland from the West Side. She told a humorous story about her parents' first meeting that further illustrates the increased status of a South Side versus a West Side residence. "Everybody [in my family] used to come over here on the South Side 'cause this was like the rich area or whatever. And my mother thought that my father was from the South Side. She was like, 'Okay, I found me a South Side man!' Come to find out that they had gone to the same school on the West Side. And he lived like four blocks from her."

4. This area from Memphis to Highland in the neighboring Bristol community area is where an ex–drug dealer said most of the drug dealing occurs. See chap. 4.

5. The homes that Terri is referring to are actually in neighboring Bristol. But there is also a new development of single-family town homes in Groveland. Each of the four home models is named for a prominent African American woman writer, and the name of the development itself emphasizes African American history. The development's brochures assert, "Modern Living Traditional Values." The brick homes with two to three bedrooms, one-and-a-half to two-and-a-half bathrooms, and a two-car garage cost (for early buyers) between $167,000 and $192,000, much more expensive than the older Groveland homes. The new homes in Bristol are priced even higher.

6. The day I interviewed Terri was the day that the verdicts were being given on Groveland's Black Mobsters who had been arrested in the "gang sweep." Terri made the comments in this paragraph in response to the television news coverage that we watched of the guilty verdicts handed down in those trials.

7. Xavier is a historically black Catholic university in New Orleans known for its pharmacy program and for the strength of its premedical curriculum.

8. Terri is correct in that black middle-class households are more likely to package numerous incomes to attain a middle-class standard of living (Landry 1987). However, her estimates of the sum total of those packaging strategies is high (even if it may accurately assess her family's earnings). Only 109 out of nearly 4,000 Groveland households reported incomes over $100,000 in 1990.

CONCLUSION

1. Massey (1996, 405) notes that the cities classified as "hypersegregated" in 1990 "contain 11 million African Americans, who together constitute 36% of the black population."

2. Wilson (1987, 7) writes that the presence of black working- and middle-class families "provided stability to inner-city neighborhoods and reinforced and perpetuated mainstream patterns of norms and behavior," and that "the black middle-class self-consciously imposed cultural constraints on lower-class culture" (1987, 55), and, finally, that in vertically integrated neighborhoods, there were a "sufficient number of working- and middle-class professional families to absorb the shock or cushion the effect of uneven economic growth and periodic recessions on inner-city neighborhoods" (1987, 144).

3. For example, Roberto Fernandez and David Harris (1992, 274) examine the characteristics of the friends of poor and nonpoor African American men and women who live in poor Chicago neighborhoods. They find that a slight majority (56.9 percent) of the friends of nonworking poor black males are indeed working, and that 44 percent of the friends of nonworking poor black females are working. Fernandez and Harris recognize that the nonworking poor actually do have social ties to working friends. They state that "the isolation of the nonworking poor from people with mainstream char acteristics is far from complete." Yet the remainder of their discussion focuses on the isolation of this group within their large proportion of nonworking peers. Fernandez and Harris do identify a subpopulation within the nonworking poor whose isolation is more complete. For example, nearly 35 percent of nonworking poor black women have no working friends. This subpopulation might be the group on which urban poverty scholars focus, but it is clearly a very small subset of African Americans in poor neighborhoods.

EPILOGUE

1. Sampson's (2012) research confirms this middling description of Groveland by using an extremely broad array of survey and other quantitative data. However, because he identifies Groveland by its real name, I do not direct the reader to particular page numbers or figures where Sampson illustrates these findings. The important point is that the position of many black middle-class neighborhoods as privileged relative to other black neighborhoods, but in peril relative to white neighborhoods of all class compositions, is empirically supported with respect to Groveland specifically in Sampson's work, and nationally in the studies that I reference throughout this epilogue.

2. Index crimes include murder, aggravated assault, aggravated battery, robbery, and criminal sexual assault (which are all classified as violent crimes); and burglary, theft, motor vehicle theft, and arson (which are nonviolent crimes).

3. Lacy argues that elite black middle-class identities in the suburbs are situational rather than fixed. For example, in cross-racial interactions within the predominately white suburb of Lakeview, her black subjects activate their "suburban identity"; this highlights values of property upkeep and relatively insular social interactions that bond them all together against city residents. In other situations, such as when shopping or house hunting, her respondents activate their "class-based identities" by dressing professionally or dropping hints about their educational credentials. This serves to differentiate themselves from lower-income African Americans. In still other moments, these suburban black families seek out opportunities to expose their children to black culture, emphasizing their racial identities.

4. These citations notwithstanding, there is a considerable dearth of ethnographies of contemporary white middle-class neighborhoods. Ironically, the first Google Book result of a search of "white middle class neighborhoods" (without quotation marks) is *Black Picket Fences*.

REFERENCES

Aalbers, Manuel. 2012. *Subprime Cities: The Political Economy of Mortgage Markets.* Malden, MA: Wiley-Blackwell.

Abrahams, Roger. 1976. *Talking Black.* Rowley, MA: Newbury House Publishers.

Adelman, Robert. 2004. "Neighborhood Opportunities, Race, and Class: The Black Middle Class and Residential Segregation." *City & Community* 3: 43–63.

Agius Vallejo, Jody. 2012. *Barrios to 'Burbs: The Making of the Mexican-American Middle Class.* Palo Alto, CA: Stanford University Press.

Alba, Richard D., John R. Logan, and Paul E. Bellair. 1994. "Living with Crime: The Implications of Racial/Ethnic Differences in Suburban Location." *Social Forces* 73: 395–434.

Alba, Richard, John Logan, and Brian Stults. 2000. "How Segregated Are Middle-Class African Americans?" *Social Problems* 47: 543–58.

Alexis, Marcus. 1970. "Patterns of Black Consumption. 1935–1960." *Journal of Black Studies* 1: 55–74.

Anderson, Elijah. 1978. *A Place on the Corner.* Chicago: University of Chicago Press.

———. 1990. *Streetwise: Race, Class and Change in an Urban Community.* Chicago: University of Chicago Press.

———. 1991. "Neighborhood Effects on Teenage Pregnancy." In *The Urban Underclass,* edited by Christopher Jencks and Paul E. Peterson, 375–98. Washington, DC: Brookings Institution.

———. 1994. "The Code of the Streets." *Atlantic Monthly* 273: 80–94.

Baker, Theresa, and William Velez. 1996. "Access to and Opportunity in Post-secondary Education in the United States: A Review." *Sociology of Education* 69: 82–101.

Banks, Patricia Ann. 2010. *Represent: Art and Identity among the Black Upper-Middle Class.* New York: Routledge.

Barnes, Annie S. 1985. *The Black Middle Class Family: A Study of Black Subsociety, Neighborhood, and Home in Interaction.* Bristol, IN: Wyndham Hall Press.

Battistoni, Alyssa. 2011. "The Dirty Secret of Public-Sector Union Busting." *Salon.*

com, February 24. http://www.salon.com/2011/02/24/battistoni_public_employees/ (accessed September 22, 2012).

Baugh, John. 1983. *Black Street Speech: Its History, Structure and Survival.* Austin: University of Texas Press.

Bell, Michael J. 1983. *The World from Brown's Lounge: An Ethnography of Black Middle-Class Play.* Urbana: University of Illinois Press.

Berry, Brian, et al. 1976. "Attitudes toward Integration: The Role of Status in Community Response to Racial Change." In *The Changing Face of the Suburbs*, edited by Barry Schwartz. Chicago: University of Chicago Press.

Berry, Brian J. L., and John D. Kasarda. 1977. *Contemporary Urban Ecology.* New York: Macmillan.

Billingsley, Andrew. 1968. *Black Families in White America.* Englewood Cliffs, NJ: Prentice-Hall.

————. 1992. *Climbing Jacob's Ladder: The Enduring Legacy of African American Families.* New York: Simon & Schuster.

Blackwell, James E. 1985. *The Black Community: Diversity and Unity.* 2nd ed. New York: Harper & Row.

Blau, Francine D., and Andrea H. Beller. 1992. "Black-White Earnings over the 1970s and 1980s: Gender Differences in Trends." *Review of Economic Statistics* 74: 276–86.

Bobo, Lawrence, James R. Kluegel, and Ryan A. Smith. 1997. "Laissez-Faire Racism: The Crystallization of a Kinder, Gentler Antiblack Ideology." In *Racial Attitudes in the 1990s*, edited by Steven A. Tuch and Jack K. Martin, 15–42. Westport, CT: Praeger.

Bocian, Debbie Gruenstein, et al. 2011. "Lost Ground, 2011: Disparities in Mortgage Lending and Foreclosures." Center for Responsible Lending. http://www.responsiblelending.org/mortgage-lending/research-analysis/Lost-Ground-2011.pdf (accessed July 1, 2012).

Bogle, Donald. 1989. *Toms, Coons, Mulattoes, Mammies, and Bucks: An Interpretive History of Blacks in American Films.* Expanded edition. New York: Continuum.

Boles, Corey. 2011. "Black Caucus Warns Obama on Jobs." *Wall Street Journal*, August 31. http://online.wsj.com/article/SB1000142405311190471660457 6542272751288958.html (accessed July 1, 2012).

Botan, Carl, and Geneva Smitherman. 1991. "Black English in the Integrated Workplace." *Journal of Black Studies* 22: 168–85.

Bound, John, and Laura Dresser. 1998. "The Erosion of the Relative Earnings and Employment of Young African American Women during the 1980s." In *African American and Latina Women at Work: Race, Gender, and Economic Inequality.* New York: Russell Sage.

Bound, John, and Richard B. Freeman. 1992. "What Went Wrong? The Erosion of Relative Earnings and Employment among Young Black Men in the 1980s."

Quarterly Journal of Economics 107: 201–32.

Bourdieu, Pierre. 1977. *Outline of a Theory of Practice.* Cambridge: Cambridge University Press.

Bourgois, Philippe. 1996. *In Search of Respect: Selling Crack in El Barrio.* Cambridge: Cambridge University Press.

Bowen, Elenore Smith. 1954. *Return to Laughter: An Anthropological Novel.* New York: Doubleday.

Boyd, Michelle R. 2008. *Jim Crow Nostalgia: Reconstructing Race in Bronzeville.* Minneapolis: University of Minnesota Press.

Boyd, Todd. 1997. *Am I Black Enough for You? Popular Culture from the Hood and Beyond.* Bloomington: Indiana University Press.

Bracey, John H., Jr., August Meier, and Elliott Rudwick, eds. 1971. *Black Workers and Organized Labor.* Belmont, CA: Wadsworth.

Brake, Michael. 1985. *Comparative Youth Culture: The Sociology of Youth Culture and Youth Subcultures in America, Britain and Canada.* London: Routledge & Kegan Paul.

Brewer, Rose. 1986. "Research for Whom and by Whom: A Reconsideration of the Black Social Scientist as Insider." *Wisconsin Sociologist* 23: 19–28.

Briggs, Xavier de Souza, and Peter Dreier. 2008. "Memphis Murder Mystery? No, Just Mistaken Identity." http://www.prrac.org/pdf/MemphisMurderMystery.pdf (accessed July 1, 2012).

Burawoy, Michael. 2003. "Revisits: An Outline of a Theory of Reflexive Ethnography." *American Sociological Review* 68: 645–79.

Bursik, Robert J., and Harold Grasmick. 1993. *Neighborhoods and Crime.* New York: Lexington Books.

Burton, Linda, Townsand Price-Spratlen, and Margaret Beale Spencer. 1997. "On Ways of Thinking about Measuring Neighborhoods: Implications for Studying Context and Developmental Outcomes for Children." *Neighborhood Poverty: Context and Consequences for Children.* New York: Russell Sage.

Byrne, James, and Robert Sampson, eds. 1986. *The Social Ecology of Crime.* New York: Springer-Verlag.

Camacho, Eduardo, and Ben Joravsky. 1989. *Against the Tide: The Middle Class in Chicago.* Chicago: Community Renewal Society.

Cancio, A. Silvia, T. David Evans, and David Maume, Jr. 1996. "Reconsidering the Declining Significance of Race: Racial Differences in Early Career Wages." *American Sociological Review* 61: 541–56.

Cary, Lorene. 1991. *Black Ice.* New York: Knopf.

Cashin, Sheryll. 2004. *The Failures of Integration: How Race and Class Are Undermining the American Dream.* New York: Public Affairs.

Caskey, John P. 1994. *Fringe Banking: Check-Cashing Outlets, Pawnshops, and the Poor.* New York: Russell Sage Foundation.

Charles, Camille Zubrinsky. 2006. *Won't You Be My Neighbor? Race, Class, and Residence in Los Angeles.* New York: Russell Sage Foundation.

Chase-Lansdale, Lindsey, Jeanne Brooks-Gunn, and Elise Zamsky. 1994. "Young African-American Multigenerational Families in Poverty: Quality of Mothering and Grandmothering." *Child Development* 65: 373–93.

Chatters, Linda, Robert Joseph Taylor, and Rukmali Jayakody. 1994. "Fictive Kinship Relations in Black Extended Families." *Journal of Comparative Family Studies* 25: 297–312.

Chicago Fact Book Consortium, eds. 1984. *Local Community Fact Book, Chicago Metropolitan Area.* Chicago: Chicago Review Press.

———, eds. 1995. *Local Community Fact Book, Chicago Metropolitan Area, 1990.* Chicago: University of Illinois.

Chicago Housing Authority. 2011. "The Plan for Transformation: An Update on Relocation." http://www.thecha.org/filebin/pdf/mapDocs/4_12_11_Report_FINAL_LR.pdf (accessed July 1, 2012).

Chicago Public Schools Data Book, 1991–1992. Chicago: Chicago Panel on Public School Policy and Finance, 1991–1992.

Chung, Chanjin, and Samuel L. Myers. 1999. "Do the Poor Pay More for Food? An Analysis of Grocery Store Availability and Food Price Disparities." *Journal of Consumer Affairs* 33: 276–96.

City of Chicago, Department of Planning and Development. 1994. *Demographic and Housing Characteristics of Chicago and Community Area Profiles.* Report no. 5.

Clark, William A. V., and Frans M. Dieleman. 1996. *Households and Housing.* New Brunswick, N.J.: Center for Urban Policy Research.

Clay, Phillip L. 1979. "The Process of Black Suburbanization." *Urban Affairs Quarterly* 14: 405–24.

Clifford, James, and George E. Marcus, eds. 1986. *Writing Culture: The Poetics and Politics of Ethnography.* Berkeley: University of California Press.

Clifford, Mark. 1992. "Spring in Their Step: Nike Is Making the Most of All That Cheap Labour." *Far Eastern Economic Review* 155: 56–60.

Cloward, Richard A., and Lloyd E. Ohlin. 1960. *Delinquency and Opportunity: A Theory of Delinquent Gangs.* Glencoe, IL: Free Press of Glencoe.

Collins, Sharon M. 1983. "The Making of the Black Middle Class." *Social Problems* 30: 369–82.

———. 1989. "The Marginalization of Black Executives." *Social Problems* 36: 317–31.

———. 1993. "Blacks on the Bubble: The Vulnerability of Black Executives in White Corporations." *Sociological Quarterly* 34: 429–47.

Contemporary Sociology. 1996. "Ten Most Influential Books of the Past 25 Years." *Contemporary Sociology* 25: 3.

Corcoran, Mary, and Sharon Parrott. 1998. "African American Women's Economic Progress." In *African American and Latina Women at Work: Race, Gender, and Economic Inequality.* New York: Russell Sage.

Correll, Joshua, et al. 2002. "The Police Officer's Dilemma: Using Ethnicity to Disambiguate Potential Threatening Individuals." *Journal of Personality and Social Psychology* 83: 1314–29.

Cose, Ellis. 1993. *The Rage of a Privileged Class.* New York: HarperCollins.

———. 1997. *Color-Blind: Seeing Beyond Race in a Race-Obsessed World.* New York: HarperCollins.

Cosgrove, Stuart. 1984. "The Zoot-Suit and Style Warfare." *History Workshop Journal* 18: 77–91.

Craig, Stephen C., and Stephen Earl Bennett, eds. 1993. *After the Boom: The Politics of Generation X.* Lanham, MD: Rowman & Littlefield.

Crowder, Kyle. 2000. "The Racial Context of White Mobility: An Individual-level Assessment of the White Flight Hypothesis." *Social Science Research* 29: 223–57.

Crowder, Kyle, Matthew Hall, and Stewart E. Tolnay. 2011. "Neighborhood Immigration and Native Out-Migration." *American Sociological Review* 76: 25–47.

Cummings, Scott. 1998. *Left Behind in Rosedale: Race Relations and the Collapse of Community Institutions.* Boulder, CO: Westview Press.

Cunningham, James S., and Nadja Zalokar. 1992. "The Economic Progress of Black Women, 1940–1980: Occupational Distribution and Relative Wages." *Industrial and Labor Relations Review* 45: 540–55.

D'Amico, Ronald, and Nan L. Maxwell. 1994. "The Impact of Post-School Joblessness on Male Black-White Wage Differentials." *Industrial Relations* 33: 184–205.

Daniels, Cora. 2004. *Black Power, Inc.: The New Voice of Success.* Hoboken, NJ: John Wiley & Sons.

Danziger, Sheldon, and Peter Gottschalk. 1995. *America Unequal.* New York: Russell Sage.

Darden, Joe T. 1987. "Socioeconomic Status and Racial Residential Segregation: Blacks and Hispanics in Chicago." *International Journal of Comparative Sociology* 28: 1–13.

DaVanzo, Julie, and Frances Korbin Goldscheider. 1990. "Coming Home Again: Returns to the Parental Home of Young Adults." *Population Studies* 44: 241–55.

Davis, Theodore J., Jr. 1995. "The Occupational Mobility of Black Men Revisited: Does Race Matter?" *Social Science Journal* 32: 121–35.

Dawson, Michael C. 1994. *Behind the Mule: Race and Class in African-American Politics.* Princeton, NJ: Princeton University Press.

Dickerson, Dennis C. 1986. *Out of the Crucible: Black Steelworkers in Western Pennsylvania, 1875–1980.* Albany: State University of New York Press.

Dickson, Lynda, and Kris Marsh. 2008. "The Love Jones Cohort: The New Face of the Black Middle Class?" *Black Women, Gender & Families* 2: 84–105.

Dillard, J. L. 1972. *Black English: Its History and Usage in the United States*. New York: Random House.

Doss, Richard C., and Alan Gross. 1992. "The Effects of Black English on Stereotyping in Intraracial Perceptions." *Journal of Black Psychology* 18: 47–58.

———. 1994. "The Effects of Black English and Code-Switching on Intraracial Perceptions." *Journal of Black Psychology* 20: 282–93.

Downey, Liam. 2003. "Spatial Measurement, Geography, and Urban Racial Inequality." *Social Forces* 81: 937–952.

Drake, St. Clair, and Horace Cayton. [1945] 1993. *Black Metropolis: A Study of Negro Life in a Northern City*. Revised and enlarged edition. Chicago: University of Chicago Press.

Dreier, Peter. 2004. "How the Media Compound Urban Problems." *Journal of Urban Affairs* 27: 193–201.

Du Bois, W. E. B. [1899] 1996. *The Philadelphia Negro: A Social Study*. Philadelphia: University of Pennsylvania Press.

Duncan, Greg, Johanne Boisjoly, and Timothy Smeeding. 1996. "Economic Mobility of Young Workers in the 1970s and 1980s." *Demography* 33: 497–509.

Duncan, Greg, Timothy Smeeding, and Willard Rogers. 1993. "W(h)ither the Middle Class? A Dynamic View." In *Poverty and Prosperity in the USA in the Late Twentieth Century*, edited by Dimitri B. Papadimitriou and Edward N. Wolff, 240–71. New York: St. Martin's Press.

Duncan, Otis Dudley, and Beverly Duncan. 1957. *The Negro Population of Chicago: A Story of Residential Succession*. Chicago: University of Chicago Press.

Dymski, Gary A., and John M. Veitch. 1996. "Financial Transformation and the Metropolis: Booms, Busts, and Banking in Los Angeles." *Environment and Planning* 28: 1233–60.

Dyson, Michael Eric. 1994. "Bum Rap." *New York Times*, February 3, section A, 13.

———. 1996. *Between God and Gangsta Rap: Bearing Witness to Black Culture*. New York: Oxford University Press.

Economic Mobility Project. 2011. "Does America Promote Mobility as Well as Other Nations?" Pew Charitable Trusts. http://www.pewstates.org/research/reports/does-america-promote-mobility-as-well-as-other-nations-85899380321 (accessed July 1, 2012).

———. 2012. "Pursuing the American Dream: Economic Mobility Across Generations." Pew Charitable Trusts. http://www.pewstates.org/uploadedFiles/PCS_Assets/2012/Pursuing_American_Dream.pdf (accessed July 11, 2012).

Edin, Kathryn, and Laura Lein. 1997. *Making Ends Meet: How Single Mothers Survive Welfare and Low-Wage Work*. New York: Russell Sage.

Ellen, Ingrid Gould. 2000. *Sharing America's Neighborhoods: The Prospects for Stable Racial Integration*. Cambridge, MA: Harvard University Press.

Ellen, Ingrid Gould, Michael Lens, and Katherine O'Regan. 2011. "Memphis Murder Revisited: Do Housing Vouchers Cause Crime?" Prepared for US Department of Housing and Urban Development, Office of Policy Development and Research. http://www.huduser.org/publications/pdf/Ellen_MemphisMurder_AssistedHousingRCR07_v2.pdf (accessed July 1, 2012).

Emerson, Michael, George Yancey, and Karen Chai. 2001. "Does Race Matter in Residential Segregation? Exploring the Preferences of White Americans." *American Sociological Review* 66: 922–935.

Entman, Robert, and Andrew Rojecki. 2000. *The Black Image in the White Mind: Media and Race in America*. Chicago: University of Chicago Press.

Erbe, Brigitte Mach. 1975. "Race and Socioeconomic Segregation." *American Sociological Review* 40: 801–12.

Ermisch, John, Markus Jäntti, and Timothy Smeeding, eds. 2012. *From Parents to Children: The Intergenerational Transmission of Advantage*. New York: Russell Sage Foundation.

Fainstein, Norman, and Susan Nesbitt. 1996. "Did the Black Ghetto Have a Golden Age? Class Structure and Class Segregation in New York City, 1949–1970, with Initial Evidence for 1990." *Journal of Urban History* 23: 3–28.

Farkas, George, Margaret Barton, and Kathy Kushner. 1988. "White, Black and Hispanic Female Wage Rates and Employment." *Sociological Quarterly* 29: 605–21.

Farley, Reynolds. 1970. "The Changing Distribution of Negroes within Metropolitan Areas: The Emergence of Black Suburbs." *American Journal of Sociology* 75: 512–29.

———. 1985. "Three Steps Forward and Two Back? Recent Changes in the Social and Economic Status of Blacks." *Ethnic and Racial Studies* 8: 4–28.

———. 1991. "Residential Segregation of Social and Economic Groups among Blacks, 1970–80." In *The Urban Underclass*, edited by Christopher Jencks and Paul E. Peterson, 274–98. Washington, DC: Brookings Institution.

———. 1996. "Black-White Residential Segregation: The Views of Myrdal in the 1940s and Trends of the 1980s." In *An American Dilemma Revisited*, edited by Obie Clayton, Jr., 45–75. New York: Russell Sage.

Farley, Reynolds, and Walter R. Allen. 1987. *The Color Line and the Quality of American Life*. New York: Russell Sage Foundation.

Farley, Reynolds, et al. 1994. "Stereotypes and Segregation: Neighborhoods in the Detroit Area." *American Journal of Sociology* 100: 750–80.

Feagin, Joe R., and Melvin P. Sikes. 1994. *Living with Racism: The Black Middle-Class Experience*. Boston: Beacon Press.

Featherman, David, and Robert Hauser. 1976. "Changes in the Socioeconomic

Stratification of the Races, 1962–73." *American Journal of Sociology* 82: 621–51.

Feldman, S. Shirley, and Glen R. Elliott, eds. 1990. *At the Threshold: The Developing Adolescent*. Cambridge, MA: Harvard University Press.

Fernandez, James. 1974. "The Myth of Metaphor in Expressive Culture." *Current Anthropology* 15: 119–45.

Fernandez, Roberto, and David Harris. 1992. "Social Isolation and the Underclass." In *Drugs, Crime, and Social Isolation: Barriers to Opportunity*, edited by Adele Harrel and George Peterson, 257–93. Washington, DC: Urban Institute Press.

Fielding, Elaine, and Karl Taeuber. 1992. "Spatial Isolation of a Black Underclass: An American Case Study." *New Community* 19: 112–27.

Franklin, John Hope. Reconstruction after the Civil War. Chicago: University of Chicago Press, 2012.

Frazier, E. Franklin. 1939. *The Negro Family in the United States*. Chicago: University of Chicago Press.

———. 1957. *The Black Bourgeoisie*. New York: Free Press.

Freeman, Richard B. 1976. *Black Elite: The New Market for Highly Educated Black Americans*. New York: McGraw-Hill.

———. 1987. "The Relation of Criminal Activity to Black Youth Employment." *Review of Black Political Economy* 16: 99–107.

Freeman, Richard B., and Harry Holzer, eds. 1986. *The Black Male Employment Crisis*. Chicago: University of Chicago Press.

Freudenberg, William. 1986. "The Density of Acquaintanceship: An Overlooked Variable in Community Research." *American Journal of Sociology* 92: 27–63.

Frey, William. 2004. "The New Great Migration: Black Americans' Return to the South, 1965–2000." Washington, DC: Brookings Institution. http://www.brookings.edu/~/media/research/files/reports/2004/5/demographics%20frey/20040524_frey.pdf (accessed July 1, 2012).

———. 2011. "Melting Pot Cities and Suburbs: Racial and Ethnic Change in Metro America in the 2000s." Brookings Institution. http://www.brookings.edu/~/media/research/files/papers/2011/5/04-census-ethnicity-frey/0504_census_ethnicity_frey.pdf (accessed February 27, 2013).

Gaines, Donna. 1991. *Teenage Wasteland Suburbia's Dead End Kids*. New York: Pantheon Books.

Galster, George C. 1991. "Black Suburbanization: Has It Changed the Relative Location of Races?" *Urban Affairs Quarterly* 26: 621–28.

Galster, George, Jackie M. Cutsinger, and Ron Malega. 2008. "The Costs of Concentrated Poverty: Neighborhood Property Markets and the Dynamics of Decline." In *Revisiting Rental Housing: Policies, Programs, and Priorities*, edited by Nicolas P. Retsinas and Eric S. Belsky, 116–19. Washington, DC: Brookings Institution.

Galster, George, and Edward Hill, eds. *The Metropolis in Black and White*. New Brunswick, NJ, Center for Urban Policy Research.

Gans, Herbert J. 1997. "Best-Sellers by Sociologists: An Exploratory Study." *Contemporary Sociology* 26: 131–35.

Garfinkel, Irwin, and Sara S. McLanahan. 1986. *Single Mothers and Their Children: A New American Dilemma*. Washington, DC: Urban Institute Press.

Gargan, Edward A. 1996. "An Indonesian Asset Is Also a Liability." *New York Times*, March 16, section A, 35–36.

Garner, T., and Donald L. Rubin. 1986. "Middle Class Blacks' Perceptions of Dialect and Style Shifting: The Case of Southern Attorneys." *Journal of Language and Social Psychology* 5: 33–48.

Gaskin, Darrell J. 1999. "Safety Net Hospitals: Essential Providers of Public Health and Specialty Services." The Commonwealth Fund. http://www.the-commonwealthfund.com/~/media/Files/Publications/Fund%20Report/1999/Feb/Safety%20Net%20Hospitals%20%20Essential%20Providers%200f%20Public%20Health%20and%20Specialty%20Services/Gaskin_safety_net_hospitals_309%20pdf.pdf (accessed July 1, 2012).

Geertz, Clifford. 1973. *The Interpretation of Cultures*. New York: Basic Books.

Gilder, George. 1981. *Wealth and Poverty*. New York: Basic Books.

Ginwright, Shawn. 2002. "Classed Out: The Challenges of Social Class in Black Community Change." *Social Problems* 49: 544–63.

Glaeser, Edward, and Jacob Vigdor. 2012. "The End of the Segregated Century: Racial Separation in America's Neighborhoods, 1890–2010." Manhattan Institute Civic Report 66. http://www.manhattan-institute.org/pdf/cr_66.pdf (accessed July 1, 2012).

Glaser, Barney G., and Anselm Strauss. 1967. *The Discovery of Grounded Theory: Strategies for Qualitative Research*. Chicago: Aldine Publishing.

Goldscheider, Frances K., and Julie DaVanzo. 1989. "Pathways to Independent Living in Early Adulthood: Marriage, Semiautonomy, and Premarital Residential Independence." *Demography* 26: 597–614.

Grant, David, Melvin Oliver, and Angela James. 1996. "African Americans: Social and Economic Bifurcation." In *Ethnic Los Angeles*, edited by Roger Waldinger and Mehdi Bozorgmehr, 379–409. New York: Russell Sage Foundation.

Greenwald, Anthony, Mark Oakes, and Hunter Hoffman. 2003. "Targets of Discrimination: Effects of Race on Responses to Weapons Holders." *Journal of Experimental Social Psychology* 39: 399–405.

Gregory, Steven. 1998. *Black Corona: Race and Politics of Place in an Urban Community*. Princeton, NJ: Princeton University Press.

Gregory, Toni. 1999. Book Review of *Black Picket Fences*. *The Journal of Negro Education* 68: 590.

Grogger, Jeff. 1992. "Arrests, Persistent Youth Joblessness, and Black/White

Employment Differentials." *Review of Economics and Statistics* 74: 100–106.

Grossman, Ron, and Byron P. White. 1997. "Poverty Surrounds Black Middle Class: Upscale Neighborhood Virtually an Island." *Chicago Tribune*, February 7, section C, 1.

Gursky, Daniel. 1996. "'Uniform' Improvement?" *Education Digest* 61: 46–48.

Gusfield, Joseph. 1995. "Preface." In *A Second Chicago School? The Development of a Postwar American Sociology*, edited by Gary Alan Fine. Chicago: University of Chicago Press.

Gwaltney, John Langston. 1980. *Drylongso: A Self-Portrait of Black America*. New York: Random House.

Hagan, John, and Ruth D. Peterson. 1995. "Criminal Inequality in America: Patterns and Consequences." In *Crime and Inequality*, edited by John Hagan and Ruth D. Peterson, 14–36. Palo Alto, CA: Stanford University Press.

Hagedorn, John M. 1988. *People and Folks: Gangs, Crime and the Underclass in a Rustbelt City*. Chicago: Lakeview Press.

Hall, Stuart, and Tony Jefferson. 1976. *Resistance through Rituals: Youth Subcultures in Post-war Britain*. London: Routledge.

Hannerz, Ulf. 1969. *Soulside: Inquiries into Ghetto Culture and Community*. New York: Columbia University Press.

Hare, Nathan. 1965. *The Black Anglo Saxons*. New York: Marzani & Mansell.

Harrison, Bennett, and Lucy Gorham. 1992. "What Happened to African-American Wages in the 1980s?" In *The Metropolis in Black and White*, edited by George Galster and Edward Hill, 39–55. New Brunswick, NJ: Center for Urban Policy Research.

Haynes, Bruce. 2001. *Red Lines, Black Spaces: The Politics of Race and Space in a Black Middle-Class Suburb*. New Haven, CT: Yale University Press.

Hebdige, Dick. 1979. *Subculture: The Meaning of Style*. London: Routledge.

Heflin, Colleen, and Mary Pattillo. 2006. "Poverty in the Family: Race, Siblings and Socioeconomic Heterogeneity." *Social Science Research* 35: 804–822.

Hirsch, Arnold R. 1983. *Making the Second Ghetto: Race and Housing in Chicago*. New York: Cambridge University Press.

Hochschild, Jennifer L. 1995. *Facing Up to the American Dream: Race, Class, and the Soul of the Nation*. Princeton, NJ: Princeton University Press.

Hofferth, Sandra. 1984. "Kin Networks, Race, and Family Structure." *Journal of Marriage and the Family* 46: 791–806.

Höijer, Birgitta. 2004. "The Discourse of Global Compassion: The Audience and Media Reporting of Human Suffering." *Media Culture Society* 26: 513–531.

Holliday, Amy, and Rachel Dwyer. 2009. "Suburban Neighborhood Poverty in U.S. Metropolitan Areas in 2000." *City & Community* 8:155–176.

Hopkinson, Natalie. 2012. *Go-Go Live: The Musical Life and Death of a Chocolate City*. Durham, NC: Duke University Press.

Hout, Michael. 1984. "Occupational Mobility of Black Men: 1962 to 1973." *American Sociological Review* 49: 308–22.

Hughes, Langston. 1948. *One-Way Ticket.* Illustrated by Jacob Lawrence. New York: Alfred A. Knopf.

Hunter, Albert. 1995. "Private, Parochial and Public Social Orders: The Problem of Crime and Incivility in Urban Communities." In *Metropolis: Center and Symbol of Our Times*, edited by Philip Kasinitz, 209–25. New York: New York University Press.

Hyra, Derek. 2008. *The New Urban Renewal: The Economic Transformation of Harlem and Bronzeville.* Chicago: The University of Chicago Press.

Ianni, Francis A. J. 1971. "The Mafia and the Web of Kinship." *Public Interest* 22: 78–100.

———. 1974. "New Mafia: Black, Hispanic, and Italian Styles." *Society* 11: 26–39.

Iceland, John. 2009. *Where We Live Now: Immigration and Race in the United States.* Berkeley: University of California Press.

Immergluck, Dan, and Geoff Smith. 2006. "The External Costs of Foreclosure: The Impact of Single-Family Mortgage Foreclosures on Property Values." *Housing Policy Debate* 17: 57–79.

Institute on Race and Poverty. 2009. "Communities in Crisis: Race and Mortgage Lending in the Twin Cities." Minneapolis: University of Minnesota Law School. http://www.irpumn.org/uls/resources/projects/IRP_mortgage_study_Feb._11th.pdf (accessed July 1, 2012).

Jackson, Janice E., and William T. Schantz. 1993. "Crisis Management Lessons: Boycott of Nike by People United to Serve Humanity." *Business Horizons* 36, no. 1: 27.

Jackson, John L. 2001. *Harlemworld: Doing Race and Class in Contemporary Black America.* Chicago: University of Chicago Press.

Jackson, Kenneth T. 1985. *Crabgrass Frontier: The Suburbanization of the United States.* New York: Oxford University Press.

James, David E., and Karl E. Taeuber. 1985. "Measures of Segregation." In *Sociological Methodology*, edited by Nancy Brandon Tuma, 1–32. San Francisco: Jossey-Bass.

Jankowski, Martin Sánchez. 1991. *Islands in the Street: Gangs and American Urban Society.* Berkeley: University of California Press.

Jargowsky, Paul. 1996. "Take the Money and Run: Economic Segregation in U.S. Metropolitan Areas." *American Sociological Review* 61: 984–98.

———. 1997. *Poverty and Place: Ghettos, Barrios, and the American City.* New York: Russell Sage.

Jargowsky, Paul, and Mary Jo Bane. 1991. "Ghetto Poverty in the United States, 1970–1980." In *The Urban Underclass*, edited by Christopher Jencks and Paul

E. Peterson, 235–73. Washington, DC: Brookings Institution.

Jarmin, Ronald, Shawn D. Klimek, and Javier Miranda. 2009. "The Role of Retail Chains: National, Regional and Industry Results." In *Producer Dynamics: New Evidence from Micro Data*, edited by Timothy Dunne, J. Bradford Jensen, and Mark J. Roberts, 237–62. Chicago: University of Chicago Press.

Jaynes, Gerald, and Robin Williams, eds. 1989. *A Common Destiny: Blacks and American Society*. Washington, DC: National Research Council.

Jencks, Christopher. 1992. *Rethinking Social Policy: Race, Poverty and the Underclass*. Cambridge, MA: Harvard University Press.

Johnson, Heather Beth. 2006. *The American Dream and the Power of Wealth: Choosing Schools and Inheriting Inequality in the Land of Opportunity*. New York: Routledge.

Johnson, Valerie. 2002. *Black Power in the Suburbs: The Myth or Reality of African American Suburban Political Incorporation*. Albany: State University of New York Press.

Jones, Del. 1996. "Critics Tie Sweatshop Sneakers to 'Air' Jordan." *USA Today*, June 6, section B, 1.

Joseph, Mark L., and Robert Chaskin. 2012. "Mixed-Income Developments and Low Rates of Return: Insights from Relocated Public Housing Residents in Chicago." *Housing Policy Debate* 22: 377–405.

Journal of Blacks in Higher Education. 1997. "The Most Highly Cited Black Scholars of 1996." *Journal of Blacks in Higher Education* 16 (Summer): 18–19.

Kain, John. 1968. "Housing Segregation, Negro Employment and Metropolitan Decentralization." *Quarterly Journal of Economics* 26: 110–30.

Kakutani, Michiko. 1997. "Common Threads." *New York Times Magazine*, February 16, section 6, 18.

Kasarda, John D. 1995. "Industrial Restructuring and the Changing Location of Jobs." In *State of the Union: America in the 1990s*, vol. 1, edited by Reynolds Farley. New York: Russell Sage Foundation.

Kasarda, John, and Morris Janowitz. 1974. "Community Attachment in Mass Society." *American Sociological Review* 39: 328–39.

Katz, Jack. 1988. *Seductions of Crime: Moral and Sensual Attractions of Doing Evil*. Palo Alto, CA: Stanford University Press.

Katz, Michael B. 1989. *The Undeserving Poor: From the War on Poverty to the War on Welfare*. New York: Pantheon.

Kefalas, Maria. 2003. *Working-Class Heroes: Protecting Home, Community and Nation in a Chicago Neighborhood*. Berkeley: University of California Press.

Keith, Verna, and Cedric Herring. 1991. "Skin Tone Stratification in the Black Community." *American Journal of Sociology* 97: 760–78.

Kelley, Robin D. G. 1992. "The Riddle of the Zoot: Malcolm Little and Black Cultural Politics during World War II." In *Malcolm X: In Our Own Image*, edited by Joe Wood, 155–82. New York: St. Martin's Press.

———. 1996. "We Are Not What We Seem." In *The New African American Urban History*, edited by Kenneth Goings and Raymond Mohl, 187–239. Thousand Oaks, CA: Sage.

———. 1997. *Yo' Mama's Disfunktionall Fighting the Culture Wars in Urban America*. Boston: Beacon Press.

Kennedy, Randall. 2012. *The Persistence of the Color Line: Racial Politics and the Obama Presidency*. New York: Vintage Books.

Kitagawa, Evelyn, and Karl Taeuber. 1963. *Local Community Fact Book, Chicago Metropolitan Area, 1960*. Chicago: University of Chicago Press.

Kitwana, Bakari. 1994. *The Rap on Gangsta Rap*. Chicago: Third World Press.

Kneebone, Elizabeth, Carey Nadeau, and Alan Berube. "The Re-Emergence of Concentrated Poverty: Metropolitan Trends in the 2000s." Washington, DC: Brookings Institution. http://www.brookings.edu/~/media/research/files/papers/2011/11/03%20poverty%20kneebone%20nadeau%20berube/1103_poverty_kneebone_nadeau_berube.pdf (accessed July 1, 2012).

Kornhauser, Ruth. 1978. *Social Sources of Delinquency: An Appraisal of Analytic Models*. Chicago: University of Chicago Press.

Kotlowitz, Alex. 1991. *There Are No Children Here*. New York: Doubleday.

Kronus, Sidney. 1971. *The Black Middle Class*. Columbus, OH: Merrill.

Krysan, Maria, Reynolds Farley, and Mick Couper. 2008. "In the Eye of the Beholder: Racial Beliefs and Residential Segregation." *DuBois Review* 5: 5–26.

Krysan, Maria, et al. 2009. "Does Race Matter in Neighborhood Preferences? Results from a Video Experiment." *American Journal of Sociology* 115: 527–559.

Kuebler Meghan. 2012. "Lending in the Modern Era: Does Racial Composition of Neighborhoods Matter when Individuals Seek Home Financing? A Pilot Study in New England." *City & Community* 11: 31–50.

Kusmer, Kenneth L. 1976. *A Ghetto Takes Shape: Black Cleveland, 1870–1930*. Chicago: University of Illinois Press.

Labich, Kenneth, and Tim Carvell. 1995. "A Battle for Hearts, Minds and Feet: Nike vs. Reebok." *Fortune* 132: 90–106.

Labov, William. 1972. *Language in the Inner City: Studies in the Black English Vernacular*. Philadelphia: University of Pennsylvania Press.

Lacy, Karyn. 2007. *Blue-Chip Black: Race, Class, and Status in the New Black Middle Class*. Berkeley: University of California Press.

Ladner, Joyce A. 1971. *Tomorrow's Tomorrow: The Black Woman*. Garden City, NY: Doubleday & Company.

Lamar, Jake. 1991. *Bourgeois Blues: An American Memoir*. New York: Summit Books.

Lamont, Michèle. 1992. *Money, Morals and Manners*. Chicago: University of Chicago Press.

————. 2000. *The Dignity of Working Men: Morality and the Boundaries of Race, Class, and Immigration.* New York: Russell Sage Foundation.

Landry, Bart. 1987. *The New Black Middle Class.* Berkeley: University of California Press.

Landry, Bart, and Kris Marsh. 2011. "The Evolution of the New Black Middle Class." *Annual Review of Sociology* 37: 373–94.

Lane, Randall. 1996. "You Are What You Wear." *Forbes* 158: 42–46.

LaPoint, Velma, Lillian Holloman, and Sylvan Alleyne. 1993. "Dress Codes and Uniforms in Urban Schools." *Education Digest* 58: 32–34.

Lareau, Annette. 2003. *Unequal Childhoods: Class, Race, and Family Life.* Berkeley: University of California Press.

Larson, Nicole, Mary Story, and Melissa Nelson. 2009. "Neighborhood Environments: Disparities in Access to Healthy Foods in the U.S." *American Journal of Preventive Medicine* 36: 74–81.

Lee, E. Bun, and Louis A. Browne. 1995. "Effects of Television Advertising on African American Teenagers." *Journal of Black Studies* 25: 523–36.

Lemann, Nicholas. 1991. *The Promised Land: The Great Black Migration and How It Changed America.* New York: Vintage Books.

Leonard, Jonathan S. 1984. "Employment and Occupational Advance under Affirmative Action." *Review of Economics and Statistics* 66: 377–85.

————. 1991. "The Federal Anti-Bias Effort." In *Essays on the Economics of Discrimination*, edited by Emily Hoffman. Kalamazoo, MI: Upjohn Institute for Employment Research.

Levy, Frank, and Richard J. Murname. 1992. "U.S. Earnings Levels and Earnings Inequality: A Review of Recent Trends and Proposed Explanations." *Journal of Economic Literature* 30: 1333–81.

Lewis, Valerie, Michael Emerson, and Stephen Klineberg. 2011. "Who We'll Live with: Neighborhood Race Composition Preferences of Whites, Blacks, and Latinos. *Social Forces* 89: 1385–407.

Liebow, Elliot. 1967. *Tally's Corner: A Study of Negro Streetcorner Men.* Boston: Little Brown.

Lofland, John, and Lyn H. Lofland. 1984. *Analyzing Social Settings: A Guide to Qualitative Observation and Analysis.* 2nd ed. Belmont, CA: Wadsworth.

Logan, John R., and Richard Alba. 1995. "Who Lives in Affluent Suburbs? Racial Differences in Eleven Metropolitan Regions." *Sociological Focus* 28: 353–64. http://www.s4.brown.edu/us2010 (accessed July 1, 2012).

Logan, John R., Richard Alba, and Shu-Yin Leung. 1996. "Minority Access to White Suburbs: A Multiregional Comparison." *Social Forces* 74: 851–81.

Logan, John R., and Harvey L. Molotch. 1987. *Urban Fortunes: The Political Economy of Place.* Berkeley: University of California Press.

Logan, John R., and Brian Stults. 2011. "The Persistence of Segregation in the

Metropolis: New Findings from the 2010 Census." Census Brief prepared for Project US2010.

Longhurst, Brian. 1995. *Popular Music and Society.* Cambridge: Polity Press.

Lott, Tommy. 1992. "Marooned in America: Black Urban Youth Culture and Social Pathology." In *The Underclass Question*, edited by Bill E. Lawson. Philadelphia: Temple University Press.

MacLeod, Jay. 1995. *Ain't No Makin' It: Aspirations and Attainment in a Low-Income Neighborhood.* 2nd ed. Boulder, CO: Westview Press.

———. 2009. *Ain't No Makin' It: Aspirations and Attainment in a Low-Income Neighborhood.* 3rd ed. Boulder, CO: Westview Press.

Mare, Robert D. 1995. "Changes in Educational Attainment and School Enrollment." In *State of the Union: America in the 1990s*, vol. 1, edited by Reynolds Farley. New York: Russell Sage Foundation.

Mare, Robert D., and Christopher Winship. 1991. "Socioeconomic Change and the Decline of Marriage for Blacks and Whites." In *The Urban Underclass*, edited by Christopher Jencks and Paul E. Peterson, 175–202. Washington, DC: Brookings Institution.

Marsh, Kris, et al. 2007. "The Emerging Black Middle Class: Single and Living Alone." *Social Forces* 86: 735–762.

Massey, Douglas. 1996. "The Age of Extremes: Concentrated Affluence and Poverty in the Twenty-First Century." *Demography* 33: 395–412.

Massey, Douglas, Gretchen A. Condran, and Nancy A. Denton. 1987. "The Effect of Residential Segregation on Black Social and Economic Well-Being." *Social Forces* 66: 29–57.

Massey, Douglas, and Nancy Denton. 1985. "Spatial Assimilation as a Socioeconomic Outcome." *American Sociological Review* 50: 94–106.

———. 1988. "Suburbanization and Segregation in U.S. Metropolitan Areas." *American Journal of Sociology* 94: 592–626.

———. 1993. *American Apartheid: Segregation and the Making of the Underclass.* Cambridge, MA: Harvard University Press.

Massey, Douglas, and Mitchell Eggers. 1990. "The Ecology of Inequality: Minorities and the Concentration of Poverty, 1970–1980." *American Journal of Sociology* 95: 1153–88.

Massey, Douglas, Andrew Gross, and Kumiko Shibuya. 1994. "Migration, Segregation and the Concentration of Poverty." *American Sociological Review* 59: 425–45.

McAdoo, Harriette Pipes. 1978. "Factors Related to Stability in Upwardly Mobile Black Families." *Journal of Marriage and the Family* 40: 761–76.

McLanahan, Sara, and Gary Sandefur. 1994. *Growing Up with a Single Parent: What Hurts, What Helps.* Cambridge, MA: Harvard University Press.

Meares, Tracey. 1997. "Charting Race and Class Differences in Attitudes toward

Drug Legalization and Law Enforcement: Lessons for Federal Criminal Law."
Buffalo Criminal Law Review 1: 137–74.

Merriwether-de Vries, Cynthia, Linda Burton, and LaShawnda Eggeletion. 1996.
"Early Parenting and Intergenerational Family Relationships within African
American Families." In *Transitions through Adolescence*, edited by Julia Graber,
Jeanne Brooks-Gunn, and Anne Peterson. Mahwah, NJ: Lawrence Erlbaum
Associates.

Merry, Sally Engle. 1983. "Urban Danger: Life in a Neighborhood of Strangers."
In *Urban Life: Readings in Urban Anthropology*, edited by George Gmelch and
Walter P. Zenner, 63–72. Prospect Heights, IL: Waveland Press.

Merton, Robert K. 1972. "Insiders and Outsiders: A Chapter in the Sociology of
Knowledge." *American Journal of Sociology* 78: 9–47.

Molotch, Harvey. 1972. *Managed Integration: Dilemmas of Doing Good in the City.*
Berkeley: University of California Press.

Monti, Daniel. 1994. *Wannabe: Gangs in Suburbs and Schools.* Cambridge, MA:
Blackwell.

Moore, Kesha. 2009. "Gentrification in Black Face?: The Return of the Black Middle Class to Urban Neighborhoods." *Journal Urban Geography* 30 :118–142.

Morenoff, Jeffrey D., and Robert J. Sampson. 1997. "Violent Crime and the
Spatial Dynamics of Neighborhood Transition: Chicago, 1970–1990." *Social
Forces* 76: 31–64.

Morris, Aldon. 1996. "What's Race Got to Do with It?" *Contemporary Sociology*
25: 309–13.

Moschis, George. 1987. *Consumer Socialization: A Life-Cycle Perspective.* Lexington, MA: Lexington Books.

Murray, Stephen. 1991. "Ethnic Differences in Interpretive Conventions and
the Reproduction of Inequality in Everyday Life." *Symbolic Interaction* 14:
187–204.

Nash, Jeffrey E. 1991. "Race and Words: A Note on the Sociolinguistic Divisive-
ness of Race in American Society." *Sociological Inquiry* 61: 252–62.

Neal, Derek. 1997. "The Effects of Catholic Secondary Schooling on Educational
Achievement." *Journal of Labor Economics* 15: 98–123.

Nelson, Linda. 1990. "Code-Switching in the Oral Life Narratives of African-
American Women: Challenges to Linguistic Hegemony." *Journal of Education*
172: 142–55.

Newman, Katherine S. 1989. *Falling from Grace: The Experience of Downward
Mobility in the American Middle Class.* New York: Vintage Books.

———. 1993. *Declining Fortunes: The Withering of the American Dream.* New
York: Basic Books.

Newman, M. W., Harry Swegle, and Jack Willner. 1959. "The Panic Peddlers:
A Reprint of Articles on Racial Problems of Changing Neighborhoods in

Chicago." *Chicago Daily News*, October 13–22.

New York Times. 2011. "Under Obama, is America 'Post-Racial'?" Sept 21, 2011. http://www.nytimes.com/roomfordebate/2011/09/21/under-obama-is-america-post-racial (accessed July 1, 2012).

Nightingale, Carl Husemoller. 1993. *On the Edge: A History of Poor Black Children and Their American Dream*. New York: Basic Books.

O'Kane, James M. 1992. *The Crooked Ladder: Gangsters, Ethnicity, and the American Dream*. New Brunswick, NJ: Transaction Press.

Oliver, Melvin. 1988. "The Urban Black Community as Network: Toward a Social Network Perspective." *Sociological Quarterly* 29: 623–45.

Oliver, Melvin L., and Thomas M. Shapiro. 1995. *Black Wealth/White Wealth: A New Perspective on Racial Inequality*. New York: Routledge.

Olusola-Ajayi, Simi. 2011. "Writing Samples: Black Picket Fences." http://www.personal.psu.edu/sa05134/blogs/olusola-ajayi_simi_e-portfolio/writing-samples.html (accessed July 1, 2012).

Orfield, Gary, and Carol Ashkinaze. 1991. *The Closing Door: Conservative Policy and Black Opportunity*. Chicago: University of Chicago Press.

Osofsky, Gilbert. 1963. *Harlem: The Making of a Ghetto*. New York: Harper & Row.

Osterman, Paul. 1980. *Getting Started: The Youth Labor Market*. Cambridge, MA: Massachusetts Institute of Technology Press.

Owens, Michael Leo. 1996. "Government Jobs and Black Neighborhoods in New York City." Paper presented at the New York State Political Science Association meeting, Ithaca, New York.

Padilla, Felix M. 1992. *The Gang as an American Enterprise*. New Brunswick, NJ: Rutgers University Press.

Pattillo, Mary. 2005. "Black Middle-Class Neighborhoods." *Annual Review of Sociology* 31: 305–29.

———. 2007. *Black on the Block: The Politics of Race and Class in the City*. Chicago: University of Chicago Press.

———. 2009. "Investing in Poor Black Neighborhoods 'As Is.'" In *Public Housing and the Legacy of Segregation*, edited by Margery Austin, Susan J. Popkin, and Lynette Rawlings, 31–46. Washington, DC: Urban Institute Press.

Pattillo-McCoy, Mary. 1998. "The Invisible Black Middle Class." Paper presented at the annual meeting of the American Sociological Association, San Francisco, CA.

Pew Research Center. 2011. "Twenty-to-One: Wealth Gaps Rise to Record Highs Between Whites, Blacks and Hispanics." Pew Social Trends. http://www.pewsocialtrends.org/files/2011/07/SDT-Wealth-Report_7-26-11_FINAL.pdf (accessed September 22, 2012).

Pfeiffer, Deirdre. 2012a. "African Americans' Search for 'More for Less' and 'Peace of Mind' on the Exurban Frontier." *Urban Geography* 33: 64–90.

———. 2012b. "Has Exurban Growth Enabled Greater Racial Equity in Neighborhood Quality? Evidence from the Los Angeles Region." *Journal of Urban Affairs* 34: 347–71.

Pinkney, Alphonso. 1984. *The Myth of Black Progress*. New York: Cambridge University Press.

Pitts, Robert E., et al. 1989. "Black and White Response to Culturally Targeted Television Commercials: A Values-Based Approach." *Psychology and Marketing* 6: 311–28.

Pitts, Steven. "Research Brief: Black Workers and the Public Sector." Berkeley Center for Labor Research and Education. http://laborcenter.berkeley.edu/blackworkers/blacks_public_sector11.pdf (accessed July 1, 2012).

Popkin, Susan J., et al. 2012. "Public Housing Transformation and Crime: Making the Case for Responsible Relocation." Urban Institute. http://www.urban.org/UploadedPDF/412523-public-housing-transformation.pdf (accessed July 1, 2012).

Powers, Daniel A. 1996. "Social Background and Social Context Effects on Young Men's Idleness Transitions." *Social Science Research* 25: 50–72.

Prince, Sabiyha. 2004. *Constructing Belonging: Class, Race, and Harlem's Professional Workers*. New York: Routledge.

Pugh, Allison. 2009. *Longing and Belonging: Parents, Children, and Consumer Culture*. Berkeley: University of California Press.

Quillian, Lincoln. 2002. "Why Is Black-White Residential Segregation So Persistent? Evidence on Three Theories from Migration Data. *Social Science Research* 31: 197–29.

Quillian, Lincoln, and Devah Pager. 2001. "Black Neighbors, Higher Crime? The Role of Racial Stereotypes in Evaluations of Neighborhood Crime." *American Journal of Sociology* 107: 717–67.

Reconstruction. 1990. "Racist Censorship, Sexist Lyrics," "Why 'As Nasty as They Wanna Be' Is Obscene," "2 Live Crew and the Cultural Contradiction of Obscenity." Vol. 1, no. 2.

Rieder, Jonathan. 1985. *Canarsie: The Jews and Italians of Brooklyn against Liberalism*. Cambridge: Cambridge University Press.

Rindfuss, Ronald R., C. Gray Swicegood, and Rachel Rosenfeld. 1987. "Disorder in the Life Course: How Common and Does It Matter?" *American Sociological Review* 52: 785–801.

Rose, Tricia. 1989. "Orality and Technology: Rap Music and African-American Cultural Resistance." *Popular Music and Society* 13: 35–44.

Rose, Tricia. 1994. *Black Noise: Rap Music and Black Culture in Contemporary America*. Hanover, NH: Wesleyan University Press.

Rosin, Hanna. 2008. "American Murder Mystery." *The Atlantic*. http://www.theatlantic.com/magazine/archive/2008/07/american-murder-mystery/6872/#

(accessed July 1, 2012).

Ross, Stephen, and Margery Austin Turner. 2005. "Housing Discrimination in Metropolitan America: Explaining Changes between 1989 and 2000." *Social Problems* 52:152–80.

Royko, Mike. 1990. "No, Nike's Still Not Shaking in Its Boots." *Chicago Tribune*, October 2, section C, 3.

Rugh, Jacob S., and Douglas S. Massey. 2010. "Racial Segregation and the American Foreclosure Crisis." *American Sociological Review* 75: 629–651.

Sampson, Robert J. 1986. "Effects of Socioeconomic Context on Official Reaction to Juvenile Delinquency." *American Sociological Review* 51: 876–86.

———. 1992. "Family Management and Child Development: Insights from Social Disorganization Theory." In *Advances in Criminological Theory* (Facts, Fragments and Forecasts, volume 3), edited by Joan McCord. New Brunswick, NJ: Transaction Press.

———. 2012. *Great American City: Chicago and the Enduring Neighborhood Effect.* Chicago: The University of Chicago Press.

Sampson, Robert J., and W. B. Groves. 1989. "Community Structure and Crime: Testing Social-Disorganization Theory." *American Journal of Sociology* 94: 774–802.

Sampson, Robert J., Stephen W. Raudenbush, and Felton Earls. 1997. "Neighborhoods and Violent Crime: A Multilevel Study of Collective Efficacy." *Science* 277: 918–24.

Sampson, Robert J., and Patrick Sharkey. 2008. "Neighborhood Selection and the Social Reproduction of Concentrated Racial Inequality." *Demography* 45: 1–29.

Sampson, Robert J., and William Julius Wilson. 1995. "Toward a Theory of Race, Crime and Urban Inequality." In *Crime and Inequality*, edited by John Hagan and Ruth D. Peterson, 37–54. Palo Alto, CA: Stanford University Press.

Sampson, William A., and Vera Milam. 1975. "The Intraracial Attitudes of the Black Middle Class: Have They Changed?" *Social Problems* 23: 153–65.

Schelling, Thomas C. 1978. *Micromotives and Macrobehaviors.* New York: W. W. Norton.

Schnore, Leo F., Carolyn D. Andre, and Harry Sharp. 1976. "Black Suburbanization, 1930–1970." *The Changing Face of the Suburbs*, edited by Barry Schwartz. Chicago: University of Chicago Press.

Schwartz, Howard, and Jerry Jacobs. 1979. *Qualitative Sociology: A Method to the Madness.* New York: Free Press.

Shapiro, Thomas. 2004. *The Hidden Cost of Being African American: How Wealth Perpetuates Inequality.* New York: Oxford University Press.

Sharkey, Patrick. 2009. "Neighborhoods and the Black-White Mobility Gap." Economic Mobility Project. Pew Charitable Trusts. http://www.pewtrusts.org/uploadedFiles/wwwpewtrustsorg/Reports/Economic_Mobility/PEW_SHAR-

KEY_v12.pdf?n=1399 (accessed July 1, 2012).

————. 2011. "Spatial Disadvantage and Downward Mobility among the (New?) Black Middle Class." Paper presented at the Annual Meeting of the American Sociological Association. Las Vegas, NV.

Shaw, Clifford. 1966. *The Jack-Roller: A Delinquent Boy's Own Story.* Chicago: University of Chicago Press.

Shaw, Clifford, and Henry McKay. 1942. *Juvenile Delinquency and Urban Areas.* Chicago: University of Chicago Press.

Silver, Marc, and Martin Melkonian, eds. 1995. *Contested Terrain: Power, Politics, and Participation in Suburbia.* Westport, CT: Greenwood Press.

Skinner, Curtis. 1995. "Urban Labor Markets and Young Black Men: A Literature Review." *Journal of Economic Issues* 29: 47–65.

Skogan, Wesley. 1990. *Disorder and Decline: Crime and the Spiral of Decay in American Neighborhoods.* New York: Free Press.

Smith, James, and Finis Welch. 1989. "Black Economic Progress after Myrdal." *Journal of Economic Literature* 27: 519–64.

Smith, Jessie Carney, and Carrell Horton, eds. 1997. *Statistical Record of Black America.* 4th edition. Detroit: Gale Research Press.

Soss, Joe, Richard C. Fording, and Sanford F. Schram. 2011. *Disciplining the Poor: Neoliberal Paternalism and the Persistent Power of Race.* Chicago: University of Chicago Press.

Spear, Allan H. 1967. *Black Chicago: The Making of a Negro Ghetto: 1890–1920.* Chicago: University of Chicago Press.

Speicher, Barbara, and Seane McMahon. 1992. "Some African-American Perspectives on Black English Vernacular." *Language in Society* 21: 383–407.

Squires, Gregory. 1994. *Capital and Communities in Black and White: The Intersections of Race, Class, and Uneven Development.* Albany: State University of New York Press.

Stack, Carol. 1974. *All Our Kin: Strategies for Survival in a Black Community.* New York: Harper & Row.

Stanback, Marsha. 1985. "Language and Black Woman's Place: Evidence from the Black Middle Class." In *For Alma Mater: Theory and Practice in Feminist Scholarship,* edited by Paula Treichler, Cheris Kramarae, and Beth Stafford. Urbana: University of Illinois Press.

Steinberg, Laurence. 1987. "Single Parents, Stepparents, and Susceptibility of Adolescents to Antisocial Peer Pressure." *Child Development* 58: 269–75.

Steinberg, Stephen. 1995. *Turning Back: The Retreat from Racial Justice in American Thought and Policy.* Boston: Beacon Press.

Stith, Melvin T., and Ronald E. Goldsmith. 1989. "Race, Sex, and Fashion Innovativeness: A Replication." *Psychology and Marketing* 6: 249–62.

Stoll, Michael. 2005. "Job Sprawl and the Spatial Mismatch between Blacks and

Jobs." Washington, DC: Brookings Institution. http://www.brookings.edu/~/media/research/files/reports/2005/2/metropolitanpolicy%20stoll/20050214_jobsprawl (accessed September 22, 2012).

Strasser, J. B., and Laurie Becklund. 1991. *Swoosh: The Unauthorized Story of Nike and the Men Who Played There*. New York: Harcourt, Brace, Jovanovich.

Sugrue, Thomas. 1996. *The Origins of the Urban Crisis: Race and Inequality in Postwar Detroit*. Princeton, NJ: Princeton University Press.

Sullivan, Mercer L. 1989. *"Getting Paid": Youth Crime and Work in the Inner City*. Ithaca, NY: Cornell University Press.

Suttles, Gerald. 1968. *The Social Order of the Slum: Ethnicity and Territory in the Inner City*. Chicago: University of Chicago Press.

Swidler, Ann. 1986. "Culture in Action: Symbols and Strategies." *American Sociological Review* 51: 273–86.

Taeuber, Karl, and Elaine Taeuber. 1965. *Negroes in Cities*. Chicago: Aldine Publishers.

Taub, Richard P., D. Garth Taylor, and Jan D. Dunham. 1984. *Paths of Neighborhood Change: Race and Crime in Urban America*. Chicago: University of Chicago Press.

Taylor, Carl S. 1990. *Dangerous Society*. East Lansing.: Michigan State University Press.

Taylor, Monique M. 2002. *Harlem between Heaven and Hell*. Minneapolis: University of Minnesota Press.

Taylor, Steven J., and Robert Bogdan. 1984. *Introduction to Qualitative Research Methods: The Search for Meanings*. New York: John Wiley & Sons.

Terrell, Francis. 1975. "Dialectical Differences between Middle-Class Black and White Children Who Do and Do Not Associate with Lower-Class Black Children." *Language and Speech* 18: 65–73.

Thompson, Daniel C. 1986. *A Black Elite: A Profile of Graduates of UNCF Colleges*. New York: Greenwood Press.

Toop, David. 1984. *The Rap Attack: African Jive to New York Hip Hop*. London: Pluto Press.

Trotter, Joe W., and Earl Lewis. 1996. *African Americans in the Industrial Age: A Documentary History, 1915–1945*. Boston: Northeastern University Press.

Trotter, Joe William. 1985. *Black Milwaukee: The Making of an Industrial Proletariat, 1915–45*. Urbana: University of Illinois Press.

Tyler, Bruce. 1994. "Zoot-Suit Culture and the Black Press." *Journal of American Culture* 17: 21–33.

Urban Studies Group, Rockefeller Institute of Government. February 1997. "Working Paper on Majority-Black Urban Residential Areas." Presented at Poverty Seminar Series, Northwestern University/University of Chicago Joint Center for Poverty Research.

US Census. 2011. "Geographical Mobility: 2008 to 2009." http://www.census.gov/prod/2011pubs/p20–565.pdf (accessed September 22, 2012).

US Department of Housing and Urban Development. 2000a. "Unequal Burden: Income and Racial Disparities in Subprime Lending." http://www.huduser.org/Publications/pdf/unequal_full.pdf (accessed July 1, 2012).

———. 2000b. "Unequal Burden in Chicago: Income and Racial Disparities in Subprime Lending." http://www.huduser.org/Publications/pdf/chicago.pdf (accessed July 1, 2012).

US Department of Justice. 2011. "Justice Department Reaches $335 Million Settlement to Resolve Allegations of Lending Discrimination by Countrywide Financial Corporation." December 21, 2011. http://www.justice.gov/opa/pr/2011/December/11-ag-1694.html (accessed July 1, 2012).

Van Deburg, William L. 1997. *Black Camelot: African-American Culture Heroes in Their Times, 1960–1980*. Chicago: University of Chicago Press.

Vanneman, Reeve, and Lynn Weber Canon. 1987. *The American Perception of Class*. Philadelphia: Temple University Press.

Vecsey, Peter. 1992. "Jordan, League Fashion a Compromise." *USA Today*, November 20, section C, 4.

Venkatesh, Sudhir Alladi. 1996. "The Gang in the Community." In *Gangs in America*, 2nd ed., edited by C. Ronald Huff. Thousand Oaks, CA: Sage Publications.

———. 1997. "The Social Organization of Street Gang Activity in an Urban Ghetto." *American Journal of Sociology* 103: 82–111.

———. 2000. *American Project: the Rise and Fall of a Modern Ghetto*. Cambridge, MA: Harvard University Press.

Villemez, Wayne. 1980. "Race, Class, and Neighborhood: Differences in the Residential Return on Individual Resources." *Social Forces* 59: 414–30.

Wacquant, Loic J. D., and William Julius Wilson. 1989. "Poverty, Joblessness and the Social Transformation of the Inner City." *Reforming Welfare Policy*, edited by David Ellwood and P. Cottingham. Cambridge, MA: Harvard University Press.

Washington, Joseph R., ed. 1979. *The Declining Significance of Race: A Dialogue among Black and White Social Scientists*. Philadelphia: University of Pennsylvania Afro-American Studies Program.

———. ed. 1980. *Dilemmas of the New Black Middle Class*. Philadelphia: University of Pennsylvania Afro-American Studies Program.

Washington, Valora, and Joanna Newman. 1991. "Setting Our Own Agenda: Exploring the Meaning of Gender Disparities among Blacks in Higher Education." *Journal of Negro Education* 60: 19–35.

West, Cornel. 1994. *Race Matters*. New York: Vintage Books.

Whyte, William Foote. 1943. *Street Corner Society. The Social Structure of an Italian Slum*. Chicago: University of Chicago Press.

Wiese, Andrew. 2004. *Places of their Own: African American Suburbanization in the Twentieth Century.* Chicago: University of Chicago Press.

Williams, Jerome D., and William J. Qualls. 1989. "Middle-Class Black Consumers and Intensity of Ethnic Identification." *Psychology and Marketing* 6: 263–86.

Williams, Terry. 1992. *Crackhouse: Notes from the End of the Line.* Reading, MA: Addison-Wesley.

Willie, Charles Vert. 1979. *The Caste and Class Controversy.* Bayside, NY: General Hall.

Willis, Susan. 1993. "Hardcore: Subculture American Style." *Critical Inquiry* 19: 365–83.

Wilson, Frank. 1995. "Rising Tide or Ebb Tide? Recent Changes in the Black Middle Class in the U.S., 1980–1990." *Research in Race and Ethnic Relations* 8: 21–55.

Wilson, William Julius. 1978. *The Declining Significance of Race: Blacks and Changing American Institutions.* Chicago: University of Chicago Press.

———. 1987. *The Truly Disadvantaged: The Inner City, the Underclass and Public Policy.* Chicago: University of Chicago Press.

———. 1996. *When Work Disappears: The World of the New Urban Poor.* New York: Knopf.

Wilson, William J., and Richard P. Taub. 2006. *There Goes the Neighborhood: Racial, Ethnic, and Class Tensions in Four Chicago Neighborhoods and Their Meaning of America.* New York: Vintage Books.

Wofford, Jean. 1979. "Ebonics: A Legitimate System of Oral Communication." *Journal of Black Studies* 9: 367–82.

Woldoff, Rachael. 2011. *White Flight/Black Flight: The Dynamics of Racial Change in an American Neighborhood.* Ithaca, NY: Cornell University Press.

Woodstock Institute. May 1994. *Focusing In: Indicators of Economic Change in Chicago's Neighborhoods.* Chicago: Woodstock Institute.

Wright, Richard, Mark Ellis, Virginia Parks. 2005. "Re-Placing Whiteness in Spatial Assimilation Research." *City & Community* 4: 111-35.

Ydstie, John. 2012. "On The Economic Ladder, Rungs Move Further Apart." *All Things Considered*, National Public Radio, May 29, 2012. http://www.npr.org/2012/05/29/153918852/on-the-economic-ladder-rungs-move-further-apart (accessed July 1, 2012).

Yeung, W. Jean, and Sandra Hofferth. 1998. "Family Adaptations to Income and Job Loss in the U.S." *Journal of Family and Economic Issues* 19: 255–83.

Yinger, John. 1995. *Closed Doors, Opportunities Lost: The Continuing Costs of Housing Discrimination.* New York: Russell Sage Foundation.

Young, Vershawn Ashanti, with Bridget Harris Tsemo. 2011. *From Bourgeois to Boojie: Black Middle-class Performances.* Detroit: Wayne State University Press.

Zukin, Sharon, et al. 2009. "New Retail Capital and Neighborhood Change:

Boutiques and Gentrification in New York City." *City and Community* 8: 47–64.

Zweigenhaft, Richard L., and G. William Domhoff. 1991. *Blacks in the White Establishment? A Study of Race and Class in America.* New Haven, CT: Yale University Press.

INDEX

Aalbers, Manuel, 248
Abrahams, Roger, 265–66n7
Adelman, Robert, 256, 258
Adidas shoes, 151, 156–57, 165
adolescence. *See* youth
adult children, use of term, 53–57
advertising
    geared to African Americans, 147–
      48, 151–52, 159, 166, 280n4
    "Hare Jordan," 164
    negative effects of, 279nn1–2
    See also consumerism
affirmative action
    assault on, 1, 21, 44
    occupations affected by, 210–11
    relevance to black middle class,
      214–15
    social class and, 19–20, 215–17
African Americans
    central concerns for, 18–19
    gains for, 210
    language as connector for, 9–10
    marketing geared to, 147–48,
      151–52, 159, 166, 280n4
    research focus on poor, 1, 2, 20–
      21, 206–9
    residential preferences of, 270n14

    See also black middle class; black
      urban ghettos; culture; role
      models
Agius Vallejo, Jody, 230
Alba, Richard D., 29, 215, 260
Alcorn State University, 22–23
Anderson, Elijah, 92–94, 167
antipoverty programs
    benefits of, 217–18
    implications for black
      middle class, 30
Arthur, Lucille (pseud.), 53–54, 236
Arthur, Sarita (pseud.)
    in dramatic skits, 134–35
    on gang members, 137
    as marginal to gangsta style,
      138–39
    on school, 134
    on shootings, 136
    thrilled by gangsta style, 134–37
Ashkinaze, Carol, 256
assets, racial gaps in, 95, 251, 264n2,
    275n1. *See also* black middle class:
    resources and strategies of
Atlanta (Ga.), racial and class ge-
    ography of, 25, 250, 255–56,
    264–65n4

fashion. *See* style
fathers
    absence of, 99–100, 106, 130, 145
    military influence on, 140
    presence of, 96–97, 100, 108–10
Federal Housing Administration,
    39–40
females
    code-switching by, 265–66n7
    kin networks of, 277n9
    occupations for, 17–18, 27, 59–60
    status symbols for, 146
    street behaviors of, 111–12
    See also gender; sexuality
Fernandez, Roberto, 283–84n3
fights
    rarity of, 89
    response to, 176–77, 245
    youth group discussions of, 134
    See also crime
film
    blaxploitation type of, 125–27
    influence of gangstas in, 128, 134,
        135–36, 143, 175, 206, 281n7
    life linked to, 136–37
    nihilistic, 279n7
Folks, use of term, 83, 85, 163–64
food stamps, 96
foreclosure crisis, 247–53. *See also*
    housing
Frankfurt School, on mass marketing,
    279–80n2
Franklin, Kirk, 41
Franklin High School, 172, 177–78
Frazier, E. Franklin, 18–19, 26, 219
Freeman, Richard B., 267n3, 268n6
French family (pseud.), 55, 216–17
Fresh Prince of Bel Air (TV show), 14
Frey, William, 256, 257, 259
friendships
    black vs. white, 184

college's role in, 197–98
definition of close, 274n2
gangs and, 174–75
poverty and, 283–84n3
See also boyfriends; dating and rela-
    tionships; family

Galster, George, 240
gangbanging, use of term, 81
gangs
    awareness of, 173–75
    community response to, 80–81
    connections to, 142–43
    description of, 137
    evolution of, 192–95
    experimenting as, 132–38
    imitation of, 126–27, 143
    killings of, 91–92
    legitimization efforts of, 85–86
    members of, 68, 98, 108–9, 111
    neighborhood ties of, 68, 70–73,
        75–78, 84–90, 203–4, 275n4
    organizational meetings of, 83–84
    process for joining, 106–9, 123
    in schools, 80–81, 82, 97, 174
    social control by, 71–73, 85–89
    as street behavior, 112
    style posturing by, 280n6
    symbols of, 83, 139, 280n6
    uncertainties of affiliation with,
        276–77n7
    See also Black Mobsters; drugs
gangsta bitch, use of term, 139
gangsta rap music
    definition of, 278n5
    interpretation of, 121–22
    sex and violence in, 120–21, 122
    styles associated with, 122–24
Gans, Herbert J., 268n5
Garner, T., 265–66n7
Gaskin, Darrell, 242

Hathaway, Donnie, 120
Haynes, Bruce, 259
Hebdige, Dick, 278n3
Heflin, Colleen, 237
Height, Jeremiah (pseud.), 145
Hicks, George, 22–23
hip-hop culture, 121–22, 126. *See also*
    rap music
Hochschild, Jennifer L., 19, 44
Hofferth, Sandra, 273n4
Höijer, Birgitta, 244
Holliday, Amy, 256
homeownership
    bank loans for, 190
    cost of, 273n2
    inheritance of, 47–53
    percentage of, 4, 72–73
    rate since 1990, 240
homicide
    example of, 77–78, 206
    geography of, 29, 203, 227
    rates of, 243–44
Hopkinson, Natalie, 259
households
    income of, 273n3
    structure of, 74, 271n3
    subfamilies in, 74
    See also family; income
housing
    description of, 39–40
    developments of, 190, 282–83n5
    economic stagnation and, 36
    foreclosure crisis, 247–53
    postwar options in, 23–24
    purchased vs. rented, 33–34,
        48, 245
    racial and class segregation in, 3,
        23–30, 68
    subprime mortgage lending, 229,
        247–53
    upkeep of, 11

See also homeownership; neighbor-
    hoods; property maintenance;
    Section 8
Housing Choice Vouchers. *See* Sec-
    tion 8
Houston (Texas), racial and class geog-
    raphy of, 25, 264–65n4
hustle, use of term, 60
Hyra, Derek, 253, 259

Ice Cube (rapper), 120
Iceland, John, 258
Immergluck, Dan, 251
income
    in class definitions, 14–15, 17,
        267n1
    drug money as, 95–97, 106–7,
        126, 131, 159, 194, 276n3
    educational hopes and, 63
    extended family issues and, 55–57,
        199, 213
    geographic space and, 25–30, 34,
        37–38
    racial gaps in, 2–3, 21–22, 211,
        264n2, 268n6, 275n1
    as resource, 103
    statistics on, 37–38, 220–21, 228
individual agency
    emphasis on, 1–2, 3
    style and, 153–54
    as survival factor, 115
institutional ghetto, 17

Jackson, Bo, 159
Jackson, John, 259
Jackson, Kenneth, 248
Jackson, Michael, 40
Jackson, Tara, 270n14
Jackson State University, 141, 145
James, David E., 269–70n12
James, Rick, 120

style's link to, 126, 139
See also gangsta rap music
Raudenbush, Stephen W., 265n5
real estate speculation, segregation fostered by, 33
Reebok shoes, 151, 156, 159, 162, 165
Reed, Tyson (pseud.)
　background of, 94, 205
　consumed by gangsta style, 128–32, 144, 232
　on conversation, 93–94
　family and friends of, 95, 98–100, 113, 145
　on freelancers, 132
　gang activities of, 98, 114–16
　hopes of, 114–15
　income of, 56
　life since 1999, 232, 242, 245, 246, 254, 256
　Nike shoes and, 159–60, 165
　parental strategies for, 104
　positive factors for, 115–16, 232
　rebelliousness of, 105–8
　resources of, 103
Reeves, Keith, 270n14
religion, homeownership and, 50–51. *See also* churches
respect, maintenance of, 92–93
robbery, example of, 170–71
Robert Taylor Homes public housing, 137–38, 209, 253
Rockefeller Institute of Government (SUNY, Albany), 25, 264–65n4
Rogers, Willard, 267n1
Rojecki, Andrew, 244
role models
　created by mass market, 162–63
　gangs as substitute for fathers as, 106–8, 130, 145
　heterogeneity of, 98, 109, 204–5
　Jordan as, 157–58

positive examples of, 111, 193, 208
social organization and, 70
working adults as, 6, 103
Rose, Tricia, 122
Rosin, Hanna, 254
Rubin, Donald L., 265–66n7
Rudwick, Elliott, 267n3
Rugh, Jacob S., 251
Ruthless Mobsters, 85

Sampson, Robert J., 29, 68, 238, 244, 260, 265n5, 274n1, 284n1
Sampson, William, 19
Scarface (film), 206
Scarface (rapper), 41
schools
　college prep in, 99–102, 103, 195
　description of, 40
　differences in, 186
　dress codes in, 123, 280n6
　gangs in, 80–81, 82, 97, 174
　graduation rates and, 144, 216–17
　neighborhood intertwined in, 38, 75–76
　Nike's marketing and, 151
　rebelliousness in, 169–70
　socioeconomic status in, 28
　stability in, 35
　street and decent orientations in, 97–98
　supplements to, 140–41
　youth group discussions of, 134
　See also education; Groveland Elementary School; universities and colleges
Section 8, 244–45, 252–57
sexuality
　dangers in, 144
　discussions about, 153
　dramatic skit on, 134–35
　in gangsta rap music, 120–21, 122

on workforce, 179–84
Wattleton, Faye, 40
Webber, Chris, 165
Welch, Finis, 264n3
welfare
  reform of, 198–99
  rejection of, 96–97
West, Cornel, 148, 211
West Groveland Community Association, 33
Westside Connection (rap group), 120
White, Byron P., 215–16
white middle class
  compared to black middle class, 1–3, 9, 10, 21–22, 204–5, 210–11, 234–37, 241–42, 248–52, 261
  ghetto trance and, 132, 206
  neighborhoods of, 29–30
  residential preferences of, 270n14
  stylistic choices by, 278n2
  as voyeuristic, 118–19
Whyte, William Foote, 167
Wiese, Andrew, 259
Williams, Robin, 273–74n6
Willis, Susan, 278n2
Wilson, William Julius
  on affirmative action, 215
  on black college graduates, 267n3
  on economy's influence, 21, 267n4
  on nonpoor out-migration, 268n7
  scholars' references to, 267–68n5
  on school-to-work transition, 273n5
  on segregation, 26–27, 29, 218, 261, 268–69n9
  on social class differences, 19–20, 283n2
  on social disorganization, 68
Wofford, Jean, 265–66n7
Woldoff, Rachael, 256, 257

Woodlawn (Ill.), migrants to, 23
Wright, Richard, 260
Wu Tang Clan (rap group), 41

Xavier University, 196, 283n7

Ydstie, John, 234
Yinger, John, 248
Young, Vershawn Ashanti, 259
young single mothers
  career hopes of, 96
  household context of, 95
  peer group context of, 275–76n2
  See also childbearing, out-of-wedlock; pregnancy
youth
  challenges for middle-class, 114–16, 211–12
  choices available to, 6, 193–94
  community concerns for, 78–79
  context for, 10–12
  definition of, 57–58
  distractions for, 64–67, 140–42
  expectations of parents, 99
  flexibility of, 125, 129
  flexible family forms and, 112–14
  as focus of research, 6–7
  as gendered experience, 111–14
  hopes of, 61–63, 96, 98, 100, 102, 132
  media's influence on, 146–47, 206
  "moratorium period" for, 58–60
  neighborhood ties of, 75–78, 204–5
  as "problem," 117–19
  rebelliousness of, 104–11
  resources of, 102–4
  social organization theory and, 69
  on socioeconomic status, 14
  supervision of, 70–71, 74–75, 80, 82